CONSUMER EXPECTATIONS

Richard T. Curtin has directed the University of Michigan's consumer sentiment surveys for more than four decades. His analyses of recent trends in consumer expectations are regularly covered in the worldwide press. In this book, Curtin presents a new theory of expectations. Whereas conventional theories presume that consumers play a passive role in the macro economy, simply reacting to current trends in incomes, prices, and interest rates, Curtin proposes a new empirically consistent theory. He argues that expectations are formed by an automatic process that utilizes conscious and nonconscious processes, passion and reason, information from public and private sources, and social networks. Consumers ultimately reach a decision that serves both the micro decision needs of individuals and reflects the common influence of the macro environment. Drawing on empirical observations, Curtin not only demonstrates the importance of consumer sentiment, but how it can also foreshadow the cyclical turning points in the economy.

Richard T. Curtin is Director of the Surveys of Consumers at the University of Michigan, where he has worked for over four decades. His analysis of recent trends in consumer expectations are issued twice monthly and are regularly covered in the worldwide press. Data from the surveys are included in the US Index of Leading Economic Indicators. During his career he has consulted with a number of countries, helping them to establish comparable consumer surveys, as well as a wide range of US and international businesses and financial institutions. He received his BA from Michigan State University and his PhD in economics from the University of Michigan.

Consumer Expectations

Micro Foundations and Macro Impact

RICHARD T. CURTIN

University of Michigan

CAMBRIDGE
UNIVERSITY PRESS

CAMBRIDGE
UNIVERSITY PRESS

Shaftesbury Road, Cambridge CB2 8EA, United Kingdom

One Liberty Plaza, 20th Floor, New York, NY 10006, USA

477 Williamstown Road, Port Melbourne, VIC 3207, Australia

314–321, 3rd Floor, Plot 3, Splendor Forum, Jasola District Centre, New Delhi – 110025, India

103 Penang Road, #05–06/07, Visioncrest Commercial, Singapore 238467

Cambridge University Press is part of Cambridge University Press & Assessment, a department of the University of Cambridge.

We share the University's mission to contribute to society through the pursuit of education, learning and research at the highest international levels of excellence.

www.cambridge.org
Information on this title: www.cambridge.org/9780521181136

DOI: 10.1017/9780511791598

First published 2019

A catalogue record for this publication is available from the British Library

Library of Congress Cataloging-in-Publication data
Names: Curtin, Richard Thomas, author.
Title: Consumer expectations : micro foundations and macro impact / Richard T. Curtin.
Description: New York : Cambridge University Press, 2019.
Identifiers: LCCN 2018039109 | ISBN 9781107004696 (hardback) | ISBN 9780521181136 (paperback)
Subjects: LCSH: Consumers. | Consumer behavior. | Marketing. | BISAC: BUSINESS & ECONOMICS / Economics / General.
Classification: LCC HF5415.32 .C86 2019 | DDC 658.8/ 342– dc23
LC record availableat https:// lccn.loc.gov/ 2018039109

ISBN   978-1-107-00469-6   Hardback
ISBN   978-0-521-18113-6   Paperback

In memory of Eileen Curtin

Contents

Figures

Tables

Preface

I have always favored the unexpected. Expected outcomes offer no new information. Results that are unexpected challenge orthodox views. While most discrepancies are resolved upon detailed examination, the few that remain have the potential to lead to a new understanding of human behavior. Over the past four decades, I have held a unique position that has allowed me to directly observe how people form and act on their economic expectations as the director of the University of Michigan's consumer sentiment surveys. I initially resisted the startling implications of my observations as they were in inconsistent with accepted theories in economics and psychology. The conventional view was that forming economic expectations required conscious cognitive deliberation of the information released by federal statistical agencies, and that accuracy demanded that reason prevail over passion. Forming expectations required knowledge of past economic developments, correct interpretations of ongoing trends, and the ability and willingness to make detailed calculations. While economists, especially professional forecasters, have demonstrated all of these skills, it was the consensus that most people could not accomplish the tasks of compiling, interpreting, and calculating economic expectations. At best, ordinary people had a very limited ability to form expectations. The bounds on their abilities were thought to be so severe that their economic expectations would amount to little more than uniformed guesses. People's economic expectations were thought to be influenced more by emotion rather than reason, the nemesis of economic rationality. This dismal assessment has been shared among all social sciences, including economics, psychology, political science, and sociology.

The expectations data from the University of Michigan surveys told a surprisingly different story. The data displayed a close correspondence with the trends in the official data series produced by the federal statistical agencies.

Even more challenging, rather than simply reflect the recent past, the expectations data predicted future economic events. How could representative samples of consumers predict future economic events as accurately as professional economic forecasters? The differences in skills, interpretation, and analytic abilities were too vast to justify nearly identical results. Without credible evidence to the contrary, the dominant explanation was that the survey data must somehow represent an illusion. It took me years to finally recognize that rather than an anomaly, it was the fundamental scientific theories of how expectations were formed that were incorrectly specified. After carefully listening to how respondents described their expectations as well as how they described their reasoning, I became convinced that the current economic and psychological theories of expectations did not capture how people used their full mental faculties to form expectations. Rather than a complex and difficult process, expectations seemed to be easily and automatically formed by the least educated as well as the most educated, by the youngest and the oldest, and by the richest and the poorest. People did not need advice about how to form economic expectations, or for any other expectations that they regularly formed. Expectations were formed naturally and automatically.

Evolutionary development has provided people with an efficient means to form expectations by fully utilizing their conscious and nonconscious cognitive abilities, their emotional resources, and by social interactions. This enhanced perspective enabled a new framework for understanding the expectations voiced by survey respondents. Accuracy is still the predominant goal in this new paradigm and the driving force of the formation process. The goal of the formation process, however, shifted from national data to the economic conditions that people actually face in their daily lives. This personalization of expectations is consistent with conventional economic theory, but it is implicitly denied in nearly all empirical research. Perhaps the most surprising finding of this revised definition of expectations is not that it enabled people to anticipate the conditions that they actually faced, but that it enabled them to anticipate how those factors changed over time in the economy as a whole. This meant that even though expectations were personalized, when aggregated across the entire population, those expectations still consistently tracked national trends. Consumer expectations thus reflected both micro considerations as well as macro realities.

More importantly, the personalization of expectations forced consideration of new tenets of rationality. The emphasis shifted from an exclusive focus on national data to include a heavy dose of local economic conditions tailored to the specific characteristics of the individual. Rather than focusing on a single source of "official" information, people had to gather information from numerous, and at times conflicting, sources. Evolutionary development has provided humans the means to effectively and efficiently expand their capacity for cognition and learning well beyond the limits of conscious deliberation. Indeed, the capacity for processing information nonconsciously dwarfs the capacity of the conscious mind. There are few activities that people accomplish without the assistance of nonconscious cognition and learning, including forming and revising personalized expectations. The paradigm that emerged provided a distinctive explanation of why, how, and when economic expectations are formed.

Another major divergence from orthodox economic theory that has emerged from my research is consistent with the Aristotelian notion of holism. This principle implies that the macroeconomy cannot be fully explained solely based on its micro components. This goes against the dominant economic view that the macroeconomy is simply a sum of its micro components, the so-called micro foundations of macroeconomics. In contrast, holism implies that the macroeconomy partly determines the actions of its micro components. The focus of the University of Michigan's sentiment surveys is the prediction of macroeconomic trends, especially those surrounding economic cycles. Empirical tests center on the correspondence between the sample estimates of the changes in consumer expectations and trends in the macroeconomy. The predictive success of these tests has meant that consumer sentiment surveys are now measured in more than six dozen countries in every inhabited continent in the world. Moreover, the new paradigm also provides a scientific foundation for self-fulfilling expectations as well as the occasional penchant for irrational exuberance and irrational fears that can produce booms and busts.

I owe a great debt to George Katona, my mentor, friend, and colleague, who started these surveys at the University of Michigan in 1946. The ideas and theories in this book represent an extension of his work, although they were never advanced by Katona. Importantly, the scientific infrastructure needed to accomplish this research was developed by Katona, Rensis Likert, Leslie Kish, Charles Cannell, James Morgan, and others at the Survey Research Center. These path-breaking developments included probability methods to select nationally representative samples, robust interviewing and coding methodologies, computerized data management and statistical analysis programs. While all these elements are now commonplace, they were revolutionary innovations in the 1940s.

   Successfully completing monthly surveys that provide a consistent series of measurements over many decades is an enormous task. This accomplishment has been due to very many people at the Survey Research Center at the University of Michigan. I have benefitted from the efforts of over one thousand people over the past four decades, ranging from senior researchers and administrators to interviewers and research assistants. Most assume that the repetitive nature of the surveys would mean that it was a routine task that once learned, could be easily repeated. In contrast, nearly every month presented new challenges to complete the survey within the fixed deadlines. Moreover, maintaining data quality has been a constant challenge given that the survey research program has extended over the past three-quarters of a century, and has witnessed dramatic changes in the economy as well as changes in the finances, size, composition, and demographic characteristics of households.

   Patricia Maher and Ann Munster deserve special recognition for their tireless efforts in maintaining the survey's scientific methodology and high data quality over the past three decades. My current research staff is led by Zeynep Tuba Suzer-Gurtekin, along with Edward Ellcey, Vivian Burgett, and Jim Zajkowski. My research has also benefitted over the years from a large contingent of student research assistants.

   The most help in advancing my research was provided by the hundreds of thousands of survey respondents who shared their insights about their economic situation. The generosity of these respondents infused my research with economic substance unattainable from any other source of economic data available to me. Indeed, the success of this research would have been impossible without their willingness to share their knowledge as well as their economic hopes and fears. Their reasoning was equally as important as their passions.

   Funding for this research was provided by many corporations, financial institutions, and government agencies over the long life of the project. I had to devote much of my time to securing the necessary funds to finance this research over the past four decades. Currently, Bloomberg L.P. is the major source of financial support. The Federal Reserve Board has provided support over the entire history of the project. The intense domestic and international interest in the data is dominated by its forecasting ability. Even at the University of Michigan, interest in the project has been narrowly defined by its predictive performance, especially how its forecasts compare with other surveys or predictions based on econometric models. As a consequence, my time has been heavily dominated by these comparative concerns to secure adequate funding to continue the project for another year. No month was complete without my writing at least a mid-month and a final report on the latest movements in consumers' expectations and their implications for the national economy. Naturally, each report generated a barrage of questions and requests for data and advice from a broad spectrum of interested parties. Although assessing the predictive performance of the sentiment data is easily accomplished, these statistical tests left the basic conundrum unanswered: how can ordinary people form expectations that accurately forecast macroeconomic trends. It is this more fundamental question that this book addresses.

While interdisciplinary research is common at the University of Michigan, this research will challenge many social scientists as it emphasizes the importance of nonconscious cognitive processes, the critical role of emotions and social influences, as well as the principle that accuracy is the dominant motivation for forming and revising expectations. The interdisciplinary theory contained in this book is perfectly generalizable to a host of other expectations people form about their political and social environment. Forming expectations has benefitted from an evolutionary process that efficiently utilizes all aspects of people's mental faculties. The evolutionary goal of expectations is to maximize the potential of the most limited resource of the human mind, conscious cognitive deliberation. For this survey project to thrive in the twenty-first century, it is necessary to develop new measurement techniques that cover the full range of people's mental faculties.

All the University of Michigan survey data used in this book, including cross-section and time-series data, question wording and sample design, are available on the project's website: umich.edu/~umsurvey. The European data can be accessed by their website: ec.europa.eu/ info/business-economy-euro/indicators-statistics/economic-databases/ business-and-consumer-surveys. Special thanks go to the University of Michigan Press, OECD, and Routledge for permission to reprint small portions of my prior publications.

Expectations and the Macroeconomy

This book is about how people form economic expectations and how those expectations influence the performance of the macroeconomy. People's economic decisions are shaped by expected future changes in prices, wages, employment, interest rates, and many other economic factors. Expectations influence people's economic decisions – deciding whether to save or to incur debt, to invest in bonds or stocks, to rent or buy a home, to enter or leave the labor force, to acquire new work skills or to move to a new geographic to find work, as well as many other economic decisions. It was Plato who first explicitly identified the essential role of expectations in human decision making thousands of years ago. His observations have now become commonplace, echoed by ordinary citizens as well as central bankers. Moreover, the importance of expectations is hardly limited to economic decisions, as expectations represent an important consideration for a broad spectrum of human decisions, including voting and policy preferences, social choices, health decisions, and numerous other behaviors. Indeed, every social science has incorporated expectations into their theories of human decision making.

Despite the centrality of expectations to human decision making, there is no scientific consensus about how expectations are formed. The divisions across the social sciences are so wide and the differences are so deeply ingrained that a resolution would require a radical shift in one or more of the disciplines to achieve a consensus. The purpose of this book is to suggest a new interdisciplinary paradigm that could accomplish this task. A few of the suggested changes have already been tacitly accepted as necessary by some scholars, but none have yet been incorporated into conventional theory; other changes are more radical, and are likely to be resisted. To accept the need for a new paradigm, one must be convinced that existing views are critically deficient, and more importantly, that the new paradigm helps to account for a broader range of observed economic behavior.

Perhaps a more basic conundrum that this new paradigm addresses is the gap between people's remarkable ability to substantially improve their material living standards and people's persistent failure to make rational economic decisions. How did societies achieve such rapid economic progress over the past few centuries when it is alleged that most people make their economic decisions without the required information, in the absence of interpretative skills, and without the ability to calculate the appropriate expectation? How could evolutionary forces have left people so incapable of making decisions that serve their best interests? Why must humans always be vigilant to avoid the corruptive influence of passion on reason when making their economic decisions? Why has reason never defeated passion? Some have simply ascribed the persistent lack of rationality as an essential and unchanging characteristic of human nature.

This book suggests a completely different answer, a new paradigm that recognizes that rational decisions are based on the full mental capacity of the human mind, including passion as well as reason. The most striking departure of this new paradigm is that rationality is no longer the exclusive property of conscious deliberation but that rational decision making is also due to nonconscious cognitive activities and guided by affective processes. In this new paradigm, passion is not the enemy of reason but its handmaiden. The orthodox assumption of optimal decisions requires exclusive dependence on rational expectations formed by conscious deliberation. This is not part of the new paradigm, although the accuracy of expectations is still viewed as the sole objective of the formation process. The benefit of the new paradigm is that it allows a more robust scientific understanding of why expectations are formed, how they are formed, when they are formed, as well as a new understanding of the influence that people's expectations have on the performance of the macroeconomy.

A critical element of this new paradigm is its recognition that economic expectations are inherently social phenomena. Economic theory favors disembodied markets, stripped of the fact that they represent the interactions of people's economic behavior. While economists think in terms of market outcomes, people think in terms of the actions and reactions of other people. Evolutionary developments have given the human brain the capacity to understand the situation of other people by verbal descriptions as well as by the more commonplace and effortless displays of emotion. People have learned to be especially concerned about potential threats and have learned that the best surveillance of the environment is done by groups of people who face similar threats as well as opportunities. Experience has taught people to take precautionary measures at the first signs of danger, without waiting for confirming data from federal statistical agencies. Often, the dangers that these threats represent quickly disappear, offset by the natural heterogeneity of economic experiences across ever larger groups of people. At some times, however, social contagion responds to real or imagined threats and acts to coordinate simultaneous changes in expectations across ever larger groups of economic agents. These coordinated reactions are often associated with recessionary downturns or economic upturns, and on rare occasions, have persisted to such an extent that they have propagated sustained booms and subsequent economic busts. Such shifts in expectations, when unpredicted by economic factors, have long been thought to be anomalous and subject to quick reversal by market forces. The new paradigm holds that self-fulfilling expectations are not only possible, but occur with some regularity.

A primary objective of this new paradigm is to understand the dynamic functioning of the macroeconomy based in part on observations of its micro units. The chapters included in the first section of this book deal with how each individual forms their economic expectations; the second section deals with how expectations influence the course of the macro-economy. The analytic goal is not to predict individual behavior; the goal is to understand how expectations influence the macroeconomy. This perspective differs from the assumption that, in order to have an impact on the macroeconomy, the expectations of a significant share of the population must change at the same time and in the same direction. The macro focus shifts the analysis from the behavior of any individual agent to the behavior of the entire economy.

The more important implication of this new paradigm is that it challenges the conventional view that macroeconomic conditions are uniquely defined by the aggregation of its micro foundations. Indeed, a critical characteristic of the new interdisciplinary paradigm is that it posits an essential degree of independence between micro and macro phenomena. Macro phenomena are neither more nor less than the sum of the micro units. Instead, it is hypothesized that expectations influence the performance of the macro-economy that cannot be predicted by the simple summation of individually held expectations. This reflects the essential social dynamic of economic expectations. Various contextual factors shape interpretations and imprint macro expectations with a distinctive meaning, which acts to determine appropriate behavioral responses.

Proving the need for this new paradigm is a challenging and complex task. It is based on data drawn from longstanding surveys of consumer

expectations conducted in the United States and dozens of other countries. To the surprise of many observers, the data drawn from these
surveys have proven to be remarkably accurate predictors of subsequent
macroeconomic developments over the past half-century. Data from
the University of Michigan's surveys have been included as components
of the Index of Economic Leading Indicators for their ability to forecast recessions and recoveries. The data collected on consumer inflation and unemployment expectations have proven to be remarkably
accurate, even as accurate as the predictions of professional forecasters.
These results have always surprised scholars, a few of whom believed
there was some hidden gimmick in the data collection process that was
responsible for the accuracy of the results. How could ordinary consumers be so accurate? This was a difficult question to answer based on
the widely accepted premise that economic expectations were the sole
result of conscious cognitive deliberation. Every attempt to elicit knowledge about specific economic quantities, such as the rate of economic
growth, inflation, or the unemployment rate, generally indicated that
the consumer possessed little or no accurate knowledge about economic
statistics. How could accurate predictions be based on inaccurate knowledge? Moreover, how could poorly informed consumers ever trump
the expectations of professional economists in forecasting the course of
the macroeconomy? Nonetheless, they have repeatedly done so to the
chagrin of many scholars.

The starting point of this book is a rigorous assessment of conventional
theories of expectations to determine their strengths and weaknesses.
A new paradigm must be justified by adding strength in place of weakness,
while at the same time, preserving the strengths of orthodox theories. The
first section of this book will document the fault lines of conventional theories of expectations as well as the fundamental properties of the new interdisciplinary paradigm of why, how, and when economic expectations are
formed. The second section extends the new paradigm to include how the
economic expectations of consumers have an active and independent influence on the performance of the national economy. Conventional economic
theory holds that consumers have a passive and dependent role in shaping
trends in the macroeconomy; the behavior of consumers is simply a reaction to ongoing changes in incomes, prices, interest rates, and other economic variables. Rather than assume consumption is endogenous, the new
paradigm holds that consumers play an active role in determining macroeconomic cycles. What follows is a preview of the major tenets of the new
paradigm, leaving the detailed exposition to the subsequent chapters.

FORMATION OF EXPECTATIONS

The rational expectations hypothesis perfectly matches all other aspects of orthodox economic theory. Consumers and firms were already assumed to rationally maximize their economic benefits, whether utility or profits, based on full knowledge of the alternatives. Perhaps the biggest surprise is that it took economic theory hundreds of years to formally extend the assumptions about rationality to the formation of expectations. To be sure, conventional theory holds that economic rationality represents a normative ideal, which is only fully achieved in equilibrium. Moreover, economists have debated whether rationality is a characteristic of individual agents or of market outcomes.

Economic rationality is not determined by how expectations are formed, but whether expectations accurately reflect the actual subsequent outcomes. Other social sciences, most notably psychology, define rationality in terms of how the expectation was formed, not by the ultimate accuracy of the expectation. Economics specifies the characteristics of the outcomes and ignores the actual formation process, whereas other social scientists argue that the only choice for people is to use a rational process when forming their expectations, regardless of the accuracy of the outcome.

This difference between defining rationality in procedural versus substantive terms reflects the underlying perspectives of each discipline. Importantly, this fundamental difference has meant that the empirical evidence assembled by each discipline has been incapable of rejecting the other discipline's position. As a result, most of the ensuing debates were framed in terms of the realism and relevance of the rationality assumptions made by each discipline. Behavioral economists adopted an essentially compromise position that held that the most productive approach was to investigate the limitations, or bounds on full rationality; namely, the ability to acquire the relevant data, the ability to interpret the data, and the ability to make the necessary calculations to form a usable expectation. There was agreement by all sides of the debate, whether economists, psychologists, or behavioral economists, that held that forming expectations was primarily dependent on the ability of agents to engage in conscious cognitive deliberations.

The empirical tests of the rationality assumption involved the central hypothesis that agents who have greater ability to acquire, calculate, and interpret economic data should also form more accurate economic expectations. Proxies for cognitive ability ranged from educational attainment to comparisons between ordinary consumers and professional economic forecasters. While the efficacy of years of formal education as a proxy for cognitive abilities is questionable, no one could doubt that compared with ordinary consumers, professional economic forecasters had greater access to the required information, had routinely performed the necessary calculations, and knew how to interpret the data. Most of the published empirical findings revealed significant differences between the average levels of expectations among consumers and actual economic outcomes, and a wide dispersion of those differences across the population.

Biased levels and persistent heterogeneity have long been taken as proof that rationality was severely bounded by limitations in the cognitive abilities of consumers. However, most of these empirical findings involved static comparisons, examining differences in some economic variable at one point in time. Clearly, the most important aspect of expectations for macroeconomics is how they change over time; it is this information that influences how people need to adjust their economic decisions. To the surprise of many observers, time-series analysis has repeatedly found that the changes over time in economic expectations were both highly correlated across education levels and highly correlated with the corresponding objective economic data. Indeed, inflation expectations of the general population have been repeatedly found to match those of professional economists who specialize in forecasting. How could this be true if ordinary consumers were hopelessly outmatched in cognitive skills and expertise in interpreting data and the forecasting ability of economists? This has always been a very challenging finding. How could differences in cognitive performance only affect levels and not changes in economic expectations? The conventional theories had no mechanisms that could explain why the means could be biased but not how those means changed over time. This seeming inconsistency can be easily explained under the new paradigm.

A More Realistic Paradigm

Economic theory posits that people form expectations only about factors that could be reasonably anticipated to affect their economic decisions. Orthodox economic theory is silent on whether people would even consider forming an expectation about the future state of a variable that had no impact on their economic decisions. The variable may be valued for other reasons, say to promote an informed citizenry or simply on the grounds of expanding one's knowledge, but expectations about social or political outcomes that had no potential impact on a person's own economic situation are properly excluded from economic analysis. Orthodox theory indicates that people should form expectations about the economic conditions that they actually face. No reasonable theory could suggest that people should form expectations about every conceivable economic statistic, nor about national averages if they consistently faced a significantly different rate. Who could be considered rational if they based their expectations on the national unemployment rate when their skills were significantly different than average, or used the national inflation rate when the prices they faced in their community were quite different? These implications have often been ignored in empirical analyses, and, more importantly, these misinterpretations have constituted the basis for erroneous empirical conclusions. In particular, the use of a single or "representative" agent in conceptualizing empirical models has produced the misleading notion that agents actually face the national average inflation or unemployment rates. As a result, some analysts have misinterpreted the dispersion of expectations as an indication of irrationality rather than as a reflection of the variations in economic conditions that people actually face.

Without these interpretative flaws, it is easy to reconcile significant differences in the levels of economic expectations across individuals at one point in time with the finding that over time changes in expectations are highly correlated. Differences in expectations reflect differences in economic situations. To be a rational guide for economic decisions, expectations about future jobs and wage prospects should be different in absolute terms among low skilled workers compared with high skilled workers. The same is true for a wide range of economic indicators, including regional as well as other differences in the economic conditions people face in their own communities. Dispersion of expectations is a common fact of economic life. The mere observation that expectations differ from the figures published by national statistical agencies cannot be taken as proof of irrationality.

Given that most economic variables change in the same direction at the same time for most people, the observation that changes in expectations are similar across the population could be taken as an indication of rationality. For example, expectations about unemployment and wages, while consistently showing significant differences at any point in time due to variations in skills, tend to increase or decrease in unison over time. While the level of overall economic growth differs substantially by geographic location, expansions or contractions tend to affect all locales in a similar fashion. The overall implication of these findings is to increase our skepticism about the presumed evidence that limited conscious cognitive skills have created persistent bounds on rationality.

There are other aspects of conventional economic theory that have distorted the results of empirical research. A prime example is when

economic expectations are formed. Orthodox theory assumes that the primary instigator of forming or revising expectations is the availability of new
economic information, which is typically released by governmental agencies
on a regular schedule. The common practice has been to assert that it is the
availability of new data on an economic statistic that sparks the formation
or revision of expectations. Moreover, conventional theory has generally
assumed that everyone will update their expectations on a wide array of
economic statistics in order to be prepared to make whatever economic
decisions may arise in the future. No cost–benefit calculations are usually
cited, with the implicit implication that the benefits will always exceed the
costs. It is often treated as comparable to an insurance model: the formation
costs incurred are justified by avoiding the presumably much larger decision losses that may arise suddenly and without warning. People are therefore assumed to hold in memory a wide range of economic expectations,
and recall specific expectations whenever they are needed. The full range
of economic expectations would involve a substantial amount of time and
effort to continually revise and update with each new data release by federal
statistical agencies. Those costs are never considered, including the opportunity costs of using one's mental faculties for other purposes.

Under the new paradigm, it is the need to make a specific economic
decision that instigates the formation of the required expectations. It is the
characteristics of the decision that enables people to judge the degree of
accuracy that is required and hence an upper bound on the cost incurred to
form the expectation. For example, people would be much more willing to
invest in forming an expectation about interest rate trends if the decision was
very sensitive to future interest rates. If the decision was quite insensitive,
on the other hand, people may only be willing to invest much less, preferring to form a relatively broad "ball park" estimate. Conventional theorists,
in contrast, would argue that only forming expectations after the need is
identified would be inefficient and more costly, especially if the decision
must be made without a prolonged delay. That explanation assumes that
people only base their economic expectations on data provided by governmental agencies rather than including private data that reflects their own
actual economic experiences. When this conjecture is subjected to rigorous
testing, the general result is that private information is preferred for a broad
range of factors that influence people's economic decisions.

Conventional theories hold that the task of information processing and
computations would overwhelm any individual, making the use of official
data highly efficient, so much so that it outweighs any quibbles about its
applicability to an individual's situation. This presumption is based on the

limited capacity of conscious cognitive deliberation. The new paradigm recognizes that humans routinely process the vast majority of information nonconsciously, and can form expectations without conscious awareness. If people want to form expectations about the economic conditions that they actually face, it is likely that nonconscious processing would aid conscious deliberation in forming their own economic expectations.

Full Mental Faculties

The most restrictive conjecture of orthodox theories is that conscious cognitive deliberation is solely responsible for forming rational economic expectations. In contrast, the new paradigm holds that the formation of expectations is an innate and automatic process based on conscious as well as nonconscious cognitive activity, with emotions serving as a motivational force. Forming expectations is an innate adaptive behavior. Expectations are automatically formed from the earliest to the latest stages of life. While it is natural for academic disciplines to theorize about the process, no discipline has delved into the fundamental evolutionary purpose of expectations. The new paradigm holds that expectations act as a means to maximize the potential of the human mind by minimizing needless drains on conscious deliberation by repeatedly forming expectations of common events. Expectations are viewed as critical to the efficient functioning of the human mind. Expectations allow the human mind to maximize the use of its most precious resource: conscious cognitive deliberation. Humans are exposed to a constant stream of information about their environment. The information easily overwhelms the capacity of the conscious mind, leaving nearly all of the information to be processed nonconsciously. Indeed, the nonconscious mind has the capacity to cognitively process information, to learn, and to form most expectations. As will be documented, these nonconscious processes account for the formation of rudimentary expectations by babies as well as the most accurate intuitions of experts.

Many critics of the rational expectations hypothesis have ignored the fact that accuracy is the dominant evolutionary rationale for forming expectations. It is this essential characteristic that enables human information processing to become more efficient as well as more effective. Indeed, accuracy is the only true rationale for forming and holding economic expectations. This is not equivalent to the unrealistic notion that every expectation is formed to be completely accurate; the intended degree of accuracy reflects a tradeoff between costs and benefits. The rational response is to not waste time and effort on a degree of accuracy that cannot be justified by benefits derived from improved economic decisions. Learning how to maintain the accuracy of their expectations is accomplished by conscious and nonconscious cognitive processes. The higher the premium on the accuracy of an expectation, the more likely it will be based on conscious cognitive deliberation. Nonetheless, it would be a very rare instance in which an economic expectation was formed without being influenced in some crucial way by nonconscious processes.

Another characteristic of the new paradigm is a recognition that expectations are fundamentally context sensitive. This is another distinctive aspect of the new paradigm that sets it apart from conventional theories. Orthodox economic theory holds that expectations are context independent, meaning that exactly the same expectation exists regardless of the context in which it is elicited. An endless stream of experiments have been performed indicating that differences in context influence the elicited expectation. The so-called heuristic and biases approach that emerged was taken to indicate that expectations were not based on rational calculations. The new paradigm comes to exactly the opposite conclusion. It views expectations as context sensitive, and it is this sensitivity that makes expectations more useful decision guides. Moreover, the heuristic and biases approach simply ends the analysis with the presumption of irrationality. No attempt is made to determine how heuristics are formed, their accuracy, or their usefulness. Heuristics are simply the outcomes of nonconscious cognitive processes, and their widespread use may indicate that forming fully rational expectations was typically deemed too costly given the benefits involved. In this new paradigm, rationality only applies to expectations tailored for specific decisions. Rationality is a property of the decision.

Rationality Is Context Sensitive

The most fundamental aspect of the new paradigm is its distinctive version of the rationality hypothesis. The new version does not conform to either the process view of psychologists or the outcome view of economists. To be sure, the new paradigm involves elements of rationality as a process as well as an outcome. The formation process, however, breaks free of the bounds of conscious cognitive deliberation to include the more dominant role of nonconscious, affective, and social influences on processing information relevant to the formation of expectations. While the accuracy of the outcome is still a prime objective of forming expectations, accuracy is never absolute, but only as precise as allowed by a cost–benefit calculation.

Importantly, rather than adopt a national perspective, people are guided by a self-interested need for expectations that reflect their own situation and decision needs.

This modified form of rationality reflects how people process, interpret, and evaluate information that they find relevant to their own welfare. While not every expectation formed in this manner will prove to be accurate, people naturally and automatically modify their expectations based on continual comparisons with actual developments. Like the formation process, the revision process is ongoing and dependent on conscious and nonconscious processes. People are motivated to make continuous revisions as long as the expectation is seen as having an important potential impact on their economic welfare. For critical expectations, the data will indicate that consumer expectations are highly correlated with actual subsequent changes in the objective measures. This alignment is at the aggregate. At the level of the individual, variations in expectations reflect differences in the economic conditions that people actually face. To conform to the revised criteria of rationality, an expectation must be viewed as having an important impact on a person's own economic welfare. This implies that the benefits of accurate expectations are ultimately derived from the impact of the decision on a person's overall economic welfare.

Most measures describing some aspect of the economy are often viewed by people as having little impact on their own economic welfare. Economists may disagree with some of these judgments, but most economic models often do not consider costs as well as benefits. There are only a few factors, such as prospects for prices, employment, interest rates, and personal incomes that are highly relevant to nearly all people. Most of the thousands of other economic variables that are of interest to economists are simply ignored. Obviously, with near zero economic benefits, no costs could be justified for forming an expectation. It would be nonsensical to anticipate that people would form rational expectations about economic series that have a trivial impact on their situation. Indeed, forming rational expectations is not a trait that can be applied to every situation and every economic variable. Rationality is decision and context specific. Perhaps this is the most important insight of the new paradigm. Rationality's sensitivity to decision context means that people will use the most cost effective means available to form their expectations with the desired degree of accuracy. This may include conscious information processing and deliberation, it may include nonconscious information processing and learning, or it may include all of people's mental faculties. The least likely is the conventional assumption that the rational formation of expectations would be based solely on conscious cognitive deliberation.

ECONOMICS OF RECESSIONS

Several other fundamental aspects of orthodox economic theory are challenged in Section II. A basic tenet of conventional theory is that recessions cannot result from rational economic behavior, but rather, recessions are always the result of some exogenous shock or policy misstep. The second aspect of orthodox theory that will be challenged is that consumer behavior is endogenous, meaning it is completely determined by other economic factors. Consequently, the consumer behavior can have no independent influence on the course of the macroeconomy. The third core orthodox belief is that rational investment decisions by consumers are based on an assessment of measurable risks that are unambiguous. The fourth involves the methodological tenet that macroeconomic developments must be justified by their micro foundations. Despite these orthodox views, it will be shown that some recessions are caused by endogenous economic forces, that consumer expectations represent a powerful and independent force that is shaping cyclical developments in the economy, that people have the unique ability to make investment decisions in the face of ambiguous information, and that trends in the macroeconomy are different than the mere aggregation of the micro units.

Recessions Are Irrational

The most fundamental characteristic of the macroeconomy is its cyclical nature. Periods of economic growth have been routinely followed by downturns in production, income, and employment. Recurrent cycles of abundance and famine were first recognized by the pharaohs of ancient Egypt, who mainly attributed changes in agricultural output to variations in the weather. The prominent role of weather as a cause of output variation lasted thousands of years, and became part of the classical economic theory first introduced by Adam Smith, David Ricardo, and Thomas Malthus. Although the initial phases of the Industrial Revolution began at about that same time, it did not change the fundamental view that the genesis of recession was due to exogenous factors. Recessions required some external shock to the economy or a misstep in economic policy. The list of exogenous factors was simply expanded from weather to include all sorts of natural and manmade disasters. Each recession was viewed as the unique result of some exogenous force. These unique events could never be fully predicted in advance, making the complete prevention of recessions impossible. Enlightened economic policies could reduce the number of recessions and mitigate their impact on the economy, but recessions could never been completely avoided.

Most people view recessions as the primary existential threat to their economic wellbeing, and consumers think one of the primary tasks of government economic policies is the prevention of recessions. After all, recessions are hardly rare events. The US economy has been mired in recessions nearly one-third of the time during the past 150 years. Although recessions have lessened in frequency in recent decades, economic downturns are still an all too common occurrence and represent a significant threat to the welfare of the nation and its people. Nonetheless, equilibrium economic theory excludes endogenous factors as even a possible cause of recessions. Orthodox theory holds that the natural dynamic is toward its equilibrium rate of growth. Indeed, it is rare for an econometric model to forecast a recession to start after one, two or three years from the current date. Instead, it is assumed that the economy always returns to its trend growth rate in future years. Since no exogenous shock can be predicted in advance, and no internal mechanism can produce a recession, the only logical forecast is a return to its equilibrium or natural rate of growth.

The notion that recessions are not caused by endogenous factors represents the fundamental belief that recessions do not result from rational economic behavior. Although economic growth is held to be synonymous with rational behavior, economic contraction must be forced by some external event. This asymmetry is a crucial part of orthodox theory. Since no individual can be assumed to willingly act against their self-interests, once aggregated, no economy can be expected to do so either. This principle of methodological individualism holds that all macro theory must be justified by its micro foundations. This unification of micro and macro theory represents a mirage that is dependent on assumption that the expectations of economic agents are themselves generated by the economic system.

As will be documented in this book, some aspects of the macroeconomy can display characteristics that are uniquely different than the sum of its micro units. Groups of people respond to macroeconomic developments in a manner that does not reflect the sum of its micro units. Indeed, macroeconomic expectations are inherently social constructs, and social dynamics respond to a "rationality" that is distinctively different from self-interest. The resistance of orthodox economic theory to this distinction is surprising since economics is guided by a comparable system-wide organizing principle, equilibrium. Equilibrium conditions are not properties of any of its micro units but are only a property of the system itself. No simple summing of the economy's constituent parts can establish equilibrium. Overall, rather than an outright rejection, this book represents a more nuanced view of the rationality postulate of economics.

The Powerful Consumer

The US consumer has consistently accounted for more than two-thirds of all spending in the national economy during the past hundred years. To most observers, this fact alone indicates the critical importance of consumer spending in determining whether the overall economy is expanding or contracting. Indeed, most of the public debate about the health of the macroeconomy is framed in terms of the strength of consumer demand. Orthodox economic theory, in contrast, holds that consumers' economic decisions are endogenous; the behavior of consumers is simply a response to changes in other economic factors. Conventional theory holds that consumers cannot independently cause an economy-wide downturn nor prompt a recovery from a recession. Orthodox economic theory admits that consumer spending may constitute a proximate cause, but convention theory holds that the ultimate or true causes are changes in incomes, prices, and interest rates. Fiscal and monetary policies that change taxes or interest rates, for example, cause consumers to expand and contract their spending. In addition to the government's powerful impact on the economy, entrepreneurial activity and investment decisions of business firms can also shape prospects for economic growth or contraction. In contrast to the active and powerful role played by government and business in shaping the course of the economy, conventional economic theory holds that consumers are passive responders, having no independent influence on the cyclical performance of the economy.

The passive role of the consumer sector in conventional theory represents a holdover from the agrarian economy, which dominated during the time that the roots of the modern discipline were formed by Smith, Ricardo, and Malthus. A barely sufficient life-sustaining economy meant that consumption was constrained to less than optimal levels. At that time, sustained economic growth and rising living standards were not anticipated and so played no role in classical economic theory. While a subsistence economy has long lost its grip on developed economies, it has been replaced by the assumption that people will always prefer more goods and services, never to be satiated. This assumption is tantamount to viewing consumption as persistently less than optimal, regardless of the prevailing level of affluence. Thus, under conventional theory, consumers are still viewed as passive translators of income into spending.

The key ingredients that made business investments powerful determinants of cyclical developments were their independent and discretionary nature. Orthodox theory holds that rising investments by entrepreneurs typically spark economic growth, and falling aggregate investment expenditures often lead to economic contractions. Nonetheless, as demonstrated in Section II, business investment expenditures have been surpassed by consumer investments in durables, vehicles, and homes, dating back to the earliest empirical evidence from nearly a hundred years ago. The term "consumer investment" is used in this book to signify the companion concept to "business investment." Consumers make investments in homes, vehicles, and household durables to more efficiently produce a higher living standard (utility) just as business firms invest in plant and equipment to more efficiently produce products and achieve higher sales (profits). While this is the standard definition of business investments, a common use of the term "consumer investments" typically refers to financial holdings which are invariably excluded from consideration as investments in this book.

The dominance of consumer investments over business investments was in terms of both dollar volumes as well as in the timing of the expenditures. Moreover, there is no reason to anticipate this will change any time in the future. Conventional theory holds that business is motivated by anticipated profits, which ultimately depend on sales to consumers. It would be more straightforward for economic theory to anticipate that aggregate business investments would be responsive to expected increases in consumer demand; that is, to the likely prospects of higher revenues and profits from consumer purchases.

While this interpretation would be more consistent with the data, it would still be misleading to consider business investments as not having an independent impact on prospects for economic growth. The only argument made in this book is that it is misleading to exclude consumer investments as an independent factor that helps to determine the cyclical performance of the economy. The relative contributions of the different factors shaping the performance of the economy are complex and are often not easily disentangled. Just as in equilibrium, where one side cannot be considered to dominate the other in determining the outcome, the same is true for the comparative importance of business and consumer investments to the performance of the macroeconomy. Advances in basic technologies are an important outcome of business investments and entrepreneurial activities. However, the cyclical performance of the economy critically depends on the timing of investment expenditures. As might be anticipated based on theory, the empirical evidence suggests that changes in consumer investments often precede changes in business investments.

For conventional theory to assert that consumer investment expenditures are endogenous requires that the economic expectations on which people based those investment decisions are also endogenous. This completes the circle of passivity that orthodox theory accords consumers. Consumers make economic decisions based on rational expectations that correctly anticipate future outcomes. Markets cleanse the untoward impact of any errors in expectations and behaviors. The only issue left is to correct for any remaining impacts from exogenous shocks through enlightened economic policies. In sharp contrast, this book provides evidence that consumers have a powerful influence on determining the course of the macroeconomy because their economic expectations are not completely predictable based only on economic factors.

This is hardly a new thesis. George Katona first advanced it more than a half-century ago, even using the emblematic title *The Powerful Consumer* (1960). Katona devised a simple set of questions to measure economic expectations in the mid-1940s that are still measured today in more than six dozen countries covering every inhabited continent on earth. The data on expectations clearly demonstrate that their formation is based on the entire capacity of the human mind. More importantly, the data also indicate how consumers anticipate and cause changes in the macroeconomy as well as how changes in the economy cause changes in the expectations of consumers. While some have suggested other measurement objectives and techniques, such as the use of probability scales and more precise measures that match economic concepts, the more simple verbal scales have generally proven to be more accurate. The superiority was due to a closer match with the mental procedures people actually use to form their expectations.

An important consideration for determining cyclical changes in the economy is what information is predicting the actual turning points. Just as the economy is reaching its most favorable level, an accurate leading indicator must turn negative, and convincingly so. The same contrarian sense must drive consumer expectations upward when the economy is recording its worst performance. During these times, when consumers have an expectation that is opposite to the performance of the economy, the economic risks may not be rationally calculable due to the ambiguous nature of the situation. While a decision based on economic rationality may not be possible, this book will demonstrate why people have a natural ability to form expectations when economic conditions are ambiguous.

The Urge to Act

John Maynard Keynes was the first proponent of the view that macroeconomics was a unique branch of economics. While many of his views were consistent with orthodox theory, one of his contributions was focused on how investment decisions were made when rational calculations of potential risks were impossible. Such ambiguous situations are now commonly referred to as Knightian uncertainty. When rational decisions were stymied by immeasurable investment risks, Keynes used the notion of "animal spirits" to provide an "urge to action." Keynes emphasized that these non-rational motivations were sometimes needed to spark a recovery at the depths of an economic downturn. Keynes did not extend the analysis to consumer investments, even though, at that time, such investments were as large in the aggregate as business investments. Instead, Keynes incorrectly appealed to a "fundamental psychological law" that held that consumer spending was a function of current income. This mistaken view of consumer spending may have resulted from older notions of the subsistence economy that likely still persisted in the absence of data on consumer spending. No data from national income and product accounts existed at that time. However, as we now know, consumer investments in household durables, vehicles, and homes were common in the 1920s as was the use of debt to finance these purchases. Moreover, the same ambiguous risk assessments plagued both consumer and business decisions when economic conditions were at their worst.

The insights of Keynes led to changes in conventional theory that he might not have anticipated. The situations in which ambiguity dominated were thought so rare as to be effectively immaterial to economics as a scientific discipline. Indeed, the equilibrium nature of economic theory explicitly assumes that all decision risks are calculable, or put in another way, when risks are ambiguous, a state of disequilibrium must exist. Orthodox theory suggests that the economic system provides inducements back toward equilibrium, although the exact path back, and how long it may take, are not specified. Additionally, the guarantee of a return to equilibrium has never been proven in practice or in theory. Keynes' "urge to act" in the face of ambiguity is now viewed as an anomaly with very limited applicability. "Animal spirits," in contrast, has become a widely used label for non-rational behavior. It is hardly ever applied to investment decisions when risks are immeasurable as Keynes intended, but has become primarily associated with consumer irrationality.

Intuitions or hunches are the modern equivalent of animal spirits that prompt the urge to act in ambiguous situations as well as when risks are measurable. Humans have a long history of making decisions based on incomplete information. As already indicated and as will be presented in detail in Section I of this book, the human brain is adept at constructing expectations of future events based on limited information. Forming expectations as intuitions is not the exception, but it is the most likely manner in which people form their expectations. In Section II, the data presented indicate that consumers are just as effective in forming expectations at cyclical turning points when ambiguous information is apt to dominate. Data on consumer expectations act as a leading economic indicator precisely because they also spark an urge to act, whether those actions are to delay or resume spending. The University of Michigan's expectation measures have a predictive ability that reflect an alignment of how the questions are worded and how people actually process and interpret economic information. It will be shown that the simplicity of the questions and index formulations outperform several alternatives that have been proposed.

Conventional theory suggests that shifts in expectations that are unpredicted by economic factors will soon be reversed by market forces. While this has been observed to occur, so too have subsequent shifts in the economy that conform to prior expectations. In the past, such shifts have been termed autonomous, and have been compared to other external shocks to the economy. However, this has been limited to only those that had negative consequences. The expectation of continued economic growth is essentially viewed as a rational self-fulfilling prophecy, but the same is not true about downturns. Since recessions are not rational, downward shifts in expectations are described as autonomous shifts due to exogenous shocks. This view has begun to change in recent years among economists, making self-fulfilling prophecies of a downturn improbable but not impossible. Moreover, if secular stagnation is the result of insufficient demand, self-fulfilling prophecies about future economic growth must also be recognized.

PARADIGM SHIFT

The paradigm shift advocated in this book requires documenting both the inadequacies of current theories as well as the superiority of the new theories. A rigorous assessment of current economic and psychological theories is used to identify weaknesses and inconsistencies, and is followed by the development of new theories that are capable of accounting for the empirical data on expectations. Although old and new theories are discussed in detail to highlight the differences, the development and justification of the new theories require a more demanding exposition. Most social sciences limit themselves to conscious cognitive deliberations, whereas this book explicitly introduces the nonconscious cognitive capacity of the human mind to process information and form expectations. While expectations can be formed solely by conscious deliberation, or solely by nonconscious processes, most expectations are formed by a combination of both the conscious and nonconscious mental faculties. Since the capacity of nonconscious information processing is vastly greater than the relatively small capacity of conscious processing, the fundamental evolutionary purpose of expectations is to optimize the use of conscious deliberation. The development of this thesis occupies most of the first section of the book.

Expectations are formed about numerous future events, from the most pedestrian events to the most extraordinary events. There is no reason to anticipate that the theories underlying the formation of economic expectations should be any different from how other expectations are formed, including political, social, personal, or any other expectation. Instead, there is every reason to believe that a common process generates all expectations. The guiding principle of forming and revising expectations is accuracy. Without a reasonable degree of accuracy, the fundamental evolutionary purpose of expectation would not be served, that is, to optimize the use of the more limited mental capacity for conscious deliberation. More importantly, conventional theories about how, why, and when economic expectations are formed have constrained rather than advanced our understanding of economic decision making. A new paradigm is needed to guide a more rigorous investigation of these basic issues.

PART I

THE FORMATION OF EXPECTATIONS

Everyone forms expectations. Expectations are beliefs about the future. Plato cited this definition more than 2,000 years ago and to this day it remains the generally accepted meaning of the term.[1] Expectations are easily and routinely formed by the youngest babies and by the oldest adults. Forming expectations is an innate process. Researchers have shown that before babies are able to talk, they develop expectations based on their experiences, showing surprise and dismay when an expected event fails to occur. That same sense of surprise and dismay is also common among adults when what they expect does not happen.

Expectations enable the allocation of scarce resources to achieve desired outcomes. While this may sound like the quintessential economic rationale for expectations, this justification extends far beyond the traditional bounds of economics. The evolutionary rationale for expectations is that they enable humans to make efficient use of their most constrained and valuable resource: the capacity to make conscious deliberative decisions. The limitations on conscious awareness require humans to efficiently and effectively use this scarce resource in order to attain their desired goals. The amount of information humans can consciously consider is vanishingly small in comparison to the deluge of information confronting them. Expectations help people decide which pieces of information they should consciously process. Fully anticipated events attract little conscious attention because they contain no new information. Unexpected events usually draw more conscious attention because they contain new information that could potentially affect their ability to achieve desired goals. People do not ignore what was expected. Most of this information is still processed, some of it consciously, but mostly without conscious awareness.

[1] Plato wrote that "each man possesses opinions about the future, which go by the general name of expectations" (Plato, Laws 644c, 360 BC).

21

The term cognition refers to people's mental ability to process information, interpret that information, and make decisions. These cognitive processes can occur consciously or nonconsciously. While most information is effortlessly processed nonconsciously, people are only consciously aware of the information they processed by effortful conscious deliberation.

This basic mission of expectations is widely recognized. Most walking or driving to familiar locations occurs without conscious awareness of road conditions, traffic, or fellow travelers unless something unexpected occurs. Indeed, most people arrive at their destination without any conscious recollection of specific events along the way. The same is true for economic information. Unless an inflation or unemployment rate changes in an unexpected manner it typically receives scant conscious attention. On trips to the grocery store, for example, most people consciously focus on the items they need and do not consciously review the price of each of the many items they purchase. If the price of some particular item has changed significantly, however, then conscious awareness is much more likely. Since the amount of economic information that people are exposed to in their everyday lives is enormous, it could easily dominate their conscious awareness to the exclusion of any other topic. Expectations enable people to manage their information processing tasks so that they can give conscious attention to the most important information. Even when people do not process economic information consciously, data on prices or employment conditions that people encounter in their daily lives can be processed without conscious awareness and can be used to form expectations.

Although expectations are a ubiquitous facet of life, no comprehensive and verifiable theory of the formation process has yet been advanced. This book advances the hypothesis that expectations are based on cognitive, affective, and nonconscious elements. The relative importance of each of these elements varies with the characteristics of the person and the situation as well as other contextual factors. This is hardly a new idea as all the components of the formation process have been widely documented in the scientific literature. Different disciplines have emphasized some features to the exclusion of others. For example, the traditional assumptions of economic rationality rely solely on conscious cognitive processes, with no consideration given to affective or subliminal factors. At the other extreme, some psychologists assume that expectations may be based on intuition or feelings that are not subject to conscious deliberation. No matter the weight given to each of these factors, all have the potential to influence expectations – even among the most rational economists or the most intuitive psychologists.

The inclusion of affective and subliminal factors along with conscious deliberation is meant to create a more accurate portrayal of human decision making. These additional factors are not recognized simply to account for inaccuracies in expectations. These factors are included to more fully explain how people form more timely and more accurate expectations that best serve their needs.

The influence of affective states on the formation of expectations is pervasive. Affect is a general term that includes evaluations, moods, and emotions. All information that is relevant to a person's economic situation is automatically accompanied by a positive or negative assessment. Rather than the conventional view that evaluations are necessarily based on a conscious assessment of information, it has been found that the affective connotation of information typically precedes the conscious awareness of that same information. Along with influencing the interpretation of information, affective states may signal the need to seek additional information, to engage in more careful scrutiny of alternatives, and to determine whether the information is processed nonconsciously or by conscious awareness. This view challenges the traditional duality of "reason and passion," which implicitly asserts that passion is not the handmaiden of reason, but acts to eviscerate deliberate judgments. It has long been argued that passion elevates people's preferred outcomes at the cost of more realistic expectations. While this may be true when passion completely dominates reason, it is also true that people make no judgments that are completely free of all affective influences.

The primary scientific challenge to the study of expectations is our inability to objectively observe expectations. Expectations must be inferred either from verbal reports or from behavior. Neither is foolproof. While many have assumed that people form expectations in advance and hold them in memory until they are needed, it is far more likely that people construct expectations for a specific purpose at the time they are actually needed. Each new construction may yield a different expectation for the same future event depending on the weights given to the various factors. Even when there has been no new economic information, changes in situational and contextual factors may alter expectations. Inferences based on behavior have the same disadvantage since the observed behavior reflects the same dynamically constructed expectation.

The chapters in this section will explore these theoretical issues in detail. Chapter 2 documents the most developed theories on the formation of expectations from both economics and psychology. All of these conventional theories assume the formation of economic expectations relies on conscious cognitive deliberation. The main disagreement involves the bounds or limits on the degree of rationality exhibited in the formation process. An implication of this fundamental assumption is that people with higher cognitive and computational skills should form more accurate economic expectations. The empirical evidence does not support this basic proposition. Inflation and unemployment expectations are indistinguishable between the most and least educated consumers, and are also indistinguishable from the expectations of economists. How could ordinary consumers be as accurate as economists in their year-ahead forecasts?

Part of the answer lies in what economic information people use to form their economic expectations. This topic is discussed in Chapter 3. The usual assumption is that expectations are based on publically available data on economic conditions collected by federal agencies. The data are assumed to be widely available in the media, so much so that people could hardly avoid hearing about the latest statistic on inflation, employment, or personal income. When representative samples of consumers are asked about those official statistics, however, the data reveal widespread ignorance. Moreover, the informational content of media reports are vastly exaggerated. The typical report was found to avoid the quantitative statistic in favor of a qualitative interpretation. To be sure, those with higher education attainment typically knew more, supporting the cognitive link to the formation of expectations. But even among consumers that knew the least about these official statistics, they nonetheless expressed their economic expectations for inflation and unemployment to the same questions that proved their forecast accuracy in the prior chapter.

Rather than basing their expectations on public information, consumers typically used private information about the prices and employment conditions that they actually faced. Indeed, economic theory holds that consumers should base their decisions on the conditions that they actually face rather than the national average. When aggregated properly, of course, the conditions faced by each consumer should equal the national averages, although with much wider true dispersion than suggested by the sole "representative agent" models commonly used in economics. That is not the most important implication of consumers' reliance on private information. The most important implication is that consumers are confronted by a continuous flow of economic information relevant to their situation. Information reaches them not monthly or quarterly, but continuously.

How can people process such an avalanche of information and make sense of the bits and pieces of changes in the economic conditions that confront them in their daily lives? The human brain is an information processing engine. People's capacity to nonconsciously process information is of orders of magnitude larger than conscious awareness. There is no reason to suspect that processing economic information is any different than the many other types of information on which people depend and regularly process both consciously and nonconsciously. Chapter 4 describes people's innate ability to form expectations through nonconscious processes, including the natural ability to form numerical associations that enable them to implicitly form economic expectations. Moreover, people can nonconsciously learn patterns of association and form nascent theories based on inductive logic. While the underlying knowledge structures elude conscious awareness, people can recall the resulting economic expectation. Such expectations are often described as intuitions or hunches, or the product of habit, since people are not consciously aware of the rationales underlying their formation. While economics has long recognized this phenomenon, it is most often associated with bias and irrationality. Such a narrow view discounts the evolutionary purpose of expectations and the automatic revision process that errors spark. While some errors may well persist, few consumers can long ignore significant errors in their expectations for their cost of living, their employment, or their wages. Whereas public information on national economic trends may be more suited to conscious deliberation, the continuous flow of the more important private information on the prices, employment, and wages that people actually face may be more suited to the nonconscious formation of expectations.

Emotions are closely intertwined with people's economic expectations. Who speaks of a job loss or income decline in a detached manner? What individual greets a falling living standard due to rapidly escalating prices without a sense of dread? Chapter 5 details how affective states play an essential role in the formation of expectations. Affective states are an independent force that can react faster to assess new information than people's cognitive system. Indeed, people automatically evaluate information before they become consciously aware of the information, which is just the opposite of what conventional wisdom would suggest. Evolutionary forces have adapted the affective system to optimally influence the formation of expectations independently from people's cognitive capacity. These automatic evaluations enable the effortless combination of many pieces of information based on their intrinsic meaning to nonconsciously form more general expectations. Moreover, unlike differences in cognitive skills, there is less variation across the population in these affective decision resources since they have benefitted from a much longer evolutionary development than people's conscious cognitive abilities.

These affective states motivate information seeking, determine the processes used to evaluate information, and provide visible signals to others about people's own economic situation. At times, emotional displays promote the contagion of economic fears at an unstoppable pace across an entire population. While such collapses in confidence are rare, information transmitted by emotional displays plays a key role in shaping the dynamics of the much more common cyclical changes in consumer expectations. Passion can no longer be viewed as the enemy of reason since both are essential components of rational expectations.

The final chapter in this section deals with how and when expectations are constructed. The formation of expectations is motivated not by the availability of new information but by the need to make a specific decision. Conventional theories assume that economic expectations are typically revised with each new data release by federal agencies, with the results stored in memory, and recalled as needed for decision making. An entire "book shelf" of expectations is maintained that includes all relevant economic factors, such as the outlook for inflation, employment, wages, interest rates, and so forth. In the conventional view, economic expectations are formed by a separate and independent process. In the new view, economic expectations are formed only when needed and each expectation is formed for a specific use. While some expectations may take an extended period of time and conscious effort to construct, other expectations are formed effortlessly and instantaneously as they are based on previously acquired information. Emotions motivate the process, including what information is considered important and how expectations are formed. Rather than being confined to the conscious cognitive functions, the construction of expectations utilizes the full resources of the human mind.

No one can be realistically assumed to use an expectation based on national data when their own economic situation differs. While the "representative consumer" typically used to explicate economic theories can be assumed to have expectations that correspond to the national average, actual consumers face markedly different economic situations. No single expectation based on national data for inflation, jobs or wages could satisfy all decision needs, and no decision maker would ignore relevant information gained after the latest government release. These common sense facts are hardly controversial. Yet, the implications of these simple facts on how people form expectations are not fully incorporated into economic theory. Given that the most effective economic expectations are always tailored to the specific decision needs of an individual in a given context, private rather than public information should logically dominate the formation of expectations.

People form expectations in order to achieve desired outcomes. Economists sometimes conflate this with the desire to acquire general knowledge about the economy. People possess no natural tendency to form expectations about economic events that have no direct impact on their lives. Self-interest rules. Nonetheless, some people do seek out ancillary economic information for a variety of purposes, not the least of which is to become a knowledgeable citizen. This book, however, is mainly concerned with those economic expectations that are important to most people, most of the time, such as expectations about future changes in jobs, wages, prices, interest rates, and asset values. These are not economic statistics to people; they are the economic facts of their own lives. Prospective changes have personal consequences so people monitor whatever information they gain in their everyday lives, including specialized information associated with occupations or interests. Processing and learning from a continuous flow of information is what the human brain was designed to accomplish. While conscious reasoning represents the most flexible and most advanced aspect of mental processing, most of the work of the human mind is accomplished nonconsciously, and its actions are guided and motivated by emotions.

This more comprehensive theory on the formation of expectations is based on empirical observation, or what George Katona identified in the middle of the twentieth century as behavioral economics. Importantly, this description of how economic expectations are formed provides strong support for the economist's view that accuracy is the primary objective. Accurate expectations allow conscious reasoning to focus on other topics, expanding the depth and reach of people's command over their environment. Inaccurate expectations automatically signal the need for more deliberation in an attempt to restore predictive accuracy. People naturally employ all their mental resources, including the much greater capacity of nonconscious information processing and learning in this task. Humans have always feared the disastrous impact of negative developments more than cherished the bounty of positive change. Emotions reflect this asymmetry and are uniquely responsible for accelerating declines in confidence and slowing recoveries in optimistic expectations. This new theory recognizes the importance of conscious cognitive reasoning, unconscious information processing and learning, and emotions on how people construct their economic expectations.

This new comprehensive theory of economic expectations is best viewed as a conjecture as this book provides no conclusive scientific proof. The least of the problems involves the ecological fallacy: no scientific inference can be drawn about individual behavior from aggregate data. This is a well-known problem with all analyses based on aggregate data on consumer, producer, or investor behavior as well as the analyses of aggregate data in other social sciences. Although most of the elements of the broader theory of expectations have been investigated and confirmed at the individual level of analysis, there has been no attempt to confirm the new theory of how expectations are formed at the individual level. This is not by choice as no scientific technique yet exists that can uniquely determine the content and interaction of conscious and nonconscious cognitive processes. Future advances may enable the illumination of this "black box," but until that happens, it makes no sense to ignore its impact on shaping economic expectations. The intellectual merit of this conjecture lies in its consistency with advances in other scientific disciplines as well as its ability to stimulate further advances in our understanding of how expectations shape the dynamics of the macroeconomy.

2

Conventional Theories of Expectations

The core principles of economics have remained largely unchanged since Adam Smith identified rational self-interest more than 250 years ago as the essential driving force of economic advancement. It was only fifty years ago that John Muth (1961) extended the same core assumptions about rational behavior to the formation of economic expectations. It was a natural extension since these principles define the core of economics as a scientific discipline. At the time Muth first introduced his theory of rational expectations, few would have guessed that it would have such a profound impact. The rational expectations hypothesis has become as deeply embedded in economic theory as it has become deeply contested by other social sciences. Economists speak of the "rational expectations revolution" to signify its overarching impact on their discipline. The revolution enabled the most significant advances in macroeconomic theory during the past half century. Other social scientists have offered trenchant criticisms that the theory was incompatible with how people actually form expectations, and that such a theoretical detachment from observed economic behavior could hardly benefit any scientific discipline. Nobel Laureates in economics numbered among both the adherents and the detractors, including Robert Lucas, Thomas Sargent, Herbert Simon, Daniel Kahneman, and Robert Shiller. The debate has hardly been settled, nor is it likely to be any time soon.

A core part of economic theory is that firms maximize profits and consumers maximize utility based on a rational assessment of all relevant information. Economists make the same assumptions about forming expectations. For many economists, the continuing debate about the rationality postulate seems surreal. A rejection of rationality would be tantamount to a rejection of the integrating principle of all economic theory. It should be no surprise that economists strenuously resist such an extreme step. Indeed, a clear advantage of the rational expectations hypothesis is its theoretical strength. The hypothesis has proved to be enormously productive in advancing macroeconomic theory, since the rationality assumption enables the powerful tools of optimization to systematically expand the depth and breadth of economic theories. Rational expectations are now an important component in nearly all of macroeconomic theory, including consumption and investment, employment and wages, debt and saving, currency exchange rates, and many other topics.

From the viewpoint of other social sciences, the acceptance of the rationality postulate seemed to signal more delusional rather than coherent thinking. This critique of the psychological assumptions that underlie economic theories was made by Gabriel Tarde in his book *Psychologie économique* (1902), and those assumptions were as sharply debated at the start of the twenty-first century as at the start of the twentieth century (Lewin, 1996). The contention is that the assumptions about human behavior that lie at the core of economic theory are empirically false. People do not rationally take account of all available information to optimally construct their expectations. The costs of complete or full rationality are just too high, even if a person was capable of such a feat. People exercise a more limited or bounded rationality when forming expectations. For most social scientists, as well as some economists, it was more sensible to assume some limits or bounds on rationality (Simon, 1997; Conlisk, 1996; Kahneman & Tversky, 1982). The term "bounded rationality" was defined to recognize limits on people's conscious cognitive capacities. These cognitive limitations gave birth to the heuristic and bias approach of Daniel Kahneman and Amos Tversky. They argued that when people's cognitive capacities are overwhelmed, people resort to heuristics or shortcut strategies for making decisions. The resulting expectations are not only suboptimal based on the information available when people formed the expectation, but people's expectations reflect persistent biases and depend on the context or frame of reference in which they were elicited.

Just as important as the differences between the two camps are the areas of agreement. Conventional economic and psychological theories share the view that the formation of economic expectations is the product of conscious cognitive deliberation. Indeed, the core distinction is defined by the extent to which conscious cognitive deliberation can be used to form rational expectations. No positive role is given to nonconscious information processing or nonconscious learning in the formation of economic expectations, despite the comparatively limitless powers of nonconscious information processing. Conscious deliberation is always the gatekeeper, even for intuitions formed by fast and frugal nonconscious processes.

After a detailed empirical review of these conventional theories, this chapter arrives at several awkward conclusions. If expectations are the product of conscious cognitive deliberation, differences in economic expectations should reflect the differences in the quality of the resources used in cognitive reasoning. Surprisingly, data on inflation expectations indicate that there is little difference between the expectations of consumers and economists. If the costs of forming accurate expectations are excessive, consumers should form inferior economic expectations. The costs faced by economists are significantly less than those faced by ordinary consumers. Professional economists enjoy significant advantages in forming expectations, including easy access to the data, knowledge of the relevant theory and models, computer programs to aid in computation, and the experience required to correctly interpret the results. In contrast, economists typically assume that consumers suffer from perceptual and judgment biases, lack computational skills, and have no knowledge of the relevant theory or how to interpret the data. The same tests on inflation expectations were performed for consumers' unemployment expectations, with the empirical results for a wide range of countries showing that consumers correctly anticipated future changes in the unemployment rate.

More importantly, the reliance on conscious cognitive abilities is not supported when a detailed examination is made of consumers with presumably different cognitive capacities. All conventional theories suggest that consumers with higher cognitive abilities would form more accurate expectations. For example, those with a college degree should have an advantage in forming more accurate expectations than those with little education. Admittedly, formal education is not a perfect proxy for cognitive abilities, but it does represent broad differences in cognitive performance. The data showed that trends in inflation and unemployment expectations are essentially similar across all education groups.

Given these known disparities in cognitive abilities, how could the same degree of forecast accuracy be achieved? Until now, no one has advanced an explanation explicitly centered on nonconscious processing of economic information, with interpretations and forecasts generated by nonconscious model building. Nonconscious processes can never completely displace conscious deliberation. Nonconscious information processing is utilized to maximize the ability of the human mind to deal with the immense amount of data on issues for which consumers have self-interested motivations to have accurate expectations. Although the very nature of nonconscious processes makes them unavailable to conscious awareness, the importance of these processes forms a critical component in the formation of expectations.

Consumers cannot consciously nor even nonconsciously process every bit of available economic information. The amount of information is staggering. Public and private agencies with tens of thousands of employees publish an enormous amount of information on the economy every day. How do consumers choose which information to follow? Economic theory posits a self-interested selection based on costs and benefits. As part of that selection, people often choose between public and private information on economic trends. In this context, private sources include information about a given individual's economic situation and public information about aggregate economic conditions.

THE KEYNESIAN MANDATE

Expectations did not play a major role in economic theorizing until the publication in 1936 of the *General Theory of Employment, Interest and Money* by John Maynard Keynes. Although expectations always had a place in the economic literature, Keynes was the first to stress the importance of expectations in determining the course of the macroeconomy. Keynes advanced no specific theory on how people formed economic expectations. He used the term "animal spirits" to convey the notion that people often base their expectations on little if any actual knowledge about the future. How could anyone know with the required certainty the ten-year rate of return to make any investment? According to Keynes, people did not rationally form expectations in the presence of ambiguity, rather they formed them as the outcome of a "spontaneous urge to action." Although Keynes convinced economists that expectations must be taken into account, the term "animal spirits" is still used to connote expectations that are "irrational" and thus outside the domain of economics. Nonetheless, given that economists made expectations the centerpiece of macro theory, Keynes sparked the establishment of research programs aimed at furthering our understanding of how expectations are actually formed.

Indeed, George Katona began to measure the expectations of consumers at the University of Michigan in 1946.[1] At the end of World War II, many feared that the post-war economy would again give rise to the same type of deflationary spiral and mass unemployment that characterized the

---

[1]   The balance of this subsection is drawn from Curtin (2004:131–132). Reprinted with the permission of the University of Michigan Press.

Great Depression of the 1930s. Press headlines in mid-1945 proclaimed, "Government economists predict eight million unemployed by 1946." What actually occurred was quite different. In the first half of 1946, the unemployed numbered 3 million, not 8, and instead of deflation, the economy faced inflationary pressures. Rather than harboring the same fears as economists, consumers exhibited a great deal of confidence in the future course of the economy. Acting on that confidence, consumers spent an increasing fraction of their incomes, pushing the savings rate to a low that would not again be recorded for fifty years (Curtin, 2004).

In a post-mortem on the forecast error, the Nobel Laureate Lawrence Klein (1946) noted that the predictions were inaccurate due to a serious error in the forecast of consumer expenditures (Curtin, 2004). The error was large enough to have a disastrous impact on economic policy recommendations. As might be expected, the forecast error prompted widespread concerns about whether the underlying economic theory was correct. Klein concluded that improvements in the accuracy of forecasting models would require a more detailed specification of the factors that shape the economic expectations of consumers.

From that point forward, conventional theories on the formation of expectations moved rapidly from the naive to the sophisticated; from the naive assumption that tomorrow would be like today to the sophisticated assumption that expectations would be unbiased and efficient forecasts of actual future economic developments. It was a shift from doubting the ability of consumers to acquire, understand, and effectively utilize information on economic developments to the assumption that they were fully rational, possessed complete information, and formed unbiased expectations of future economic events. This shift from one extreme to the other occurred rather rapidly, in the twenty-five years between the publications of Keynes and Muth.

What Is Past Is Prologue

Forming expectations essentially involves processing and interpreting information. The basic assumptions are that consumers are aware of the relevant data, can perform the required calculations, and know how to interpret the information correctly. The initial theories attempted to minimize the burden of these assumptions by simply postulating that history foretold the future. People expected that whatever economic outcome they recently observed would continue unchanged into the future. This simple extrapolation model had several virtues. Incremental change is typical for most economic variables. Today's unemployment rate is much like yesterday's, as tomorrow's inflation and interest rates are similar to today's. As long as the period covered by the expectation was relatively short, yesterday's outcome could accurately approximate today's result. In addition, this model did not make excessive demands on consumers, as there was no need for interpretation or for calculations. Consumers only needed the knowledge of the current value.

The next set of models was barely more complex. People based their expectations on the extrapolation of the past several observations. This meant that consumers would take into account the rising or falling of the series when forming expectations. This model was somewhat more demanding. Consumers needed to know the recent history of the variable, and had to calculate whether and how it had changed. For most consumers, this was a natural extension since they commonly judged economic variables in terms of change, for example, whether the rate of unemployment or inflation was improving or worsening. More complex forms of the extrapolation hypothesis, however, meant giving declining weights to the more distant past than to recent observations. This entailed even more calculations, although most were quite straightforward, and people were thought to easily and naturally accommodate declining weights as memory faded.

Perhaps the most demanding of these initial models were those that viewed the formation of expectations as the outcome of a learning process. Learning models still focused only on the past history of the series, but also took into account prior errors in people's expectations (Nerlove, 1958; Cagan, 1956; Fisher, 1930). To learn from past errors involved more calculations on the part of consumers as well as an unbiased memory of their own prior expectations. These models assumed that consumers based their expectation for the next period on the recent past history of the series as well as on their own past errors, typically adding or subtracting a given amount or proportion of last period's error. The size of the error correction determined the "speed" of learning. While learning could not completely erase errors, the assumption posited that people gradually reduced the size of errors over time.

Each of these early models were essentially equivalent. Whether called extrapolative, adaptive, learning, or error correction models, these models can be shown to be equivalent to a weighted average of past realizations by the Koyck (1954) transformation. What differed was the specification of the process used by consumers to form their expectations. The specifications were not detailed enough to indicate the expected size of the various effects, so any estimated coefficient significantly different from zero was taken to be consistent with the hypothesis. Unfortunately, given that all shared the same reduced form model, the inability to uniquely specify the various hypotheses meant that the empirical tests could not robustly distinguish between the competing alternatives.

For economists, error learning models held the greatest appeal since they believed that experience brought expectations in line with subsequent realizations. That hope, however, was misplaced since the reliance on past changes produces systematic biases. Systematic prediction errors result since expectations tend to underestimate or overestimate the true change whenever the underlying variable is trending upward or downward. In response to this deficiency, augmented models were proposed, which incorporate information on other variables that are assumed to influence the formation of expectations. The use of this additional information can help to offset the tendency toward systematic prediction errors. Needless to say, such augmented models greatly increase the presumed burden on consumers for collecting even more information, making more calculations, and interpreting more complex models.

More importantly, these augmented models took on characteristics that were similar to the rational expectations hypothesis. The key difference was in how they were empirically tested. One tested against the backward sources of expectations, the other tested the forward accuracy of expectations. Thus, empirical analysis of the augmented models tested whether any of the variables had a predictive association with subsequent expectations, while the rational expectations model tested whether expectations could accurately predict subsequent realizations. The former tested the process used to form expectations but not the accuracy of expectations, while the latter tested the accuracy of expectations but not how people formed expectations.

It should be no surprise that changing economic conditions influenced the outcome of the empirical tests. The early findings from the research program at the University of Michigan indicated that expectations had both backward- and forward-looking components. Most of the time, expectations followed past changes. Since yesterday's economy was very similar to today's conditions, tomorrow's expectations were much like today's outcomes. Empirical tests confirmed this obvious relationship. At other times, expectations could not be predicted from past trends. These discontinuous shifts reflected the incorporation of newly emerging economic trends. Since the US economy has mostly exhibited stable growth conditions in the past half century, empirical tests favored the adaptive expectations model.

RATIONAL EXPECTATIONS HYPOTHESIS

John Muth began his classic article on rational expectations by noting that survey data on expectations were as accurate as the elaborate models of economists (Muth, 1961). His basic insight was that economic agents form their expectations so that they are essentially the same as the predictions of the relevant economic theory. The assumption that people formed expectations rationally was for Muth the natural extension of core economic principles. Nonetheless, Muth noted that rationality was an assumption that was testable by the systematic comparison with alternative theories in explaining observed expectations.[2]

Compared with tests of utility maximization, expectations have the unique advantage that they can be estimated and subjected to empirical tests. The rigor of the tests of the rational expectations hypothesis ranges from tests of biases and predictive accuracy to how efficiently people used every possible piece of relevant information in forming the expectations. No one has performed such comparable tests on utility or profit maximization. Even casual observers know that consumers often make choices that decrease their welfare and often base their decisions on incomplete information. Hardly anyone believes that people actually maximize utility in a rational manner. Despite this fact, the assumption of rationality plays a positive and useful role in economic theory as well as in practical applications – at least according to economists.

Other social sciences hold just as strong opposing views. These differences are rooted in the respective scientific methodologies of the disciplines. Milton Friedman (1953) declared in his celebrated essay on methodology that the validity of an economic theory is independent of its psychological assumptions. Predictive accuracy was the true test of theory, not the realism of the embedded assumptions. Friedman used the example of an expert pool player. A model that had good predictive performance is based on the physical laws of velocity, momentum, and angles. Expert pool players shoot as if they know these equations of motion. If asked, however, they will undoubtedly deny any knowledge of these physical laws. Yet, more realistic assumptions about their behavior would not improve the predictive accuracy of the model.

Nonetheless, there are differences among economists about how rational expectations should be empirically tested. Three types of tests have been

---

[2] This paragraph is drawn from Curtin (2010:34). Reprinted with the permission of Routledge Press.

proposed. The most common is a time-series test that compares changes in an expectation with subsequent changes in the economic variable. The second type is based on repeated observations on the same person since the rationality postulate is assumed to hold for each individual. Such panel data would avoid offsetting differences across individuals that could bias the outcome of the tests. The third type of test is based on the premise that rational expectations are market outcomes, not properties of an individual's expectation. For example, inflation expectations are derived from the inter-action of buyers and sellers of inflation-adjusted securities, not from an individual's bid or even the bids across groups of individuals. The market tests of the rationality hypothesis are excluded from any further discussion since the consensus is that rationality should be conceptualized as a prop-erty of individual economic agents.

How Should Rationality Be Tested?

Perhaps the most significant difference is whether rationality is conceived as a characteristic of the process or as a characteristic of the outcome. One definition focuses on the process of forming expectations, the other on the outcomes of the formation process. One judges rationality by how expectations were formed, regardless of the outcome, the other by whether expectations accurately predicted future outcomes, regardless of how they were formed. How should rationality be judged? Psychologists have gener-ally favored process over outcomes, and economists favor outcomes over process. The essential argument of psychologists is that the future is so uncer-tain that tests of rationality must focus on the process, while economists claim that for the purposes of decision making, tests of rationality must focus on their accuracy. It would be a mistake to label one approach correct and the other incorrect. They simply constitute different perspectives on the same topic. Indeed, in an ideal world, a rational process would produce a rational outcome, which one integrated theory could describe.

Economic theory starts from a premise and deduces testable behavioral propositions. When empirical evidence does not support the proposition, a modification of the theory is indicated. Economic theory relies on the power of predictions to test theories, not on the relevance of the assumptions used to generate the predictions. The opposite is true for psychology. Rather than being solely focused on the behavioral outcomes, psychology concentrates on the processes utilized in forming expectations. For psychology, it makes no sense to dismiss the realism of the embedded assumptions. If the process used was rational, psychologists usually judge the outcome rational as well.

The methodological debate has not been resolved. Moreover, we cannot expect a resolution in the future due to deeply ingrained differences between the disciplines. The only core principle that all conventional theories agree on is that the formation of economic expectations is the outcome of an information processing task. This task typically assumes that conscious deliberation and interpretation of economic information are required. Nonconscious processing and emotions play no positive role in conventional economic theories. Indeed, they are viewed as a persistent source of misperception and bias that conscious deliberation must overcome. Conventional expectation theories strictly adhere to the long held primacy of conscious reasoning over emotion and intuition.

The basic challenges to the rational expectations hypothesis are based on the high cognitive costs of forming expectations in this manner. Information has to be gathered, calculations made, and the data interpreted correctly in order to form each of the several economic expectations needed to make rational decisions. Many people are simply not capable, it is argued, of calculating and interpreting economic data. Even among those that have the capacity, the opportunity costs of devoting resources to rationally forming each expectation would be so high as to preclude many other deliberative tasks. Since higher costs are generally associated with more accurate expectations, people would generally not seek to maximize accuracy, but suffice with fewer well-crafted expectations (Simon, 1987).

Economists have recognized these constraints but countered that information on important economic series, such as inflation or unemployment, is widely and freely disseminated by the mass media, and expert interpretation often accompanies these releases, making it relatively easy for consumers to interpret the data and, if necessary, to revise their expectations. For economists, people must compare the costs of updating expectations with the benefits derived from updating. Updating expectations may be relatively infrequent if there is no need for updating, or it may be very frequent when the benefits of up-to-date expectations are high.

Private versus Public Information

There is no parity between the expectations of consumers and economists for most economic variables. Parity may only exist where consumers have direct experience with the economic variable, such as inflation, employment, and income. Expected changes in these variables are an important source of information to incorporate into current decisions. This notion has been incorporated into economic theory as the permanent income or life-cycle hypothesis. These concepts imply that when consumers plan their consumption and savings behavior, they take into account their long-term expectations. If this is an accurate assumption, then consumers have a self-interested motivation to form expectations about future changes in prices, employment, and incomes as well as the costs of credit and returns on assets. Consumers do not have such high self-interested motivations to form expectations about many other future economic events that will not materially affect their own economic situation.

This distinction is important as it indicates that consumers are more likely to use private rather than public information in forming their expectations. The most powerful private information is specifically tailored to their own situation. It is not the general inflation rate that matters, but the prices that people face for the goods and services that they actually purchase. It is not the overall rate of growth in jobs, but jobs for which they are qualified and in the areas in which they live that are most important. Why would people base their expectations on prices or wages that they would not actually face? In contrast, economists base their expectations on national data, not self-interested private sources of information. The distinction between private and public information has been a constant source of confusion when economists evaluate empirical tests of consumer expectations. When comparing, for example, self-interested inflation expectations with government statistics, nearly all consumers would have either higher or lower estimates even if consumers' aggregate expectation was perfectly accurate. The same is not true for the analysis of economists' expectations, and empirical analyses have often shown much smaller variations in their expectations about the government's published rate. Note that this difference is just about the variance in expectations, and not about the accuracy of the midpoint of the entire distribution of responses. If all consumers accurately reflected their own spending, the total would mirror the aggregate amount. Although the dispersion of consumers' expectations can be expected to be much larger than economists' expectations, there may not be any inherent bias making the midpoint of the distribution any less accurate.

An important characteristic of private information is that it arrives in a constant flow of bits and pieces – for example, as the prices of the products and services consumers purchase every day, information from family, friends, and acquaintances, or as the news from the mass media about past and prospect price trends. Conventional theories posit that consumers revise their expectations with each public announcement, with the implicit assumption that consumers ignore the constant flow of information about their own economic situation. While announcements of public information on inflation can hardly overwhelm the capacity of conscious deliberation, most conventional theories assume that the constant flow of information on prices would far exceed the capacity of conscious attention. As will be shown in the next few chapters, nonconscious information processing is ideally suited for such a task.

Empirical Models

The formation of expectations depends on two factors: informational inputs (I) and the model or process of transforming information into expectations (f). Let an economic expectation (E^e) formed by the ith individual be defined as:

$$E_t^{e_{t-1}} = f(I_{t-1})$$

where the subscript t on E^e indicates the period for which the expectation applies, and the expectation formed based on the information that was available in a prior period, denoted by the superscript e_{t-1}. The dominant specifications of this equation are the rational expectations hypothesis and the extrapolative, adaptive and error learning models (Curtin, 2010).

The following autoregressive distributive lag representation summarizes the various adaptive, extrapolative, and error learning models:

$$E_t^e = \alpha + \sum_j \beta_j E_{t-j}^e + \sum_j \gamma E_{t-j} + \epsilon_t$$

where E^e is the expectations of an actual economic event E, j is the lag length, and ε is the error term, with the i subscript dropped for convenience. Other variables that are part of the relevant information could also be included in the equation. Defining the unique characteristics of the various models involves the specification of coefficients α, β, γ, and ε.

Empirical tests of the rational expectations hypothesis are much more rigorous than tests on adaptive or learning models. Rather than simply finding a significant relationship, rational expectations require a rigorous series of empirical tests. Rather than being supported by any significant relationship, the theory requires the observation of a series of specific point estimates. Unbiased expectations under the rational expectations hypothesis demand that the coefficients α and β are zero and one, respectively, in the equation:

$$E_t = \alpha + \beta E_t^{e_{t-1}} + \epsilon_t$$

This does not necessarily mean that an individual's expectation is perfectly accurate, it simply assumes that an inflation rate could not have been more accurately formed based on the available information than when $\alpha = 0$ and $\beta = 1.0$. Moreover, the strong test of rationality requires that all of the available information has been efficiently and optimally used in forming the expectation, in order to produce the best possible forecast. This involves tests on the statistical properties of the prediction errors to determine if they are consistent with those stipulated by the hypothesis (orthogonality, efficiency, consistency, as well as unbiasedness). Tests of this assumption take the form:

$$\zeta_t = \alpha + \sum \beta_j E_{t-j} + \sum \gamma_j Z_{t-j} + \epsilon_t$$

where ζ is the prediction error, the coefficients β and γ are expected to be zero, and the prediction errors are serially uncorrelated. This expresses the notion that if any of the available information was systematically related to the prediction errors, the information was not efficiently and optimally incorporated into the formation of the original expectation. It should be no surprise that empirical tests have often failed to support the more rigorous requirements of the rational expectations hypothesis.

Importance of Accuracy

Forming expectations is a burdensome task. People exert the effort because accurate expectations are useful when making economic decisions. The benefits must justify the costs. While most theories have paid critical attention to the costs of forming expectations, variations in the benefits have recently received attention as well. How are benefits defined? Presumably by the positive impact on economic decisions from correct expectations. Leaving aside how to evaluate the impact on decisions, who would repeatedly exert the effort to knowingly form inaccurate expectations? This does not imply that perfect accuracy is required for the effort to be undertaken, nor that people do not anticipate learning from their past errors. The notion of accuracy must be defined with respect to the costs and benefits involved. Few consumers would consider their expectations inaccurate if they were off the mark by a relatively small amount, and a few would be satisfied if their expectations were in the same ballpark. You might think that no one would form expectations if the best efforts they undertook were always inaccurate. That presumption would be incorrect. It would depend on the degree of error compared with the benefit derived even with that likely error. Nonetheless, the goal of any economic agent is to form accurate expectations.

Costs and Benefits of Updated Expectations

Economists realize that rational expectations are costly to form and the benefits from continuously updating expectations may be overstated (Curtin, 2010). As long as there is any positive cost involved in collecting and processing information, some agents will sometimes choose to hold less accurate expectations. Economists have described the impact of costs on the formation process by the terms "sticky information" or "rational inattention" (Bacchetta & van Wincoop, 2005; Sims, 2003; Mankiw & Reis, 2002). These theories postulate that rational consumers may find that the costs associated with updating their expectations exceed the benefits. At any given time, some people will find it worthwhile to incur the costs, especially if that information is critical to a pending decision. Most of the time, however, rational inattention is the optimal course. Alternatively, agents may base their expectations on imperfect information, which is less costly than perfect information. Whatever the cause, the process creates staggered changes in expectations, whereby at any given time expectations reflect a combination of current and past information across different people.

The concept of "inferential" expectations has also been proposed to account for the staggered pace that expectations are updated (Menzies & Zizzo, 2009). The core idea is that consumers determine whether new, relevant information warrants a change in their current expectations. Newly released economic data is noisy and is often subject to revision. It would be inappropriate and too costly to revise expectations with every wiggle in the data. Revisions are treated like statistical hypotheses. Consumers only revise their expectations when the cumulative evidence indicates a significant change has occurred. Otherwise, consumers leave their expectations unchanged.

Some economists view disagreement across people in their expectations at any given time as an indication of such a process (Mankiw et al., 2004). Some have modeled the disagreements as the result of factors other than costs, such as an epidemiological process in which "expert opinion" spreads slowly through a population like the spread of a disease (Carroll, 2003). Costs can also be assumed to vary across demographic subgroups, as some encounter lower costs for acquiring and using information, and other more economically active subgroups derive greater benefits from updating their expectations more frequently. This interpretation of disagreements or inaccuracies in expectations addressed the mistaken inference that the very existence of differences indicated non-rational expectations (Souleles, 2001).

A wide range of processes that either encourage or discourage agents from updating their expectations could create staggered changes. A common hypothesis for staggered updating holds that it is due to asymmetric responses to economic information, with agents updating their expectations much more quickly in response to bad news. Consumers perceive bad economic news as containing more potentially relevant information about their financial situation (Akerlof et al., 2001). Some models estimate that negative economic news may have twice the impact of positive news (Kahneman & Tversky, 1982).

The volume of news also matters – especially the volume of bad news – as well as news that represents a sharp and negative break from the past (Carroll, 2003). Based on information theory the tone and volume of economic reporting affects expectations beyond the information contained in the reports (Sims, 2003). It is not clear when the news media creates expectations and when their reporting simply responds to ongoing changes in expectations. Like any other business, the news media caters to consumers' preferences (Hamilton, 2003). For example, large shifts in expectations for future changes in the unemployment rate changed in advance of shifts in media reports about unemployment (Curtin, 2003). Revisions in expectations have been shown to respond equally to the news heard by consumers as well as to macroeconomic announcements by the state statistical agencies (Lahiri & Zhao, 2016).

One hypothesis states that the same staggered information flows result from uncertainty about the correct structural model of the economy. Since model uncertainty is costly to resolve, it results in less frequent updating of expectations (Branch, 2007). Although the data that indicates disagreement in expectations is similar to what could be expected to result from model uncertainty, these two concepts are distinct. More importantly, the prevalence of disagreement may be much more variable over time than uncertainty.

The models developed to capture the impact of staggered information are similar to consumption models that incorporate the division between "rule of thumb" and rational consumers. In this context, the switching models capture the difference between those that update their expectations regularly and those that base their expectations on pre-existing information. Mankiw and Reis (2003), Carroll (2003), Khan and Zhu (2002) and Curtin

(2010) estimated that rather than continuously updating their expectations, most people update their expectations only a few times a year.

Staggered updating of expectations may result from variations in the perceived benefits rather than the costs of updating. Consumers who are about to make major purchases or investments are thought to be more motivated to update their economic expectations so as to make more informed decisions. Those planning to buy a home or invest in a business, for example, may be more motivated to form accurate expectations about future economic trends.

Despite the rationales for differences in expectations across populations, these modifications still adhere to the underlying notion of a single information source. While staggered information and model uncertainty may result in heterogeneity of expectations, there is no theoretical basis for expecting heterogeneity among those that have recently updated their expectations. These modifications still assume that the same information is available to all agents and all agents use the same models to generate expectations about the future. The allowance of private in addition to public information provides a theoretical reason to expect heterogeneity in expectations to persist, even among recent updaters.

Each of these refinements still holds the formation of expectations to be rational, but that consumers may not have updated any particular observation due to a cost–benefit calculation. In essence, this means that the strict tests cited above for the rational expectations hypothesis may be inappropriate in practice.

Refinements of Expectations Models

A more careful consideration of the costs and benefits of accurate expectations has prompted several refinements in the empirical tests of the expectations hypothesis. Some other modifications reflect the elimination of naive suppositions about the formation process. The initial models of expectations were the most restrictive in their assumptions about the formation process: a common source of information was assumed to be available to all people, the information was thought to be costless to obtain, the benefits were expected to be much greater than the cost of processing and interpreting the information, each revision was triggered by the announcement of the latest data by a federal statistical agency, and each newly revised expectation was held in memory (or in any other form) until it was needed. Since each individual would behave similarly, the expectations of the entire population would be updated at about the same time. With few variations, this same procedure was subsumed in empirical tests of the rational expectations hypothesis as in tests of adaptive, extrapolative, and error learning models.

Take unemployment expectations as an example. All models assumed that people update their unemployment expectations each month based on the latest national unemployment rate announced by the Bureau of Labor Statistics. The information is assumed to be freely and widely distributed by the news media such that it would be hard to avoid hearing about the latest data and how it had changed from the prior measurement. People would assess the meaning of the data and revise their expectations accordingly, expecting the benefits of updated expectations to exceed the costs. Rational expectations models would require the most effort to process and interpret the data, while adaptive and error learning models would require less effort, and extrapolative models require the least effort. People would repeat this same process each month as new unemployment data became available. The same process would hold for all economic expectations.

Reification of Economic Data

Empirical tests on such simplified models created as much confusion as insight. Perhaps the most basic issue was the assumption that economic expectations can be conceptualized as resulting from one common source of information. It is an artifact of the simplified model that all agents focus on the same definition of inflation, unemployment, or economic growth; that one common source of economic information is the data from the government's statistical agencies. This assumption reflects the widespread tendency toward the reification of economic data – that is, treating conceptual measures as if they had a concrete existence (Curtin, 2004; 2010). While economists justifiably have strong preferences for the measures they have developed, it does not follow that all individuals should adopt the same set of indicators. The relevant economic theory indicates that consumers should use the measure which best reflects their own economic situation. It would make no sense for consumers to take into account future prices that they will never face in the marketplace. People should form expectations about employment opportunities that utilize their own skills and experience in their own geographic areas. Expectations based on national averages, for example, would mean holding expectations that were consistently biased and proved to be an inaccurate guide for their own decisions. Empirical research has confirmed a good deal of variance in actual costs of goods and services or employment conditions across different population groups and across different geographic areas due to differing demand or differing supply conditions.

The counter argument is that even if a bias exists for individuals, those differences would cancel in the aggregate since the data based on representative population samples would match national totals. This would only be true in time-series tests of the correspondence of sample mean expectations and the data from the statistical agencies. It would not be true if the tests were conducted at the individual level using panel data, testing whether a given person's expectation corresponded with one common measure. This problem has been endemic in tests based on panel data, and the cause of widespread misinterpretation. Even in aggregate time-series tests, some have misinterpreted the significant divergences between a person's expectation and the national average as an indication of non-rational expectations (Bryan & Venkatu, 2001; Souleles, 2001).

Another manifestation of the same underlying issue is whether tests of expectations should be based on the initially released (real time) data or if expectations should be based on the subsequently revised data. National agencies revise most economic data and revise them a number of times. For national income and product accounts, multiple revisions occur within months, as well as annual and benchmark revisions. Most analyses of expectations use the currently available data, meaning that the data represent mostly revised data with only the latest observations represented by unrevised data. Some have proposed that empirical tests of expectations should be based only on the initially released data since that is the information that was most likely used to form expectations (Mehra, 2002; Stark & Croushore, 2002; Keane & Runcle, 1990; Zarnowitz, 1985). Others have argued that if past data are revised, people must take into account those revisions when revising their expectations. The basic rationale for isolating the impact of initial from revised data on expectations was to provide a more robust test of the initial announcement effect on expectations. That goal was largely stymied since the latest data is typically reported as a change from the revised prior reading. Overall, there is little empirical evidence that consumers revise their inflation expectations each time the government issues new monthly estimates, revises old figures or revises its measurement methodology. Rather than primarily basing their expectations on public data, consumers have demonstrated a preference for using private information sources.

There is a longstanding tradition in economics of recognizing both private as well as public sources of economic information. People gain economic information about prices, employment, and the overall pace of economic activity, for example, from their many daily interactions in the marketplace. People share economic information among family members, friends, neighbors, coworkers, and a variety of acquaintances they interact with each day. These sources of information have much greater saliency since they more closely reflect people's economic situations. The impact of private information has been found to be pivotal in the formation of unemployment expectations (Curtin, 2003).

One way of exploring the impact of private versus official information is to compare changes in expectations with the official release dates. The key analytic issue is how to devise a proxy measure of the unobserved inflation rate, for example, prior to the official announcement. This issue is easy to solve; the best estimate of the current month's inflation rate is the official inflation rate. Moreover, the hypothesis is easily testable since consumers' expectations data are collected in any given month prior to the official announcement of the statistical agency. The current month's inflation expectation should be dominated by last month's release of the inflation rate for the hypothesis of the primacy of official information to hold. In contrast, the current month's inflation expectation should be dominated by the yet unreleased inflation rate for the same month if the hypothesis that private information dominates. As it will be demonstrated, such a test provides little support for the notion that consumers base their expectations on the official announcement.

Data on Economic Expectations

Inflation Expectations. The University of Michigan has collected data on the inflation expectations of consumers for more than fifty years. The survey asks all consumers two questions about expected price changes: the expected *direction* of change in prices and the expected *extent* of change. The survey has asked the question on the expected direction of change in a comparable format since 1946, while it has modified the question on the extent of change several times. In the 1940s and 1950s, the question simply asked whether prices would go up a little or go up a lot; from the 1960s to the mid-1970s, the question included a series of fixed percentage intervals from which the respondent was asked to choose; and from the mid-1970s to present, the question simply asked the percentage rate of inflation that the consumer expected. This analysis focuses only on the data collected since 1978 for the open-ended question on inflation expectations. Importantly, these detailed quantitative estimates of inflation expectations are compatible with the most rigorous tests of the rational expectations hypothesis as well as the adaptive hypothesis.

Unemployment Expectations. The survey asked consumers only about the expected direction of change in the national unemployment rate, and whether unemployment would increase, decrease, or remain unchanged. Importantly, the wording of the question asked by the University of Michigan was essentially equivalent to the questions asked in European countries. The response distributions were converted into "balance scores" or "diffusion indexes." The indices are constructed as the difference between the proportions who expect the unemployment rate to increase minus those who expect it to decline. This type of index is the standard method used to report expectations data. The only difference between the US data and the data for other countries is that the neutral baseline in the US data is 100 and it is 0 in other countries; this difference in the published data has no impact on time-series correlations. Since these data only measure the expected change in unemployment, not the magnitude of the anticipated change, the data are not sufficient to rigorously test the rational expectations hypothesis. The data is nonetheless useable in determining whether unemployment expectations are more consistent with the rational expectations or the adaptive hypothesis.

Are Expectations Backward or Forward Looking?

Perhaps the most basic question about the formation of economic expectations is whether they have predictive value or simply reflect past developments. Are economic expectations forward or backward looking? Or both? To be forward looking, today's expectation must correspond to tomorrow's outcome. If consumers based their expectations only on past changes and had no predictive ability, such backward-looking expectations would not be of much interest. Indeed, labeling them expectations would be a conceptual error since they simply represent perceptions of past changes. While such perceptions may still influence behavior, calling them expectations would be a misnomer. Of course, typical hypotheses on expectations are grounded in both past developments and predictive of future change.

Tests of whether economic expectations represent a backward- or forward-looking process have typically been examined in separate equations, with the analyst having the responsibility to judge the comparative evidence. There is a way to test both hypotheses in the same reduced form equation by regressing current expectations on both past and *future* changes in the actual inflation or unemployment rates. Strong support for the adaptive hypothesis would be demonstrated if past but not future changes in the actual inflation rate were significant predictors, while support for forward-looking expectations would be shown if future but not past changes in the actual inflation rate were significant predictors. The resulting equation is simply another method to test for "Granger causality" (Geweke et al., 1983). For the data on consumer inflation expectations (Curtin, 2010), the estimated equation fitted using US data from 1978 to 2005 was:[3]

$$P_t^e = \frac{0.895}{(0.276)} + \frac{0.291}{(0.106)}\sum_{j=1}^{4}P_{t+j} + \frac{0.318}{(0.148)}P_t - \frac{0.089}{(0.151)}\sum_{j=1}^{4}P_{t-j}$$

$$+ \frac{0.172}{(0.252)}\sum_{j=1}^{4}P_{t-j}^e \qquad \overline{R^2} = 0.954$$

The estimated equation for the US data on unemployment from 1978 to 2012 was:

$$U_t^e = \frac{35.7}{(9.22)} + \frac{7.57}{(2.35)}\sum_{j=1}^{4}U_{t+j} - \frac{1.89}{(3.88)}U_t - \frac{3.32}{(2.45)}\sum_{j=1}^{4}U_{t-j}$$

$$+ \frac{0.700}{(0.077)}\sum_{j=1}^{4}U_{t-j}^e \qquad \overline{R^2} = 0.823$$

The data strongly support a forward-looking orientation of consumer inflation and unemployment expectations. The empirical results indicate a highly significant association between current expectations and future changes in the inflation and unemployment rates. The coefficients for the four-quarter lead (indicated by t ranging from +1 to +4) in the rate of inflation and unemployment were both positive and significant, at more than twice the standard error shown in parentheses. A separate chi-square test on their exclusion of the four-quarter lead was easily rejected for both inflation ($p = 0.006$) and unemployment ($p = 0.001$).

In contrast, the data provided no support for the notion that expectations were backward looking. The coefficients for the four-quarter lag (indicated by t ranging from −1 to −4) were clearly insignificant. Moreover, the coefficients were negative, exactly the opposite of what the adaptive hypothesis would predict. How could consumers ignore past developments in forming their current expectations? Prior expectations could capture some of the influence of the past, although the four-quarter lagged expectations

---

[3] This paragraph and estimates for the inflation rate are drawn from Curtin (2010:53). Reprinted with the permission of Routledge Press.

were only significant for the unemployment equation. In addition, the contemporaneous change in the inflation and unemployment rates could have incorporated past developments, although the survey data has always been completed well in advance of the official announcements. Finally, consumers may be utilizing private information on the prices and employment conditions that they actually face in the marketplace rather than relying on government announcements of the inflation and unemployment rates. A subsequent chapter will explore in detail the importance of private compared with public economic data in forming economic expectations.

Rational Expectations: Economists versus Consumers

Tests on whether the University of Michigan data on inflation expectations meet the rigorous criteria imposed by the rational expectations hypothesis have been repeatedly conducted during the past quarter century.[4] The data have never given unequivocal support to the rational expectations hypothesis, with the primary failing being the lack of efficient use of all available information.[5] Thomas (1999:141–142) summarized his findings by noting that "consensus household inflation forecasts do surprisingly well relative to those of the presumably better-informed professional economists." Indeed, the median consumer forecasts of year-ahead inflation rates "outperformed all other forecasts in the 1981–97 period on simple tests of accuracy as well as on tests for unbiasedness." Mehra (2002:35) also finds that Michigan's median inflation expectations outperforms the expectations of professional economists and forecasters: "They are more accurate, unbiased, have predictive content for future inflation, and are efficient with respect to economic variables generally considered pertinent to the behavior of inflation." As noted at the start of this chapter, findings such as these originally motivated Muth to advance the rational expectations hypothesis.

The finding that consumers' performance at forecasting the inflation rate is comparable to forecasts by economists is troublesome. The basic thrust

---

[4] See Mehra (2002), Grant & Thomas (1999), Thomas (1999), Roberts (1997), Baghestani (1992), Batchelor & Dua (1989), Bryan & Gavin (1986), Gramlich (1983), Lott & Miller (1982), and Noble & Fields (1982).

[5] Cukierman and Meltzer (1986) have suggested that this is not a clear violation of the rational expectations hypothesis, since households may not always correctly distinguish between temporary and permanent shocks and thus their forecasts could exhibit serially correlated errors.

Similar comparisons were done for year-ahead forecasts of the national unemployment rate. Curtin (1999; 2003) found that consumers' forecasts of the year-ahead unemployment rate outperformed those of professional forecasters as well as forecasts from two prominent macroeconomic models.

of the critique of the rational expectations hypothesis is that the cognitive demands far exceed the capacity of ordinary consumers. Indeed, the very notion of bounded rationality is based on the limitations of conscious cognitive deliberation. Moreover, it is quite difficult to argue that the costs of collecting and processing information are not significantly lower for economists than for consumers. Not only are costs lower for economists, but the professional benefits of accurate expectations are also higher for economists. So why is the accuracy of consumers' inflation expectations comparable to economists?

There is one significant difference between the inflation expectations of economists and consumers: there is much greater dispersion in the expectations of consumers than of economists. Some consumers expect unusually high rates of inflation, others unusually low rates. The dispersion of inflation expectations among economists is quite small compared with consumers; indeed, it is an order of magnitude smaller. This would be even more troublesome if one assumed that all consumers based their expectations on the information released by federal statistical agencies. Greater variations, however, would be expected if consumers based their expectations on the inflation rate they actually faced. In this case, it would be rational to assume that different individuals in different economic circumstances, living in different geographic locations, or with distinctive spending habits would have different expectations about inflation. In contrast, it can be assumed that economic forecasters invariably base their expectations on the official series published by the government, and therefore could be expected to have a smaller dispersion in their expectations. It could be argued that if someone were to base their expectation on just one other consumer or just one economic forecaster, they would be much better off picking one economist. Almost every economist's inflation expectation is fairly close to the average of all economic forecasters, but that is not true for every consumer.

EVIDENCE OF COGNITIVE LIMITATIONS

The underlying rationale for theories of bounded rationality is that many people do not possess the necessary cognitive skills to form accurate economic expectations. The best available survey proxy for cognitive differences is the amount of formal education each person has attained. The more years of formal schooling correspond to greater cognitive performance in a wide range of tasks (Ceci, 1991). Those with greater formal schooling, such as those who have obtained college degrees, would have a greater robust ability to understand and interpret public data on economic variables, and would thus produce more accurate expectations than those who may not have graduated high school. Needless to say, there are many exceptions to such an assumption. Legends abound about titans of industry that had little formal education but nonetheless used cutting edge and creative techniques to produce innovative products. John D. Rockefeller, Andrew Carnegie, Henry Ford, and Thomas Edison never finished high school, and more recently, Bill Gates and Steve Jobs were college dropouts. More commonly, we have all known people who had little formal education but were astutely aware of economic developments and had the ability to interpret and forecast future prospects. Nonetheless, more formal education is usually associated with greater cognitive ability.

The empirical tests were replicated based on the US data on inflation expectations (see Table 2.1). The findings confirm the prior results based on quarterly observations from 1978 to 2005 (Curtin, 2010). Two statistical tests were performed: whether inflation expectations were unbiased predictors of the actual future changes in the Consumer Price Index (CPI) inflation rate, and whether people efficiently used all available information. The first test required that the coefficient on expectations be equal to 1.0 and the constant be equal to 0.0; this means that for expectations to be rational they had to be equal to the actual inflation rate. The second test required that any errors in inflation expectations be unrelated to any available information on past inflation rates at the time the expectation was formed.[6]

The results of the analysis indicate that the year-ahead inflation expectations for the entire sample of US households as well as for each of the education subgroups formed an unbiased estimate of the actual inflation rate. The null hypothesis that inflation expectations were a biased estimate was rejected for every education subgroup at the 95% confidence level: every constant term was insignificantly different from zero, and every estimated coefficient on inflation expectations was insignificantly different from one. Only among the least educated, those with less than a

---

[6] Given that survey data usually involve some aggregation errors, the regressions were calculated using nonlinear least squares to estimate a moving average error term, using a consistent estimate of the covariance matrix that allows for serial correlation and heteroscedasticity. The overlapping forecast intervals generated by the survey questions could produce serially correlated errors even among perfectly rational agents (Croushore, 1998). In fact, a significant first-order moving average error term was found in all equations. The residuals are also tested for the inefficient use of information on inflation, but no tests were attempted for the inefficient use of other relevant information (what is called strong efficiency).

Table 2.1 *Tests of Rational Expectations Hypothesis Based on University of Michigan's Inflation Expectations Data (Quarterly Data, 1978–2005)*

Population Subgroup	Unbiased $\Rightarrow \alpha = 0$ & $\beta = 1$ $P_t = \alpha + \beta P_t^{E_{t-4}}$					Efficiency $\Rightarrow \delta = 0$ & $\varphi = 0$ $e_t = \delta + \varphi P_{t-5}$		
	A	β	Θ	R^2	χ^2 for H_o	δ	φ	R^2
All Households	−0.414	1.184	0.655*	0.884	1.538	0.030	−0.035	0.005
	(0.533)	(0.181)	(0.108)		[0.464]	(0.158)	(0.039)	
Education								
Less High School	−0.323	1.148	0.574*	0.800	0.722	−0.551*	0.091*	0.051
	(0.692)	(0.221)	(0.091)		[0.697]	(0.195)	(0.033)	
High School	−0.482	1.208	0.611*	0.866	1.895	−0.121	0.001	0.000
	(0.610)	(0.189)	(0.076)		[0.388]	(0.167)	(0.037)	
Some College	0.082	1.064	0.607*	0.850	1.946	−0.105	−0.009	0.000
	(0.635)	(0.208)	(0.118)		[0.378]	(0.204)	(0.037)	
College Degree	0.113	1.049	0.568*	0.853	1.960	−0.048	−0.021	0.000
	(0.514)	(0.175)	(0.172)		[0.375]	(0.187)	(0.049)	
Graduate Studies	0.061	0.998	0.712*	0.876	0.107	−0.027	−0.022	0.000
	(0.588)	(0.189)	(0.081)		[0.948]	(0.195)	(0.058)	

Note: Standard errors in parentheses; probability level of χ^2 in brackets. All standard errors and covariances calculated using the Newy-West procedure. All estimated equations included a moving average error term. An asterisk indicates significance at the 0.05% level; significance tests on all coefficients except β were for differences from 0.0 and tests on β were for differences from 1.0. R^2 adjusted for degrees of freedom.

Source: Curtin (2010:56). Reprinted with permission of Routledge Press.

high school degree, was there any evidence of the inefficient use of information about the inflation rate that was available at the time they formed their expectations.

A summary of the overall findings from this analysis are similar to Muth's analysis in his classic article: consumers' inflation expectations are forward looking, they are generally as accurate as the forecasts of economic models, and they more closely correspond to the hypothesis of rational expectations than to the backward-looking hypothesis of adaptation.

These results have always been met with disbelief. How could consumers manage this feat? How could the inflation expectations of ordinary consumers be as accurate as those of economic forecasters? Is there some unique feature of the University of Michigan data that makes this result possible? Are US consumers more motivated, are the data more widely available, or are consumers more economically sophisticated? If these findings are so theoretically improbable, how could they be repeatedly replicated over the decades? Before discussing why the results are theoretically probable, the same basic findings are extended to other countries as well as other economic expectations. The other most commonly cited aspect of macroeconomic performance is the unemployment rate, for which data exists on dozens of other countries.

Unemployment Expectations

The survey question on unemployment expectations does not ask for quantitative estimates like the question on inflation expectations. The question only asks consumers for the expected direction of change in unemployment. As a result, a rigorous analysis of the rational expectations hypothesis is not possible as was done for inflation expectations. Fortunately, this does not mean that the ability of these expectations to predict future changes in the unemployment rate cannot be rigorously tested. Clive Granger developed such a statistical test, for which he won the Nobel Prize in economics in 2003. While it is commonly referred to as the Granger causality test, the use of the term "causality" is not meant literally. It only tests whether one variable has the ability to predict future changes in another variable over and above what could be predicted from the variable's own prior changes. Five lags of the unemployment rate and unemployment expectations were used to test whether past changes in the unemployment rate can predict changes in expectations, and whether past changes in expectations can predict future changes in the unemployment rate. It would be natural to anticipate that both would be true: people form their unemployment expectations based on what happened in the past, and their expectations predict future changes in the unemployment rate.

The data provides more convincing evidence that people's expectations predict subsequent unemployment rates than that people base their expectations on past changes in the unemployment rate. Statistical tests show strong support that expectations predict subsequent changes in unemployment, over and above the influence of the past history of the unemployment rate (see Table 2.2, the column for all respondents). Nonetheless, in about half of the countries, past changes in unemployment predicted changes in expectation; in comparison, in all but three of the fifteen countries, expectations predicted subsequent changes in the unemployment rate. This relationship was far from perfect, but demonstrated the predictive power of consumers' unemployment expectations.

The same statistical tests were performed for three education subgroups: those with a high school degree or less, those with some college or vocational education beyond high school, and those with a college degree. Since education is related to greater cognitive skills, it could be anticipated that college degree holders could form unemployment expectations more readily. The statistical results were the same: the predictive power of unemployment expectations was not rejected for any of the educational subgroups. The accompanying Figures 2.1a–2.1d show the trends in expectations and the actual change in the unemployment rate for all US consumers as well as for the three education subgroups. Since the survey question asked about the expected change in unemployment during the year ahead, the unemployment rate is plotted as the change from the prior year's level. It is hard to discern a differential pattern between the education subgroups that would indicate that cognitive ability had a significant impact on forming unemployment expectations (see Figure 2.1). Indeed, the unemployment expectations of the three education subgroups are highly correlated, with an average inter-correlation of 0.90.

To provide a more comprehensive assessment, the same tests were performed for fourteen other countries, which asked comparable questions on unemployment expectations. The countries selected were limited to those that had asked the expectation question for more than fifteen years and published the data within educational subgroups. For each country that data was obtained, a series of VAR regressions were run to test Granger causality between unemployment expectations and the unemployment rate. The expectations variable was defined as a "balance score," meaning that the score was equal to the percentage point difference between the sample proportions that expected a decreasing and an increasing unemployment

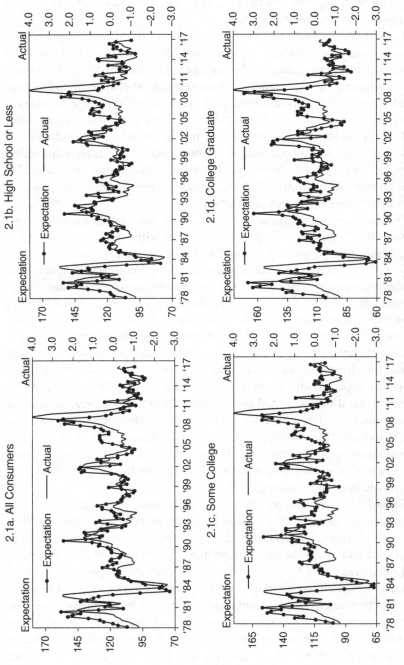

Figure 2.1 Unemployment Expectations and Change in Unemployment Rate in the United States, 1978–2016

rate during the year ahead. This conforms to how sponsoring organizations regularly publish the data. Five lags of both variables were entered into each regression; the contemporaneous changes were not used so that there was a true time separation between the survey measured expectation and the officially announced unemployment rate for each country – although the survey measure was completed well before the statistical agency announcement. There was no attempt to maximize the observed relationship in each country. By including five lags of both variables, the ability of unemployment expectations to forecast the unemployment rate was tested by simultaneously taking into account the predictive power of the prior five observations of the unemployment rate. The main goal was to ascertain the informational content of the measure of unemployment expectations in a comparable manner across countries. Each country has some unique factors that influence the relationship between consumer expectations and subsequent changes in unemployment. Countries may differ in terms of the degree to which they publicize official statistics: some countries could have employment regulations that decrease people's concerns about potential job losses, or some countries could have more job and income opportunities outside of the official economy on which statistics are based.

First, just considering the results for all consumers in each country, unemployment expectations provided predictive information about future changes in the unemployment rate in twelve of the fifteen countries. The strongest relationships at the country level were found for the United States, the United Kingdom, France, Spain, Austria, Belgium, Greece, Ireland, Denmark, the Netherlands, Germany, and Portugal (see Table 2.2). The countries that showed no significant ability of expectations to predict the unemployment rate were Finland, Italy, and Sweden. Italy and Sweden were distinctive in that the data indicated no relationship at all, in either direction. The data for Italy and Sweden, however, indicate that expectations at times led and at other times followed actual changes in the unemployment rate (see Figures 2.2a–2.2n). This inconsistency meant that neither expectations nor actual changes in unemployment could dominate. The situation in Finland is more complex in that the expectations for every education subgroup were significant predictors of changes in the unemployment rate, but that same pattern was not significant for all consumers.

Perhaps more surprising was the finding that past changes in the official unemployment rate showed even less correspondence with subsequent unemployment expectations. In just seven of the fifteen countries, did past changes in unemployment significantly relate to unemployment expectations at the conventional 5% significance level. The only

Table 2.2 *Predictive Performance of Consumer Expectations for Unemployment in Fifteen Countries for the Total Sample and by Education Subgroups*

Country	Date[a]	Expectations Predict Unemployment Rate				Unemployment Predicts Expectations			
		All	Education			All	Education		
			Primary	Secondary	Tertiary		Primary	Secondary	Tertiary
Austria	1995–2016	0.003	0.002	0.002	0.004	NS	NS	NS	NS
Belgium	1985/86–2016	0.003	0.008	0.002	0.003	NS	NS	NS	NS
Denmark	1985/86–2016	0.007	NS	0.015	0.005	NS	0.028	NS	NS
Finland	1989/95–2016	NS	0.017	0.008	0.008	0.017	0.035	0.014	0.017
France	1985/86–2016	0.000	0.005	0.005	0.001	0.002	0.014	0.014	0.011
Germany	1991–2016	0.039	0.035	0.034	NS	0.003	0.003	0.001	NS
Greece	1998–2016	0.007	0.005	0.008	0.019	0.029	NS	NS	0.001
Ireland	1985/86–2016	0.007	0.032	0.033	0.027	NS	NS	NS	NS
Italy	1985/86–2016	NS	NS	NS	NS	NS	NS	NS	NS
Netherlands	1985/89–2016	0.031	0.043	0.015	0.009	0.026	0.018	NS	0.041
Portugal	1986–2016	0.041	0.028	0.022	0.013	0.011	0.023	NS	0.006
Spain	1986–2016	0.000	0.001	0.000	0.000	NS	NS	NS	NS
Sweden	1995–2016	NS	NS	NS	NS	NS	NS	NS	NS
UK	1985/90–2016	0.000	NS	0.030	0.006	0.000	0.000	0.000	0.000
US	1978–2016	0.000	0.000	0.000	0.000	NS	NS	NS	0.007

[a] Second start date refers to information on education.

Note: Table entries represent the probability of rejecting the hypotheses that expectations do not predict subsequent unemployment rates or that unemployment rates do not predict subsequent expectations. NS indicates it was not significant at the 5% level (0.050).

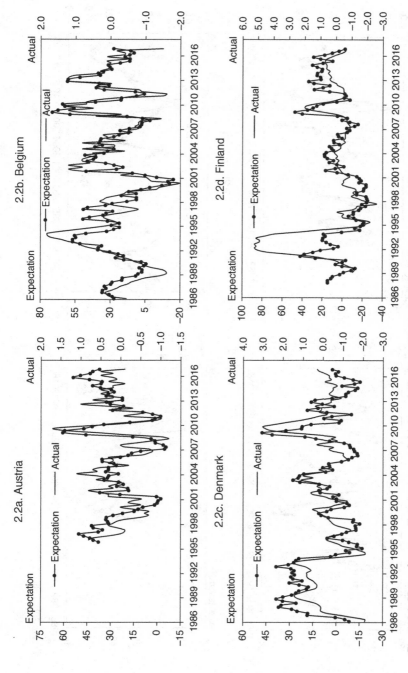

Figure 2.2 Unemployment Expectations and the Actual Change in Unemployment Rates

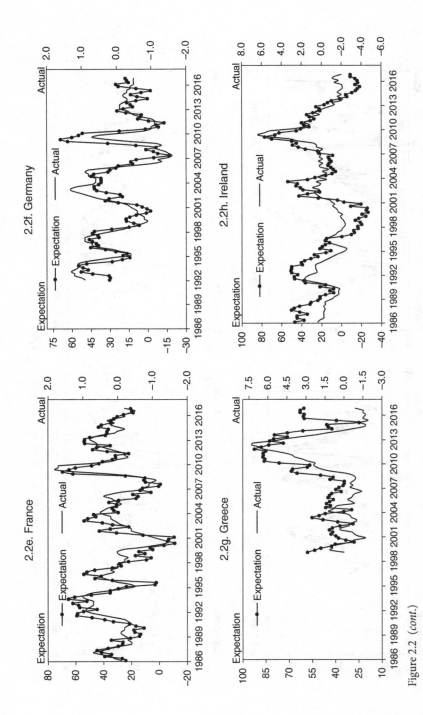

Figure 2.2 (*cont.*)

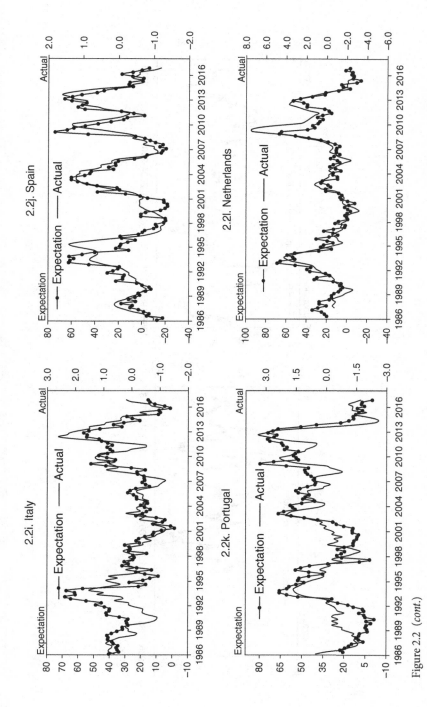

2.2i. Italy

2.2j. Spain

2.2k. Portugal

2.2l. Netherlands

Figure 2.2 *(cont.)*

61

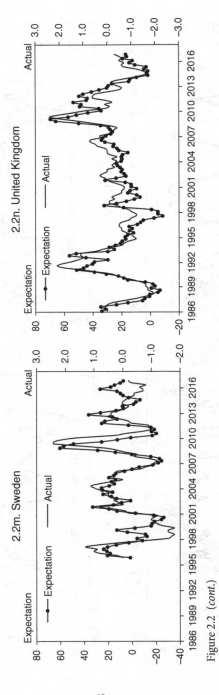

Figure 2.2 (cont.)

countries to demonstrate a significant impact were the United Kingdom, France, Germany, Portugal, Finland, the Netherlands, and Greece. While it is true that the data suggest that expectations are generally more likely to predict subsequent changes in unemployment than expectations simply conform to past changes in unemployment, this test cannot completely dismiss the influence that past unemployment changes have on expectations. Moreover, the empirical results are sensitive to the number of quarters the variables are lagged in the regressions. It could be true that most information on recent changes in the official unemployment rate is more promptly incorporated into expectations rather than having a prolonged or staggered impact on expectations. Nonetheless, the Granger tests provide evidence that expectations do not simply reflect past developments.

The same Granger causality tests were also performed within educational subgroups for each country. Unemployment expectations were available for the European countries for three educational groups: primary (less than a high school degree in the United States), secondary (high school degree), and tertiary (college degree). The data provide strong evidence that cognitive ability as proxied by education had little impact on the accuracy of unemployment expectations with the exception of the data from Italy and Sweden. There was partial evidence that cognitive ability mattered in Denmark and the United Kingdom as the unemployment expectations among the lowest educational subgroup were not significantly related to subsequent changes in the actual unemployment rate (see Table 2.3).

Perhaps the clearest rejection of the importance of cognitive abilities in forming unemployment expectations is the virtually identical trends across the three education groups (see Table 2.3). The average time-series inter-correlation within each of the fifteen countries was 0.96. The lowest average correlations were for Denmark (0.87) and the United States (0.90). Excluding these two countries, the average inter-correlation was 0.98. Since the unemployment expectations were nearly identical across educational groups, the accompanying figures would look identical if they were replicated for each education group in each country. Nearly identical time trends, however, do not mean identical levels. Indeed, the lower the education, the higher the expected unemployment rate since education also serves as a proxy for workplace skills. These demographic differences will be discussed in detail in a later chapter.

Over the past quarter century, the average US unemployment rate for those without a high school degree was more than three times higher than for those who had a college degree – 9.3% versus 2.8% from 1992 to 2016. In the European Union (fifteen countries) from 2000 to 2016, those with only

Table 2.3 *Correlations of Unemployment Expectations by Education Subgroups*

Country	Dates	Education Levels			
		Low & Middle	Low & Top	Middle & Top	Average Inter-Correlation
Austria	1995–2016	0.98	0.96	0.99	0.98
Belgium	1986–2016	0.99	0.98	0.99	0.99
Denmark	1986–2016	0.82	0.81	0.98	0.87
Finland	1995–2016	0.99	0.98	0.99	0.99
France	1986–2016	0.99	0.97	0.97	0.98
Germany	1986–2016	0.99	0.95	0.96	0.97
Greece	1986–2016	0.96	0.93	0.98	0.96
Ireland	1986–2016	0.99	0.98	0.99	0.99
Italy	1986–2016	0.99	0.96	0.98	0.98
Netherlands	1989–2016	0.98	0.95	0.98	0.97
Portugal	1986–2016	0.96	0.96	0.96	0.96
Spain	1986–2016	0.99	0.97	0.99	0.98
Sweden	1995–2016	0.98	0.97	0.98	0.98
UK	1990–2016	0.97	0.95	0.97	0.96
US	1978–2016	0.91	0.87	0.91	0.90

a primary education had unemployment rates that were more than twice as high as those in the highest education group – 13.8% versus 5.1%. Although those with the least education may have cognitive limitations in forming expectations, their need for accurate employment forecasts is higher, and presumably, their willingness to incur costs is greater when forming these expectations.

Weak Evidence for Cognitive Limitations

The data on inflation and unemployment expectations provide convincing evidence that most consumers in developed economies do not suffer from the high costs of gathering, processing, and interpreting information on trends in inflation and unemployment. Indeed, consumers' inflation and unemployment expectations were remarkably accurate in most of the countries studied. The limitations or bounds on economic rationality appear to be very loose. How could this be? Why did differences in cognitive skills not translate into differences in economic expectations?

The first caveat to note is that only a fraction of the countries that currently collect data on consumer expectations were included in the analysis. To be included, countries had to collect data on unemployment expectations over a sufficient period of time to enable robust statistical tests, the data had to be available by educational subgroups, and the official unemployment rate measured by the country's statistical agency had to be available and based on internationally accepted standards. For most of the countries excluded, the data on consumer expectations have been collected for a relatively brief period of time. Additionally, many of the excluded lesser developed countries did not sample their entire population, but restricted interviewing to a few major urban areas, and some of the countries do not regularly collect or publish data on unemployment rates as conventionally measured. While there is no reason to expect negative results from these other countries, a robust empirical assessment was not possible.

The observed accuracy of consumers in forecasting inflation and unemployment has sometimes been attributed to other special factors rather than skill. Some people have suggested that it was simply luck. That explanation may be plausible for one survey in one country. It is improbable to assert that over the past several decades, the results were due to lucky guesses by hundreds of thousands of survey respondents in dozens of countries. Another common explanation is that it is due to the superior performance of groups over individuals, the so-called "wisdom of crowds" (Surowiecki, 2004). Economists and consumers were both represented by groups in the empirical tests, although the size of the consumer samples was much larger. Why would larger groups of consumers be more accurate year-ahead forecasters? Large groups of consumers are not necessarily more informed than smaller groups of economists, nor could we expect that larger groups of consumers have higher average mental capacities than smaller groups of economists. It is unlikely that group size alone accounted for the difference.

Another explanation invokes the theory of self-fulfilling expectations. Given some inflation or unemployment expectation, consumers may behave in product and labor markets in such a way as to make that expectation come true. Central banks do fear a renewed "inflationary psychology" that promotes higher inflation by affecting economic decisions, and seek to establish low and stable inflation expectations that help to contain inflation. There has also been a concern following the Great Recession that consumers may view labor markets so inhospitable that some people may have changed their job seeking behavior. The fear is that stagnation could become a self-fulfilling prophecy.

Importantly, most of the sparse evidence about self-fulfilling expectations is about how negative expectations could produce negative economic results. Economic theory excludes the possibility that positive expectations can act as a self-fulfilling prophecy, even though the positive impact of consumer optimism on the economy is typically part of the explanations offered by laymen and professionals alike. If credence was given to self-fulfilling prophecies that would imply that economists are essentially forecasting the expectations of consumers! The influence of self-fulfilling expectations on the functioning of the macroeconomy will be discussed in detail in Section II of this book.

Another explanation involves differences in the motivations of consumers. While education has been used as a proxy for cognitive abilities, it can also serve as a proxy for workplace skills. While those with the least education may have cognitive limitations for forming accurate expectations, their need for accurate employment expectations is higher since the likelihood of unemployment is substantially greater. Given that the benefits are much higher, the costs these individuals are willing to incur may be much greater and these extra efforts may offset their cognitive limitations. There is no evidence, however, that the least educated are very knowledgeable about the unemployment rate published by government agencies.

The cognitive burden would be reduced if rather than being faced with the tasks of acquiring, processing, and interpreting official data, people based their economic expectations on information they encountered in the course of their everyday life. Such private information would be tailored to their own situations and formatted in a manner that they could easily understand. It would be foolhardy to suggest that all people use private information, or that all people use public information to form their expectations. Many, if not most, people use a mixture of both public and private sources of economic information. Given the ubiquitous nature of economic information, there is no empirical analysis that could prove one always dominates the other. What can be done is an assessment of people's knowledge of official economic statistics to determine whether people possess accurate knowledge of publically available economic statistics. This task is undertaken in the next chapter. It should be no surprise that few people possess accurate knowledge of publically available economic statistics on unemployment, inflation, and the rate of overall economic growth.

The simple shift from public to private information does not solve all the cognitive challenges involved in forming expectations. Indeed, compared with the parsimonious public information, private information is composed of many small bits of information. Economic theory assumes that the deluge of information would quickly overwhelm people's conscious cognitive resources, and thereby create a preference for summary statistics provided by state agencies. Even under these circumstances, forming economic expectations could still overwhelm people's capacity to form expectations by conscious deliberation. As a result, some have proposed modifications that lower the costs or limit the degree of deliberation, such as Simon's satisficing approach or Kahneman and Tversky's heuristic approach. Such rules-of-thumb substitute for conscious deliberation, but expectations formed in this manner are typically inaccurate and subject to persistent biases. The accuracy of inflation and unemployment expectations makes a strong case that conscious reasoning is aided by some other features of the human mind. Subsequent chapters will advance the notion that nonconscious processing of economic information and nonconscious learning enable people to form economic expectations that serve their own interests. While nonconscious processes can never completely displace conscious deliberation, it would be senseless to omit from consideration the vastly greater capacity and cognitive power of the nonconscious mind.

3

Private and Public Sources of Economic
Information

The natural inquisitiveness of people was noted long ago when Aristotle began his book Metaphysics by saying "All men by nature desire knowledge" (Curtin, 2008).[1] Acquiring information about economic conditions has been a common facet of life since the dawn of civilization. Even before governments devised economic accounts, people utilized information about economic conditions in their decisions about bartering and trade, borrowing and lending, as well as in many other decisions that influenced their economic wellbeing. Simply because it was not measured by an official statistical agency of the state, there is no reason to doubt that people sought out and used such information.

In those earlier times, however, there was no reason to expect that all people would arrive at the same estimate of inflation or the same rate of economic growth (Curtin, 2008). Information was scarce, costly to obtain and process, and there were no accepted paradigms to interpret the data. Indeed, national income accounts are a relatively recent innovation, with the first accounts published by William Petty in 1665. Modern national income accounts were only devised in the first half of the twentieth century by Simon Kuznets and others (Vanoli, 2005). The availability of national income and product accounts, including data on conditions in labor and product markets, reduced the cost of economic information and increased its quality and timeliness. Information on economic conditions is now often viewed as nearly costless to obtain since people are constantly exposed to

---

[1] This chapter combines the results from interviews conducted in 2009 with an earlier data collection conducted in 2007. Small portions of the text in this chapter were drawn from an OECD conference paper (Curtin, 2008) as well as the text describing the replicated questions with the permission from OECD, Public Affairs and Communications Directorate. Based on the results of a question wording experiment, the published 2007 data were revised to be consistent with the 2009 survey as described in this chapter.

official government statistics by the mass media. Indeed, it is argued that exposure is so complete that people would have to actively ignore the available information to be unaware of economic data. Unlike in earlier times, there is reason to believe that everyone would now be fully aware of the official data on the key indicators of the performance of the national economy (Curtin, 2008).

Economic crisis has always provoked an intense public interest in the performance of the economy, and the financial crisis that began in 2008 was no different. Public interest was heavily oriented toward news about the economy in 2008. According to national surveys of public interest in different news stories, eight of the top fifteen news stories rated by the public's interest in 2008 were about the economy, three stories were about the election of Obama, three were about floods and hurricanes, and one was about the Olympics (Pew, 2009). This heightened interest did not simply represent an intellectual curiosity or a citizen's interest in determining which public policies would best resolve the economic crisis; in fact, these concerns sprang from a direct financial stake. The crisis affected nearly every person, if not from income declines, job losses, or foreclosure and bankruptcy, then from the evaporation of accumulated wealth in homes, investments, and pension accounts. Nearly nine in ten respondents in a representative national sample of US residents wanted to know about recent economic developments in late 2008 even if it was bad news, and nearly eight in ten reported that they needed to know about these economic developments in order to make more informed financial decisions (Pew, 2009).

People's intense demand for economic information has been met by seemingly endless reports in the mass media on nearly every wiggle in every economic statistic imaginable. It would seem reasonable to conclude that the worst economic crisis since the Great Depression has prompted the public to become more knowledgeable about the main statistical indicators on the performance of the economy. Who could not have heard news about changes in gross domestic product (GDP), unemployment, or the inflation rate? Unfortunately, that has not been the case. Even during the most widely reported economic crisis in nearly a century, people were surprisingly uninformed about official economic statistics.

Nearly every profession – whether political scientists, physicians, mathematicians, physicists, or economists – has been disappointed with the amount of knowledge ordinary citizens possess. It is an all too frequent occurrence that some survey finds that a surprisingly high proportion of people could not name their representative in the legislature (Delli

Carpini & Keeter, 1996), have accurate knowledge about common medical conditions (Lucas, 1987), know about planetary orbits (Lucas, 1988), know how to do rather simple arithmetic operations (OECD, 2006), or know the current rate of inflation or unemployment (Curtin, 2008; Blinder & Krueger, 2004; Blendon et al., 1997). The lack of knowledge has been variously attributed to the limitations in the cognitive capacity of the public, the challenging technical and mathematical jargon used in official announcements, the high costs and low benefits from updating knowledge of official economic statistics, the absence of a perceived importance of official statistics to people's everyday lives, and even the lack of credibility of the nation's statistical agencies.

The assumption that people utilize official sources of economic information reflects the widespread tendency toward the reification of economic data – that is, treating conceptual measures as if they had a concrete existence. It should be no surprise that few people think in terms of GDP in chained 2000 dollars, or even know what that concept signifies. Few know that people have to be actively looking for work to be counted as unemployed, and few people understand the differences in inflation rates based on a fixed market basket or people's actual expenditures on goods and services. It does not follow, however, that people do not actively seek and use information about the performance of the national economy in making their economic decisions. While economists justifiably have strong preferences for the measures that they have developed, it does not follow that all people should adopt that same set of indicators. Indeed, economic theory suggests that people adopt whatever measures prove most useful, considering both the costs of obtaining the information and the benefits that can be achieved by more informed decisions.

For most consumers, the most relevant information is about their specific economic situation (Curtin, 2008). In contrast, the concepts of Gross Domestic Product, the Consumer Price Index, and the unemployment rate, for example, were devised as appropriate measures of conditions in the macroeconomy for the representative consumer. Rather than macro data, people typically base their decisions on a different information set, namely the strength of the local economy, the change in the prices they actually face, and job prospects for people with their same skills and abilities. Of course, when aggregated across all communities and people, the data would approximate the national averages that economists favor.

It makes no economic sense to assume that people pay attention to an inflation rate that is higher or lower than the one they actually encounter. Empirical research has confirmed a good deal of variance in actual inflation rates across different demographic groups (Hobijn & Lagakos, 2005; Hagemann, 1982; Michael, 1979). Most of the differentials are based on the differential inflation rates for specific products or services, such as higher health care costs among the elderly, or in specific areas of the country, such as price differentials between rural and urban areas. Indeed, the *Dallas Morning News* ran a story entitled "Consumer Price Index may not reflect your family's reality," and directed readers to a link that calculates the change in the Consumer Price Index (CPI) based on how the family actually allocates their spending across eight major categories. While many of the price differentials do not persist over extended periods of time and people's circumstances change as they age, it is unreasonable to expect that people would ignore these important differences. The same may be said for employment conditions, as people would naturally pay more attention to job opportunities that are relevant to their own skills and abilities. The national unemployment rate may be quite meaningless to workers living in areas or working in an industry that has a distinctly different outlook for employment, whether it is better or worse than the national average. While relevant information about prices and employment conditions are, in principle, available from the state statistical agencies at no cost, in practice, the cost to acquire and process this information is high. The cost to acquire and process private information, however, may be significantly lower and the potential benefit of that information may be significantly higher, leading people to prefer private over official data sources (Curtin, 2003).

The measurement of people's knowledge about the performance of the economy does not depend on a direct translation of the economist's definition into survey questions, but on the ability of the resulting measure to accurately reflect the underlying economic concept. This is more than simply rephrasing questions to use "population language" or decomposing complex economic variables into more manageable measurement objectives; it also means constructing questions that are based on the same conceptual framework used by ordinary people in making their economic decisions.

This chapter will document what people knew about several key aspects of the economy based on survey data collected in the United States just before the crisis began in 2007 and during the crisis in 2009. While it may be naive to anticipate widespread public knowledge of economic statistics in 2009, there could hardly be a more compelling situation than the recent economic crisis to motivate people to acquire accurate information about key economic indicators. Most of the important criteria that influence public knowledge remained unchanged, such as the prevailing cognitive limitations or the jargon used in the official releases; those factors could be considered to be unchanged for the population as a whole from 2007 to 2009. What did change was the performance of the economy, and the change was large enough to demand the attention of nearly every person. Of course, no "natural experiment" is ideal, but the radical shift in the performance of the economy presented a unique research opportunity.

The most important hypotheses about the acquisition of knowledge involve the costs and benefits of economic information. The economic crisis has presumably made the cost of acquiring information about official economic statistics lower, and the benefits of accurate knowledge higher. This implies that the benefits would exceed the costs to a greater extent in 2009 than in 2007, and prompt more people to update their knowledge about the economy. It is important to stress that the economic crisis was expected to raise both the supply and demand for quantitative information about the key economic indicators.

The data suggest that most people did not know the exact figures contained in the official releases on the rate of unemployment, the rate of change in consumer prices, or the rate of growth in the overall economy in 2007 or 2009. Indeed, only a minority of people could report a specific figure for the current rate of unemployment, inflation, or economic growth, and a surprisingly large portion reported that they had never heard of the statistic or the statistical agency that publishes the data. The data indicated that knowledge about official statistics was viewed as burdensome, difficult to acquire, and for most people, knowing the official statistics was seen as providing little if any additional benefit to the individual. The economic crisis has had little impact on the state of knowledge. Most people were nearly as uninformed about the performance of the economy during the economic crisis as before it started.

Does the data suggest that people simply ignore these economic indicators when making their economic decisions? No. It is not the information that they ignore, but the source. Most people favor informal sources of information tailored to their own economic situation. Even for those people who professed to having never heard of an official statistic, when asked about their expectations for the same economic topic, nearly every person could provide an estimate. Information on inflation, unemployment, and economic growth was crucial for their planning, but it was usually not the official information provided by the federal agencies. It was information gained from private rather than public sources.

Just as surprising were findings about the media's role in disseminating the latest federal statistics on the performance of the economy. Most conventional theories of expectations view the costs of acquiring information as trivial because of the role of the mass media. However, unlike the presumptions of the conventional models, a search of transcripts of television broadcasts and articles in newspapers could not confirm the universal dissemination of the official *rates* of unemployment, inflation, or economic growth. Media reports about the economy were more often qualitative rather than quantitative in content. Economic growth is typically reported to have slowed or improved, without quantifying the numerical extent. Presumably, if the numerical change was larger than usual, the media may say growth had jumped or crashed, but still without providing any quantitative information. The same is true for the inflation and unemployment rates. Instead of publicizing the numbers, the media emphasizes how the economy has affected individual families. The media long ago decided the best way to communicate with their audience was not with numbers but by how those events affect others just like themselves. To be sure, some people do want those exact numbers, and there are media outlets that cater to their needs. The *Wall Street Journal* and cable business shows, for example, meet those needs. Most of the media that reach the majority of US households, however, report only on the qualitative interpretation of federal economic statistics, not the actual numeric figures.

The key implication is that for most people, the cost of acquiring the numerical figures for economic statistics, which conventional theories assume are the required building blocks to form expectations, is well above zero. The cost of acquiring *quantitative* information on the official statistics were found to be surprisingly high since most newspaper and television reports failed to include the numerical estimates in their reports, preferring to summarize the data in qualitative rather than quantitative terms. Overall, the data suggest that the costs of obtaining official economic statistics were higher than had been widely alleged, and the benefits of knowing the official statistics lower than typically assumed.

SURVEY METHODOLOGY

Reliable and valid measures of what people know about economic conditions are subject to all of the problems usually associated with sample surveys. Aside from the more general issues of survey methodology, the crucial measurement issue involves judgments about the capacity of individuals to provide meaningful responses. Questions that measure people's knowledge of economic conditions can be phrased in a number of ways, each differing in the cognitive burden placed on respondents. Increasing the precision of the measures also increases the extent of information that respondents must access from memory, the required computational skills, and the motivation of respondents to provide accurate responses.

This research took two distinct approaches to the measurement of people's economic knowledge. The first set of questions asked about the respondents' knowledge of the official rates of unemployment, inflation, and economic growth. If a respondent replied that they did not know the official rates of unemployment, inflation, or economic growth, they were asked if they had ever heard of the official measures. For an economist, it was hard to imagine anyone who had not heard of the unemployment rate or the inflation rate. The hypothesis was that people had simply not heard of the most recently announced rate, which was thought to be more likely in 2007 than in 2009.

The second set of questions was quite different in that the questions did not refer to an official rate produced by some government agency but instead asked about the same underlying economic concept. These questions were part of the regular monitoring of consumer expectations and were asked before the questions on their knowledge of the official rates. Perhaps the most striking difference was that these questions were phrased in "population" language and avoided any mention of official rates, the government agencies responsible, or how the measure should be defined. These questions were designed to capture public as well as private information about the economic measures. These questions was asked before the other questions as part of the regularly repeated standard questionnaire.

All of the questions were asked as part of the University of Michigan's Surveys of Consumers. The survey samples are representative of all households in the United States, with every adult given an equal probability of being selected for an interview. The data were collected in May and August of 2007 and in April and May of 2009, and included a total of 2,016 cases.[2]

---

[2] The report on the 2007 survey was based on the April and May 2007 surveys (Curtin, 2008). Since the April survey included a methodological experiment relating to the cognitive burden of asking questions about official economic statistics, which was found to have a significant effect on the data results, the May survey was repeated in August 2007, and then again repeated in April and May of 2009. The exclusion of the April 2007 survey meant there was consistent wording in the four remaining surveys. It should be noted that this also means that the previously published data for 2007 is slightly different than the survey results included in this article. See Curtin (2008) for the details on this experiment.

Knowledge of Official Data on the Economy

The survey measured people's awareness of the official national unemployment rate, the CPI, and the rate of growth in the GDP. Each question included three core elements: it defined the economic indicator, it identified the official governmental agency responsible for collecting the data, and asked for the most recently published figure. The wording of the questions were as follows:

First, the Bureau of Labor Statistics counts people as unemployed if they are not currently working but have been actively looking for work during the prior four weeks. What was the most recent rate of unemployment published by this government agency?

Another economic indicator published by the Bureau of Labor Statistics is the Consumer Price Index, or the CPI. Compared with a year ago, what was the percentage change in overall prices as measured by the Consumer Price Index, or CPI, published by this government agency?

The Bureau of Economic Analysis regularly publishes data on the total amount of goods and services produced in the U.S. This figure is called the Gross Domestic Product and is often abbreviated as GDP. Compared to a year ago, what was the percentage change in the Gross Domestic Product, or GDP, published by this government agency?

Note that the first question asked was expected to be the easiest to answer: the unemployment rate is widely discussed in the media and the percentage is not a rate of change but a simple proportion. In contrast, the CPI, while widely publicized, is always expressed as a rate of change, and that rate is variously published as a simple month-to-month change, an annualized month-to-month change, or a year-to-year change. This implies that the information about the CPI may require more processing and calculation before it is useable as an answer to this question. The final question was the most difficult since it concerns a quantity that does not directly impinge on people's economic lives like inflation or unemployment, giving them less incentive to track the measure; moreover, the figure is repeatedly revised, and variously reported as an annualized quarter-to-quarter change or annual change, and adjusted for seasonal variations and inflation. It is also important to note that unemployment and inflation express negative outcomes, and people have been found to pay more attention to negative rather than positive economic developments.

Some people may not have provided answers because they did not have knowledge about all three elements of the questions. People may not have known how the rate they knew was defined, may have never heard of that particular federal agency, or may not have heard an announcement for some time. While each of these possibilities was not investigated, a follow-up to each question was asked of everyone who did not know the official figures:

Have you ever heard an announcement of the ...
... unemployment rate by the Bureau of Labor Statistics?
... the Consumer Price Index, or CPI, by the Bureau of Labor Statistics?
... the Gross Domestic Product, or GDP, by the Bureau of Economic Analysis?

Respondents could have replied that they had heard of the economic indicator, but just did not know the current figure. This may have simply reflected rational inattention in 2007, but that hypothesis is more difficult to sustain in 2009 due to the widespread interest reported by people in the performance of the economy as well as the intense media reporting on the economic crisis. A "no" answer could presumably mean either that they had not heard of the official indicator or that they did not know of the government agency, or both. Nonetheless, given that the research objective was to determine if people paid attention to the releases from federal agencies, naming those agencies seemed an important aspect for a robust test.

Reported Awareness of Official Economic Statistics

If you thought that the greatest economic crisis since the 1930s had significantly raised the public's overall awareness of official economic statistics then you would be incorrect. The only economic indicator of which people were marginally more likely to report awareness was the unemployment rate (see Table 3.1). The proportion of US adults that reported that they thought they knew of the most recently published official rate of unemployment rose to 58% in the 2009 survey, up from 47% in 2007. While this was a statistically significant increase in awareness, it was still rather small given the extent of the rise in the unemployment rate – the unemployment rate more than doubled, rising from 4.5% in May of 2007 to 9.4% in May 2009, which was at that time the highest unemployment rate in more than a quarter century.

There was no change in people's awareness of the official statistics about the performance of the economy or consumer prices, regardless of whether those perceptions were accurate. Awareness of the latest GDP figures rose by an insignificant amount, from 23% in 2007 to 25% in 2009, despite the fact that the economy was in a steep recession in 2009 (–6.1%) but in 2007 the economy was still expanding (+3.2%). The data indicated that

Table 3.1 *People's Knowledge of Official Measures of Economic Performance*

What is the rate of ...	Unemployment		Consumer Price Index (CPI)		Gross Domestic Product (GDP)	
	2007	2009	2007	2009	2007	2009
Provided rate answer	47%	58%	27%	22%	23%	25%
Heard of, but didn't know current rate	33	26	40	41	40	39
Never heard of official rate or agency	19	15	31	34	36	33
DK; NA	1	1	2	3	1	3
Total	100%	100%	100%	100%	100%	100%
Cases	1,005	1,011	1,005	1,011	1,005	1,011
Addendum (medians)						
People's reports of official rates R_{it}	5.0%	8.5%	3.0%	2.9%	3.3%	1.5%
Absolute percentage point error in people's reports $\lvert R_{it} - A_t \rvert$	0.68	1.09	0.78	3.08	1.42	2.83

Note: the actual official rates (A_t) reflect the latest data release available on the date the interviews were conducted and do not reflect subsequent revisions.

marginally fewer people said they knew the rate of CPI inflation in 2009, falling from 27% in 2007 to 22% in 2009, as CPI inflation fell from 2.7% to -1.0%. Perhaps the most surprising finding was that one-third of all adults reported in both 2007 and 2009 that they had never heard of the official statistics on GDP growth or CPI inflation. Never having heard of the official unemployment rate declined from 2007, but it was still unexpectedly high at 15% in 2009 given the widespread concerns about joblessness at that time. The most generous interpretation was that people had never heard of the federal agency responsible for publishing the official statistics rather than not having heard of the actual statistics. Nonetheless, this would still imply that these people might not be able to distinguish what represented the official statistics favored by economic models.

Among those that did provide a rate answer, the median estimated unemployment rate jumped to 8.5% in 2009 from 5.0% in 2007 (see Table 3.1). These sample estimates were very close to the actual rates announced by the Labor Department at the time of the surveys: 8.5% in 2009 and 4.5% in 2007. To more accurately assess errors in people's knowledge, the absolute difference was calculated between what people reported (R_{it}) and the latest release of the official statistic (A_t) in percentage points. The median absolute errors treat both overestimates and underestimates equally.

The median absolute percentage point error in people's estimates of the unemployment rate increased in 2009 to 1.09 from 0.68 in 2007. People's estimates of the CPI inflation rate were also less accurate, with the absolute error rising to 3.08 in 2009 from 0.78 in 2007. The same was true for GDP: the median absolute error rose to 2.83 in 2009 from 1.42 in 2007. Unlike in 2007, the headline CPI inflation rate at the time of the survey in 2009 was negative, although the core inflation rate was still positive. While people reported a slightly lower inflation rate and a much lower GDP growth rate in 2009, those declines still left the 2009 estimates further away from the actual levels than in 2007. Indeed, whereas in 2007 one-third of all respondents that reported a rate of CPI inflation were within half of a percentage point of the actual rate, just one in ten were as accurate in 2009. The same results held for GDP reports: in 2007 one-third were within half a percentage point of the actual rate but only one in ten in 2009. The higher degree of inaccuracy may have been due to the negative rates of growth in both prices and the economy in 2009.

The negative rates of change in the CPI and GDP statistics in 2009 represented a greater cognitive challenge than the positive rates of growth in 2007. Negative numbers appeared for the first time during the Han Dynasty (202 BC–AD 220) and only became common in Europe in the seventeenth century (Dehaene, 1997). Knowledge of positive numbers has an intuitive basis as a counting device, present in all people, from infants to those with little or no formal education (De Cruz, 2006). Negative numbers do not have a natural intuitive basis, and understanding negative numbers relies more on explicit training than on an automatic cognitive process. It is of some interest to note that one of the first rationalizations of negative numbers was as a measure of debt (Dehaene, 1997), but most people still have trouble conceptualizing debt as negative savings. The key difference is that the comprehension of positive numbers is more likely to be an effortless cognitive process and the comprehension of negative numbers is more likely to be an effortful conscious process.

The distribution of people's estimates of the rates of unemployment, inflation, and economic growth indicates that the CPI rather than GDP was more inaccurate. Among those that reported a specific GDP rate, 45% reported a negative rate of GDP growth in 2009. In contrast, among those that reported a specific CPI rate, just 16% reported a negative rate in 2009. The substantial difference in reports of negative rates of change weakens the hypothesis about the higher cognitive burden of negative numbers but cannot totally reject the impact. A higher core rate of inflation may have skewed people's CPI estimates upward, with most of the declines in the headline CPI due to falling energy prices.

Nonetheless, it is somewhat distressing that during the worst recession in modern history, one in eight respondents reported the official statistics for the GDP growth rate as over 8% in 2009. This level of inaccuracy among those who purported to know the latest GDP figure is quite amazing. Because it is never socially desirable for respondents to admit ignorance, the survey may have encouraged people to make a wild guess. This tendency may be offset, though, by motivations to avoid the embarrassment of an incorrect answer to a knowledge question when the respondent could assume that the interviewer knew the correct answer. It was impossible to disentangle these two hypotheses with the collected data. The methodological experiments that were conducted provided considerable evidence that the majority of respondents viewed the questions about official economic statistics as burdensome.

DEMOGRAPHIC CORRELATES OF KNOWLEDGE OF OFFICIAL STATISTICS

It is of some interest to determine the demographic correlates of people's knowledge as they may indicate differences in costs or benefits of acquiring information. Although the conscious cognitive capacity of the US population could not have meaningfully changed in just two years, people may have been less proficient at reporting the negative rates of change that were common in 2009 but not in 2007. The demographic characteristics of the respondents reflect a combination of differences in cognitive capacity, interests, and differences in the benefits of accurate knowledge of official statistics. People with college degrees can be assumed to have a higher cognitive capacity than high school graduates. Although education is a very rough guide to differences in cognitive capacities, it is the closest proxy that was available in the survey. Experience is also a great teacher of the importance of economic information. Older respondents are likely to have more economic experience and a greater appreciation of understanding the benefits of accurate knowledge of economic statistics. Higher income households make more economic decisions that would benefit from accurate information, although lower income households may suffer greater proportionate risks if their decisions proved faulty. Socialization may have caused differences between males and females in their attention to government statistics.

The most obvious variable to investigate for differences is the absolute error in people's perceptions of the official statistics. Given that few people actually provided a numerical answer to that question, the analysis needs to be supplemented by investigation of those who reported that they knew of the statistic but did not know the current rate, and an investigation of the demographic correlates of those that reported that they had never heard of the official statistics.

Specific Rate Answers

The errors in perceptions of official economic statistics among people who provided a response were smaller as education increased, among older people, and among those with higher household incomes. Moreover, the same pattern was present in 2007 and 2009 (see Table 3.2). This consistent relationship indicates the stable impact of cognitive capacity, interest, and differences in the benefits derived from accurate knowledge of economic statistics. Not surprisingly, the largest errors occurred among the lowest income groups, the youngest, and the least educated in both 2007 and 2009. Nonetheless, the errors contained in the 2009 reports on official statistics were significantly higher than in 2007 across all demographic groups, even among the most educated, the oldest, and the highest income groups. There is no credible hypothesis that would explain why the 2009 errors were significantly larger than the 2007 errors. Greater public attention to news about the economy in 2009 did not yield more accurate knowledge of official economic statistics. This does not imply that people did seek and obtain more information that was relevant to their own economic decisions. It does mean, however, that people did not place greater emphasis on obtaining accurate information on official economic statistics.

Lack of Knowledge about Economic Statistics

Education, age, and income had more success at explaining who admitted no up-to-date knowledge of economic statistics and who reported that they had never heard of the official statistics. Indeed, these few demographic variables were able to explain twice as much compared with their ability to account for differences in the accuracy of the reports.

Higher educated respondents were consistently less likely to report that they had never heard of the economic statistics, and generally more likely to report that they simply did not know the most recent figure. Although education and income are correlated, income was still a significant predictor

Table 3.2 *Median Absolute Errors in Estimates of Economic Statistics among Demographic Subgroups*

	Unemployment Rate		Consumer Price Index (CPI)		Gross Domestic Product (GDP)	
	2007	2009	2007	2009	2007	2009
Household Income						
Bottom third	1.08	1.45	0.88	3.70	1.94	5.37
Middle third	0.90	1.41	0.82	3.13	1.46	2.35
Top third	0.56	0.88	0.76	2.65	1.10	1.90
Age						
18–34 years	0.90	1.60	1.28	3.02	1.49	3.84
35–54	0.81	1.26	0.80	3.06	1.43	2.91
55 or older	0.56	1.00	0.69	3.17	1.22	2.28
Education						
High school or less	1.12	1.45	2.06	3.02	1.73	5.08
Some college	0.62	1.14	0.78	2.84	1.30	2.11
College graduate	0.55	0.93	0.60	3.10	1.02	2.11

because it is a proxy not only for cognitive ability but also for the degree of engagement in the economy. Higher income respondents were more likely to simply not know the current figure for each statistic and significantly less likely to have never heard of these official economic measures. Even apart from education, the data indicate that higher income households may have a vested interest to give more attention to economic statistics, may face lower costs in acquiring economic information, or may garner greater economic benefits from updating their information more regularly.

The age of the respondent also had a widespread impact on these responses. Older respondents were significantly less likely to report having never heard of these economic statistics, and were generally more likely to report that they knew of them but did not know their current levels. This probably reflects the greater life experiences of older adults, especially those experiences of several decades ago when inflation and unemployment were at double-digit levels and GDP fell sharply.

IMPORTANCE OF INFORMATION ON OFFICIAL ECONOMIC STATISTICS

While economic models usually include an assumption that all agents have full knowledge of official economic statistics, the data above indicated that official information is not widely known. It is useful to check the underlying assumption that people value exact information on official statistics as well as whether they trust the official statistical agencies to provide accurate data to the public. Following the questions on knowledge of official statistics, respondents were asked whether they thought it was important to know exact information on official economic statistics, whether they would like additional information on these topics, and whether they trust official statistics to be accurate. The wording of the questions were as follows:

How important is it for a person like you to have exact information about the rate of unemployment, the rate of change in prices, and the rate of change in the Gross Domestic Product – would you say it is extremely important, very important, somewhat important, not very important, or not important at all?

Would you like to be more informed about these topics or would you not want any more information about these topics?

In general, on a scale of one to ten, where one is "do not trust at all" and ten is "trust completely," how much do you trust official government statistics to accurately measure the rate of unemployment, the rate of change in prices, and the rate of change in the Gross Domestic Product?

Somewhat surprisingly, respondents viewed the importance of official information on the exact rate of unemployment, inflation, or economic growth as only slightly more important in 2009 than in 2007 despite the heightened levels of uncertainty about prospects for the economy (see Table 3.3). Moreover, there was no change in the percentage of people who desired more information on official economic statistics in 2009. Although half of all people reported that they would like more information about the performance of the economy in both years, the economic crisis did not increase the felt need for more official information. It might have been expected that people would have accorded a much higher level of importance to information about the performance of the economy whether the hypothesis about staggered updating was true or false. Moreover, the median absolute errors in people's reports of the rates of unemployment, inflation, or economic growth were unrelated to the importance of the official data or the felt need for more information. It was true, however, that people who could actually recall a specific rate of unemployment, inflation, or economic growth were also somewhat more likely to find official information more important than those who could not report a rate.

Two-thirds of all people reported a middling or slightly higher degree of trust in the accuracy of official economic statistics in 2009 – this question was not asked in 2007. Many fewer people were on the extremes, either having complete trust (9%) or complete distrust (12%). Importantly, people

Table 3.3 *Importance of and Trust in Official Statistics and Most Common Sources of Economic Information*

Importance?	2007	2009	Trust Official Statistics?	2007	2009
Extremely important	6%	8%	Do not trust at all (1–2)	NA	12%
Very important	20	23	Mostly distrust (3–4)		15
Somewhat important	37	42	Middle position (5–6)		33
Not very important	25	21	Mostly trust (7–8)		31
Not important at all	10	6	Trust completely (9–10)		9
DK; NA	2	0	Total		100%
Total	100%	100%			
Want More Information?			**Source of Information**		
Yes, want more	50%	49%	Television	80%	87%
Do not want more	48	50	Newspapers	62	62
DK; NA	2	1	Internet	42	48
Total	100%	100%	Family, friends, etc.	31	40
			Radio	38	35
			Magazines	15	13
			Never obtain information	10	5

who reported that they mostly trusted the accuracy of official statistics had the smallest absolute errors in their reports of the rates of unemployment, inflation, and economic growth. It is of some importance to note that the significance of the relationship of trust in the accuracy of the official data had a significant impact even after the demographic characteristics of the household were taken into account for unemployment and inflation rates. Nonetheless, there is no reason to anticipate that trust significantly declined in 2009 from 2007 thus producing more errors in 2009. The most common sources of information about the performance of the economy in both 2007 and 2009 were hearing the news on television, followed by newspapers, and the internet (see Table 3.3). More people reported obtaining information from family and friends or from personal experience than from hearing reports on the radio in 2009 (40% versus 35%); it was the reverse in 2007. While 10% of all people said that they had never obtained information about the performance of the economy in 2007, this figure dropped to just 5% in 2009. These self-reported sources of economic information closely match the results from media studies. The Pew Research Center has estimated that in 2008, 84% of US adults obtained economic news from television, 64% from newspapers, 48% from the internet, and 40% from family and friends (Pew, 2009).

The change between 2007 and 2009 was largest for obtaining information from family, friends, and co-workers (+9 percentage points), followed by television (+7) and the internet (+6). While the increase in television and the internet as a source of economic information is hardly surprising, the increased importance of family, friends, and co-workers suggests that informal sources of information on economic statistics rose during the crisis. This increase could reflect cognitive limitations that are overcome by a friend's "translation" into terms that could be more easily understood, or it could reflect the importance of tailoring the information to the individual's own circumstances, or to the advantage of social groups to discern threats to group members.

COVERAGE OF OFFICIAL ECONOMIC STATISTICS IN THE MASS MEDIA

A critical assumption in testing whether people have accurate knowledge of the current rates of unemployment, consumer prices, and economic growth is that those rates are communicated by the government through the mass media. In an attempt to test this assumption, television transcripts and newspaper archives were searched to determine if they contained a report that cited a specific number for the official statistics on the day it was released by the government agency, or during the following three days. A four-day window was chosen because most US newspapers are morning editions that are printed before the 8:30 a.m. release time of the statistical agency, and since some releases occur on Fridays, a four-day window was needed to include the following Monday. A report on the official statistic that did not mention the exact official rate was not counted even if it did occur in the four-day window. The same searches were done in 2009 as in 2007. The TV transcripts and newspapers were searched over two sixteen-month periods, from January 2006 to April 2007 and from January 2008 to April 2009.

News reports from the five major broadcast networks – ABC, NBC, CBS, CNN, and Fox – were searched. Total viewership for the prime time nightly newscasts on ABC, CBS, NBC, CNN, and Fox totaled 26.1 million in 2008 (Pew, 2009). All-business networks (such as CNBC) were not included, even if they were owned by one of the five networks that were included. The official release of the unemployment rate was reported every time on CNN and 92% of the time by ABC and Fox in 2008–2009 (see Table 3.4). Although the official unemployment rate was the most frequently reported number in 2008–2009, the percentage of times the exact unemployment rate was reported averaged 83% in 2006–2007 and declined to 60% in 2008–2009. Exact figures for the CPI were reported much less frequently

Table 3.4 *Media Reports of Economic Indicators from Official Statistical Agency*

	Unemployment Rate		Consumer Price Index (CPI)		Gross Domestic Product (GDP)	
	2007	2009	2007	2009	2007	2009
Television – Average 5 networks	83%	60%	35%	35%	46%	51%
ABC	63	82	19	18	44	24
CBS	56	12	63	0	25	12
NBC	100	24	13	0	31	18
Fox	94	82	31	71	50	100
CNN	100	100	50	88	81	100
Newspapers – Average 22 papers	51%	75%	57%	49%	40%	52%
USA Today (circulation 2.2 million)	44	59	63	65	50	53
Wall Street Journal (circulation 2.1 m)	100	100	88	100	81	100
New York Times (circulation 1.0 m)	100	100	100	100	94	100
Los Angeles Times (circulation 0.7 m)	75	100	100	88	75	76
Washington Post (circulation 0.7 m)	100	100	100	100	100	100

Note: 2007 data drawn from Curtin (2008).

than the unemployment rate, with the 2008–2009 average falling to just 35%. This was equal to the 2006–2007 average, but the distribution was much more skewed in 2008–2009 as NBC and CBS never reported exact figures and CNN and Fox reported the CPI figure about three-fourths of the time.

Exact GDP figures were reported about half the time in both periods, but again in the 2008–2009 period there were considerable differences across the networks: CNN and Fox reported GDP figures for every release while ABC, CBS, and NBC reported exact figures for one-fourth of the releases. Overall, more exact figures for all figures were reported by CNN, followed by Fox News. Notably, however, CNN and Fox had just a 13% share of total viewership of the nightly newscasts. If the 2009 figures were adjusted for differences in viewership, the average proportion of newscasts that included the exact unemployment rate was 47% (down from 60%), the exact CPI rate was reported by 15% (down from 35%), and the GDP rate was reported by 29% (down from 51%). Who would have guessed that people would report exact figures for these key economic indicators less often during the Great Recession?

The generally infrequent reports of exact figures for these economic statistics stand in sharp contrast to the greater coverage devoted to the economy by all five networks. From the start of 2007 to the end of 2008, the proportion of news coverage on the economy rose from 0.5% to 26.3%

Table 3.5 *Responses to Expected Inflation Question by Knowledge*
of the Official CPI

Knowledge of Official CPI	Could Not Provide Answer to Question on Inflation Expectations (%)
Knew of CPI, and provided latest official rate	9
Heard of, but didn't know official CPI rate	9
Never heard of official CPI rate or agency	19
Total sample	12

across all news media (Pew, 2009). Rather than focusing on the official statistics on unemployment, inflation, and economic growth, the news reports focused on the financial crisis, declines in housing and stock prices, subprime loans, foreclosures, bankruptcies, Wall Street and auto bailouts, and a myriad of other economic problems. Overall, the many facets of the economic crisis appear to have overwhelmed and displaced the more traditional measures of the performance of the economy.

The declining number of newspapers and declining readership in 2009 negatively affected the replication of the 2007 search of news stories in US newspapers. A total of twenty-seven newspapers were searched in 2007, each having a circulation of more than 400,000 as of March 2006. Only twenty-two of these newspapers were still published and met the much reduced 2009 circulation criteria of just 250,000 as of March 2009.[3] The total circulation of the newspapers was 21.1 million at the start of 2006, and just 13.4 million at the start of 2009. Table 3.5 also includes the statistics for the five top papers in terms of circulation. Note that *USA Today*, the paper with the highest daily circulation, more closely mirrors the average reporting habits of all twenty-two of the largest US newspapers.

Newspapers are often read by more than one person, with a 2006 estimate that on average 2.3 persons read each copy (according to the Newspaper Association of America). Ignoring that some people read more than one paper each day, the number of people reading each copy in circulation was

---

[3] The newspapers included in both the 2007 and 2009 searches, in order of 2009 circulation, were: *USA Today, Wall Street Journal, New York Times, Los Angeles Times, Washington Post, New York Daily News, New York Post, Chicago Tribune, Houston Chronicle, Arizona Republic, Denver Post, Long Island Newsday, Dallas Morning News, Minneapolis Star Tribune, San Francisco Chronicle, Boston Globe, Plain Dealer, Philadelphia Inquirer, Newark Star-Ledger, St. Petersburg Times, Atlanta Journal Constitution*, and the *San Diego Union-Tribune*.

48.6 million in 2007 and 30.8 million in 2009, a decline of 37%. The overall level of newspaper readership was estimated to be barely higher than the 26.1 million that viewed nightly newscasts on TV.

Three papers in the 2008–2009 period cited every release of the official rates for unemployment, inflation, and economic growth (*Wall Street Journal*, *New York Times*, and the *Washington Post*), an improvement over just one paper in the 2006–2007 time period (*Washington Post*). *USA Today*, the paper with the largest circulation, cited the official figures just over half the times in both periods. Across all papers searched, the unemployment rate was reported more frequently in 2008–2009 than in 2006–2007, rising to 75% from 51% of the official releases. The official figures for the CPI were reported slightly less frequently in 2008–2009 (49%, down from 57%), and the official figures for GDP were reported more frequently (52%, up from 40%). While newspapers reported the official statistics somewhat more frequently, the rise in frequency hardly matches the severity of the 2009 recession or the professed interest in the economy by the public.

The AP and UPI wire services carried reports for every release of the latest official rates of unemployment, the CPI, and GDP in both 2007 and 2009. If we presume that the twenty-two papers with the largest circulations and the five television networks all had access to the wire reports, the lack of complete coverage would be an active decision of the editors not to publish the numeric figures. It was likely to reflect a judgment about the newsworthiness of the latest figures given their viewers' interests. Given that the *Wall Street Journal*, *New York Times*, and *Washington Post* all have readers with higher than average education and incomes, these papers may have included the exact figures due to judgments about their reader's interest, with the opposite decision made by papers like *USA Today*. Nonetheless, most of the media preferred to emphasize the qualitative and more subjective aspects of these economic statistics rather than report the exact figures.

The simultaneous internet releases of the official statistics have supplanted the distribution functions of the AP and UPI wire services in recent years. The news wires (and others) still have the advantage of viewing the results early (in a locked room) so they can also provide commentary at the time of the release. Nonetheless, people from around the globe can access the same data the instant it is released via the internet. Moreover, a rising number of people favor getting the news about the official statistics on the internet, whether from the official site or from the many other websites that post similar information. Like television and newspapers, some websites report full information, some partial, and some mixed with commentary.

An assessment of the frequency of reports of the official figures on the internet is both straightforward and complex. The straightforward answer is 100% since the statistical agencies first report the official releases of the unemployment, inflation, and economic growth rates on the internet. The answer is more complex in that in the many versions of the official releases that most people actually access, the official number may or may not be included. While using an internet search engine, such as Google, one would find numerous mentions (and interpretations) of all the official reports, though it would require some additional effort to locate the official number.

The total number of accesses of the official news releases on the Bureau of Labor Statistics and the Bureau of Economic Analysis websites provides some gauge of interest in the official figures. The news release of the unemployment rate by the BLS was accessed 23,056 times on May 8, 2009, well above the 8,243 accesses on May 4, 2007. The news release for the Consumer Price Index, also posted on the BLS website, was accessed 8,522 times on May 15, 2009, down from 11,959 accesses on May 15, 2007.[4] These differences mirror the lower television and newspaper coverage of the CPI figures compared with the official unemployment rate. These are relatively small numbers, but unlike TV viewership or readers of newspapers, every release contained the appropriate numbers. Still, the number that directly access the official releases would disappear when calculating the total mass media audience. Overall, this review of the dissemination of official economic data suggests that people's lack of knowledge about official economic statistics is attributable in part to the inadequate communication of that information by the mass media. The unemployment rate was the exception, with reports of the official unemployment rate more frequently reported, and people's knowledge of the unemployment rate was more accurate. The coincidence is suggestive but does not prove causation given that there may have been higher demands on the part of the public for accurate knowledge rather than just a greater supply of information.

The one conclusion that is inescapable is that there are substantial costs that people incur when updating information about economic statistics, significantly higher than the near zero cost that is typically assumed in economic models.

[4]   The GDP figures were posted on the BEA website on May 29, 2009, with the news release on May 29, 2009 having 11,849 accesses (no 2007 data are available). The data are from personal communications with Reggie Simons of the BLS Division of Enterprise Web Systems and Alec Minor, Web Manager, Bureau of Economic Analysis.

PRIVATE KNOWLEDGE ABOUT THE PERFORMANCE
OF THE ECONOMY

The questions about people's knowledge of official data released by federal agencies can be compared with other questions that simply ask about unemployment, prices, and economic growth. Unlike the prior questions, which identified the official governmental agency responsible for collecting the data and asked for the most recently published figure, these alternate questions simply asked respondents about likely changes in unemployment, prices, and the economy. Less technical jargon was used to define each of these economic concepts, and the questions focus on the next twelve months rather than changes over the past twelve months. It should also be noted that these questions were asked prior to the questions on the official economic statistics, and the questions were separated in the questionnaire by dozens of other questions that took more than five minutes to ask. The wording of the questions were as follows:

How about people out of work during the coming twelve months – do you think that there will be more unemployment than now, about the same, or less?

During the next twelve months, do you think that prices in general will go up, or go down, or stay where they are now? By what percent do you expect prices to go (up/down) on the average during the next twelve months?

Now turning to business conditions in the economy as a whole – do you think that during the next twelve months conditions will be better, or worse than they are at present, or just about the same?

The questions on expected trends in unemployment and business conditions were measured using qualitative scales while the question on expected inflation is based on a quantitative response scale. The high degree of forecast accuracy for the responses to the questions on inflation and unemployment expectations were covered in the last chapter. It is worth emphasizing that consumers' inflation expectations were repeatedly found to be unbiased, efficient and as accurate as professional economists' forecasts. Curtin (1999; 2003) found that consumers' forecasts of the year-ahead unemployment rate outperformed those of professional forecasters as well as forecasts from two prominent macroeconomic models. Consumers' expectations for the GDP growth rate also have an excellent prediction track record that earned it a place in the US composite index of leading economic indicators (Curtin, 1999; 2003).

The cognitive barriers presented by the questions of the official measures of unemployment and GDP virtually disappeared when the questions on these same topics were phrased in everyday language (see Table 3.5). In sharp contrast to the high degree of professed ignorance of the official figures, the percentage of the population that reported that they could not answer or did not know what to expect totaled just 1% in both 2007 and 2009 for the questions on unemployment and GDP growth. It would have been reasonable to anticipate that people would know more about economic events that already took place and for which information was readily available than to be knowledgeable about future prospects for those same economic performance measures. Nonetheless, year-ahead expectations for unemployment and GDP were held by virtually all consumers.

The question on inflation expectations was much more difficult. It asked for a quantitative estimate of next year's inflation rate. Whereas the questions on unemployment and GDP growth only asked about the direction of expected change, the inflation question also asked about the extent of change. Most consumers knew whether they anticipated an increase or decline; nearly all of the question's difficulty involved identifying a specific quantitative estimate of the expected change. The data provide an estimate of the additional difficulty involved in forecasting next year's inflation rate compared with knowledge of last year's inflation rate. Among respondents who reported that they knew last year's inflation rate, just 9% did not report a specific estimate of next year's inflation rate (see Table 3.5). In other words, just 9% of those who viewed themselves as knowledgeable about the current rate of inflation did not provide a quantitative estimate of next year's inflation rate. Some found the question too difficult, and some were simply too uncertain about what to expect to suggest a specific number. Interestingly, the same level of difficulty in providing a quantitative inflation expectation was obtained from those who reported having heard of the CPI but did not know the most recent data. One might have expected a level somewhat higher than 9% since these people specifically said that they had no knowledge of the most recent official inflation rate. After all, most conventional theories base the formation of expectations on people's awareness of the most recently available official information. If staggered updating is assumed as well as the tendency of consumers to use outdated expectations in response to the question, an identical 9% would require such responses by everyone. Even if the proportion was only marginally higher than 9%, it would lend some credence to the conventional theories that put a heavy emphasis in empirical models on the public dissemination of statistical releases by federal agencies.

Among those who said that they had never heard of the CPI, 19% did not report a specific inflation expectation for the year ahead. While this result is more in line with conventional theories, it still meant that 81% of those who professed no knowledge whatsoever of the official CPI nonetheless had no trouble in answering a question on the expected inflation rate for the year ahead. This appears to be a significant rejection of the importance of public information since one-third of the total sample reported no knowledge of the CPI. The number that reported no knowledge of the official CPI is no doubt an overestimate given the number of media reports, whether qualitative or quantitative. Just because someone hears a report based on the latest CPI data, there is no guarantee it was attributed to the responsible federal agency. The media could have simply reported that "prices are up," for example, or that "prices were unchanged." Moreover, the very name "consumer price index" sounds generic, so that even if it were attributed, consumers may have not realized it was an official designation. Despite these nuances, it is still hard to believe that one-third professed ignorance. Perhaps the best defense of conventional theories is that consumers simply did not know they knew. But even this defense can only apply to general qualitative knowledge of the current inflation rate, not the specific quantitative knowledge assumed by the conventional theories.

ASSESSMENT OF PEOPLE'S KNOWLEDGE OF OFFICIAL STATISTICS

What do people know about official economic statistics? Only a minority of people could report a specific figure for the current rates of unemployment, inflation, and economic growth, although the majority had heard about these official statistics. When they did report a specific figure, it typically differed from the official statistic by half a percentage point to three percentage points, depending on the economic statistic. People reported more accurate figures for the unemployment rate, and less accurate reports of the inflation rate and GDP growth rates. The unemployment rate had the advantage of requiring fewer cognitive resources to understand simple percentages rather than rates of change, and fewer cognitive resources are required to comprehend positive numbers rather than negative figures.

People make decisions about whether to update their information on the economy depending on the costs of acquiring, processing, and interpreting new information compared with the potential benefits of the new information. Given that the 2007 data were collected when unemployment, inflation, and economic growth were relatively favorable and stable, most people might not have been willing to undergo the costs of updating for the minor benefits they could anticipate. It was expected that the worst economic downturn since the 1930s would motivate people to acquire updated information about the economy. Unfortunately, people were no more knowledgeable of official economic statistics in 2009 than in 2007, and their knowledge of economic statistics was much less accurate in 2009. This negative conclusion is based on the premise that the cost of updating information about official statistics was lower, the benefits higher, and the cognitive burdens of obtaining and processing information were constant over the two year period. This implies a decisive rejection of the assumption that official statistics were for most people the most relevant measures for people to use in making their own financial decisions.

The errors in perceptions of official economic statistics were smaller among the more educated, among older people, and among those with higher household incomes in both 2007 and 2009. This unchanged relationship indicates the consistent impact of conscious cognitive capacity, interest, and differences in the benefits derived from accurate knowledge of economic statistics. Nonetheless, the errors contained in the 2009 reports on official statistics were significantly higher than in 2007 across all demographic groups.

The cognitive resources needed to acquire and process information on official statistics had presumably remained unchanged in 2009 from two years earlier. The costs of acquiring the latest statistics, however, were still high for most people. There was a surprising lack of mass media reports on the official quantitative rates of unemployment, inflation, or economic growth. The mass media did enlarge their qualitative descriptions of the economic crisis rather than highlighting the official figures. There is no question that a determined consumer could obtain the exact information on the economic statistics, but that would usually take additional time and effort. Only those who regularly subscribe to few national papers or who regularly watch cable business shows would be exposed to the latest economic statistics in the cost-free manner suggested by conventional expectation formation models.

Moreover, most people did not judge having more exact information on economic statistics as important. Indeed, people were nearly evenly divided between such information being important versus unimportant. Surprisingly, the 2009 economic crisis did not make people more desirous of having up-to-date information than in 2007. Distrust in the accuracy of official statistics played a role, although people remained slightly more trustful than distrustful.

Perhaps the most important factor limiting people's knowledge of official statistics is the benefits they would derive from basing their decisions on national estimates. There is no reason to expect that people would seek out information about an inflation or unemployment rate that they did not face. Indeed, rather than economy-wide information, it is more likely that local information is more appropriate. Local unemployment rates for jobs that individuals are qualified for are more important than national unemployment rates, and people that consume a greater proportion of their incomes on certain products or services would naturally view the potential benefits of information on those products or services greater than information on overall inflation. The primacy of information that is specific to their own economic situation increases the importance of what economists call "private" compared with "public" information.

The survey included other economic measures more aligned with people's usual economic experiences. Answers to questions about trends in unemployment, inflation, and economic growth were nearly universal, standing in stark contrast to responses to the knowledge questions on the official rates. The general lack of knowledge of the official rates did not mean that people were unaware of the performance of the economy, only that they did not know the official rate most recently published by a governmental agency. Private knowledge about expected price trends, as well as unemployment and economic growth, was widespread, and past analyses have shown those expectations to be relatively accurate.

Such a complex overall assessment of the public's knowledge of economic statistics is much less surprising than the premise that people would consistently use their scarce resources to monitor official economic statistics published by government agencies. Consumers do desire knowledge about their economic situation, as Aristotle noted long ago. The next chapter examines how people can use their total mental capacity to monitor the economic factors that have an important impact on their own financial situation.

4

Processing Economic Information

The human brain is an information processing machine. Evolutionary adaptation has meant that no element of the human mind can be dismissed as superfluous. Humans use both conscious and nonconscious processes to acquire information about their environments. The most common distinction is that deliberation by the conscious mind is effortful whereas it is presumed to be effortless by the nonconscious mind. That is not the most important difference. Conscious reasoning, which enables the most advanced decision skills, is a scarce resource when compared with the nearly unlimited capacity of the nonconscious. It is simply impossible for people to make every economic decision by conscious deliberation. Most decisions are based on nonconscious mental processes. There are not enough hours in the day for people to consciously deliberate about all of life's decisions. Indeed, it is the exception rather than the rule when behavior is the sole result of conscious reasoning. How do humans decide when to use their scarce attentional resources? Expectations help them to decide which pieces of information they should consciously process. Events that are fully anticipated attract little conscious attention because they contain no new information. Unexpected events draw more conscious awareness because they contain new information that could potentially affect an individual's ability to achieve desired goals. People do not ignore what was anticipated. Most of this information is still processed, some of it consciously, but most of it without conscious awareness.

Nonconscious processing of information clearly dominates the more limited capacity of conscious awareness. The advantages of the nonconscious mind to process information are overwhelming. It has been estimated that people can process hundreds of thousands of bits of information per second nonconsciously compared with the dozens of bits of information that people can process consciously. Some have estimated the advantage as high as 11.2 million to 40 bits of information per second (Dijksterhuis, 2004; Wilson, 2002). Scientists base these estimates on the number of receptor cells of each sensory organ and the nerves that go from these cells to the brain. Most of these bits of information are visual rather than auditory or tactile, about 10 million of the 11.2 million bits of information. These estimates are imprecise since no exact measure of the processing capacity of the unconscious mind yet exists, and will not exist until future developments in neuroscience provide a more definitive answer. No one doubts that the nonconscious processing capacity is orders of magnitude larger than conscious awareness (Lewicki et al., 1992).

A primary function of the brain as an information processing engine is to make judgments rapidly and effortlessly (Montague & Berns, 2002). Evolutionary development has meant that everyone routinely forms expectations to efficiently allocate their scare attentional resources. People learn over time how to best handle expected events, and gradually develop rules of thumb that operate nonconsciously to automate these decisions. The use of such decision heuristics has somehow achieved more notoriety for their biases than for their efficiency. These heuristics are no different in principle than the statistical models used by economists to generate forecasts. These statistical models, in contrast, have achieved more notoriety for their accuracy. Nonetheless, both heuristics and statistical models have long histories of inaccurate predictions. Despite these shortcomings, economists as well as consumers use these "models" because they efficiently utilize their scarce resources based on their current state of knowledge. The clear advantage of statistical models is that they lay bare all assumptions that were used in the estimation process. Each assumption can be tested to determine whether and how much it improved the accuracy of the resulting forecasts. The problem with decisions made by nonconscious processes is that people cannot explain the underlying rationale for their decision to themselves or to others. They may well cite some justification, but by its very nature, nonconscious knowledge cannot be known by the conscious mind. Nonetheless, this lack of conscious awareness does not mean that nonconscious information processing is not an essential element of everyday economic life. Nor does it mean that it is any less accurate than conscious reasoning. Indeed, cognitive processes themselves are not necessarily conscious. Cognition is defined to include all processes by which sensory input is stored, transformed, recovered, and used (Neisser, 1967). People accomplish most of these cognitive tasks nonconsciously. Given that nonconscious processing is automatic and effortless, no one can avoid this process and no one can afford to ignore its results (Bargh & Ferguson, 2000; Bargh & Chartrand, 1999).

Nonconscious processing of information is evolutionarily much older than conscious information processing and has benefitted from hundreds of thousands of years of refinement (Reber, 1992). The nonconscious capacity of the human brain developed millions of years ago as an automatic survival guide. The prefrontal cortex, the area of the brain primarily associated with conscious deliberation, developed about two hundred thousand years ago. Consciousness is not a replacement for nonconscious processes; it acts in combination with nonconscious processes to enhance the chances for survival and advancement. While conscious deliberate action may be a distinctive human achievement, this does not diminish the vital importance of the subconscious for human functioning. The cognitive nonconscious is more stable and resilient, functioning despite various limitations to conscious awareness such as traumatic brain injury, amnesia, autism, and Alzheimer's disease. The cognitive nonconscious is independent of age, with infants and the elderly showing no less functioning, and it is independent of intelligence measures such as IQ. Its long evolutionary development is responsible for smaller differences among people in their nonconscious cognitive capacities than in their conscious reasoning abilities. Humans share this capacity for unconscious information processing with many other species and it is as necessary for their survival as it is for ours.

Unconscious processing so dominates the information acquired by people that it can no longer be routinely dismissed as an unimportant source of economic expectations. The acquisition of information, however, is only part of the power of the unconscious cognitive system. People automatically learn something about the structure of the information they process nonconsciously. Learning about complex interrelationships is automatic, and results in abstract representations that people can utilize to form expectations (Reber, 1967). People can nonconsciously form associations among events, and routinely form models to understand current economic developments and to help anticipate future changes. This implicit knowledge is not accessible to conscious awareness, but it nonetheless influences people's expectations and actions. Even though people may be consciously aware of what they expect to happen, they cannot consciously recall the reasons for holding those expectations. The knowledge from such learning is stored in implicit memory, documented by neuroscience to be in different regions of the brain from memories that are accessible to conscious recall. It should be no surprise that nonconscious acquisition of information and its structural representation is an indispensable component of knowledge (Lewicki & Hill, 1989; Lewicki, 1986).

What role does nonconscious information processing and interpretation play in the formation of economic expectations? Clearly, for some people in some situations, it plays no role whatsoever, at least according to them. Since nonconscious processes are outside of conscious awareness, who could know with certainty? Nonetheless, economists as well as a wide array of other people have a strong predilection for conscious deliberation of economic matters. While these people may engage in conscious deliberation much more than other people, even the most dedicated do not have enough time to consciously consider every aspect of their economic environment, let alone all other important areas of their lives. An absolute preference for conscious reasoning would imply a very inefficient allocation of mental resources and much less effective overall decision making.

At the other extreme, there are people who readily admit that they never really think about economic matters – at least in terms of the usual technical jargon of the economics profession. Nonetheless, these people are often quick to give their estimate of the future inflation or unemployment rates. When asked to explain the basis of their expectations, they can only say that it is a hunch or gut feeling. While some may disparage such expectations simply as wild guesses, these expectations may actually reflect nonconscious learning. Then there is the vast middle who admit to a moderate interest in economic issues. While their expectations may well result from nonconscious processes, some have argued that every expectation undergoes a conscious review before they use it to make an important decision (Kahneman, 2011). This may be possible if people had unlimited conscious resources so that every decision could be checked and rechecked. As long as nonconscious expectations had proved to be reasonably accurate in the past, why would people undergo the costly process of consciously second guessing their own expectations? Indeed, nonconscious processing of economic information is best described as having been learned from conscious processing (Cleeremans et al., 1998). Only if their expectations had misled them in the past would people allocate their precious conscious resources and expend the necessary effort to form more accurate expectations.

The major premise of this chapter is that the formation of expectations is an innate and necessary part of human life. From the youngest of babies to the oldest of adults, people acquire and interpret information about their environment and effortlessly form expectations. This automatic process enables them to dynamically allocate their scarcest and most valuable mental resources to best serve their self-interests. While conscious reasoning is their most precious mental resource, people entrust the vast majority of their everyday decisions to nonconscious processes. To be sure, conscious learning informs and shapes nonconscious processes, just as nonconscious learning informs and shapes behavior. Nonconscious learning is based on associations, on the covariances among events. To deal with the inevitable mathematical calculations, humans possess a natural number sense. People of all ages perform simple arithmetic operations; even before infants develop language skills they know how to add and subtract. An important aspect of this natural ability is people's preference for frequencies rather than proportions or probabilities. Natural frequencies are the form in which people observe events and it is the acquisition of that type of information that powers people's inferences and forms the basis for their expectations.

The covariance detection techniques used by the nonconscious mind are essentially similar to the latest forecasting models developed by econometricians (Stock & Watson, 1998; 2002; 2007; Sargent & Sims, 1977). The forecasts based on these econometric techniques, called factor models, are comparable to those generated by nonconscious learning. Neither depends on prior knowledge of the underlying structural properties since no causal relationships are assumed. The estimates rely solely on the covariances. Some economists think the lack of structural models is a critical deficit since they can provide no explanation of the results in terms of causal relationships. Others think of it as an advantage since these forecasts avoid the most common errors due to the incorrect specification of the causal model and structural instability. This is essentially the same debate about the merits of conscious and nonconscious information processing and learning.

Most readers would not dispute most of the points made so far, save one. Not all decisions are equal. Some decisions have far greater consequences and therefore would get far more conscious attention. Indeed, economists have long doubted the importance of nonconscious processes when the decision involved significant financial stakes. What person would put life and limb at risk, let alone his or her financial wealth, by allowing their behavior to be governed by nonconscious processes? Surely, the processes developed for survival on the savanna thousands of years ago no longer apply to the much more complex decisions required by life in the twenty-first century. The complex decisions of modern life require the expanded capabilities of conscious reasoning. Perhaps not all economic decision's require conscious attention, as many are either repetitive or trivial, but surely people would consciously consider the critical decisions that could have a significant economic impact on their lives. Major purchases such as homes and vehicles could pave the way to future happiness or bankruptcy. Saving and investment choices could mean financial windfalls or hardship. Surely, conscious deliberation is required when the financial life or death of a family is at stake. Or is it? The answer to this question may surprise you. It is best explained by an example that everyone commonly experiences.

SUBLIMINAL TRAVEL

Imagine you are commuting to work, school, or your favorite coffee shop. You could be driving, biking, or even walking. You take a familiar route and are aware, from past experiences, of the busy intersections, the stop lights you will encounter, and the likely volume of traffic. When you reach your final destination, you may find that you have difficulty in recalling specific events along your commute. Did you have to stop to allow traffic to pass at a certain intersection, or did traffic stop for you? Were there any other people at the crosswalk you used? How many red lights did you encounter? Like you, many people would find it difficult to remember every aspect of their normal commute. This is because most people typically process such information nonconsciously, and the appropriate behavioral response is automatically performed without conscious deliberation. People automatically stop when the light is red, and automatically turn at the correct intersection. If asked, most people would insist that while driving they were always alert and attentive to changing road conditions. When pressed about the details of their trip, some would simply admit that they must have forgotten. That same lack of recall, however, is not true if they experienced a problem along the way.

If something out of the ordinary were to occur, this unexpected event would automatically activate conscious awareness. Perhaps there is a driver who is speeding dangerously, or a dog runs unexpectedly into the roadway. These unexpected events trigger conscious processing and cause you to take defensive actions, such as switching lanes or applying the brakes. Such a dramatic reminder is usually not necessary for people to understand that life and limb are at stake, even on the most familiar terrain. While people may well modify their prior expectations to take into account new experiences, no one abandons the use of nonconscious processing and the use of expectations to trigger the need for conscious awareness. No one can afford to since no one can be consciously aware of every possible detail. People innately and automatically form expectations. These expectations are dynamically tailored to past experiences as well as the road conditions you are likely to encounter on that day. Did you leave early or during rush hour? Are weather conditions good or are roads snow covered? Such contextual factors shape your expectations. While some driving expectations may apply to all trips, no one would ignore additional, relevant information. People automatically and effortlessly tailor their expectations to the specific situations they face.

Everyone has an appreciation of the importance of past experience in forming appropriate expectations that permit safe driving. New and young drivers need to devote much more of their conscious resources to this task. Until suitable experience forms expectations, distractions to their constant attention to driving conditions can have hazardous results. The same is true for experienced drivers who visit an unfamiliar city. Navigating highways in unfamiliar cities demands more conscious and effortful attention. Since some aspects of the unfamiliar streets and intersections cannot be automatically processed, this greatly increases the demands on conscious attention. People handle such situations by turning off the radio, ending conversations, or otherwise lessening the distractions to their conscious attention. They may even ask a fellow passenger to help lessen the information processing demands by watching for street signs or keeping a lookout for merging traffic. People know that such driving is more effortful and tiresome, and some wonder why anyone would want to live in such an environment. The past experiences of residents, of course, have enabled them to form expectations that allow them to process most of the information nonconsciously and still enjoy the music or an engaging talk show on the radio while commuting to work even on the busiest of freeways.

For most people, driving is a normal part of their daily routine, and not given any special consideration. When traveling on familiar routes, most people are willing to leave the majority of their driving decisions to their nonconscious processing capabilities. If these potentially life-and-death decisions are routinely made nonconsciously, there is little reason to think that the majority of economic expectations are not formed by nonconscious processes as well.

The same subliminal process occurs when people do their weekly grocery shopping. People typically buy so many items that the shopping carts are full and often overflowing. Most of the time, grocery shoppers do not consciously review the current price of every product to determine if and how it had changed from the last time they bought the item. If people undertook such a process it would greatly expand the time required to do their weekly shopping for groceries. Most prices are processed nonconsciously. Nonetheless, when a product's price is unexpectedly high or low, people become consciously aware of the difference and deliberate whether they should still buy the product, buy a substitute or another brand, or in the case of a price decline, decide if the decline represents a temporary or permanent reduction and whether to purchase an additional amount. The same underlying principle holds: if the product's price conforms to expectations, nonconscious processes dominate, leaving the shopper to focus their conscious faculties on other matters, but when the price is unexpected, it sparks the need for conscious deliberation. There are numerous other examples of how nonconscious processing of information is routinely used by people, reserving their more limited and more precious ability to consciously deliberate only when the new information was unexpected. The driving example, however, makes the case that people depend on nonconscious processes not just for trivial decisions but for decisions about their survival.

People build their repertoire of nonconscious processes based on prior experience, monitor those automatic judgments for accuracy, and adjust their expectations when necessary. There is nothing unique about economic expectations that would set them apart. Just like any other expectation, reasonably accurate economic expectations are essential to maximize human potential. And just like any other expectation, people form economic expectations that are specifically tailored to their own situation. People innately and automatically base their expectations on conscious and nonconscious mental resources as the situation demands. The goal of this chapter is to give credence to the position that nonconscious information processing and nonconscious learning are important elements in the formation of economic expectations.

CONSCIOUS, PRECONSCIOUS, AND SUBLIMINAL PROCESSING

What is consciousness? Although the concept of consciousness has been discussed throughout recorded history, it was René Descartes (1596–1650) who identified the concept as it is now commonly understood. Despite its long history, there is no widely accepted definition of consciousness or any empirical measure that can reliably detect its presence. Consciousness has often been associated with awareness, although awareness is not always accompanied by consciousness. Importantly, for present purposes, when people have conscious knowledge of some economic information, they can verbally report that information and consciously use the information in their deliberations. Consciousness permits explicit and deliberate decisions for which people can explain their reasoning. Conscious decisions are commonly thought to be superior since they can utilize the full power of reasoning and can be based on all relevant information. Accordingly, the most accurate expectations are thought to be the result of conscious information processing and deliberation.

The terms subconscious or unconscious have been commonly used to describe the absence of conscious thought. These terms, however, were for many years associated with psychoanalysis of primitive sexual and aggressive impulses which was popularized by Freud. Although the term nonconscious is now used to avoid these associations, it is not strictly preferred to the older terms. In this book, the terms nonconscious, subconscious, and unconscious are used interchangeably to denote the absence of conscious thought.

Unconscious preparations for even the simplest of actions occur before people become consciously aware of the actions they are about to perform. Rather than the popular notion that actions are the result of conscious decisions, action often precedes conscious awareness (Bargh & Morsella, 2008). In the driving example, when a dog darts in front of the car, drivers typically begin to apply the brake before they become consciously aware of the event a fraction of a second later. External events can directly and unconsciously activate information processing systems as well as initiate a behavioral response. The unconscious mind represents a sophisticated and adaptive behavioral guidance system. Given that nonconscious control of behavior existed well before consciousness, it is likely that the conscious mind represents an adaptation of the nonconscious for specific purposes.

Although nonconscious information cannot be part of conscious awareness, sleep enables the consolidation and integration of information. This interaction leads to a selective gain in conscious knowledge on the basis of nonconsciously learned information, especially if its connection to behavioral choice is highly salient (Fischer et al., 2006; Wagner et al., 2004). When faced with a difficult or complex decision, people commonly refer to "sleeping on it" before making the decision. Sleep enables them to merge the necessary conscious and nonconscious information (Stickgold, 2005; Walker & Stickgold, 2004). Even then, people have no conscious recollection of their unconscious knowledge, but they became consciously aware of the resulting decision.

It is useful to divide the nonconscious state into two parts: the preconscious and the subliminal (Dehaene et al., 2006; Kihlstrom, 1987). Preconscious means that information is potentially accessible to consciousness, but it is usually not consciously accessed. It is the preconscious processing of information that partly determines whether an event should be consciously considered. Preconscious is likely to direct a stimulus event to conscious awareness if it was unexpected or highly salient, but conscious awareness is less likely if the stimulus event was fully expected or very low in saliency. For example, when driving or walking to work, most information is routinely processed but only unexpected events arouse conscious awareness. Salience of the events also matters so that people are more likely to be consciously aware of a highly salient event, even if it was expected. The exposure time to a stimulus event is also important. Exposure over a very short duration may not be recognized consciously, such as a brief glimpse at some price information, but exposure to the same information over a longer period may result in conscious awareness, such as a shopping trip to the grocery store. Even long exposures do not guarantee conscious awareness, as people may not be aware of prices of the things they had just purchased. Importantly, there may be a long delay between preconscious awareness and the conscious realization of that information. An associated development may suddenly bring to conscious awareness an event that was initially observed even in the distant past.

Most information is processed nonconsciously or subliminally. Subliminal denotes that the information processed is not accessible to the conscious mind. The term subliminal simply means "below the threshold" of consciousness. The comparable term, supraliminal, meaning "above the threshold" of consciousness, however, is not commonly used. What is unique about the subliminal is that the information processed and knowledge gained can be used in decision making but the individual has no conscious awareness of that knowledge. Researchers have proven this in many experiments. For example, Betsch et al. (2001) asked subjects in their study to focus their attention on sixty advertisements that appeared on a computer screen. While the advertisements were displayed, seventy-five pieces of information on changes in the market value for five different stocks were shown on the side of the screen. The subjects were told that the purpose of the exercise was to test their ability to recall information from the ads; the information on the stocks was meant to be a distraction. At the end of the study, the subjects were also asked about the relative performance of the stocks. Although the subjects could not accurately recall the information on changes in the value of each stock, they were able to correctly rank the order of the performance of the five stocks from best to worst.

The distinction between conscious, preconscious, and the subliminal is important for the study of the formation of economic expectations. There is no question that people can and do form expectations based on conscious information processing. That not only agrees with convention but it is the way most people describe the process, even if it simply represents a rationalized story that justifies their decision after the fact (Nisbett &

Wilson, 1977). What is less recognized is the importance of deliberation without conscious attention. What is even more surprising to most observers is that the more complex the economic decision, the more likely the expectation will be formed nonconsciously.

OPTIMAL USE OF COGNITIVE RESOURCES

Whether people process information to form expectations by conscious or nonconscious mechanisms is the result from the solution to an optimization problem. The choice reflects how best to maximize the use of the more constrained conscious cognitive processes as well as the more unlimited nonconscious capacity to form economic expectations. Conscious deliberation is effortful. Computations are required of the raw economic information, and its interpretation requires knowledge of economic models and the interrelationships among the variables to form the expectation. More importantly, conscious awareness has an opportunity cost that vastly exceeds the costs associated with the more unlimited capacity of nonconscious processes. In contrast, nonconscious cognition is effortless. In most situations, nonconscious processing of information is costless, but even with its enormous capacity, it does have some opportunity costs. Importantly, nonconscious information processing is ideally suited to incorporate complex data and relationships, automatically learning how best to represent the data for future use in forming expectations. Nonetheless, many believe that conscious cognitive processing has significant advantages, and would be the preferred means if its capacity were not so constrained.

The preference for conscious decision making should not be taken to indicate that conscious processes are necessarily superior to nonconscious processes. The common bumble bee has been shown to make judgments under uncertainty when foraging that exactly mirror the type of rational decisions that human nonconscious processes are typically thought incapable (Brase et al., 1998). Even if conscious and nonconscious processes would yield the same decision, people may still prefer conscious decisions because they could cite the reasons for their decisions and so justify the decision to themselves and others.

People's ability to consciously make a series of rational decisions over short periods of time may be quite limited. An individual's capacity for intentional self-regulatory behavior is quickly depleted. It is just not true that people are capable of making repeated rational choices as long as they are in a conscious state. Even small and rather trivial conscious choices exhaust people's ability to make conscious self-regulatory choices in subsequent, entirely unrelated decisions (Baumeister et al., 1998). How do people cope with such limitations and still take actions that serve their best interests? People accomplish this by fully utilizing both their conscious and nonconscious mental resources.

How do people decide on the best allocation of their mental resources? People rely on their expectations. The old adage about only what's new is news applies. Unexpected events are more likely to be processed consciously, and expected events are more likely to be processed unconsciously. People are less likely to consciously attend to an economic event that is indistinguishable from past outcomes, unless of course, if a significant change occurred. An unchanged unemployment or inflation rate that was expected is unlikely to be processed consciously, but people are much more likely to become consciously aware of those rates when they post an unexpected change. Even small changes, which at first may elude conscious attention, can accumulate over time in the nonconscious and may finally reach a threshold that triggers conscious awareness.

There is no symmetry, however, in how people respond to positive and negative economic news. It has been long known that negative news has a much greater impact, as much as twice the impact of positive economic news. In the University of Michigan's surveys, consumers are asked to name any economic developments of which they had recently heard. The news reported tracks changes in recent cyclical economic developments in inflation, unemployment, and the like. When all of the references are cumulated over longer time horizons, negative news was reported about twice as frequently as positive news. This result conforms with both economists' predictions based on prospect theory (Kahneman & Tversky, 1979) and psychologists' findings that negative events attract much more attention than positive developments (Smith et al., 2003), and that negative events result in more frequent conscious attention than positive developments (Schwarz & Clore, 1996). As shown in the next chapter, people's affective states have a significant impact on whether they choose to become consciously aware of new information.

The conventional economic view of how people handle their limited conscious cognitive resources is completely different. An optimal division between conscious and nonconscious processing is not the goal. People simply aim to diminish the burden on conscious deliberation by using a shortcut. People utilize well-worn rules of thumb to make "fast and frugal" decisions (Gigerenzer, 1996; Kahneman et al., 1985). Rather than optimization, people aim toward satisficing, which means finding a solution that will permit some satisfaction even if it is not the optimal choice (Simon, 1955). The use of heuristics introduces systematic biases, but people judge the more manageable demands on their limited capacity to make fully rational decisions to offset these losses. The implication of bounded rationality is that those with greater limits on their cognitive capacity to acquire, calculate, and interpret economic information would use these decision shortcuts more intensely, and therefore form less accurate expectations. This assumption was found to be largely false in the prior chapter as the least educated held just as accurate expectations for inflation and unemployment.

Economists have typically used the term "habits" to describe behaviors that do not result from conscious thought and deliberation. Habitual behavior is thought to be involved in a wide range of issues important to the functioning of the macroeconomy, contributing to theories of sticky prices and wages, spending and saving, asset prices, and economic growth, as well as shaping the impact of fiscal and monetary policies. Habits are learned, and once learned, they tend to persist even in the face of contrary information. The consistent use of a rule of thumb simply represents a habit, and like heuristics, this enables a fast means to form expectations without depleting scarce conscious resources.

While it is clear that such decision heuristics are widely used to form economic expectations, what is unclear is whether these rules of thumb are learned from personal experiences or inculcated by socialization and popular culture. Given that the underlying purpose is to improve personal decisions by substituting commonly accepted standards, combined with the deference of economics to representative agents and national data, the conventional view has been that these shortcuts are independent of people's own situations. These rules of thumb are often claimed to be based on economic facts that provide a distilled statistical guide to decision making. Others have hypothesized more dynamic standards, with expectations depending not on fixed rules but expert opinion. Information from news commentaries on what experts think the latest data may mean for the future is then consciously adopted (Carroll, 2001). If the methods used or sources followed fail to predict the future, people will simply choose to adopt their expectations from different experts. There is no shortage of economic pundits in the media. There is an overabundance. More distressing to the viewer who aims to adopt the expert's view as their own expectation, there is an overabundance of conflicting opinion.

Some observers who have emphasized the influence of intuition on expectations, have also highlighted the importance of nonconscious processes. When the decision maker is an expert on a particular topic, these nonconscious processes create accurate intuitive judgments in that area. For most people, however, the common belief was that nonconscious processes are incapable of improving the accuracy of their expectations. Whether prompting greater accuracy or not, intuitive decision making has been defined as essentially equivalent to nonconscious learning. Robin Hogarth (2001) found intuitive decision making to be nonconscious, rapid, used for decisions that involve multiple dimensions, based on past experience, not easily explained afterwards, and often made with a great deal of confidence. Insofar as intuition or fast and frugal heuristics are hypothesized in this way, they are equivalent to nonconscious learning. Indeed, brain scans have revealed the close connection between intuition and nonconscious learning and memory (Lieberman, 2000).

Expectations Are Innate

The formation of expectations is an innate part of the human condition. Humans continuously form expectations about their environment throughout their lives. It is a matter of survival. Over many thousands of years, evolutionary developments have honed the processes that people use to form and revise their expectations. In the earliest days of mankind, survival depended on quick reactions to unexpected events. The unexpected appearance of a hungry competitor, then as now, could be a life-changing event. Knowledge about expected outcomes enables people to take precautions. More importantly, knowing which actions are more likely to meet with success, and which actions are more likely to fail, enables people to take more effective actions and more efficiently achieve their goals.

Thousands of years ago, even before language was developed, people distinguished between the expected and unexpected developments. Hunters expected prey more frequently in some areas, and expected danger more frequently in other areas. Evolutionary developments were responsible for shaping the mechanisms needed to form expectations. Since inaccurate expectations can have disastrous results, it has always been a central concern to hold as accurate expectations as possible. There is every reason to believe that the evolutionary process acted to provide mechanisms that would continuously revise expectations to minimize or eliminate inaccuracies.

A basic problem is that humans are exposed to more information about the environment than they can possibly process. Selective attention is required. The issue is how to choose, not only among competing events but also whether to use conscious or nonconscious resources. While conscious processing may be preferred, it is a scarce resource, whereas the capacity to nonconsciously process information is substantially greater. Efficient use of mental resources would require that people only devote their conscious awareness to the most important information. Importantly, what people view as critical information largely depends on whether the information was expected or unexpected. Novel or unexpected events are more likely to be processed consciously, and expected events are more likely to be processed unconsciously (Velmans, 1991). Importantly, nonconscious attention does not rule out a response, as behavioral reactions to some unexpected events originate as unconscious decisions, with conscious awareness, if any, occurring fractions of a second later.

Think again about driving or walking to work along a familiar route. You process most information about your travel nonconsciously. When you arrive at work, if nothing out of the ordinary happened, you barely remember whether you had to stop at some intersection to allow traffic to pass or if traffic stopped to allow you to proceed through the intersection. All of the events you expected, and your correct actions at every intersection were based on nonconscious processing and nonconscious decisions. However, if something out of the ordinary happened, this unexpected event would automatically activate your conscious awareness. For example, when a vehicle makes an unexpected turn into your path of travel, you may have already subconsciously begun to apply your brakes when you become consciously aware of the situation a fraction of a second later. The unexpected or novel event may turn out to be a false alarm or may represent a serious life-threatening accident, or anywhere in between. If such events repeatedly occur, your expectation of danger may change and you may now regard a specific intersection as so dangerous that it always requires your conscious attention.

Expectations help people to maximize the use of their conscious and nonconscious processing resources. Of course, people's expectations may be incorrect and those mistakes may lead to disastrous consequences. While the formation, use, and revision of expectations appear to be innate features of humans, the content of expectations about the environment must be learned. This is as true for economic expectations as any other expectation. When making a common and routine purchase, say for gasoline, the price is much less likely to enter conscious awareness if it was expected than if the price had unexpectedly jumped or plunged. That does not mean the price was ignored nonconsciously, but that based on the expectation, it was not deemed to warrant conscious attention. When first learning about gasoline prices, however, any price may arouse conscious attention, or even some other event can compel conscious awareness, like a disruption in the supply of oil or the imposition of a new tax.

In the driving example, young drivers must first learn by repeated experiences which situations they can handle nonconsciously and which demand conscious attention. New drivers must confront all situations with constant attention to build up their repertoire of expected and unexpected events. This is perhaps why cell phones and passengers are more dangerous for teenage drivers than for older, more experienced drivers.

Expectations are so central to cognitive functioning that even newborns form expectations. Indeed, most studies of cognitive development among infants prior to the development of any language skills have been based on what infants consider novel or unexpected outcomes. Studies of infants have settled on "looking time procedures" as the standard scientific measure of cognition (Onishi & Baillargeon, 2005; Spelke et al., 1992). Infants looked longer at what was unexpected or novel. In studies of the numerical ability of five- to eight-month-old infants, after a training period to set expectations, when experimental conditions indicated either a correct or an incorrect conclusion, the incorrect conclusion drew longer attention by infants. For example, when showing infants the addition of one puppet to another puppet on a stage, the correct answer would be a stage with two puppets. When researchers incorrectly showed the infants a stage with one or three puppets, the attention infants gave to the incorrect answers was significantly longer than they gave to the correct answer. Their puzzlement reflected a failed expectation, and presumably that their expectation needed to be revised.

What causes humans to form expectations? Developments in neuroscience have placed expectations at the center of theories involving the neurotransmitter dopamine. Dopamine transmits information from one nerve cell of the brain to another by modulating the sensitivity and efficacy of the signal transmission of other neurotransmitters (Di Chiara, 1997). The dopaminergic brain pathways, long thin bundles of cells in the mid brain, are very old in evolutionary terms and exist in all mammals. There are three dopaminergic pathways that transmit dopamine from one region of the brain to another: the mesolimbic system, involved in learning and behavior in response to incentives, the nigrostriatal system, involved in learning to automatically execute complex behaviors, and the mesocortical system, involved in conscious attention and short-term memory (Di Chiara, 1997).

It is in the mesolimbic system, involved in learning in response to incentives, that dopamine has been hypothesized to respond to the gap between what is expected and what is experienced. This theory, known as the reward prediction error hypothesis, related dopamine to learning. This hypothesis represents a version of Thorndike's (1911) classic learning hypothesis. Thorndike hypothesized that learning can occur whenever a stimulus is repeatedly paired with a reward or punishment. The prediction error hypothesis replaced the temporal contingency of the stimulus with the expectation of the outcome as the basic learning mechanism. Such a trial-by-error learning mechanism has become a central building block of modern learning theory. Under the prediction error hypothesis, dopamine reinforces learning when the outcome exceeds expectations, and acts to eradicate learning when expectations exceed outcomes. When expectations are met, there is no prediction error and the behavior is maintained. As the expectation more accurately predicts the subsequent occurrence, the dopamine response recedes. The response of dopamine critically depends on expectations in humans (Montague & Berns, 2002). Dopamine is thus hypothesized to be a carrier of information on expectations.

During initial learning, a positive outcome itself activates dopamine, but the activation may be conditioned to react to an associated stimulus, rather than the reward that follows the stimulus. It is the expectation based on the stimulus, rather than the outcome itself, that then activates dopamine. Context-dependent stimuli can modify dopamine responses (Nakahara et al., 2004). Researchers demonstrated this in a study of the dopaminergic neurons in thirsty monkeys as they learned to associate a tone with the onset of fruit juice. During initial learning, dopamine neurons fired in response to the juice reward. After several trials where the monkeys learned that the tone predicted the arrival of juice, dopamine responded to the tone, rather than the juice (Mirenowicz & Shultz, 1994). In this case, dopamine releases responded to the expectation rather than reward, and the dopamine response changed based on whether the expectation was predictive of the outcome. This is similar to the finding in economics that it is the expectation of a change in taxes, for example, that is the proximate cause of a change in behavior rather than the actual change in taxes.

Some economists have pointed to what they presume is the crucial role of dopamine in choice, learning, and belief formation (Caplin & Dean, 2008; Camerer et al., 2005). There is no scientific consensus about whether dopamine plays a causal role in learning or if dopamine simply reflects learning that takes place in other areas of the brain. Other hypotheses that indicate a noncausal relationship with dopamine are consistent with the data as well, for example the "incentive salience" (Berridge & Robinson, 1998) and "attention switching" theories (Redgrave & Gurney, 2006).

Whatever turns out to be the ultimate truth, the formation, use, and revision of expectations are innate parts of the human condition.

Inherent Numerical Sense

Forming economic expectations would seem to require a basic comprehension of numbers. How else can people make sense of data on income, inflation, or unemployment? How much mathematical ability is required to form expectations? Does this limit the formation of economic expectations to conscious rather than unconscious processing? Can people form economic expectations without numbers, relying not on exact quantities but on relative comparisons? The answers to these questions may surprise you. People inherently possess a basic knowledge of numbers that develops naturally soon after birth. These numerical abilities are universal, span all cultures, and are even present in the most isolated societies. Arabic numerals and word representations of numbers are processed nonconsciously and automatically as quantities (Dehaene & Akhavein, 1995). This numerical capacity represents our common evolutionary history.

Dehaene (1997) and others have maintained that people develop a core "number sense" even before they are able to understand verbal communications. Pre-verbal infants, without any conscious knowledge of numbers, are able to process quantitative information and even do basic arithmetic operations before they acquire language skills (Simon et al., 1995; Starkey et al., 1990). Infants automatically attend to colors, sounds, shapes, and movements as well as the number of distinct colors, sounds, shapes, and movements. Very soon after birth, human infants develop the ideas of zero, one, two, and many. These have been detected experimentally at various points between the development of vision and six months (Carey, 2001; Wynn, 1992). By the age of two months, infants can learn simple statistical patterns in visual data (Kirkham et al., 2002), and by six months they can learn statistical patterns in sounds (Kuhl, 2004). Five- and six-month-old infants can perform basic arithmetic operations such as addition and subtraction (Dehaene et al., 1998; Simon et al., 1995; Wynn, 1992; Starkey et al., 1990).

It is still unknown whether natural quantitative ability depends on an abstract notion of numerosity or if it is based on the ability of infants to accurately track small numbers of objects or events (Xu & Spelke, 2000). Indeed, small cardinal numbers may be independent of language (Varley et al., 2005). This is suggested by the literal displays of the numbers 1 to 3 as vertical lines in the Roman numbering system (I, II, III) and horizontal lines in Chinese (−, =, ≡). Interestingly, in most numbering systems, arbitrary symbols denote numbers larger than 3, such as IV instead of IIII in

Roman notation. This suggests that humans have an innate ability to differentiate easily between small values (1 to 3), but that this skill declines with larger numbers. In fact, our innate abilities with small numbers is reflected by their dominance in print, with the numbers 1 to 3 occurring twice as frequently as all other digits combined. This innate accuracy with small numbers, however, does not extend to larger numbers.

People possess two number systems, one for small numbers and another for large numbers (Feigenson et al., 2004). The first is for the precise representation of a small set of cardinal numbers, 0 to 3. People know these numbers intuitively and use them with precision. Larger quantities quickly exceed the processing capacity of this innate system. To illustrate, researchers have experimentally shown that it takes less than half a second to perceive the presence of one, two, or three objects. Beyond three, speed and accuracy in citing the number of objects fall dramatically (Dehaene, 1997).

The second system for large numbers is called the "mental number line" (Dehaene, 1997). Rather than the precise representation of the first system, large numbers are represented as approximate magnitudes on the mental number line. These two separate systems independently process large and small numbers differently, and neuroimaging has confirmed that these two processes occur in different parts of the brain (Presenti et al., 2000). Moreover, even the large number system can operate nonconsciously, as these capacities have also been found in aboriginal speakers of languages lacking numbers greater than 5 (Pica et al., 2004 on the Amazonian Indigene; Gordon, 2004 on the Pirahã tribe). For numbers greater than 3, humans can make nonconscious approximations of large numbers that are often valid by using the "mental number line."

The "mental number line" represents the meaning of numbers (Dehaene, 2003). The various mechanisms that humans have developed to assess differences in quantities share a common element – the "just noticeable difference." This quantity is proportionate to magnitudes evaluated. For example, suppose at a 90% degree of accuracy, humans can distinguish between the quantities 10 and 13. If we wanted to keep the same level of accuracy for other sets of numbers, we would have to proportionately increase both numbers, for example, by doubling both to 20 and 26. This is sometimes referred to as Weber's Law, after the German physician E. H. Weber, who is considered a founder of experimental psychology. The law implies that as quantities increase, their meaning is interpreted logarithmically. The eye senses brightness approximately logarithmically, and the ear senses loudness by the logarithmic scale of decibels. The same logarithmic characteristics apply to the mental number line. As a result, the capacity to accurately distinguish between two very large numbers is limited, and becomes more limited as the quantities increase. In contrast, distinguishing between small numbers is very fast and accurate. Although people's ability to distinguish magnitudes grows substantially as they age, it reaches a limit in early adulthood (Feigenson et al., 2004; Starkey et al., 1990).

The implications of the mental number line on economic expectations are obvious. Few people can cite the current size of the Gross National Product in trillions of dollars, or can readily assess the meaning of the absolute change from last quarter. Meaning derives from a logarithmic transformation of the data (Izard & Dehaene, 2008). Nearly everyone can assess the meaning of a 5% change compared with a 10% gain, which simply represents the differences in the logarithms of the absolute numbers. Mental number lines thus provide people with the ability to determine what constitutes "reasonable" accuracy: it is the smallest relative amount they usually perceive.

Preference for Frequencies

There are other limitations to this innate numerical capacity. Neither the core number system nor the mental number line supports negative numbers, fractions, square roots, or a host of other elements that people must learn consciously. More general, conceptual knowledge of mathematics only appears after people acquire some logical skills. Moreover, people's nonconscious operates on an inductive basis, accumulating natural frequencies and making associations across events or objects. What is stored in memory is not the probability or the percentage of times some event occurred but the frequency with which a particular event has happened (Gigerenzer, 1998). With this basic information, people can calculate a probability, but the reverse is not true. Based on only a probability, it is impossible to calculate the frequency of an occurrence. It is always better to retain the frequencies and sample size than to simply remember the proportion or probability of an event.

Indeed, humans had no regular exposure to numerical information in the form of probabilities and percentages until the second half of the twentieth century (Gigerenzer et al., 1989). Whereas evolutionary development has meant that people can process frequencies automatically and nonconsciously, probabilities require more effortful conscious reasoning (Hasher & Zacks, 1984). Indeed, the mind has evolved over time to develop abilities specifically designed to make informed statistical judgments based on natural frequencies (Brase et al., 1998). Even infants under one year old have been shown to use frequency information to make predictions about future events (Xu & Garcia, 2008; Teglas et al., 2007; Aslin et al., 1998). The term "ecological rationality" describes the use of natural frequencies in a Bayesian analysis that conforms to economic rationality (Gigerenzer & Hoffrage, 1995).

Frequencies are the privileged representational format. Natural frequencies are in the form in which people observe events and allow the sequential acquisition of information on events. Natural frequencies have been shown to foster statistical insight and allow people to become "intuitive statisticians" (Gigerenzer & Hoffrage, 1999; Cosmides & Tooby, 1996; Nisbett et al., 1983). These innate abilities do not diminish with age. In comparison with conscious cognitive skills that increase in childhood and decline in old age, nonconscious processing abilities remain largely unchanged over the entire life span (Midford & Kirsner, 2005). The speed at which people process information also shows marked variations. Given that the speed of information processing mainly reflects the cognitive capacity devoted to the task, it should be no surprise that the speed shows much greater declines for conscious than unconscious processing among older adults.

The same nonconscious quantitative processing capacities are common to many species and have a shared evolutionary origin (Gallistel & Gelman, 1992). Researchers have confirmed similarities in human and animal number processing with experiments similar to those performed with infants, and through fMRI scans. Researchers found that humans and macaques have analogous regions in the brain for basic arithmetic functions, and the impairment of these regions leads to impairment of arithmetic ability (Dehaene et al., 2004). They also found that monkeys and rats can learn and distinguish magnitudes up to a ratio limit (Feigenson et al., 2004), and that animals, human infants, and human adults share nonconscious number processing and very basic arithmetic abilities (Dehaene et al., 1998). Furthermore, some animals can count and assess relative magnitudes (Gallistel & Gelman, 1992). This suggests that at least some basic ability to nonconsciously process numerical values and perform arithmetic was determined by evolutionary developments and transmitted genetically.

NONCONSCIOUS LEARNING AND MODEL BUILDING

Forming expectations according to conventional economic theories requires more than just knowledge of current information and performing some calculations. The interpretation of the observed data is also a crucial element. Conventional theories assume that people use some sort of a model to interpret the latest economic data. An important corollary of conventional theories is that people base their economic expectations on the national data provided by federal statistical agencies. Since there is just one public announcement for each statistic each period (aside from revisions), the cognitive tasks required are assumed to be manageable. The revised theory of expectations presented in this book emphasizes that expectations are tailored to the economic situations faced by each individual. There is no evidence that most people have knowledge of the official rates of inflation or unemployment, but there is every reason to believe that they form expectations that accurately anticipate future changes in inflation and unemployment. The information that people find relevant to forming their expectations is more likely to be about the prices of the goods and services they actually purchase and the income and employment conditions in the communities in which they live. This is the type of information that is most relevant to the economic decisions they need to make. The problem is that rather than one piece of information per month, people face massive amounts of data every day. Moreover, the data are often inconsistent, as, for example, some prices move in opposite directions and some job and income prospects improve as others worsen. How people interpret such piecemeal data is an even more challenging task; economists would rightly claim that it would take computer programs as large as those used by the official statistical agencies! Such an enormous and complex data processing task is thought to be impossible. How can people make sense out of such massive amounts of information?

While such an enormous and complex data processing task would overwhelm the conscious cognitive capacities of most people, the use of nonconscious information processing could accomplish this task. Without conscious intent or realization, people can accumulate the frequencies of certain economic events as they are encountered, and in the process become sensitive to certain regularities and associations in the data. This nonconscious learning of regularities is accomplished without any intention to learn, and without conscious awareness that it has taken place, and the resulting knowledge is not consciously accessible so it cannot be verbally expressed. The process has been variously called unconscious learning, implicit learning, implicit or tacit knowledge, or implicit memory (Lewicki, 1986; Reber, 1967). This knowledge is popularly called intuition, instinct, or a gut feeling. People commonly admit that they are unaware of the basis or the rationale for their intuitions, but experience has taught them to rely on their instincts as a guide for their behavior.

Milton Friedman's famous example of the billiard player who can make the most difficult of shots without having any explicit knowledge of the physics involved serves as an illustration of this point. He gained this knowledge implicitly from experience, unknowingly, and he cannot express the knowledge other than by example. Nonetheless, the player's shots display the most complex aspects of the underlying theory, and he performs them seemingly effortlessly and more quickly than a person could consciously calculate the optimum trajectory, speed, and spin on the ball. Of course, Friedman was not making a statement about implicit learning; his purpose was to declare irrelevant the realism of the assumptions embedded in a model. For Friedman, prediction was the only reliable test of theories. In the present context, the accuracy of expectations is the most reliable test that proves implicit learning has taken place. Nonconscious learning allows people to develop models of economic events that are reasonably complex and reasonably accurate.

Friedman tackled an age-old question: how do we learn whether one event predicts another? Nearly every scientific discipline is based on a deductive methodology, but human information processing and nonconscious learning is based on an inductive system. People count frequencies and observe associations to draw conclusions. This is a system that has been crafted and tested by evolutionary forces. Extinction would have threatened our survival, as well as the survival of other species, without the ability to predict events. Is associative learning, also called contingency learning, up to the task? It is not surprising that from an evolutionary perspective, associative learning has been shown to approximate optimal solutions (Rescorla & Wagner, 1972). Learning theories also have a strong tradition in economics, although there is some disagreement on whether the optimal solution is reflected by an individual agent or by the behavior of markets.

How do the properties of conscious knowledge differ from nonconscious knowledge? If conscious and nonconscious knowledge were represented in the brain in the same manner at the same locations, then either one would be equally easy or difficult to elicit. This is demonstrably untrue. Explicit memory allows conscious retrieval; implicit memory cannot generally be consciously accessed. Although nonconscious knowledge itself is inaccessible, that knowledge supports the performance of cognitive and motor tasks (Lewicki, 1986; Reber, 1967). Experience plays a more decisive role in expanding implicit knowledge and performance whereas verbal instruction is more likely to expand explicit knowledge but not performance (Berry & Broadbent, 1984).

Most people understand this essential difference. Learning to drive a car, to become a chef, or to play a piano can only be accomplished with actual practice, and greater proficiency typically means long hours of practice. There is no verbal or written test that can access driving, cooking, or playing skills, even if some explicit knowledge is needed about the rules of the road, the ingredients, or the notes in a musical scale. Just as "the proof of the pudding is in the eating" for some tasks, for other tasks "book learning" is more appropriate.

Most tasks require a mixture of both explicit and implicit knowledge, indicating that however independent, these systems typically work in harmony. Although explicit and implicit memories are in dissociable brain regions, these two systems during learning appear to work in a parallel fashion. Sleep substantially enhances explicit and implicit memories through consolidation of learning. Importantly, during sleep some types of implicit knowledge can become explicit and available to conscious thought (Fischer et al., 2006; Wagner et al., 2004).

The building blocks of nonconscious learning are automatic frequency and covariance detection. People can not only directly register associations between events but can also automatically use transitive inference rules (Lewicki et al., 1994). To encode any type of information, it must be processed in terms of covariances; the only way to nonconsciously interpret the meaning of an economic event is to learn how its features covary with other events. Nonconscious learning means that information about covariations are detected, processed, and stored without conscious awareness; the information can nonconsciously influence behavior, and the knowledge cannot be consciously controlled or directly examined (Lewicki, 1986). Compared with consciously controlled cognition, the nonconscious acquisition of information is much faster and more sophisticated in that it is capable of efficiently processing multidimensional and interactive relations between variables. Importantly, the conscious appraisal of the meaning of perceptions of economic events is independent from the associated structural knowledge that is automatically and unconsciously generated. Moreover, nonconscious learning does not depend on age or skill development. From a very early age, infants have the capacity to nonconsciously learn associations and infer structural properties among events as do very old adults.

Conscious learning of associations among economic events is of course quite common. Indeed, it could be argued that most of the most important economic relationships are the subject of conscious deliberation. Conscious processing is more likely to occur the higher the salience of the information, but most economic information can be expected to be processed nonconsciously. It is like driving or walking to work: only unusual or unexpected events demand conscious deliberation, all other events are more likely to be processed nonconsciously.

Importantly, even if an event is consciously considered, this does not mean that same event will not also be processed nonconsciously with regard to its covariations and structural relationships. As will be described in more detail, most experiments that have documented nonconscious learning were conducted with the conscious awareness of subjects to the various stimuli. This awareness does not interfere with nonconscious processing of the information and the automatic detection of covariations.

Attention to Information

All learning, whether conscious or nonconscious, requires some attention (Hoffmann & Sebald, 2005; Turk-Browne et al., 2005). It is simply not possible to process all information about the surrounding environment. People's goals determine where attention is directed since information is required to accomplish economic goals. Other than for the most salient events, practice is required for goals to automatically activate attention; enough practice so that it becomes habitual. Nonconscious learning is based on experience and is task related. There is no reason to expect that people would routinely acquire information on economic events that do not directly influence their lives in some way. In this sense, implicit learning is neither automatic nor passive, but rather occurs in response to the task requirements (Cleeremans et al., 1998). Implicit learning is more likely the more meaningful the underlying task is to the individual (Roßnagel, 2001; Mathews et al., 2000; Lewicki et al., 1997). Emotion plays a significant role in how meaningful tasks are perceived, a topic that will be discussed in detail in the following chapter.

Nonconscious learning can incorporate biases just as conscious cognition can (Kahneman et al., 1985). A surprising feature of nonconscious learning is that small sample sizes may actually improve the sensitivity of humans to detect correlations (Kareev et al., 1997). This has an obvious survival advantage when new developments require an appropriate behavioral reaction. Mistaken generalizations from small samples can also create a persistent bias, and these nonconscious generalizations may sometimes become self-perpetuating (Lewicki, 1986). This may be due partly to the fact that association does not mean causation. In any event, it warns against the unwarranted assumption that nonconscious learning is free of all the foibles associated with conscious learning.

Nonconscious Learning

The oldest and most widely replicated paradigm to study nonconscious or implicit learning is artificial grammar (Reber, 1967 for a review). Subjects are presented with a series of nonsensical strings of letters that, unbeknownst to them, were formed according to a set of rules. After some amount of practice with the strings of letters, researchers inform the participants that there exists a system to the formation of valid strings. Researchers then ask subjects to either generate valid strings or to categorize strings as valid or not. Subjects perform this task at significantly better than chance levels. They are unable, however, to verbalize the rules of the grammar, or even guess some reasonable approximation to the rules. Researchers interpreted this skill to mean that subjects have learned the underlying structure of the grammar nonconsciously, automatically, and independently of any conscious effort. Such nonconscious knowledge can be retained for a long time – in one study, a brief period of exposure yielded better-than-chance performance in testing after a two-year delay (Allen & Reber, 1980).

Another longstanding and just as widely replicated research paradigm focuses on the nonconscious detection of covariations (Lewicki, 1986 for a review). The general purpose of these experiments was to determine whether people could gain knowledge about covariations across events or objects without conscious awareness. To test for this possibility, people were exposed to relatively complex auditory, verbal, or visual materials. These materials included many features that could be potentially interrelated, but most were designed to be independent. Only a few selected features were designed with embedded correlations, and these features were hidden so as to make their conscious detection as difficult as possible. Following exposure to the materials, researchers asked people to engage in completely unrelated tasks designed to eliminate any impact of short-term memory on the subsequent tests. Since implicit knowledge is not accessible to conscious awareness, people answered questions that could determine if nonconscious knowledge of the covariation affected their responses. For example, some characteristic of pictured people, such as a characteristic of their appearance, was embedded with an association to a specific characteristic, such as kindness. The subsequent questions were designed to determine if the same association persisted on an independent task. Typically, the embedded correlation was observed at a significantly higher than chance level.

Another experiment exploring nonconscious learning about economics is referred to as the "sugar factory." The sugar factory is a computer game whose object is to control various inputs to a "black box" production mechanism to maximize profits (Berry & Broadbent, 1988). People learned to manage the factory by practice. They learned to control production by manipulating the number of workers and other inputs; they also had to learn more complex relationships that involved the lagged impact of some inputs on production and profits. Participants never knew the underlying rule that generated profits, but with enough practice, participants learned to control the system and perform at much better than chance levels. Even those who mastered the game could not verbalize the full set of underlying rules, suggesting that they gained the knowledge implicitly. To be sure, participants could answer questions about some of the obvious manipulations they performed, but they could not answer questions about the lagged relationships. In a variant of the same experiment, each participant at the start of the experiment was explicitly told the rules that generated production and profits. Rather than more quickly enhancing their performance, it actually slowed the participant's learning of how to best control production (Sterman, 1989; Reber et al., 1980).

People can also learn how to balance risk and reward nonconsciously. Consider drawing cards from one deck that provided large gains and losses but netted long-term losses, or another deck that provided small gains and losses but netted long-term gains (Bechara et al., 1997). As experience increased with each hand played, people came to favor the deck that netted positive long-term gains. Subjects acquired the nonconscious knowledge piecemeal, gradually accumulating, nonconsciously forming covariances between decks and net winnings. Even as they learned the essential difference, people could not express what they had learned but nonetheless changed their behavior. Some people were included in the experiment who had damage to the prefrontal cortex, preventing the nonconscious mind from learning from experience. These people continued to make poor choices and lose money. More generally, the ability of the nonconscious to learn from experience and generate an intuitive guide to behavioral decisions is crucial to avoid nonadaptive decisions (Damasio, 1994).

Similarities to Econometric Methods

You might think that only fools would rely on economic expectations that were partly formed by consciously unknowable information and processes. For important financial decisions, people need to know the data, do the calculations, and interpret the information using the best forecasting models. This is the method that has been used by macro econometric models, once viewed as the best way to produce economic forecasts. Model-based expectations, however, proved remarkably vulnerable to errors, and these mistaken expectations were at times extraordinarily large. Christopher Sims (1980) attributed the forecasting errors to the identifying restrictions that were needed to estimate the structural models by the usual econometric techniques. He found these restrictions not only theoretically incredible but also unnecessary to produce accurate forecasts. David Hendry (Hendry & Krolzig, 2005) championed the view that it was the instability of the structural models that has been the major cause of large forecast errors, and detecting and avoiding these breakdowns is a prime objective when trying to produce more accurate expectations. Sims as well as James Stock and Mark Watson have suggested that more accurate expectations would be generated not by pre-specifying the structure of the model but by allowing the estimates to be dynamically determined by the observed associations among the variables. Such dynamic factor models, now in wide use in the profession, are based on the premise that the true model is best conceptualized as a relationship among latent or unobserved components. It also implies that economic expectations cannot be reliably deduced from a structural model but rather must be induced from the observed relationships.

The parallels to what has been discussed in this chapter are remarkable. The most accurate methods used by econometricians as well as ordinary consumers rely on learning from observed covariances. Neither impose a specific causal model to interpret the data; both simply rely on the associations among the variables. Each method obtains the most accurate expectations when based on observations of a large number of variables, and each provides estimates that are more robust in the face of data revisions and biases as well as contradictory observations. Both use the accuracy of expectations as their sole criterion; neither cares about whether the procedures conform to conventional economic theories. Each is descriptive; neither can be used as a normative standard for forming rational expectations. Perhaps the most important similarity is that neither method provides the type of justifications that economists and consumers prefer when asked to explain the reasons underlying their expectations. Everyone naturally wants to cite specific causal relationships. Although none are truly available, this hardly deters consumers and economists from offering some plausible causal explanation. Consumers unabashedly offer such justification and so do economists. Economists have never felt confined by the lack of realistic behavioral assumptions and have always focused solely on the models' predictive power as a justification of the underlying theory. Why should people act any differently when forming and justifying their own expectations?

This convergence represents a triumph of conscious reasoning. Scientific methods and advances in computing power have enabled economists to estimate expectations using methods comparable to those that humans have acquired over millions of years of evolutionary development. Of course, the purpose of this chapter was not to trumpet the capacity of the nonconscious mind. It was to emphasize that the nonconscious mind completely dominates the mental capacity of humans to process information and shape behavioral responses.

THE AUTOMATICITY OF EXPECTATIONS

People do not need to be taught to form economic expectations. Forming expectations is an inherent part of living. There is no reason to assume that economic expectations only appear after a certain age or a certain level of cognitive development. People form their first expectation soon after birth, automatically and without conscious deliberation. Even young children engage in barter and exchange, often before they are able to talk or walk. Millions of years before the advent of national economic statistics, people of all ages sought information on potential changes in their economic circumstances. People have always obtained this information in bits and pieces, and the most important information is always directly tied to people's own economic situations. Some of this information immediately benefits from their conscious attention, but most of it is attended to nonconsciously. Nonconscious processes enable people to digest massive amounts of data and to effortlessly determine associations and contingencies among the various bits of information. Although forming accurate expectations is a complex undertaking, the human mind is uniquely designed to accomplish this task. Just as conscious cognitive skills can be expanded by learning from experience, so too can the cognitive skills of the unconscious mind.

Accuracy has always been the overriding goal of economic expectations, whether it was judging the size of the herd in the African savanna or income prospects in modern America. To obtain a reasonable degree of accuracy, the unconscious mind forms expectations based on observed frequencies and inductive logic, while conscious reasoning favors probabilities and deductive logic as the superior method. While both logical approaches offer efficiency and reasonable accuracy, only the latter can also accurately report the underlying factors used to form the expectation. Life involves tradeoffs, and most people choose accuracy over explanation when they judge the opportunity costs of using conscious deliberation is too high. Given the severe limitations on their conscious cognitive resources, people choose to regulate most of their everyday behavior by mental processes outside of their conscious awareness.

Only one factor that would prompt people to revise their expectations has so far been identified: new information. This conforms to conventional economic models. Affective and emotional influences also play a critical role in how and when people revise their expectations. Experts often disdain and simply dismiss the role of passion, the so-called animal spirits, as incompatible with rational expectations. At best, such emotional influences are considered exogenous factors, forced into economic models by evidence of a significant impact that cannot be explained by more traditional economic variables. This is comparable to the tradeoff between accuracy and explanation mentioned above, with modelers wanting the increased accuracy for their forecasts, even if they cannot offer any coherent theoretical justification for their inclusion.

This chapter began with the observation that evolutionary adaptation has meant that no element of the human mind can be dismissed as superfluous. Not only does the emotional system have a profound impact on how economic information is processed, but the automatic display of human emotions acts to transmit each person's economic assessments to other people. Mirror neurons give people the natural ability to recognize and understand these displays. This recognition may cause a reassessment of their own economic expectations and prompt a broadly coordinated cascade of expectations that could result in a sudden collapse of confidence. The next chapter will examine these affective influences on expectations in more detail.

5

Affective Influences on Expectations

Who considers the possibility of a job loss in an emotionally detached manner? Who speaks dispassionately about reducing their living standards due to an expected increase in inflation? Emotions have always been inseparable from people's assessments of their economic situation. Long ago, philosophers identified reason and passion as the central features of human decision making. And for just as long, the conventional wisdom has been that reason must always triumph over emotion when making economic decisions. Humans have long struggled to eliminate the influence of passion on their decisions, but they have never been successful. Their failure was not due to a lack of willpower. It was a fool's errand, an impossible task. Antonio Damasio (1994) found that reason and emotion were both essential to rational decision making. The sole reliance on reason was what he termed "Descartes' error." Damasio examined people with frontal lobe damage that impaired their emotions but left the decision-making region of their brain untouched. He found convincing evidence that even with all the necessary information to make a decision, people with these impairments were unable to make a choice. The emotional system provides information that is critical for decision making, including what people prefer and what people want to avoid. Without this affective information, the choices people make lack meaning, resulting in an inability to choose. It should be no surprise that evolutionary adaptation has meant that our emotional system cannot be dismissed as superfluous to rational decision making.

Emotions play an essential role in forming rational decisions and can no longer be simply dismissed as superfluous for the scientific analysis of decision making. It is not as though economists have never recognized the impact of emotions on economic decisions, but they have always argued that emotional influences would lead to less than optimal expectations. Reason is associated with conscious cognitive deliberation, and passion with nonconscious impulses that promote irrational decisions. Indeed, the term "animal spirits," popularized by Keynes (1936), is still used to signify how irrational decisions can influence the macroeconomy (Akerlof & Shiller, 2010). It is of some interest to note that "animal spirits" was initially a medical term, probably borrowed from Descartes, who used it to capture the impact of subconscious emotions (Koppl, 1991). This dismissal of emotion is closely tied to the dismissal of nonconscious processes in decision making. The nonconscious and emotions were viewed as equivalent and irrelevant, just as consciousness has been viewed as the sole genesis of rationality.

Although emotions are critical to rational decision making, purely emotional decisions are unlikely to be rational. In the mythical Minnesota town of Lake Woebegone, all the women are strong, all the men are good-looking, and all the children are above average. Who would be surprised to find that these people held positive expectations about their spouses or children? The Lake Woebegone effect reflects the natural human tendency to overestimate one's own capabilities or hold unrealistic expectations. These expectations represent hopes and dreams. In some cases, it may be better to hold optimistic views even if they are unrealistic. Nonetheless, it would be surprising if all residents of Lake Woebegone expected above average income growth and based their economic decisions on that unrealistic expectation. What benefit would people derive from forming economic expectations that consistently proved to be inaccurate?

It is of some importance to recognize that the influences of affective states on economic expectations operate independently of the cognitive capacities of individuals. The most and the least cognitively gifted individuals have affective capabilities that are more equal. There is less variation across the population in these affective decision resources due to their longer evolutionary development than variations in people's conscious cognitive abilities. People use their affective systems to automatically evaluate economic information, influence what information they seek, and prioritize and motivate the timely formation of expectations. Evolutionary forces have adapted the affective system to optimally influence the formation of expectations independently from people's cognitive capacity.

Instability in the macroeconomy due to sudden and large changes in expectations has always been difficult, if not impossible, for conventional economic theories to predict in advance. A sudden collapse in confidence is usually ascribed to exogenous forces or animal spirits, and beyond the purview of economics. The abruptness and speed of the collapse is due to the affective or emotional component of expectations, especially for negative shifts in expectations. Long ago Darwin (1872) identified social communications as the adaptive function of emotions. Emotional expressions enable people to quickly and effortlessly communicate the essential meaning of economic events. People have an inherent ability to understand emotional expressions, present even among the youngest of infants. This native ability forms the basis for social contagion. Indeed, imitation is among the most basic instincts of humans, and herding behavior is a common facet of economic life. While cascades in economic expectations have resisted explanation by conventional theories, there is no reason to delimit economic theory with claims of irrational exuberance or irrational fears. The sudden collapse or boom in confidence is no less important to economic theory even if its precursor is more affective than cognitive.

The next section defines the most important affective influences on the formation of economic expectations. These factors provide automatic evaluations of economic information, help to determine whether the information is consciously processed, and effectively substitute for cognitive deliberations when an immediate decision is imperative. Subsequent sections provide a more detailed examination of these topics as well as supporting data. Finally, this chapter will examine how emotional displays foster social contagion and the development of cascades in economic expectations.

This chapter does not advance an emotional theory of expectations to replace cognitive theories. The purpose of this chapter is to detail how affective components influence cognitive processes as well as how cognitive processes influence the affective components that shape economic expectations. The integrating principle is that humans have learned to optimally use the entire capacity of their brains to efficiently and accurately form expectations for making decisions about their own economic situations.

WHAT ARE AFFECTIVE INFLUENCES?

Affect is a general term that includes evaluations, moods, and emotions. Each of these aspects has an identifiable and distinct impact on the formation of economic expectations. Importantly, these affective influences represent an evolutionary adaptive mechanism to guide behavior that is more accessible and faster than cognitive processes. These affective states are automatically produced by nonconscious processes. Without conscious awareness, they prompt instant reflexive actions in the face of potential threats, or when the danger is not imminent, they can prompt information seeking behavior. They motivate goal-directed behavior by providing a compelling urge to act. They guide the smallest of everyday choices as well as the most important life-changing decisions. Importantly, these affective influences can act to increase or to decrease the need to devote conscious attention to the formation of an economic expectation.

Affective influences on expectations are pervasive. Compared with cognition, affective influences derive their strength from greater accessibility as well as faster initial responses. Affect can quickly galvanize mental resources to form expectations, and prompts individuals to tailor their expectations to their own needs. Moreover, these affective influences evolve and develop though experience. People learn which economic threats are the most dangerous to them personally as well as which opportunities are most valuable to them. Affect automatically triggers people's attention when they encounter information that is relevant to their own economic situation. Affect provides a quick and efficient means to identify personally important economic information, and more importantly, an effortless means to discard from consideration the massive amounts of personally irrelevant economic information confronting people every day.

Affect thus provides an information-sorting mechanism that makes forming expectations more efficient. Whereas conventional theory assumes that people base their expectations on full and complete economic information, this revised theory assumes that people base their expectations on all personally relevant information. This assumption accords with the theoretical view that to be useful decision guides, people must tailor their expectations to the economic prospects that they actually face. The implications for the formation of expectations are also quite different from bounded rationality. Bounded rationality indicates the limitations on the use of conscious cognitive processing in forming expectations. Like conventional theory, bounded rationality completely ignores the critical importance of affect in forming expectations. Bounded rationality simply provides a justification for imperfect expectations due to the limitations on conscious cognitive processing. The addition of affective influences allows a more complete explanation of how people actually form their economic expectations.

Evaluations

All information that is relevant to a person's economic situation is automatically accompanied by a positive or negative assessment. People effortlessly generate these evaluations even before they become consciously aware of the information itself. Rather than the conventional view that evaluations are always based on a conscious assessment of economic information, the affective connotation of economic information precedes conscious awareness of the information. People immediately and effortlessly classify economic information as good or bad; this is done unintentionally by dedicated neural circuits and without conscious awareness (Zajonc, 1980; 1984). Although nonconsciously processed information is generally not available to conscious recall, these automatic evaluations that are based on that information can be consciously accessed.

These automatic evaluations of economic information have a significant impact on shaping economic expectations. They act as a common currency to integrate separate pieces of information in order to form an overall economic expectation of say, inflation, job or income prospects. This role of evaluations as an integrating principle was first noted by Katona (1951). In addition to the impact of the information itself, the affective connotation of the information can also influence behavior (Schwarz & Clore, 2003). These affective evaluations act as strategic signals; they focus conscious attention on searching for specific information as well as motivate the search for additional information (Ross & Dumouchel, 2004).

Moods

Whereas evaluations are tied to specific pieces of economic information, mood represents a more general affective state. Mood typically lacks a single identifiable cause, and has a more pervasive impact on human functioning. The defining characteristic of mood is that it reflects a persistent nonconscious evaluation of the current environment (Bargh & Chartrand, 1999). Moods last longer than the more fleeting individual evaluations. The affective influence of mood is more stable, and moods are largely the result of nonconscious processes.

Perhaps the most important aspect of mood for the formation of expectations is that mood determines how information is processed. Whether people are in an optimistic or pessimistic mood, or whether the mood reflects uncertainty or fear, has an impact on how they interpret new information. A pessimistic mood signals that the current situation is problematic and more frequently fosters the use of conscious processing to determine the potential impact of any change in the economic environment. Uncertainty promotes more conscious information searches and more careful weighting of alternatives. Fear is closely associated with uncertainty, but fear focuses attention solely on the source of the fear itself. In the presence of fear, attention is so concentrated on the source of the threat that it reduces attention to other economic information. For example, when someone fears losing their job, all other aspects of the economic environment decrease in importance or are evaluated in terms of its employment implications. Fears of high and rising inflation cause people to evaluate nearly every economic event in terms of its impact on future prices.

Needless to say, such focused fears of job loss or inflation are accompanied by economic actions that would not have occurred otherwise. Fears of rising inflation in the 1970s promoted the widespread reaction by consumers of buying in advance of additional price hikes, which in the aggregate only acted to accelerate the pace of inflation. Fears of potential job loss typically cause consumers to postpone some discretionary purchases as a precautionary measure, and those lost sales result in an economy with fewer jobs and less income. These reactions, of course, confirm people's initial fears of job and income losses and act to accelerate the economic downturn.

An optimistic mood, in contrast, favors less conscious information processing, even of contrary information. When the performance of the economy is positive, people see little need to closely monitor every potential deviation. As long as the economy proceeds as expected, people devote fewer conscious resources to an ongoing examination of changes in their economic situation. Optimistic consumers do not ignore unfavorable developments, but they implicitly discount these negative economic signs as having meaning for their own situation. An overall favorable outlook for jobs does not mean that every job category is expanding, nor does a low inflation rate mean some products will not increase in price. Indeed, the behavior of optimistic consumers is sometimes described as resilient in the face of potential economic dangers. This confident reaction of consumers promotes more spending and hence greater employment and higher incomes, helping to generate a self-confirming cycle.

It is important to emphasize that mood shifts themselves cannot create optimism or pessimism. The driving force of mood shifts involves how people judge their future economic situation. Mood shifts follow these changes in economic prospects. Mood does influence the speed at which people adopt optimistic or pessimistic expectations, with shifts toward pessimism being much more abrupt than gains in optimism.

Emotions

Emotions are intense, arise quickly, are generally brief, and have an identifiable referent. Emotions focus conscious awareness on specific topics.

Although a person may or may not be able to verbally express their emotions, everyone is consciously aware of their emotions. Importantly, emotions are not fully accessible to conscious control, and may persist even in the face of people's conscious attempts to alter their emotions. Emotions can signal an urgent need for conscious awareness, act as strategic signal, motivate behavior, prioritize goals, or can be a source of information for decision making (Ross & Dumouchel, 2004; Schwarz & Clore, 2003; Elster, 1998; Damasio, 1994; Frijda, 1986).

Emotions help ensure that expectations are formed in a timely manner when prolonged indecision could be disastrous or entail high and unacceptable opportunity costs. At times, everyone faces the need to make an immediate decision before all relevant information is available, such as purchasing a product at a discount that would not be available if they delayed the decision. Emotions serve the essential function of forcing the formation of an expectation before all necessary information about potential benefits and costs has been collected and fully analyzed. Essentially, emotions serve as a functional equivalent for the cognitive faculties that they displace (Elster, 1998).

This substitution of emotion for conscious deliberation to make immediate decisions takes advantage of the faster processing of information and the ability of emotions to quickly galvanize action. Humans learned long ago that decisions that entailed lengthy cognitive deliberation could risk their life or limb. This is just as true today as it was in ancient times. People must make instantaneous decisions without conscious reflection to avoid death both in modern urban areas and in the primeval jungle. It is nonsensical to suggest that the evolutionary development of emotions was so maladaptive that it would favor irrational reactions. The bold assertion that conscious deliberation alone produces rational expectations and that emotions invariably promote irrational expectations is simply not tenable.

AUTOMATIC EVALUATIONS OF ECONOMIC INFORMATION

Robert Zajonc (1980; 1984) was the first to demonstrate that people automatically evaluate information before they become consciously aware of the information. He advanced the idea that people have an independent affective information processing system that is powerful and faster than people's cognitive system. This accounts for people knowing their preferences before they are able to explain the reasons for holding those preferences. Zajonc famously observed that "preferences need no inferences." This view challenged the still widely held belief that inferences drawn from cognitive deliberation were required before people could determine their preferences. This conventional view reflects the presumed supremacy of the conscious mind and rational decision making. The revised view reflects the evolutionary advantages of parallel processing by the affective and cognitive systems. To be sure, people can and do change their evaluation after conscious reflection. Nevertheless, to think that these initial evaluations are automatically irrational makes no sense. This may well be true on some occasions, but it can hardly be thought of as a chronic condition as that would constitute maladaptation. This does not imply that economic preferences are somehow immutable. Casual observation as well as scientific studies have shown that these automatic evaluations are learned and revised based on past experiences. It does imply, however, that people's emotional systems, like their cognitive systems, adapt to changes in circumstances. Just as some cognitive beliefs about the economy resist change and others quickly respond to new information, the same can be said for the affective influences on expectations.

Theorists have long viewed the supremacy of conscious control as necessary so that reason can overcome passion when making rational decisions. This presupposes that the affective information processing system may respond to irrational impulses rather than reflecting an evolutionary adaptation that facilitates rapid decisions that are consistent with the goals and objectives of the individual. Some have suggested that the mind rescues conscious control from the grips of passion before any action is taken. A review process does this, whereby decisions that do not originate from conscious deliberation are reviewed to determine if the decision meets rational criteria before an actual choice is made (Kahneman, 2011). Not every choice rates a conscious review; it depends on other factors, such as the importance of the decision or the person's past experiences with that type of decision. Indeed, if every evaluation was reviewed, the mental capacity of most people would be so overwhelmed that little else could be accomplished. Moreover, in some cases, not only does an evaluation precede conscious awareness, but a behavior response is also set in motion before people become consciously aware of the situation. If reasoned inferences always preceded evaluations and actions, an important adaptive advantage of the human mind would be lost.

A secondary, but no less important, benefit of these automatic evaluations is that they enable a good deal of diverse economic data to be effortlessly combined. Each piece of information is automatically encoded with a positive or negative valence. The individual's own situation determines how the information is encoded as well as the importance or weight given to the information. This encoding process can occur consciously or nonconsciously. This common currency provides the means to integrate diverse economic information based on its common affective component. This enables people to combine information across a broad range of economic data so they can form expectations about their own overall economic prospects. This automatic process allows people to easily distill and aggregate thousands of bits and pieces of economic data based on their own personal experience. The adaptive purpose of this process is to facilitate learning. Aggregation allows people to more reliably identify underlying associations and trends on which to base their expectations.

Interestingly, economists face the same problem and use a comparable process to aggregate diverse economic information. Their weighting function is based on monetary units. Monetary units are a fairly new innovation on an evolutionary timescale and are unlikely to ever completely displace people's affective evaluation units used to effortlessly process information. If any convergence can be expected in the future, it is likely that societies will move away from judging economic performance in dollar terms. In recent years, there has been a concerted attempt to move beyond the sole reliance on monetary measures by incorporating more subjective measures of economic welfare, spearheaded by economists Joseph Stiglitz and Amartya Sen.

Consumer Confidence Measurements

These automatic evaluations by the affective system proved to be the workhorse of consumer confidence surveys. The questions about personal finances as well as overall conditions in the economy were not designed to be based on these automatic evaluations, but they have nonetheless benefitted by tapping these automatic evaluations. The guiding principle of these surveys was to design questions that were phrased in a way that allowed most people to easily understand the basic underlying economic concept. Economic jargon was avoided, with the economic concepts described in normal population language. Just as important, the response scales needed to capture what respondents thought were meaningful differences in their assessments. No one was asked to respond in the type of exacting quantitative details favored by economists. The goal was to obtain the best data without undue burden. The more exacting the question and detailed the response codes, the greater the burden and the more likely respondents are unable or simply refuse to provide codeable data. The objective was to word questions that provided an accurate assessment without causing an undue cognitive burden. Although the objective was not to appeal to people's automatic evaluations, the response scales chosen were typically evaluations that ranged from better to worse or good to bad.

These same questionnaire decisions were not only made by the University of Michigan, but also independently by research institutes and statistical agencies throughout the world. Many countries initially judged that because of differences in culture, the educational or demographic composition of their populations, or experience with market economies, that different wording would be more appropriate to their country's situation. After trial and error, all countries have uniformly settled on the use of the same evaluative response scales, although not on the same wording of the questions themselves. This reflects the underlying advantages of phrasing the questions in terms each population could easily understand and basing the response scales on these automatic evaluations.

Interviewers conducting the consumer sentiment surveys at the University of Michigan have had the most difficulty with respondents who happened to be economists! Asking any economists for their expectations about prospects for inflation, interest rates, and unemployment as well as the overall outlook for the economy over the next five years generates long, detailed, and qualified answers. They answer the questions from a professional perspective, and they wonder how an ordinary consumer could ever answer such questions. In contrast, ordinary consumers have no trouble answering these questions; even the least educated or the oldest consumers. Economists often assume that most consumers simply give an answer that pops into their mind at that moment. It was assumed that they were offered out of polite cooperation with the task of providing an answer to each question asked. The answers obtained, however, were alleged to be simply random guesses. Many economists initially suggested that such random responses would mean obtaining as many positive as offsetting negative replies. The resulting time trends would be flat and independent of changes in the economic series that the question was about. That assessment was easily and quickly proved incorrect.

Economists were correct to assert that consumers did not have accurate knowledge of official economic statistics. They were incorrect to assume that this ignorance of official economic statistics would hamper their ability to form accurate expectations on which to base their economic decisions. The avoidance of jargon and the reliance on population language had the unintended consequence of shifting the focus from knowledge about official economic statistics to how people experienced those same underlying economic events in their everyday lives. This switched the emphasis from economic information that they did not know and did not use to the information on economic conditions that they actually faced and used to form their expectations.

It was equally difficult to comprehend how consumers could offer accurate expectations so quickly and so easily. Human rationality is limited and the burdens of the conscious deliberative processes are too high for the average consumer to easily and quickly navigate. How could they provide accurate answers in a matter of seconds to economic issues most experts had to ponder long and hard before answering? How could they provide what amounted to instantly available answers to very difficult questions? Given that we know they do hold reasonably accurate economic expectations, the obvious answer is that these expectations were preformed and could be easily recalled. What everyone had discounted was the important role played by nonconscious processing and learning; otherwise, the same limitations on conscious reasoning would apply.

THE INFLUENCE OF MOODS ON INFORMATION PROCESSING

The Consumer Sentiment Index published by the University of Michigan has been described as reflecting the mood of the consumer. This is an apt description. Consumer sentiment has all the essential characteristics of mood: it represents a general affective state, it is an evaluation of the overall environment, it is more stable than its individual components, it influences how new information about the economy is processed, and it is subject to cyclical swings.

Mood not only influences consumers but it has been long known to influence all decision makers, including those assumed to make rational decisions when trading stocks. Sunshine, for example, was first related to the establishment of a good mood among stock traders more than a hundred years ago (Symeonidis et al., 2010). While the overall impact from weather on stock prices is small and short-lived, it is predictable (Hirshleifer & Shumway, 2003). Importantly, sunshine does not directly influence the willingness of traders to bid up prices. It affects prices indirectly by how weather-induced moods influence the manner that relevant information is processed by stock traders.

People cannot consciously choose their mood toward the economy; it arises unintentionally and automatically. It represents a compilation of individual economic events integrated by their evaluative outcomes. Although moods may arise through nonconscious processes, moods influence whether people process additional information consciously or nonconsciously. A positive mood is typically associated with more heuristic processing and increased reliance on the top-down use of pre-existing knowledge structures (Bless et al., 1996). Situations that present no problems mean that there is no need for detailed conscious analysis. In such benign situations, there is an automatic shift toward nonconscious processing to minimize the load on scarce conscious resources. The opposite is true when the mood of the consumers is pessimistic. Conscious processing of economic information is more typical when people fear for their jobs or are worried about income losses. In an evolutionary perspective, the adaptive purpose of moods may be to put people on notice that constant surveillance is required for potentially threatening economic developments.

Economists have known for some time that negative economic news garners greater interest than positive developments, but few have added that negative news is subject to greater conscious deliberation than positive developments. The larger risks associated with negative economic developments require greater conscious attention when economic decisions are involved. It is not that people totally ignore positive developments, but that people devote fewer of their scarce conscious cognitive resources to these developments. People are more likely to nonconsciously process positive developments when the assessment of the overall economic environment is favorable. This is true even if some economic event runs counter to the prevailing positive mood. In contrast, when evaluations of the overall economic environment are negative, not only is every bit of economic news scrutinized for its implications, but it is repeatedly analyzed. People have been known to excessively dwell on these potential dangers. Since pessimism signals a high risk of continued deterioration in the economy, people seek out any information that could have a potential impact on their economic situation, however remote. It simply does not matter if your job is currently at stake, or if the prices of the goods you purchase have already risen. Negative economic developments command more conscious attention.

This asymmetry does not represent a failure of human rationality. This preference has evolutionary roots and is reinforced by everyday economic decisions. People have learned to be more sensitive to negative developments. It was and still is a matter of economic survival. One might think that today's economy does not present the same life-and-death situations as long ago, but economic losses can still shatter lives and leave them in ruins.

Psychologists as well as economists have only recently recognized the greater importance of bad economic news. Ben Bernanke (1983) suggested the "bad news principle" to describe the greater importance of potentially unfavorable developments when making irreversible economic decisions. The information asymmetry reflects risk aversion. For example, if immediately after making a large purchase, a person's financial situation suddenly and unexpectedly worsens, they are likely to regret making this decision. The reverse is not true, however. If after that same purchase, a person's finances unexpectedly improve by a substantial amount, people rarely experience post-purchase regret. This is especially true for irreversible purchases. While you might resell a vehicle and incur a small loss, a vacation once taken cannot be returned.

Even reversible purchases, such as the purchase of a home, are affected. If a home purchase was being considered when a consumer had a negative outlook on the economy, much more time and conscious deliberation would be devoted to the decision. Many things could go wrong. Would the purchaser suffer a future job loss or a cutback in income? Would the price of the home decline soon after the purchase? What about the neighborhood and community, would services be cut back or taxes increased due to an economic downturn? It is hardly surprising that home purchases were postponed even by those who were ultimately untouched by the economic downturn. Few want to risk the consequences of a bad decision.

In contrast, when consumers are in a positive mood about the economy, they might make the decision to purchase a home without as much conscious consideration of all the potential negative economic consequences. While most people are not impervious to economic adversity, during favorable economic times most people assume that it will continue to go well for them economically. The decision is about finding the right home in the right neighborhood, not about worrying how they might find themselves without a job and facing foreclosure. Economic optimism means that people do not devote most conscious cognitive resources to the expected course of the economy but rather to the other non-economic characteristics of the purchase. While such automatic expectations may at times encourage unsustainable housing booms, the same is true of persistent housing busts due to excessive worry about the future economy.

Kahneman and Tversky's prospect theory (1979) provided a more comprehensive view of the asymmetry of information. They first hypothesized that decisions are based on a reference point: a comparison standard that adjusts with experience. This is a sharp departure from conventional economic assumptions that define the reference point at zero. Any positive news has value in classical economics. This would mean that news of a 1% rate of growth in GDP would be viewed as a positive development, although not as positively as a 5% growth rate. With comparison standards defined by recent experience, it is not readily apparent whether people would consider a 1% or even a 5% growth rate in GDP as favorable or unfavorable news. If the reference standard was 3%, for example, the 1% is likely to be viewed negatively and the 5% positively. The same is true for the inflation and unemployment rates or any other economic statistic. Reference standards adapt to changes in economic circumstances and seamlessly become part of people's nonconscious reference standards.

The second key insight was that for equal departures above and below the reference standard, losses loomed larger than gains. That is, people would judge news of GDP growing at two percentage points below the reference point as having much greater negative consequences compared with growth of two percentage points above the reference point. Indeed, people judged the losses to be about twice the size of the gains. This means that even minor negative changes have the same impact as much larger positive changes. News about potential negative economic developments simply has a greater absolute impact on expectations than positive developments.

Negative News Dominates Conscious Recall

What evidence suggests that consumers not only find negative news more informative but also actually devote more conscious attention to potentially negative economic developments? The University of Michigan surveys have regularly asked respondents whether they have heard any news of recent economic developments, and if they have, they are asked to identify what news they had heard. The survey does not offer any preselected answer categories so each respondent has to describe the news they have heard in their own words. One might expect that in good economic times, the balance of reports about recent developments would be favorable, and in bad times, the balance would be negative. Moreover, although there have been eight recessions since 1960, for the vast majority of time, the US economy has been in expansion. Indeed, the annual average GDP growth rate from 1960 to 2016 was 3.1%, and real after-tax personal incomes rose by an annual average of 3.2%. This meant that over the fifty-seven-year period, GDP and personal incomes have quintupled. The average American would surely report their awareness of such a positive economic record. Or so it would seem.

Despite the generally positive economic environment, respondents reported on average nearly twice as many negative as positive economic developments. Over the past fifty-seven years, negative developments were reported by 51% compared with just 28% who reported positive economic developments. It has been a rare situation when reports of positive news items outnumbered negative references, typically just after the end of a recession. Even when the economy was expanding at a robust pace, consumers nonetheless chose to report more negative economic threats. Only in eleven of more than 228 quarters from 1960 through 2016 did a majority of respondents report favorable economic developments. The ratio of bad to good economic news reports was 1.8 over the fifty-seven-year period. This is remarkably close to the oft-stated implication of Kahneman and Tversky's prospect theory that for equal sized divergences, negative economic developments have twice the impact of positive developments.

The overall news balances as reported in the surveys averaged a negative twenty-three from 1960 to 2016, that is, the percentage citing negative developments exceeded the percentage reporting positive developments by twenty-three percentage points. Instead of being more common, reports of favorable economic developments were the clear exception over the past half century. Across all surveys, favorable news dominated just 18% of the time. In comparison, negative economic developments dominated in eight in ten surveys. In 2% of the 228 quarters, people reported positive and negative developments equally. The eight recessions that occurred since 1960 lasted a total of ninety-three months, or 14% of the time, as determined by the National Bureau of Economic Research (NBER), and the economy was in expansion during 591 months or 86% of the time. Ironically, the share of time that the economy has in and out of recession was nearly the reverse of the time people reported good and bad economic developments.

Negative news dominated each category of economic events that respondents identified. The free responses have been coded over the years into 100 different categories depending on the respondent's reply. There are many different ways people talk about employment. Some reported job changes at their own employers, or by the employer of their spouse, friends, or neighbors. Others reported employment trends in some industry. Still others reported changes in work hours. And some reported hearing the latest official reports on job gains or job losses. These broadly diverse reports about one aspect of employment or another reflect how people learn about and interpret the meaning of the underlying trends. The same is true of inflation, credit conditions, the performance of stocks and investments, and even how they anticipate whether changes in economic policies will affect the economy. In each of these categories of news, respondents more frequently mentioned negative than positive developments (see Table 5.1). Note that news about employment dominated all other categories. Indeed,

Table 5.1 *Reports of News about Recent Economic Developments, 1960–2016*

	Positive Reports (%)	Negative Reports (%)	Balance of News
Employment	11.0	21.3	−10.3
Inflation	1.1	4.4	−3.3
Economic Policies	2.1	5.5	−3.4
Retail Sales	2.3	3.3	−1.0
International Trade	0.5	1.7	−1.2
Stock Market	2.0	2.4	−0.4
Credit Conditions	2.2	2.6	−0.4

the average proportion of respondents to mention negative employment developments averaged 21% across the entire fifty-seven-year period, about four times the next highest percentage. During periods of high inflation, consumers reported more negative news about various price increases, at levels comparable to unemployment. The data indicate the clear dominance of bad news, especially news about potentially unfavorable developments that could directly affect people's own finances.

The lack of reports of favorable developments certainly suggests people's inability to consciously recall favorable economic developments. Why do people more easily recall negative economic developments from memory but not positive developments? Indeed, people's reactions seem to imply the lack of any memory of positive economic developments that they could consciously recall. Rather than reporting good economic news, people simply responded that they had heard of no recent economic developments. This professed lack of conscious knowledge was much more common than would be anticipated given the generally favorable performance of the US economy. On average, 45% of all respondents over the fifty-seven-year period reported that they had heard of no recent economic developments. This is astonishingly high. While this cannot prove that they were nonconsciously aware of positive economic developments, there are plenty of other behavioral indicators that confirm their awareness. Furthermore, it is clear that most people were consciously aware that they had made substantial economic progress during most of the past half century.

Overall, the data strongly suggest that consumers process the economic information used to form expectations differently depending on whether their moods are optimistic or pessimistic. When consumers' moods are optimistic, they relegate their attention to ongoing economic developments to nonconscious processes. Only when a consumer adopts a pessimistic view is conscious attention more likely to be devoted to economic developments. Consumers can only recall and report economic events that they consciously perceive. It is not that consumers completely ignored positive economic events. It simply reflects the fact that people cannot consciously recall information that they had processed nonconsciously. Despite their inability to recall positive developments, those same respondents held favorable expectations for the overall economy. In comparison to the minuscule number of quarters since 1960 in which a majority of consumers reported hearing about favorable economic developments, nearly half of all respondents characterized prospects for the economy as "good" during that same time period. The key difference is that unlike responses to the news question, consumers had no trouble providing their automatic evaluations of economic prospects even if they were based on information not consciously available.

Mood and Cyclical Changes in Confidence

A primary characteristic of trends in people's economic expectations is that they move in repetitive cycles from peaks to troughs. Sustained expansions in economic confidence are followed by sustained contractions. While the cyclical trends primarily reflect changes in economic conditions, the mood of the consumer plays a part in generating the underlying upward or downward momentum. Mood can facilitate continued change in the same direction as well as provide resistance to the establishment of opposing trends. Consumers are said to be resilient when they ignore unfavorable developments during an upturn, and anxious when they dwell on every potentially negative event in a downturn. A resilient consumer promotes continued optimism, and an anxious consumer amplifies pessimistic trends. Mood thus acts to confirm pre-existing views, and in doing so, boosts momentum. In the extreme, mood can promote economic booms as well as busts.

This dynamic is enabled by differences in information processing strategies depending on the mood of the consumer. Upward trends in economic expectations would normally be quite vulnerable to bad economic news. Who could ever expect every element in an economy to improve? At any given time, some aspects of the economy are in decline, even if on balance, most factors are improving. How do consumers ignore these unfavorable economic events and continue to judge economic prospects ever more favorably? Economists readily suggest that it is a matter of proportion: based on monetary weights, the negative events are simply less important than ongoing positive developments. In popular parlance, people use rose-colored glasses, with the tint determined by monetary units. An alternative explanation is that when an optimistic mood prevails, people are much more likely to process the information nonconsciously. Nonconscious processes are prompted by incremental change; conscious processing is required for large or sudden change in expectations. For some economic event to have a dramatic impact on expectations, it must be processed consciously. Resilience can thus be conceptualized as a component of an optimistic mood.

What role does mood play in determining the turning points in consumer sentiment? When the economy is at a cyclical peak, what causes the mood of consumers to turn from positive to negative, and just as important, what causes consumers to change toward optimism when the economy is at its worst? Even at cyclical peaks or troughs, the University of Michigan surveys have never recorded perfect consensus among consumers. There are always some who remain positive or negative when most other people have the opposite view. There are always substantial shares of households who expect financial setbacks even in good economic times, and there are always households who expect financial gains even when the economy is in recession. While the net position across all respondents is a good proxy for the overall mood of consumers, the affective influence of mood on expectations operates at the individual level.

Two factors are responsible for shifts from optimism to pessimism or from pessimism to optimism. The most important factor is changes in economic conditions. Social contagion then amplifies and accelerates the impact on expectations of even small changes in the opposite direction. For example, when the prevailing mood is optimistic, the small portion of the population that holds pessimistic expectations begins to expand. The expansion of negative expectations is slow at first, but after reaching some threshold, quickly grows by social contagion. Naturally, those who have suffered the initial economic reversals are among the first to become more pessimistic, but the shift is often led by sophisticated economic observers who have not yet been harmed. Although the reverse of the same process produces shifts in the opposite direction, positive shifts develop more slowly across the population.

The impact of social contagion is usually more powerful during downturn, meaning that the degree of expressed pessimism at the troughs is much greater in relative terms than expressed optimism at the peaks. Social contagion can also produce booms, but this happens much more rarely and only after a prolonged period of robust economic growth. This means that fears of economic reversals can incite a pessimistic mood much faster than hopes can stir a renewed sense of optimism. Economic confidence can collapse overnight, as the recent financial crisis has again demonstrated, but it takes years of improved economic conditions to rebuild optimism. Not only are more conscious resources devoted to negative economic developments, but as the accompanying uncertainty increases, it greatly heightens the felt intensity of the potential threats. Uncertainty triggers a sense of fear, and once aroused, these fears cause people to accentuate their search for other potential economic dangers.

EXPECTATIONS NEED EMOTIONS

Emotion is the antithesis of reason. Accurate expectations result from reason, not passion. Passion is the source of biased expectations. Those beliefs have represented the bedrock foundation of all theories about economic expectations for more than 2,000 years. Such a blanket disregard of emotions is not justified by modern theories of decision making. Emotions can and do bias expectations as people sometimes substitute what they hope and wish would happen for what they could reasonably expect to happen. Expectations based solely on reason may be the ideal, but without some passion, humans would never be motivated to form expectations. Traditional theories simply assumed that people always maintain accurate economic expectations. This assumption conveniently excludes the main role of emotions, which is to motivate people to form and revise their economic expectations. It is the force of emotions that compels people to seek out information, to prioritize their competing economic goals, to consciously consider the impact of alternative outcomes, and to ensure the timely formation of expectations.

Nonconscious processes effortlessly generate emotions that are automatically displayed by facial, vocal, postural, and body movements. These displays serve two essential roles. They provide people with tangible evidence about how they feel about economic events in their own lives, even if they cannot verbally express their feelings. At the same time, emotions provide visible displays to others about what people think is important or threatening about their economic environment. Since people have little conscious control of their emotions, most observers have more confidence in the truthfulness of emotional displays rather than conflicting verbal descriptions. For example, an upbeat verbal description of someone's job prospects combined with a facial display of fear and anxiety would lead most people to discount the words in favor of the emotional display.

Communication is the primary adaptive role of the visible display of emotions. This form of communication existed long before spoken languages, and its evolutionary development has refined and honed the ability of humans to use a multitude of sometimes very minor facial or body movements to communicate detailed and complex messages about actions, intentions, and emotions. Even without the ability to hear what a person is saying, just seeing their facial and body movements can be sufficient. The old adage that "a picture is worth a thousand words" captures the power of emotional displays to effectively and efficiently communicate. These emotional displays play a critical role in coordinating changes in expectations and setting the pace of change across large groups of people. The expression of a particular emotion makes it as clear to the individual involved as well as to other people that some economic event is beneficial or problematic and demands immediate attention. Fears about financial safety, for example, motivate the adaptive reaction of escape, and when people display this emotion, it motivates others to do the same even if they did not know the precipitating cause. Fads and fashions, whether in products or investments, prompt similar reflexive actions to buy or sell based on nothing other than the knowledge of what other people have done. Humans are essentially social creatures. Understanding the actions and emotions of others is essential to our survival.

Scientists have attributed the ability to instinctively understand the meaning of another person's behavior to a unique capacity of parts of the brain called mirror neurons. A mirror neuron fires both when a person performs a certain action and when the person observes the same action performed by another person (Rizzolatti & Craighero, 2004). The name comes from people's ability to replicate or mirror the actions of others. Mirror neurons not only enable people to imitate the actions of others but they also provide them with the ability to understand those actions. It gives people information on the motives, intentions, and emotions of others. People gain this knowledge not by conceptual reasoning or thinking but by direct stimulation and feelings. Mirror neurons are part of the cognitive system present from birth that is entirely devoted to processing social information (Lepage & Théoret, 2007). Such information is crucial to forming people's own economic expectations. Long ago, Keynes recognized the importance of "beauty contests" whose objective is to determine the economic expectations of others before forming your own expectations. What Keynes did not realize was that this was a natural function of the human brain. The spread of economic expectations by social contagion is not a virus that people need to use reason to overcome but is a benefit that evolution has provided to form more accurate expectations. Feelings, rather than being the antithesis of reason, are actually an integral component of the mental processes people use to form economic expectations.

Self-Motivation

Experts generally believe that the basic categories of emotions are universal, but how they are evoked and expressed depends on culture (Darwin, 1872). The most basic and universal emotions include anger, disgust, fear, sadness, surprise, and happiness (Ekman, 1992). Note that although most of these emotions are negative, it does not imply that people are more likely to actually experience negative emotions. It does suggest that evolutionary development places greater weight on identifying potential threats to survival rather than potential benefits. This is still true today as indicated by the excessive awareness among consumers of negative economic developments, even when economic conditions are quite favorable. There is a relation between the strength of an emotion, especially negative emotions, and its ability to arouse conscious attention and motivate action.

The last chapter highlighted the critical role the emotion of surprise played in motivating people to revise their economic expectations. The emotion of surprise represents an inherent mechanism that automatically monitors expectations for accuracy and motivates people to revise their expectations accordingly. The surprise of an unexpected economic event, whether positive or negative, informs people about the accuracy and usefulness of their expectations. There is a relation between the size of the gap between expectations and outcomes and the strength of the emotion, and consequently, people's motivation to revise the expectation. Negative gaps arouse greater concerns for immediate revisions, whereas positive gaps command less urgency.

Fear and anger are two other emotions that have a significant impact on expectations. Fear has long been associated with the evolutionary adaptive response of escape. Fear has a powerful and instantaneous impact on people's ability to organize and direct their cognitive resources. Fear creates a "tunnel vision" that is so concentrated on the source of the threat that it reduces conscious awareness of all other information. When consumers fear job losses, all other aspects of the economy are judged in terms of their impact on employment. Even among those who may not be directly affected by job losses, fears dominate the intensive search for news on employment and how it could affect them. Even minor changes, such as news that a few employees lost jobs, has an exaggerated impact on their

conscious deliberations. The same is true when consumers fear high inflation. In the 1970s, consumers judged nearly every economic change by how
it might influence the inflation rate.

Anger is another emotion commonly related to unfavorable economic
events. Anger and fear have distinctive impacts on economic behavior.
It has been found that fear affects judgments about risk but not blame,
whereas feelings of anger affect judgments about blame but not risk
(Gallagher & Clore, 1985). Although the 9/11 terrorist attacks generated
both fear and anger among the US population, those that mainly expressed
fear rather than anger also expressed greater precautionary savings motives
to reduce their future economic risks (Lerner et al., 2004). Expressions
of greater anger compared with fear were associated with approval of
retribution.

A similar process occurs with regard to consumers' views on overall economic policies. Anger over poor economic performance causes consumers
to direct their complaints toward the government whereas economic fears
cause people to focus on how they can immediately protect their economic
situation. In the past half century, anger with a poor economy has been
mainly directed at the president and his administration. Since the election
of President Kennedy in 1960, the performance of the economy has been a
central issue in elections, and a major cause for Presidents Carter and Bush
to lose their reelection bids. The reelection of President Obama in 2012,
despite poor economic conditions, may have been due to the lack of anger
toward his administration, even if most people were still fearful about the
future course of the economy.

Social Contagion

People learn by observing the behavior of others. Imitation is common.
Exhibiting the same behavior may be due to people reacting in a similar
manner to the same external stimulus (herding behavior) or people
disregarding their own information and decision-making processes and
simply adopting the same actions as others (informational cascades).
Herding and informational cascades describe how large numbers of
people can revise economic expectations in the same manner at the same
time (Easley & Kleinberg, 2010; Bikhchandani et al., 1992). For example,
people may react in a similar fashion to an announcement by a federal
statistical agency about the latest change in inflation, unemployment, or
the pace of overall economic growth. The same is true for how people
quickly adjust their expectations in a similar way to announcements of a

new federal tax policy or interest rate policy. Such herding behavior is the most commonly assumed mode of learning in economics as it is attributed to individual rational agents who happen to base their expectations on the same external information and come to the same conclusion. Similar expectations are not due to social coordination but simply result from the rational reactions of each individual to the same information.

The theory of cascades makes the opposite assumption: people simply adopt the expectations of others, disregarding whatever independent information they may possess. In this case, the information on some specific economic expectation cascades across a population. People do not act as independent agents but simply revise their expectations to conform to pre-existing beliefs. An important assumption about informational cascades is that people do not have access to the information known to others; they can only observe the behavior of others. For example, people sometimes accuse the media of manufacturing a cascade by initially reporting some expert's economic forecast and then subsequently reporting ever larger numbers of people who have adopted that same expectation. Typically, it involves the incessant drumbeat of bad economic news; hardly anyone has ever complained that the repetition of good news stories was responsible for robust economic growth! The key characteristic of cascades is that people adopt an economic expectation without knowing the underlying economic rationale. That is viewed as a desirable property of informational cascades since cascades are seen as capable of explaining why masses of people sometimes adopt irrational expectations. Indeed, economists typically use informational cascades to understand the irrational excesses of booms and busts in everything from financial markets to fads and fashion. They do not use cascades to describe why masses of people quickly adopt rational expectations.

The recent discovery of mirror neurons provides a third view between the solitary rational actor of herding theory and the unthinking social conformity of cascades. This form of learning is based on a more complete understanding of other people's assessments of their economic circumstances. This form of learning is much more powerful than imitation. Every school curriculum recognizes the limitations of rote memorization compared with a basic understanding of the underlying principles. Imitation represents memorization of a specific reaction to a specific event in a specific situation. People cannot easily transfer what they learned to another situation. Learning by understanding enables the generalization of the core principles to other situations and other economic events (Katona, 1940). Mirror neurons give people the inherent ability to understand other people's actions and evaluations of economic events. This transfer of information does not depend on the existence of a prior relationship as it can occur between total strangers (Zajonc, 1965). Who hasn't instinctively understood the joy or the despair shown by a stranger when they got a sought after job or lost a long-held job? And who hasn't automatically discounted that joy or despair when someone gained the job by unfair advantage or lost the job by incompetence? While mirror neurons are most often associated with empathy, the understanding provided by mirror neurons is not blind to contextual and other factors.

What role does understanding the economic concerns of others play in the formation of people's own economic expectations? The primary role is to motivate people to reconsider the adequacy of their current economic expectations. While people's economic situations may not be fully comparable, it is the emotional connotations that provide a common yardstick that indicates the need for change. People effortlessly and automatically acquire this information, even those who have no direct social interaction other than visual cues. While process is independent of conscious reasoning, the cascades in expectations it can create are not mindless. They are the result of a fast and effective way for humans to communicate. Indeed, evolutionary development has made this form of emotional communication an inherent component of the human mind.

The excesses of cascading economic expectations, whether toward booms or busts, have received the greatest attention. The more important and far more common situation is the role of emotional contagion in producing turning points in the cyclical evolution of consumer expectations. What causes people to decide the economy is about to sink despite ongoing economic growth, and what causes people to expect an economic upturn when the economy is at its worst? Without this prescience, consumer expectations could not forecast subsequent changes in the economy. As already noted, consumers do not form their economic expectation by exclusively focusing on national economic statistics. People want to form expectations that they tailor to their own economic situation. The best sources of information involve how economic conditions are changing for people similar to themselves. What better gauge of local economic conditions than information from other people in the same community who share essentially similar economic circumstances. The connection may be as slight as shopping at the same stores or as deep as working for the same company. The greater the connection, the deeper the understanding gained from observing their nonverbal cues, even if people have no direct personal contact. Long before a downturn or upturn can even be noticed in aggregate economic statistics, a small number of people gain or lose jobs, experience income increases or declines, or find their living standards have changed for better or worse due to shifts in prices. The emotional displays that are generated are the seeds of contagion.

PASSIONATE EXPECTATIONS

Economic expectations must be based on rational and not emotional considerations. This core principle has long been justified by the importance of accuracy. People understand that accurate expectations enable them to make better economic decisions. Nevertheless, what person could view their own economic prospects dispassionately? Passion is an inevitable part of the formation of economic expectations. The essential message of this chapter is not that people base their expectations on the emotional appeal of some outcome, but that the formation of expectations is motivated and shaped by affective processes that operate in parallel with cognitive processes. Each system provides crucial advantages to human decision making. The affective system can process information faster, automatically and effortlessly make assessments, and motivate actions even before people become consciously aware of the information. The cognitive system is unmatched in its ability to identify the most appropriate data, to interpret and assess alternative scenarios, and to learn from past errors. If cognitive resources were unlimited, people would base all economic expectations on the use of these mental resources. Unfortunately, conscious cognitive resources are severely limited. Rather than being the enemy of rational expectations, the affective system promotes the efficient use of mental resources and motivates people to optimize benefits from the perspective of the overall economic decision.

The most pervasive influence of the affective system is that a positive or negative assessment automatically accompanies all information relevant to a person's economic situation. These automatic evaluations are not arbitrary. They represent what a person has learned from past experiences. These basic evaluations allow people to effortlessly combine a good deal of diverse economic data in ways that make future assessments more sensitive to the individual's own economic situation. More importantly, these automatic evaluations help people decide whether to undergo the additional effort required by conscious deliberation. People are more likely to incur these additional costs when the balance of their economic expectations begins to shift in the positive or negative direction around cyclical turning points. While a conscious assessment of emerging economic trends is always present at turning points, more consumers simultaneously arrive at such points in downturns than in upturns. This reflects the greater sensitivity and the faster response of the affective system to negative economic developments.

While the impact of automatic evaluations on conscious deliberation is dependent on the flow and content of individual pieces of information, mood automatically generalizes the need for more or less conscious awareness of economic developments. The impact from optimistic and pessimistic moods on information processing is asymmetric. Economic pessimism is more highly associated with conscious processing than economic optimism. This reflects the greater affective importance of avoiding negative developments. Mood thus automatically enables more efficient mental processing by taking into account the higher costs of negative developments. Nonetheless, as economic expansions and contractions lengthen, consumers become more sensitive to countervailing trends. The optimistic or pessimistic mood begins to dissolve along with shifts in the balance of their automatic assessments of ongoing economic developments. Most consumers do not consciously choose to be optimistic or pessimistic, nor do they consciously choose to shift from one to the other.

The final affective influence examined does not promote more efficient use of mental resources, but motivates people to update their current economic expectations. Emotions help to set priorities among competing goals as well as motivate the accomplishment of goals. Conventional economic theory uses the concept of utility maximization as the primary motivation, but this concept is confined to preferences among alternative outcomes. Emotions play a much more important role. Perhaps the most important characteristic is that emotions are not fully accessible to conscious rational control. While this is not bothersome when used to define what people desire, it is quite troublesome for conventional theories when emotions are considered to act in some instances as the functional equivalent of cognitive faculties. Moreover, communication is the primary adaptive purpose of emotional displays. Humans have an inherent ability to understand these emotional expressions, and use this ability to gauge the motives and expectations of others. This form of communication predates language, and its long evolutionary development has enabled communication through even slight nuances of facial muscles or posture. These messages represent a powerful force in motivating people to reassess their economic expectations. Rather than relying on official statistics to form their expectations, people place greater weight on their own experiences and the economic experiences of other people. Importantly, these emotional displays can spark cascades in expectations whereby sizable portions of the population abruptly change their economic expectations. While it is rare that such cascades ultimately lead to irrational booms or busts, in every cyclical upturn and downturn, consumers place considerable weight on the expectations of others when forming their own economic expectations.

It is no longer tenable to conceptualize the formation of economic expectations as the sole product of conscious rational deliberation. Expectations are based on affective as well as cognitive systems. Since these systems operate in parallel, it should be no surprise that different outcomes from the two systems may occur at times. Whenever the differences are large, people are motivated to resolve the difference. If they cannot close the gap, this difference forms the basis of subjective uncertainty that is inexpressible in terms of the probabilities of the two outcomes.

6

The Construction of Expectations

Explaining economic behavior without the driving force of expectations is unthinkable to economists. Of all the social sciences, economics has placed the greatest emphasis on explaining today's decisions by what may happen in the future rather than by what occurred in the past. People form economic expectations so they can make more efficient and more effective decisions that serve their own best interests. This practical purpose requires that expectations be tailored to the needs of specific economic decisions, and that the expectations be reasonably accurate. Such tailored expectations can be constructed only after decision needs are identified, and then formed by the least costly method to achieve the desired benefits. This cost–benefit approach to expectations is the hallmark of economics, and represents the core theoretical framework for describing how expectations are constructed.

This description of expectations is clearly based on widely accepted tenets of economic theory. Conventional theory holds that accurate expectations enable people to maximize the utility they derive from their economic decisions, and that expectations are formed as the outcome of an information processing task that seeks to balance costs and benefits. The critical differences that have been raised in the prior chapters do not relate to the core theory but rather how the theory has been conceptualized in practice. The differences involve the mechanisms used by people to acquire, process, and interpret information. The new conceptualization is more inclusive by recognizing that the full potential of the human mind is utilized in the construction of economic expectations. Conscious cognitive deliberation, which represents only a part of the mental resources people use to form expectations, has completely dominated theory and empirical research on the formation of expectations. The contribution of nonconscious processes has been greatly undervalued, with scant research on how these processes

can automatically accumulate data and produce expectations by associative learning. Moreover, emotions in conventional theories have been
solely viewed as a source of bias and irrationality. Little attention is given
to the role of emotions in shaping how economic events are perceived and
interpreted or to the role of emotions in setting economic priorities and
galvanizing resources to quickly revise expectations when warranted by a
sudden change in circumstances.

The first topic of this chapter will be to describe how the various
components of the human mind operate in parallel to produce coherent
economic expectations. While expectations can be the sole outcome of conscious deliberation, or solely based on nonconscious processes, or even the
singular result of affective influences, it is far more likely that expectations
represent the influence of all three components. When all subsystems point
to the same expectations, people commonly have a deep sense of confidence in their judgments. Such unanimous agreement among the mental
subsystems is not always achieved, as people sometimes recognize a difference in what they "think" will happen as opposed to what their intuitions
anticipate or what their emotions lead them to expect. These differences
reflect a type of uncertainty that is quite different from an economist's
notion of uncertainty as risk. It is more similar to what an econometrician
would call "model" uncertainty, since people are uncertain about the correct
model to use to interpret the inconsistencies in the data that are available
to them. In such situations, some people may favor conscious deliberation,
others may trust their intuitions, and still others may put more weight on
their feelings. Given that forming accurate expectations is a complex task in
a constantly changing economy, it should be no surprise that a unanimous
agreement is not always forthcoming. Indeed, if unanimity was always the
result, there would be no adaptive purpose for maintaining interdependent
mental subsystems.

The second topic of this chapter is how and when expectations are
constructed. In the conventional view, the formation process is always independent of the intended purpose for which the expectation may be used.
In the new conceptualization, expectations are formed to meet the needs
of a given decision within a specific context. This seemingly minor difference has a profound impact. In the conventional view, people are assumed
to revise their expectations when new information is released by a federal
statistical agency. A full array of revised expectations based on the latest
data on unemployment, inflation, income, GDP, and so forth, is then stored
in memory (or on paper, computer disk, or by any other means). These
expectations are retrieved whenever people need to make an economic

decision. In contrast, the new conceptualization assumes that people form expectations in response to their own specific needs, and it is the decision context that determines how information is interpreted and weighted in the construction of economic expectations for that specific use. This means that two people who differ in age or geographic residence, for example, may hold different expectations for inflation or unemployment, and that the same person, when confronted by different economic decisions, may accept different accuracy levels in their expectations. Traditionally, context dependence has been considered a source of bias; in this new conceptualization, context dependence represents an innate flexibility that people automatically utilize to tailor their expectations for a specific purpose.

The third topic covered in this chapter is the accuracy of expectations. The benefits of accurate expectations are ultimately gauged in terms of their impact on the economic decision for which they were formed. The benefits from the outcomes of specific decisions determine the level of desired accuracy. If the outcomes are quite sensitive to the accuracy of the expectations used in making these decisions, people would willingly devote more of their mental and other resources to the task. The benefits from greater accuracy justify higher formation costs. If, at the other extreme, decision outcomes are relatively insensitive to the accuracy of a particular economic expectation, people would not be inclined to use many of their valuable resources to refine the expectation. Indeed, the minimization of costs based on the sensitivity of expectations to decision outcomes is an important part of the rationale for tailoring expectations to specific decisions. While economic theory points toward the importance of the benefits derived from the decision in comparison to costs, nearly all empirical studies have been conducted in terms of the accuracy of the expectations themselves, completely ignoring variations in derived benefits. While such a simplifying assumption may have been appropriate within the context of a single representative agent model, it is theoretically inappropriate when applied to the more general case of how heterogeneous agents handle the benefits–costs tradeoff.

The fourth topic concerns the fact that the formation of economic expectations is inherently a social process. From the earliest times on the African savanna to the current digital age, people have always based their economic expectations partly on the actions and beliefs of others. Economic survival is enhanced by social communications. Even before language, people automatically communicate their economic expectations through emotional displays. Even in the digital age people routinely use pictorial representations of facial expressions, called emoticons, to succinctly convey their emotional interpretation of events. No one has to be taught what emotional displays mean. Mirror neurons give people the innate ability to understand the meaning of the communicated emotions (Enticott et al., 2008). The fear and anxiety caused by job loss are routinely conveyed by facial and body language as is the joy and relief when that person finds a new job. Conventional economic theory places no weight on this source of nonverbal information in forming expectations. Nonetheless, such emotional displays represent an important source of information for individuals. Moreover, the automatic transmission of emotions can greatly accelerate the pace of change in economic expectations across entire populations, especially with the advent of television and other electronic media. No person can easily ignore the meaning of such nonverbal displays from another person in a similar economic situation; people naturally see such information as having a potential impact on their own situation. No one needs to understand the quantitative details to react to facial and body language. This may explain the dominance in the mass media of qualitative reports on economic statistics as they rely more on the emotional interpretation than the knowledge of the statistics themselves.

The final topic deals with an assessment of the strengths and weaknesses of conventional economic theories on the formation of expectations. The clear strength of the rational expectations hypothesis is that it holds the accuracy of expectations to be paramount. This is clearly in accord with the primary function of expectations, which is to maximize the capacity of our mental resources to make decisions. Another somewhat surprising strength of the rational expectations hypothesis is that it leaves the actual formation process undefined, thus allowing the potential influence of nonconscious and affective influences – although most economists would view such influences as outside the scope of their discipline. Perhaps the biggest deficit is not with the theory itself, but its conceptualization through the use of representative agents and its failure to correctly account for accuracy in the context of decision outcomes. In contrast, the strength of the bounded rationality theory is its recognition of the limits on conscious deliberation and its begrudging acknowledgment of the importance of intuitions. Unfortunately, even among psychologists, only conscious cognitive deliberation is capable of reliably forming bias-free expectations. Theories about how people learn to form and revise their expectations must be freed from the confines of conscious deliberation.

To accomplish this transformation requires a paradigm shift from the favored deductive logic of orthodox theory to explain the formation of expectations to the more widespread use of inductive logic favored by the cognitive nonconscious.

THE MASTERPIECE OF EVOLUTION

The human brain is the masterpiece of evolution. No other species is capable of the intellectual or artistic achievements of humans. The brain is a massive parallel processor that can assimilate enormous quantities of information at the same time and achieve multiple goals simultaneously. Theories about how the brain functions in decision making have never fully accommodated the fact that separate brain modules can focus on achieving separate, and at times, conflicting goals. Some theorists have tried to avoid and simplify the problem by hypothesizing that there is a central control function that directs all brain processes to achieve desired goals. Such a majordomo (homunculus) is impossible. If there were a central control function, its serial operation would inevitably represent a bottleneck, slowing information processing and decision making. Distributed processing is conducted by semi-autonomous brain modules that have the ability to call in other resources when they encounter unusual situations. The remarkable achievement of the brain is that its distributed processing works without a central control function. Think of typing some text in an email, playing a piano, or simply walking with a friend: how could a central control function serially process the many millions of instructions that need to be executed simultaneously by every part of the body, from limbs to internal organs, precisely coordinating your movements with those around you, while you communicate by voice and body expressions, recognize the presence of other people or objects, and plan for your next sentence or movement? Separate parallel processing is required, and these overlapping systems can produce reliable, stable, and adaptable behaviors without central control. Parallel processing implies that people have no definitive hierarchy of goals that rigidly controls their behavior; instead, people simultaneously pursue a variety of sometimes conflicting goals.

Just as decentralized markets can coordinate economic decisions across an entire economy more efficiently and effectively without a central planning function, the dynamics of the brain's parallel processing system can more efficiently and effectively create the wide array of expectations needed for decisions in the modern economy. Not all markets function perfectly, and the same is true for the parallel modules of the brain. Sometimes, all modules must be galvanized in response to a specific stimulus, such as flight or fight in response to danger – or in the modern economy, for example, the loss of a job. Most of the time, the conflict across subsystems do not pose serious problems for economic expectations. Conflicts are often sensed by people as an uneasy feeling about some expectation; they may signal a difference between a conscious expectation and an intuition. As with unexpected events, such differences motivate the need for greater attention until the divergence between conscious expectations and subconscious intuitions is eliminated.

The human brain has evolved over 6 million years. Initially, the human brain was quite primitive, similar to the neural structure found in today's reptiles (Massey, 2002). The mental capacity of the first humans was limited to the brain stem and cerebellum, which controlled autonomic functions such as the respiratory and cardiovascular systems as well as some basic instinctual behaviors. Limbic systems were then added, surrounding the brain stem and cerebellum. The functions of the limbic system include storing and coordinating sensory information, relaying information to other parts of the brain, and the expression of emotions. Like the workings of the initial brain structure, the various functions of the limbic system work without conscious awareness to process information and generate the affective states that influence the formation of expectations. The final and outermost layer, the neocortex, was added as recently as 150,000 years ago to consciously process sensory information. Obviously, the limbic system did not replace the functions of the brain stem and cerebellum, just as the neocortex has not replaced the functions of the limbic system. Although each brain module commands some aspects of human behavior, the systems are not independent nor are they redundant. Each provides unique information and processing capacities.

The prefrontal cortex is the part of the neocortex that is capable of the type of mental activity associated with conventional theories on the formation of expectations. Interpreting data, performing calculations, and selecting appropriate models require the type of conscious rational thinking that is in the province of the prefrontal cortex. The emotions produced nonconsciously by the limbic systems, it has been argued, could only diminish the accuracy of economic expectations formed by conscious deliberation. While this has been the firm belief of scholars ever since this view was first advanced by the ancient Romans, it is now known to be an impossible task. The neural structure of the brain implies that the capacity for conscious deliberation necessarily rests on the nonconscious and emotional foundation of the limbic system (Massey, 2002; Turner, 2000). It is much more likely that emotional considerations will prevail over rational considerations since the neural connections linking the limbic system to the neocortex are far greater than those linking the neocortex to the limbic system (Carter & Frith, 1998). The emotional brain also precedes the rational brain in the perception and evaluation of new information (Massey, 2002). When the rational brain finally becomes aware of new economic information, the emotional brain has already added information that affects its interpretation (Zajonc, 1980). The affective states automatically produced by the emotional brain are a vital component in the formation of expectations. Moreover, the sole focus on conscious reasoning ignores the nonconscious cognitive capacity of the brain to process and interpret information; conventional theories implicitly conflate these nonconscious cognitive abilities with emotion as sources of bias.

Dual-Process Models

Since passion cannot be stamped out of reason, scholars have proposed several theories to accommodate the inevitable presence of nonconscious and emotional elements in the formation of economic expectations. Freud (1900) first proposed a dual theory of information processing more than one hundred years ago, and the dual system approach has now become an integral part of cognitive neuroscience (Kahneman, 2013; Stanovich & West, 2000; Epstein, 1994). While it is still true that only conscious deliberation is capable of rational judgments in these models, the dual system approach recognizes the existence of another mental system that can process information and form expectations. Economists have generally interpreted dual-process models as juxtaposing the use of reason with emotion, with some version of "willpower" determining which process is used. The more willpower, the theories hold, the more likely the expectation was formed by conscious deliberation. This enables economists to model the determinants of the necessary willpower that would ensure rational deliberation as well as the circumstances in which emotion would dominate rationality in decision making.[1] Others have proposed a "corrective" dual model, whereby intuition produced by nonconscious processes is subject to a review by conscious deliberation and revised as needed (Kahneman, 2013). All dual-process and corrective models commit "Descartes' error" by assuming that

---

[1] Economists have proposed a number of dual-process models ranging from the planner-doer model (Shefrin & Thaler, 1988), the hot-cold model (Bernheim & Rangel, 2004), automatic and controlled processes (Camerer et al., 2005), and the affective and deliberative processes (Loewenstein & O'Donoghue, 2004). For an overview of dual-process theories see "Dual-Process Theories in Social Psychology" edited by Chaiken & Trope (1999).

reason can be free of emotion (Damasio, 1994). Every choice involves the assessment of relative value defined by subjective preferences. Even the choice to elevate economic rationality above all other criteria reflects a strong emotional commitment. Rationality and emotion are not separate dimensions of behavioral choice (LeDoux, 1996). Emotions act to galvanize the necessary mental resources, command selective attention to the relevant issues, and motivate people to change their economic expectations. A more appropriate dual model would be a "consolidated" design whereby expectations are formed by interdependent processes that produce as timely and as accurate economic expectations as warranted by costs and benefits (Gilbert, 1999).

Humans have an extraordinarily limited capacity for conscious reasoning, especially when compared with the relatively unlimited capacity to process information nonconsciously. And even the limited conscious reasoning capacity can be quickly exhausted by comparatively simple and brief cognitive tasks (Baumeister & Vohs, 2004; Bargh & Chartrand, 1999). Too much attention has been given to the costs of overcoming the deliberate effort required by conscious reasoning and too little attention to the high opportunity costs inherent in people's limited capacity for conscious reasoning. A more accurate assessment would be to compare the losses from the costless use of intuitions enabled by nonconscious processes with the opportunity costs incurred from not consciously attending to other important decisions. Just as important, the integrated structure of the human brain means that conscious deliberation can never be free of influences from the emotional brain, nor from the cognitive activities undertaken subliminally.

Unfortunately, the consolidated design has received the least attention in the economics literature. The theories of bounded rationality, first proposed by the Nobel Laureate Herbert Simon, implicitly recognize the limitations on conscious deliberation in the formation of expectations. This was not an endorsement of the power of the unconscious, however, but simply the recognition of the significant barriers for people to consciously form fully rational expectations. Theories of bounded rationality simply accepted the limitations on conscious rational deliberations due to the lack of complete information and people's inability to make the necessary calculations or to correctly interpret the data. To form economic expectations despite the limitations on conscious reasoning, these theories assumed that people use some mental rules of thumb or heuristics to form their expectations. It is assumed that these mental shortcuts are learned, and in some cases, particularly among experts, could become reasonably accurate. For most observers, however, using heuristics to form economic expectations was believed to result in biased expectations. The "heuristics and bias" approach gives no credence to the efficiency of unconscious information processing and learning, no acknowledgment of the important role played by affect in the construction of expectations, and no recognition of the need to maximize the use of people's relatively limited conscious mental resources. The heuristics approach was simply meant to describe how people could form expectations without detailed knowledge of the data and their inability to calculate and interpret the results. Heuristics is simply the name for the "black box" of expectation formation; few were interested in explaining how specific heuristics developed, say toward inflation or unemployment, or how heuristics changed along with economic developments.

Social Resources

Humans are social animals. No description of the human condition can be complete without the recognition that the interactions among humans are critical to their existence. While conventional economic theory often makes the simplifying assumption that the preferences of each agent are independent, that assumption is poorly suited for the study of the formation of expectations. There are substantial reasons to believe that people would take into account the expectations of others when forming their own expectations. If most other people expect negative economic developments, for example, and are cutting back on their spending, people may want to take precautionary measures as well, even if they did not initially expect the same unfavorable economic changes. The importance of such Keynesian "beauty contest," where the goal is to correctly anticipate what most other people expect, has long been recognized. There is another, perhaps more important, reason for people to heed the expectations of others. Other people who are in economic situations that are very similar to yours offer an independent perspective on how your situation may change in the future. Other people act as proxies for forming expectations about an essentially shared economic situation.

Social groups can act as more efficient and effective information processors to form or revise economic expectations (Bargh & Williams, 2006). Moreover, groups are especially adept at processing complex information by sharing resources and pooling relevant information (Hinsz et al., 1997). While a few people may belong to formal groups such as investment clubs, it is far more likely that people depend on much more informal grouping or networks. Network members may possess information on one or more economic topics, such as job prospects or investment opportunities. Even within households, some members may specialize in one topic or another so they can process the needed economic information more efficiently. Importantly, the critical information gained by group members is communicated just as all other information in social situations, automatically and nonconsciously. People are most interested in the evaluative summaries, not the details, and the most persuasive and powerful evaluations are those underscored by emotions.

It is of some interest to note that Keynes chose a "beauty contest" to illustrate his point. Such contests primarily rely on facial and other body language to communicate. These contests are the antithesis of rational deliberation. These interpersonal signals have evolutionary roots that have made this form of communication nearly universal and equally shared across populations (Ross & Dumouchel, 2004). These signals to the emotional brain facilitate the rapid transmission of economic information, and at times cause sudden and sharp changes in economic expectations across entire populations.

Long before the development of language, humans communicated visually. To this day, the human senses are dominated by vision, whereas most mammals are olfactory dominant. The brain is wired to subordinate other sensory information to visual information which has conferred on humans an evolutionary advantage (Turner, 2000). The bipedal stance of humans enhanced our ability to communicate though body gestures as well as by facial expressions. Charles Darwin (1872) proposed that communicating by visible emotional expressions was an innate skill of humans. No one has to be taught what emotions mean; mirror neurons make the meaning of the communicated emotions clear to any observer (Enticott et al., 2008; Rizzolatti et al., 2001). Mirror neurons automatically connect people to each other in a fundamental way since the activity of mirror neurons are identical whether a person performs an action or observes another person performing the same action.

With the addition of the neocortex, language developed as the natural extension of visual communication by emotional displays. Importantly, language did not replace emotion as a form of human communication. Spoken language accompanied by emotional expressions represents the most powerful form of human communication. Indeed, nonverbal communication is at least as important as the words a speaker uses; some estimate that the nonverbal content accounts for nearly all of what is actually communicated. Even casual conversations that motivate action not only require a sound message but also a consistent facial expression, tone of voice, hand gestures, and other appropriate body movements. Someone who communicated with a flat tone, aloof manner, and a passionless delivery will not convince many people even if the message is sound. These mannerisms act to convince the listener that the speaker does not truly believe the message and it can be safely ignored.

Unlike the wide variety of languages, which need to be learned to be understood, the meanings of expressed emotions are universal. For example, humans only need a few brief milliseconds of seeing the devastating impact of unemployment on a person's face to understand its meaning; no words need to be spoken. In contrast, people could read about the same impact of unemployment on a person without sensing the same devastation that one look would communicate. Language expands our ability to communicate, but it does not replace or supersede emotional communications. While emotions are difficult to express by spoken language, they are displayed nonconsciously by facial and bodily expressions. Emotional communication adds emphasis, and through the action of mirror neurons, a profound understanding is instantly and effortlessly communicated.

The most primitive human is likely to have communicated economic expectations by emotional displays in much the same way as modern man. The adaptive purpose of this innate facility to understand the economic situations of others is not to enhance our feelings of empathy, but to enhance our survival. Emotional displays force people to recognize and understand in detail what others have experienced. Insofar as they signal an unexpected gain or loss, these displays motivate people to immediately reassess their own economic expectations. Humans are experienced in noticing even minor changes in these facial and body expressions. Indeed, the unemployment rate, for example, does not have to actually increase before people's emotional expressions of uncertainty and fear are clearly understood by others as a cue to adjust their expectations. Facial and bodily expressions can act as an early warning system or a leading indicator, prompting observers to seek information and potentially change their own expectations. Importantly, it is emotional communication by facial and body expressions that is responsible for abrupt changes in the economic expectations across the entire population.

It should be no surprise that these sudden shifts in economic expectations are faster and more abrupt when the change is in the negative direction. This may reflect the fact that most emotions are negative rather than positive. The universal and most basic emotions have been identified by many scholars since the dawn of Western and Eastern civilizations. A typical list includes fear, anger, sadness, disgust, happiness, and surprise (Ekman, 1972). There are more extensive lists of emotions, but these are nearly universal and many other emotions are combinations, such as anger and disgust to form contempt, or subsumed in a broader definition, such as joy within happiness.

Preference for Conscious Deliberation

Why would people choose to form economic expectations by the effortful task of conscious deliberation rather than simply base their expectations on intuitions? The most common answer by scholars involves the accuracy of the resulting expectation. Conscious rational deliberation holds a greater promise of accuracy and, more importantly, allows people to scrutinize the factors and procedures underlying their expectations, and facilitates learning from past errors. Conscious deliberation has higher costs, but also has higher anticipated benefits in terms of accuracy. While this represents a standard analysis, it is necessarily incomplete since it avoids the high opportunity costs of using a scarce resource. The ability to rationally deliberate is a limited mental resource, and these limits make it impossible to consciously form all of the expectations that people require. No one can devote the prohibitive share of consciousness to forming expectations covering every possible event in the economic, political, and social spheres of their lives, let alone to consciously revise their expectations with each new data release or event. The substantial opportunity costs mean that every expectation cannot be consciously formed and repeatedly revised. People must set priorities, and the priorities must dynamically reflect variations in people's lives as well as external events. The assumption that every person consciously maintains a complete and up-to-date set of economic expectations is untenable as it would represent a wasteful and uneconomic use of their scarce mental resources.

The traditional argument for the sole reliance on conscious rational deliberation to form expectations is as overblown as the traditional aversion to nonconscious processes. All nonconscious processes are by definition not considered rational and thus an impediment to accuracy. The argument that only conscious deliberation can be rational is false. This bias may reflect the misleading notion that cognitive activity is restricted to consciousness, that unconscious cognitive processes are not shaped by learning and experiences, or that the unconscious is not capable of performing complex data analysis and interpretation. Even if only a modest degree of accuracy for a limited number of economic expectations could be obtained from nonconscious processes, it would have a significant impact on how people maximized the use of their mental resources. While the intuitions of experts have been shown to be as accurate as more deliberate conscious analysis by those same experts, the ability of nonconscious processes to learn from experience among ordinary people has not received much attention in the social science disciplines. The so-called "intuitive statistician" has been treated as an anomaly rather than incorporated into mainstream theory on the formation of expectations. There is reason to believe that people can achieve much more than a minimal level of accuracy, as demonstrated by the accuracy of their inflation and unemployment expectations analyzed in Chapter 2.

When do people choose to engage in conscious deliberation? There are some people who engage in conscious deliberation more often than others due to their higher cognitive capacities, because conscious reasoning about economic events is their preferred style, or they want to be able to verbally explain the factors behind their expectations. Although this set of characteristics may well describe social science theorists, it also applies to a broad range of individuals as well. People do differ in their "need for cognition," or their preference to engage in effortful conscious cognitive activities, which psychologists have conceptualized as a generalized personality trait (Petty et al., 2009; Cacioppo & Petty, 1982). Most people, however, do not hold such strong preferences for conscious cognitive reasoning about expected economic events. Nonetheless, even among those with a high cognitive capacity and a preference for cognitive deliberation, conscious deliberation is still a limited resource that is selectively used.

Differences in these characteristics may describe variations in average levels of conscious deliberation across population groups, but they do not describe what factors propel individuals to use conscious deliberation. The use of conscious deliberation is determined by whether the information represents a new or unexpected event, by the economic and emotional importance attached to that information, and by the expectations other people have about the same event. While there is no question that it is the economic information itself that commands attention, how people respond to the information depends to a large degree on emotions: whether it is the surprise of an unexpected economic event, the emotional significance of an economic change or emotional communications by facial and bodily expressions of other people. While these are not the only motivators of conscious deliberation, the critical role played by emotions is to galvanize people to promptly seek out other relevant information and revise their expectations.

It would be a mistake to view the decision to engage in conscious deliberation as tantamount to forming an expectation using only conscious resources. Most economic expectations are sufficiently complex so that both conscious and nonconscious information processing are typically involved. Indeed, the greater resources of the unconscious are more adept at handling the most complex problems. For example, people may consciously gather information but only come to a conclusion after nonconscious processing and learning. People often describe this process as the need to "sleep on it" before making a decision (Fischer et al., 2006; Wagner et al., 2004). Since unconscious information processing is designed to mirror the same conscious processes usually undertaken by individuals, the more a person becomes consciously adept at some task, so too does the unconscious. Given that the unconscious mind automatically produces intuitions about expected economic developments, the task of the conscious mind is either to accept or reject the unconscious mind's intuitions (Kahneman, 2011).

The choice to use conscious or nonconscious reasoning is also made in more passive ways. After starting to consciously deliberate, people may end the process short of its goal or simply get sidetracked to another topic. Simultaneous conscious processes tend to be disruptive because the capacity of conscious deliberation is limited. Nonconscious processing, in contrast, does not suffer as much when other tasks are simultaneously undertaken. Moreover, an end to conscious processing does not necessarily imply that the expectations will not be ultimately formed. As long as some minimal level of attention is maintained nonconsciously, the processing will continue uninterrupted.

Integrated Mental Resources

This new theory of how expectations are constructed is based on the seamless integration of conscious and nonconscious mental processes as well as on the cognitive and affective systems of the human mind. The complete array of mental resources may not be utilized in the construction of every economic expectation, as some are mainly formed by conscious cognitive deliberation while others are mainly constructed by nonconscious processes. The same applies to the relative importance of cognitive and affective influences, as some expectations are shaped more by affective processes. It is an impossible task to parse the relative importance of conscious versus nonconscious processes as well as the influence of cognitive versus affective processes on the formation of any given economic expectation. No one has the resources to make every economic decision by rational deliberation, nor would anyone have the inclination to use their mental resources so inefficiently. People learn how to balance the use of their mental resources so as to achieve a reasonable degree of accuracy in their expectations. To be sure, there are pathological cases where people avoid conscious deliberation to their detriment as well as cases where people excessively deliberate about the pros and cons of a decision well beyond any potential benefit.

It has often been claimed that when the size of the financial stake was large or the decision was important, people would form their expectations in a manner consistent with rational deliberation. People would simply not be satisfied with a fast intuitive judgment based on nonconscious processes when the consequences of a misjudgment are high. This is clearly consistent with a view that the costs must be justified by the benefits, with larger financial stakes prompting more conscious deliberation. A careful review of experimental evidence, however, found no support for this view (Camerer & Hogarth, 1999).

Other than for the most trivial economic expectations, it is impossible to parse how much of the processing occurred consciously and how much nonconsciously. To reiterate, the most complex economic expectations are handled more efficiently by nonconscious rather than conscious processes. The nonconscious mind has the advantage of a much greater processing capacity that can handle more dimensions of a complex decision and continue uninterrupted over longer periods of time. Rational deliberation by the conscious mind, in contrast, cannot easily handle multiple dimensions nor can people devote long periods of continuous processing due to competing demands on conscious awareness as well as growing fatigue from the mental effort itself.

The brain has evolved over millions of years to optimally make decisions. Despite the evolutionary gains in the capacity of the human mind for rational deliberation, there is no reason to anticipate that it has or would eventually displace the important role of the nonconscious or the critical role played by emotions in the formation of expectations. It is not just that the relevant economic information reaching people will always exceed their conscious processing capacity, but also for the optimal use of mental resources, people will always find it more efficient to process some information nonconsciously. Moreover, emotions will always be required to define preferences and to motivate human behavior, not the least of which is to motivate rational deliberation. The conscious, nonconscious, and emotional components of decision making are all required to maximize the potential of the human brain.

Attention: Conscious and Nonconscious

Attention to economic information is essential for people to form expectations. Everything about the modern economy must be learned. People must learn which aspects of the economy are likely to have an impact on their welfare, and which aspects they can safely ignore. This learning process starts early in life and it continues throughout people's lifetimes, reflecting changes in their economic circumstances as well as changes in the economic environment. Monitoring changes in economic conditions for potential opportunities and threats is as common now as when our ancestors first roamed the African savanna. Conscious awareness as well as nonconscious cognitive processes require some degree of attention. An efficient deployment of people's mental resources would imply that while some information would enter their conscious awareness, the much larger capacity of people's nonconscious processing capacity would be utilized for most information. As people become more adept at gathering the necessary economic information, the process becomes increasingly routinized and accomplished with less conscious control. People learn to mirror the same conscious means they use to form expectations, automatically and effortlessly by nonconscious processes (Hodgkinson et al., 2008; Bargh & Chartrand, 1999). Even if a modest degree of accuracy is obtained when people form their expectations nonconsciously, it would have a significant impact on how people maximize the use of their mental resources.

Attention is required to process information either consciously or nonconsciously (Koch & Tsuchiya, 2006). Some events automatically command attention, but most do not. Even the much larger processing capacity of the nonconscious has its limits. It is simply not possible to process all available information. People must choose based on their motives and goals. While most people automatically attend to information about their own income and job prospects or about prices of the goods and services they purchase, few people are motivated to regularly pay attention to aspects of the economy that have little or no bearing on their own situation. People learn which sources of information allow them to anticipate changes in their incomes, jobs, prices, or whatever other factors they deem important for their future livelihood. Some people are also motivated to be knowledgeable about more general issues for a variety of reasons, including personal interests, civic engagement, and informed voting. In all cases, persistent attention to a particular set of economic factors requires an equally persistent motivating force. Motivations are defined by and derive their sustaining strength from people's emotional makeup. Without the motivating force of emotions, there would be no rationale for the cognitive processes to form expectations.

There is nothing especially demanding about learning to nonconsciously acquire, interpret, and learn about the economy compared with the countless other tasks that confront people every day. People learn to nonconsciously process information and make correct decisions in real time across a wide array of tasks. Indeed, some tasks that people easily accomplish by nonconscious control would be impossible if done consciously. There is no person who can play a piano composition by consciously thinking of which finger was needed to press which key for each note, just as no driver could consciously calculate the probability of an impending accident and then consciously deliberate on their best reaction to limit damage and still have time to avoid the accident. These skills need to be learned by every new piano student and beginning driver. Learning to accomplish these skills nonconsciously is never directly taught; it is accomplished indirectly and automatically as people actually perform these tasks. These nonconscious abilities are not perfect, and people often realize the need for conscious intervention. There is a seamless interplay between utilizing conscious and nonconscious mental processes. While the efficient use of mental resources favors nonconscious processes for most learned tasks, conscious deliberation is more likely to be reserved for departures from expected events.

The same is true for how people learn about future economic prospects. Take inflation expectations as an example. The conventional view is that no person could adequately track changes in the prices of the hundreds of different products and services they purchase. This is a formidable task even for a single shopping trip as people typically leave grocery stores and other retail outlets with shopping carts full of different products. Moreover, it would be a daunting task to correctly estimate the overall share of your budget represented by each product or service so you could compute an inflation rate. These are powerful arguments for people to rely on information from federal statistical agencies. Nonetheless, the data suggest that most people pay less attention to the official inflation rate and more attention to their own market experiences. How could this be true? While people may not have learned to nonconsciously process every price of every product they purchase, the nonconscious mind has the capacity to process vast quantities of information and distill overall trends from the embedded associations. Shoppers learn to do this task automatically and effortlessly. Just as people become consciously aware of unusual circumstances when driving, large price changes are likely to arouse conscious attention, and are more likely to cause shoppers to reconsider their purchase. Certainly, this process is far from perfect, but it provides information that is tailored to the decision needs of the shopper. Moreover, such private information has been shown in Chapters 2 and 3 to have high informational content by the strong correspondence consumer inflation expectations have with actual inflation rates.

This does not imply that everyone, or even most people, become experts at forming accurate economic expectations. Subconscious processing of information depends in part on conscious learning. For someone who has quite naive expectations, for example, that today's price will be the same as yesterday's, there is no reason to expect that the subconscious would process the information any differently. Another person who has a very complex algorithm for computing inflation expectations can be anticipated to nonconsciously process information in much the same manner. Higher conscious cognitive ability is mirrored in the capacity of the cognitive subconscious. This accords with the common observation that the intuitions of experts are more accurate than the intuitions of amateurs.

Nonconscious acquisition of information is quite different from nonconscious learning. Nonconscious perception is simply monitoring changes in the economic environment. Nonconscious learning is automatically accomplished and requires only minimal levels of attention to the stimuli itself (Berry & Dienes, 1993). Importantly, unlike nonconscious perception of information, implicit learning could lead to the development of new conclusions about the future. While agents can report their "expectations" regardless of whether they were formed consciously or nonconsciously, only those that formed their expectations consciously could report on the underlying reasons for holding the expectation. It is often true in population surveys that respondents cannot explain the underlying reasons for their expectations. These respondents simply repeat the same expectations in different words but offer no explanation, or simply say it was a hunch or a guess. Nonetheless, if pressed for an answer, most people could offer a number of factors to rationalize their expectation.

This new view does not consider conscious and unconscious information processing as independent, nor does it view the cognitive and affective systems as necessarily producing different expectations. Indeed, nonconscious processing of economic information represents learned behavior, learned from the same information that was used when expectations were formed consciously. Just as people's driving behavior can be effectively controlled by nonconscious processes, so too can the accumulation and interpretation of data relevant to forming economic expectations. And just as the sudden sense of danger while driving can immediately prompt conscious awareness, the sudden realization of an unexpected economic development can immediately spark conscious awareness. Such unexpected economic events can reflect sudden surges or crashes in gas or stock prices, or any other dramatic economic event. More typically, however, the unexpected event represents a small departure from what was expected and results in people's awareness that their expectations were incorrect. The same is true when driving: accidents are rare in comparison to the many small adjustments made by drivers in anticipation of potential problems. Finally, it is of some importance to emphasize again that people are motivated to form expectations about economic events that have a direct bearing on their lives. Expectations about their own job prospects or wages or about the outlook for the prices of goods and services they actually purchase guide their economic decisions. Forming expectations about economic statistics which do not have a noticeable impact on their own financial decisions is another matter.

TAILORED EXPECTATIONS

No one can directly observe the mental processes that people use to form their economic expectations. We can only observe an expectation when it is elicited either verbally or behaviorally, and deduce properties of the formation process from other observable evidence available at the time the expectation was elicited. Economic theory provides two basic guidelines that govern the formation of expectations: the payoff from forming expectations is derived from their beneficial impact on economic decisions, and the costs of forming expectations must be no larger than the anticipated benefits. The term tailored expectations is meant to encompass these two theoretical guidelines. People are assumed to construct expectations that are tailored to a specific economic decision in a given context. Tailored expectations can only be constructed after decision needs are identified, and are then formed by the least costly method to achieve the expected benefits. People may intentionally form less accurate expectations given the relative insensitivity of the decision to the expectation. Who could justify the increased costs for greater precision when it would not have a meaningful impact on the resulting decision, or if the cost exceeded the benefit? Indeed, an important part of the rationale for tailoring expectations to specific decisions is the minimization of the formation costs for the degree of accuracy desired.

The conventional conceptualization of expectations is based on the same theoretical foundation, but assumes the primacy and universal applicability of national data. Thus, rather than using the yardstick of decision outcomes, the conventional approach relies solely on the accuracy of expectations in terms of the national data. The implicit argument is that if the expectation proves to be an accurate predictor of the national data, it will provide the maximum improvement to the average individual's economic decisions. The benefits of forming expectations based on national economic data were justified by their universal applicability, and the costs are believed to be low due to the widespread dissemination by the media. These assumptions were demonstrated to be empirically false in Chapter 3. Nonetheless, it is hard to deny the appeal of these restrictive assumptions since they allowed analysts to compare prior expectations with independent observations of subsequent realizations. Inflation, employment, income, and the rate of economic growth can be impartially observed and compared with what was previously expected. While such impartial comparisons are possible in other areas, such as election outcomes, most other social science disciplines do not have an independently verifiable source of outcome data.

Some economists have argued that people derive direct utility from economic expectations as well as indirect utility by virtue of better decision making that is enabled by accurate expectations. The direct utility derived from expectations is justified on grounds of general knowledge or good citizenship (Karlsson et al., 2009). Insofar as the objective is to cast more informed votes or otherwise influence decisions on public policies, the costs of forming these expectations are still ultimately justified not just by the utility derived from voting but from the adoption of favored public policies. A belief that your vote will not be decisive lowers the perceived benefit and thus lowers the costs you are willing to undertake to become a more informed voter. While any knowledge does provide some direct utility, the economic expectations that are discussed here have the sole objective to enable people to make more optimal economic decisions.

When Are Expectations Formed?

What triggers the formation or revision of economic expectations? Is it the availability of new economic information that sparks the revision process, or is it the need to make some specific economic decision, or both? There is a strong tradition in economics and psychology that expectations are formed when new information becomes available; the newly revised expectations are then recalled from memory whenever they are needed. People are implicitly considered to have a "memory shelf" full of different economic expectations, all updated to include the latest information. This has been called the "file draw" theory of expectations. People are motivated to update their file of economic expectations whenever new national data are available. The timing of revisions is predicated on the release of economic data by federal statistical agencies. Most analysts typically assume that expectations are revised shortly after the new data are publicly released. While some accept the fact that people may base their expectations on partial and incomplete data that is available before the official release, they typically assume that people nonetheless revise their estimates based on the latest available data from the state statistical agencies. Economic data services even maintain histories of the first data released as well as all the subsequent revisions for use in analyses, with analysts hoping to uncover whether expectations were based on the initial release or the latest revision.

Data on income, consumption, and production from the national accounts are subject to frequent revisions according to a set schedule. In three consecutive months, the releases are called the advance estimate, the preliminary estimate, and the final estimate, which are then subject to annual revisions and less frequent comprehensive benchmarking. The consumer price index and the unemployment rate are not subject to the same high frequency of revisions. The conventional assumptions mean that updating even just the most important economic expectations would require a substantial amount of conscious effort to process all of the revised information, interpret its meaning, and do the calculations to produce revised expectations. Moreover, people are assumed to undergo the costs required to revise their economic expectations regardless of an intended decision use for the expectation. Overall, this implies a frequently used file draw to maintain a complete set of updated expectations.

Since the costs of constantly updating expectations may be prohibitive, some economists have proposed a process of updating expectations that is irregular because their need is not evenly distributed but staggered over time (Bacchetta & van Wincoop, 2005; Sims, 2003; Mankiw & Reis, 2002). Only when an economic decision requires an updated expectation will people undergo the cost of the revision. Such a process would implicitly exclude all decisions that are not planned in advance so as to allow the necessary time to gather the latest information and form their revised expectation. Others have countered that all people obtain information when it becomes available but that the most recent data may be insufficient to cause them to change their expectations (Menzies & Zizzo, 2009). Only when they infer that the recent data would result in a significant change in their expectation will the revision occur. This view puts more weight on the interpretation of economic data, and the need to make judgments about how much noise is contained in the latest data. While staggered updating may well lead to a reduced burden, the latter view still requires a considerable amount of time and mental effort to accompany each data release. The costs are still viewed as minimal since mental activity is considered costless in these theories, including the implied opportunity costs.

The alternative view is that expectations are formed only when they are needed, and the costs are minimized by constructing expectations that exactly meet the needs of the specific decision. Rather than being geared to public releases of national economic data, revisions to expectations are dominated by the timing and specific needs of private economic decisions. Tailored expectations match the prospective benefits to the formation costs. Some people in some situations will demand greater accuracy and are willing to incur higher costs. In other situations, people will be content with a less accurate expectation and a correspondingly lower cost. The desire for accuracy mainly reflects how sensitive the outcome of a decision is to an economic expectation, and how large an impact the decision will have on people's financial situation. Experience and learning can alter the costs of forming expectations, as can changes in the availability of the relevant economic information. Expectations may not be formed in any single way by all people, or in a single way by the same person in all situations. The only constant across all people and all situations is a cost–benefit calculation that requires a degree of accuracy for a given cost.[2]

Even if people wanted to tailor economic expectations to their own situation, it could be argued that the proper starting point is the national data. If such a two-step process accurately described the formation of tailored expectations, the national data would then be preeminent. With the primacy of national data, conventional theories of how expectations are constructed would not only be a good first approximation, but would also be accurate at the macro level since variations in individuals' economic situations could be expected to cancel in the aggregate. Such a proposition could be used to describe the accuracy of inflation and unemployment

---

[2] Just as there is no single method that all people use in all situations, there are multiple criteria that can be used to judge the appropriateness of expectations. Based on normative considerations, economists have long favored "rationality" as that criterion. Some behavioral economists believe an important goal of economic decisions is the avoidance of losses. Minimizing losses rather than maximizing gains makes decisions dependent on past reference points. Prospect theory posits that utility depends on departures from a reference point, with negative departures having twice the impact as positive departures, or what is known as loss aversion. There has been observed a larger negative impact when people feel personally responsible for outcomes (Kahneman & Tversky, 1982) and when the outcomes are unexpected (Kahneman & Miller, 1986).

expectations documented in Chapter 2. What was shown in Chapter 3, however, was that people do not generally base their expectations on the published data from national statistical agencies, nor does the media widely distribute the quantitative results of these releases. If anything was reported by the media, it was typically a terse evaluative summary of the results, indicating, for example, that the statistic was higher, lower, or unchanged. More detailed reports on inflation or unemployment do occur, but these reports generally focus on how an individual or family is coping with higher prices or job loss, not a more detailed examination of the quantitative figures. This suggests that such media reports act as a signal to alert people to the availability of new economic data, and people would then seek out the information by other (costless) means.

Source of Economic Information

There is another answer to when new information becomes available. It simply recognizes the obvious fact that people are exposed to a continuous flow of economic information. New information about inflation is gained on every shopping trip, in countless advertisements, in personal conversations, and news media reports. The same is true for many other facets of the economy. Indeed, the typical day contains an avalanche of economic information for most people. It would be an enormous burden for people to consciously update their expectations with each new bit of information. Nonetheless, the future orientation of expectations demands attention to ongoing economic developments, expert forecasts, and ongoing economic developments conveyed by the media, even if that information contains a good deal of noise. Aside from public information, people could rely on private sources of information gained from personal experience and first-hand knowledge. The advantages of private information are that it is more detailed and more applicable to an individual's own economic situation. For example, people generally know more about their own income prospects than they can infer from public information on economy-wide income growth, and know more about the prices of goods and services they actually purchase or know more about their own job prospects in the communities where they live (French et al., 2013).

There are exceptions, of course, where information about national events trumps personal experience. News about droughts affecting crop yields, production shortages due to strikes, lockouts, or natural disasters, or a newly proposed federal tax policy, to name a few, can directly affect prospects for prices, jobs, and incomes. Nonetheless, as shown in a prior chapter, the national data provided by federal statistical agencies is not the most important source of economic information for most people. Private information commands much more attention than public information whenever it has a higher probability of affecting people's own economic situation.

Context Shapes Expectations

It is well known that verbally elicited expectations are not invariant to the frame or context in which the question was posed. Priming, framing, and anchoring effects are said to represent biases since expectations are not invariant to the measurement procedure. These effects have been extensively documented by Kahneman and Tversky as well as many others. These violations have been termed "elicitation effects" or "procedural invariance" since conventional theory assumed that expectations should be invariant to the context in which they were elicited. Perhaps the most famous examples have been observed differences in expectations depending on whether the question was framed in a positive (gain) or negative (loss) context. Another approach, most often favored by economists, is to avoid the potential bias of verbally elicited expectations by deriving expectations from behavior. For example, inflation expectations can be derived from data on US Treasury Inflation Protected Securities or TIPS. The value of these securities is tied to the Consumer Price Index; the returns increase with inflation and decrease with deflation. In addition, futures markets provide price estimates for a wide range of commodities. Other prediction markets, such as Intrade and the Iowa Electronic Market enable measures of a variety of social, political, and economic events. Expectations derived from these markets enjoy a high credibility among economists since they are based on informed participants who back up their expectations with monetary wagers, even if the amount of money involved is sometimes trivial. The underlying behavioral assumption is that economic decisions are not context dependent, and that eliciting behavior in different contexts would not produce different results. That assumption, however, does not hold as expectations are as dependent on the context in which they are elicited regardless whether they were deduced from behavioral or verbal reports.

Rather than viewing context dependence as a flaw of elicited expectations, it could be argued that it is the result of people's natural inclination to form expectations that are tailored to their overall perceptions of their situation. From the perspective of the outside observer, elicited expectations may well appear "context dependent," but from the viewpoint of the individual themselves, their expectations were simply tailored to be "context sensitive" (Schwarz, 2007). People automatically, and typically nonconsciously, adjust their responses to framing, priming, and anchoring effects since those factors determine the implied meaning of the question or goal of the behavior. This is not a shortcoming but an adaptive trait of human decision making. This adaptive purpose requires that expectations be tailored to the demands of specific economic decisions. Contextual factors do not bias their expectations, but act to tailor their expectations to specific circumstances and decision goals. The finding of ubiquitous framing and context effects should have signaled the possibility of a faulty theoretical premise rather than biased responses. What is so shocking about the proposition that different contexts are interpreted as meaning different decisions that require different responses?

The contextualization of expectations is consistent with how humans process and store information. Economic information that is maintained in memory is tagged with an emotion and associated with a specific context (Turner, 2000). This helps to ensure that appropriate information is used in different contexts. For example, the price of an identical product may depend on where it is purchased, the price of an identical house on where it is located, or the wage for identical work on where it is performed. Moreover, contextual references enhance our ability to recall information. It is a common occurrence that certain experiences that initially resist recall may be finally remembered by thinking about the context or the associated emotion. More importantly, these contextual referents enable greater specificity in creating associations and nonconsciously distilling information about underlying trends. Since contextual information is a required part of mental processes, why should it be surprising when people initially form expectations that are context dependent?

When people construct their economic expectations, three aspects of the decision context are of special importance. The first is that the context delineates exactly what economic expectation is required to make a specific decision; the second is that the context helps to determine how sensitive the outcome of the decision is to the accuracy of the expectation; and the third is that the context determines the importance of the decision's accuracy. These factors reflect the anticipated benefits as well as the costs people are willing to undertake in order to form the expectation. Economics has typically assumed that national data met the specifications for the required expectation, and without foreknowledge of the actual decision or its importance, fully accurate expectations are assumed to produce the best possible decision. These suppositions were byproducts of the simplifying assumption of a sole representative agent model commonly used in economics combined with the assumption that the costs of forming expectations were near zero.

It is a rare situation in which a person would think that national data on inflation, employment, or income would yield more accurate expectations than information on the prices, employment conditions, or income prospects that they actually face. Moreover, few people would think it optimal to base a specific purchase decision on expectations for prices of all goods. It is common knowledge that the prices for some goods or services rise faster or slower than the overall rate of inflation, or even decline while most prices increase. Even the least sophisticated buyer of electronic goods knows this to be true, and what consumer expects the prices of food or energy to match trends in non-core inflation?

Many purchase or investment decisions require a number of expectations, especially decisions that could have a significant impact on people's future economic welfare. The purchase of a home is a prime example. The decision to purchase a home depends on expectations about future prices and interest rates as well as prospective income and employment trends. What home buyer would use national data on the overall inflation rate, or even the overall rate of appreciation in home values, to estimate the future appreciation of the home they are considering? The most important information to form this expectation is data for specific neighborhoods, not national averages. The same is true for income and job prospects: what lender ignores personal data in favor of national data to determine whether a buyer is credit worthy? National data is sometimes relevant as changes in local mortgage interest rates, for example, are determined by national markets. For the most part, however, the relevant economic expectations are not as easily obtainable as the national headline data provided by federal statistical agencies. Private sources of information are needed, with the information designed to meet specific requirements.

People may purposely hold more negative economic expectations so as to err on the side of caution when making certain decisions. People could deliberately decide to incorporate expectations of a higher probability of job loss or a lower likelihood of income gains when making some decisions but not others. If expectations were elicited in the context of these risk-averse decisions, these economic expectations would be different than if the same expectations were elicited in the context of a risk-neutral decision.

An elicited expectation would naturally reflect the decision context as well as the socioeconomic and demographic characteristics of respondents. It is amazing that someone could expect the same verbal or behavioral response regardless of how an economic expectation was framed, primed, or anchored. Indeed, how decisions are framed, primed, and anchored represents critical characteristics of the decision context. And even more amazing is that they would consider differences to solely represent bias rather than adaptive processes. Needless to say, elicited expectations are unlikely to be free of bias, but the bias cannot be simply estimated as differences from the national figures. Homogeneity of expectations reflects the flawed reasoning spanned by the use of sole representative agent economic models. No person would rationally use an inaccurate measure of the economic conditions rather than information on the conditions that they actually faced. Heterogeneous expectations are the rule not the exception.

Accuracy of Expectations

Economic expectations are estimates of uncertain future outcomes. People's primary objective is to form accurate expectations since correct expectations allow them to maximize the allocation of their mental resources as well as achieve the highest utility from their behavioral choices. Faulty expectations can have serious repercussions. People recognize that all economic expectations are error prone, motivating them to constantly revise their expectations as new information becomes available. Although people would prefer to understand the underlying causal factors, their first-order concern is to correctly anticipate the future state of the economy given the currently available information. Judgments about accuracy are inextricably bound to assessments of costs and benefits. What is a reasonably accurate economic expectation depends on the benefits it confers and well as the costs it exacts.

Conventional economic theories typically assume that the benefits derived from economic expectations are high relative to the formation costs. This is largely due to the assumption that the formation costs are near zero. This assumption is justified since information about national economic conditions is distributed by the mass media at no marginal cost to the public. Moreover, conscious deliberation is assumed to be costless in an economic sense (although still effortful). Even a marginal benefit would be enough for people to form economic expectations, and to repeatedly revise their expectations as the latest federal data is made publically available. These assumptions have not only been applied to a wide range of economic series but to many other aspects of the political economy as well. As a result, people are assumed to hold a full array of economic expectations due to the positive ratio of benefits to costs. Importantly, conventional theories assume that assessments of accuracy are independent from any decisions for which the expectation was used. It matters little whether the expectation is a critical factor in a decision or has only a marginal impact on the decision since expectations are assumed to be formed for any and all potential uses. Overall, these assumptions lead to the inescapable conclusion that the best test of accuracy is a comparison of a person's economic expectations with data on national realizations. This rationale has long dominated empirical tests of the accuracy of economic expectations.

The new theory advanced in this book does not disagree with the final result as much as the underlying rationale. Indeed, the purpose of this book is to offer a more robust explanation of how ordinary people could form economic expectations as accurately as economists. How could consumers correctly anticipate changes in the inflation and unemployment rates as well as a professional forecaster, or as accurately anticipate whether the entire economy was poised to slip into recession or shift toward recovery? It is well documented that the average citizen does not know the latest national economic statistics, understand rudimentary economic theory to interpret the data, have the computational skills to calculate an expectation, or even have an interest in performing these tasks. Ordinary people, however, accomplish these tasks in ways never anticipated by conventional theories. People do not base their expectations on national data, but tailor their expectations to the economic conditions they actually face. Unlike their indifference to national data, people are highly motivated to anticipate changes in economic conditions that directly affect their own welfare. It is only when the economic expectations of each individual are properly aggregated that their expectations closely match the national data. Of course, not every series of interest to economists is monitored by every individual. People's attention is limited by their judgments on whether the economic series plays an important role in their decisions; as benefits approach zero, so does their attention. As long as benefits are positive, formation costs are incurred until they are, at most, equal to the anticipated benefits. Since formation costs are a function of desired accuracy, people effectively reduce the accuracy of their expectations to conform to the prospective benefits. Reasonable accuracy is defined in terms of an acceptable range of expected outcomes, which grows wider as the anticipated benefits shrink. Moreover, judgments on the reasonable accuracy of expectations are decision and context specific, and are based on a current reassessment of all available information. The basic rationale for tailored expectations is that they minimize the formation costs.

The accuracy of expectations at the macro level of analysis has been traditionally divided into two parts: differences in the average levels and differences in how closely expectations actually track actual economic developments over time – the *alpha* and *beta* of the rational expectations hypothesis. As detailed in a prior chapter, significant differences have been observed in the average levels of inflation and unemployment expectations among socioeconomic subgroups. For example, less educated consumers expected higher unemployment on average than college graduates. From the standpoint of conventional theory, these *alpha* differences were interpreted as indicating biased expectation, which happened to offset in the aggregate. Based on the new conceptualization, these expectations simply mirrored the actual conditions faced by people with different levels of education and their expectations reflected this fundamental fact. Nonetheless, the changes over time in inflation and unemployment expectations were virtually identical across education subgroups and were predictive of the actual future developments in the national data. These differences were not surprising based on the new conceptualization that assumes that people form expectations about the economic conditions that they actually face in order to make optimal economic decisions. Lower-skilled workers actually do face much higher unemployment rates than college graduates during both good and bad economic times over their entire lives. As long as these variations in average levels persist over time, these subgroup differences will not have a significant impact on macro-level analysis.

The data published by the US government on unemployment rates by age and education support this contention (see Tables 6.1 and 6.2). The monthly unemployment rate in the twenty-five years ending in December 2016 for those aged between twenty and twenty-four averaged 10.2%, while unemployment among those over age fifty-five averaged 4.1%. Such large persistent differences in the average level of unemployment would be hard to ignore by individuals when forming their expectations. Despite these large and persistent differences in average levels, how the unemployment rate changed over time was nearly identical for all age subgroups. Indeed, the time-series correlations among age subgroups were nearly perfect, ranging from 0.97 to 0.98. The same was true for unemployment rates across educational subgroups. The average unemployment rate in the twenty-five years ending in 2016 for workers with less than a high school degree was 9.3% compared with just 2.8% for college educated workers. As with age, there were significant and persistent differences in the levels of unemployment across the subgroups. The time-series correlations across education subgroups were also quite high, ranging from 0.93 to 0.98, indicating that the unemployment rates in each subgroup followed nearly identical time trends. It is this high correspondence in actual trends that enables

Table 6.1 *Unemployment Rates among Age Subgroups,*
Monthly US Data, 1992–2016

Age	Mean	Correlations among Age Groups			
		20–24	25–34	35–44	45–54
20–24	10.2				
25–34	6.1	0.97			
35–44	4.8	0.97	0.98		
45–54	4.2	0.97	0.98	0.98	
55 or Older	4.1	0.97	0.98	0.97	0.98

Source: Bureau of Labor Statistics.

Table 6.2 *Unemployment Rates among Education Subgroups,*
Monthly US Data, 1993–2016

Education	Mean	Correlations among Education Groups		
		Less High School	High School	Some College
Less High School	9.3			
High School	5.8	0.96		
Some College	4.8	0.95	0.98	
College Degree	2.8	0.93	0.97	0.97

Source: Bureau of Labor Statistics.

people's expectations to predict future changes in the national totals, even if the average level of their expectations are more closely tailored to their own economic situation.

Minimizing the Cost of Accuracy

Accuracy is costly. How do people decide how much mental effort and other resources should be devoted to forming their expectations? People gauge the level of accuracy by how much the expectation will influence the final decision. People aim at achieving the degree of accuracy that balances the formation costs with the decision benefits. Thus, interest rate expectations are more critical when considering a variable rate mortgage than a variable rate credit card loan on a new household appliance. While each expectation may well represent an unbiased and efficient use of the available information, in one case the band of allowable error would be much smaller. People can vary the cost of forming expectations by changing the amount of effort they devote to the task. Conventional theories, however, have always maintained that only conscious deliberation is capable of producing accurate expectations. This implied that any use of nonconscious processes would inevitably involve bias.

Is accuracy better served by the deductive logic of rational deliberation or by the inductive logic of nonconscious empirical associations? Deductive logic is favored by economists since it can help to identify the underlying causal structure rather than simply estimate the correlations among variables. Deductive logic has long been held as a requirement for the advancement of science (Popper, 1935). This strong preference has meant that when scientists conjectured how people form their economic expectations, they proposed causal models. This same predilection for causal models is typically expressed by ordinary people. When asked to explain their expectations, people usually cite some underlying causal factors. It should be no surprise that the conscious rational mind prefers the deductive logic of the scientific method.

Accurate predictions, however, do not require an understanding of the underlying causal model. Milton Friedman long ago recognized that predictive accuracy was more important than the realism of the model's assumptions. Who would deny the expert ability of a pool payer even if he had no inkling of the underlying physics involved? The same is true for economic expectations. The dominating concern for predictive accuracy has led to a growing acceptance among economists of the logic of association to produce more accurate forecasts (Stock & Watson, 1998; 2002; 2007; Sargent & Sims, 1977). This preference was not based on theory, which always favors the deductive logic of causal models. It was based on more practical tests of accuracy. Correlation is not causation, and simple associations may be misleading. But that loss must be judged against the losses due to poorly specified causal models as well as instability in the estimated casual pathways. To be sure, science has not forsaken causal models, but it has admitted that forecasts based on the inductive logic of association can at times be more accurate.

That same acceptance of inductive logic is implicit in the actions of people. Nonconscious learning is based on inductive inferences that are derived from numerous observations. No causal model is needed to interpret or understand the data as the predictions are based on associations, not causal relationships. The mechanisms used are essentially similar to how econometric factor models employ observed relationships to make predictions. Furthermore, just as people may use conscious deliberation to give their intuitions a final review, economists may also review forecasts based on factor models to insure causal plausibility. For the sole purpose of prediction, both inductive and deductive methods are useful. The costs of nonconscious processes compared with conscious deliberation are lower for the individual, however. These cost differentials favor the use of inductive methods, assuming equal levels of accuracy. The problem is that people cannot describe the factors supporting their expectations, just as Reber's (1967) subjects could classify new strings as grammatical or not but were unable to identify the underlying rules of grammar, and participants in "sugar factory" experiments implicitly knew how to maximize profits but could not verbalize the rules. The same occurs when people express economic expectations based on nonconscious information processing as they implicitly know what they expect without being able to describe why they hold those expectations. People can certainly offer rationalizations after the fact, which may or may not correspond to the underlying nonconscious processes. People simply have no conscious knowledge of these processes.

The recognition of the importance of nonconscious processes has a greater impact on theories of bounded rationality rather than the rational expectations hypothesis. Rational expectations are about outcomes; the theory does not specify how those expectations are formed. Theories on bounded rationality are about the process that people use to form expectations. The core of bounded rationality is the limited ability of humans to understand, calculate, and interpret economic data. Bounded rationality is uniquely about the inability of humans to perform conscious cognitive deliberations using causal models. No allowance is made for nonconscious processing and learning.

It could be surmised that expectations would evolve more slowly over time if the change was produced by associative learning rather than by causal models. After all, it should take more time for people to accumulate enough evidence from specific examples to justify an underlying change in expectations. Yet, the turning points in economic expectations have been shown to arise more quickly from consumer surveys than econometric models. Indeed, it is this characteristic that makes consumer expectations a leading economic indicator. Most of the time, associative learning produces slowly changing economic expectations. This is not surprising since most of the time the economy is expanding; recessions are uncommon events. Nonetheless, recessions can have a devastating impact and are justifiably feared. People don't wait for the official announcements of statistical agencies to alert them to threatening economic events on the horizon. People engage in constant monitoring of the ongoing flow of information, and a significant departure from prior expectations immediately signals the need for conscious processing. Automatic evaluations of new information spark an emotional response that commands heightened conscious attention to economic events. The pessimistic mood which develops promotes a heightened and persistent need to acquire more information so that expectations can be promptly revised. This is why large negative shifts in consumer expectations can abruptly occur in advance of econometric models that are based on official data releases.

Importance of Social Interactions

People look toward other people for information about what economic conditions they may face themselves. This is true for two quite important reasons. First, people who face similar economic conditions may have knowledge about potential economic developments that are directly relevant to another person's situation. Other people in comparable situations are good proxies for how people should change their own economic expectations. Moreover, it is more efficient and less costly to rely on a broad range of people to indicate any potential threats on the horizon. Second, even if a person believes that their economic situation is immune to a particular threat faced by others, the fact that others plan to take some defensive action in response, such as spending cutbacks, could directly affect your economic situation. For example, even if a person does not work for the dominant local employer, a plant shutdown will mean many community members will experience some falloff in their own economic prospects. Most of the time, even hints of a future slowdown in employment is enough to cause community-wide apprehensions.

A common greeting when meeting another person is "How are you doing?" While this expresses concern for another person, the question is also motivated by people's concerns for potential changes in their own situation. It is no surprise that some people also get questions based on their occupation or interests. "How's business?" or "How's the economy doing?" and even "Where's the stock market headed?" are common questions asked of people thought to have expertise or interests in these areas. They could simply be a worker in a plant who may have knowledge of future production schedules, a business executive, an avid stock investor, or someone who is known to be always knowledgeable about the economy. Like media reports that favor the subjective meaning rather than the objective economic statistics, these conversations rely heavily on evaluations, with a prominent role given to nonverbal communications by facial and body language. People possess an intuitive mechanism to automatically process information from observing the actions of others. These mirror neurons can easily and quickly comprehend the meaning of the response from gestures and other nonverbal communications even if the verbal response was brief and incomplete. Overall, mirror neurons are a fundamental building block of economic behavior since they enable people to understand the intentions and emotions of others by just observing their actions (Iacoboni et al., 2005; Gallese et al., 2004).

SCIENTIFIC LAMENT

What is unique is the near universal denial of the important role nonconscious cognitive processes play in the formation of expectations. This is natural and anticipated. Since nonconscious processes cannot be consciously known, people cannot attribute with any degree of certainty the factors underlying any expectation that was formed by a nonconscious process. People often cite some rationale that they think is consistent with the expectation, commonly called a "rationalization" because they could not consciously know the truth underlying reasons (Nisbett & Wilson, 1977). The offered rationale, however, may nonetheless be close to the truth since nonconscious processes are learned, and that learning may be reflected in their stated rationales. Importantly, rather than citing some causal factor, people may simply cite "intuitions" or "gut feelings," or even that the expectation represents a "wild guess." Such responses are an implicit recognition that other processes were responsible, processes of which the person had no conscious knowledge. Pure fantasy may dominate some expectations, but this is much less likely for events that affect a person's economic welfare. If they did hold such fantasy expectations, the disastrous decisions that resulted would normally cause an immediate revision.

While social scientists may regret that nonconscious processes are not easily subjected to scientific scrutiny, there is no reason to deny the critical mental functions that are performed nonconsciously. The essential rationale for the exclusions of nonconscious processes is what cannot be measured, cannot be part of any theory; only hypotheses that can be refuted by empirical tests are relevant to the advancement of science. This is a false claim as far as economics is concerned. Economic theories on the formation of expectations posit observable inputs that are transformed by the "black box" of the human mind into observable outputs. For economists, it is the relationship between inputs and outputs that is the theory's core, not the "black box" that transforms one into the other. The rational expectations hypothesis epitomizes the economist's view. The hypothesis ignores the "black box" and simply tests whether the available information was fully and accurately exhausted in the formation of expectations. The rational expectations hypothesis places no restrictions on how information is processed by the "black box." While few if any economists would emphasize the importance of nonconscious processes, the dominant theory is indifferent to how information is processed.

Unfortunately, some of these conjectures about the role of the unconscious or emotions cannot be proven definitively, at least not yet. While scientists are starting to unravel the workings of the nonconscious mind, it will be some time before specific pieces of information can be definitely associated with conscious or nonconscious processes in forming expectations. Insofar as unconscious information processing is learned and mirrors conscious processes, the same empirical tests for the presence of, say, rationality or adaptive processes can be implemented and interpreted in the usual way. In the conventional analysis, the information is simply assumed to be processed consciously. No evidence is provided that this was the case, but the presumption has been so strong that it has never been contested.

The main alternative to this hypothesis defines rationality by how information is processed, not by the rational characteristics of the resulting expectation. Bounded rationality and learning theories are primarily concerned with how the "black box" transforms inputs into outputs. These theories restrict attention primarily to factors that influence conscious deliberation, including the ability to interpret and understand relevant data, perform the required calculations, learn from past errors, and so forth. Importantly, these alternatives are confined to conscious processes. Nonconscious processes, although largely left undefined, are associated with biased expectations. The biases result from the abandonment of conscious rational deliberations in favor of heuristics or intuitive rules of thumb. The explicit exclusion of nonconscious processes would not be a problem if economic expectations mainly resulted from conscious deliberation. If, however, nonconscious processes play a significant role, the implications from these theories are misleading. Indeed, it was the inability of the presumed bounds on cognitive deliberation proxied by education to satisfactorily account for the accuracy of inflation and unemployment expectations that motivated this book's more intense examination of the potential contribution of nonconscious processes.

The new view is that conscious and nonconscious processes work in tandem, and that partnership produces more accurate economic expectations that efficiently use all mental resources. Of all of the processes, perhaps nonconscious information processing is the most widely accepted (although still rare). Everyone can recognize that they have nonconsciously processed some information on which they based some decision. Where one finds widespread disbelief, however, is with the proposition that the nonconscious mind can effectively utilize such information in forming an economic expectation. The calculations and interpretations that are necessary to turn implicit knowledge of a series of economic events into a well formed and accurate expectation have been much harder to accept.

REQUIRED PARADIGM SHIFT

The theory of economic expectations advocated in this book represents a major divergence from conventional theories. The theory is based on a more comprehensive view of how people process information as well as a more inclusive view of the workings of the human mind. Since time immemorial, passion has been viewed as the enemy of reason and nonconscious processes as the opponent of reasoned deliberation. These rigid divisions have impeded as well as distorted our understanding of how economic expectations are formed. Separating the inseparable has a long history of thwarting scientific progress, and conceptual unification has been the engine of scientific advancement. Long ago Galileo and Newton disposed of the rigid distinction between celestial and terrestrial, and Darwin disposed of the distinction between the evolution of the mental and the physical (Tooby & Cosmides, 1992). The barriers erected between the social and natural sciences are still largely intact, although they have become more porous. This book advocates that a full understanding of how expectations are formed requires the unification of cognitive processes, whether the cognitive activity is undertaken consciously or nonconsciously, as well as the unification of cognitive and affective influences on expectations. Rather than an abandonment of rationality and optimization as the core principles of economics, this book argues for a more comprehensive view of how the human brain uses all of its resources to form accurate expectations that enable people to maximize the outcomes from their economic decisions. The paradigm shift that this unification represents will no doubt be met by strong objections. Nonetheless, the mounting empirical evidence that affective and nonconscious processes exert a powerful influence on the formation of expectations can no longer be denied.

The standard justification for the exclusion of affective and nonconscious processes has been the claim that accuracy is the unique outcome of conscious rational deliberation. To be sure, conscious deliberation based on deductive logic is humankind's most prized accomplishment. It is, however, not the only notable achievement that enables humans to accurately and quickly respond to changes in their environment. Indeed, most of the decision-making capacity of the human brain is governed by nonconscious processes, with conscious deliberation playing little if any role. These nonconscious processes prove their merit by providing accurate and prompt behavioral responses for most decisions. If nonconscious processes did not take over most information processing and learning, people's lives would be hamstrung by the constant onslaught of having to use their scarce conscious resources to repeatedly make essentially the same decisions. Moreover, such nonconscious processes do not simply reflect the adoption of habits as they encompass much more than a fixed response to a given stimulus. The cognitive nonconscious is capable of discerning associations and learning about changing relationships so that people can automatically form and revise their expectations. Nonconscious processes are just as dynamic as conscious deliberation. People come to rely upon the automatic adaptation of expectations to changing economic conditions and naturally favor shifting the mental burden of information processing to their virtually costless nonconscious. It would be senseless to presume that evolutionary changes in the functions and capacity of the human brain would be maladaptive.

This does not mean that errors do not frequently occur from nonconscious processes. Misperceptions, new developments, unique or unanticipated events regularly characterize the complex dynamics of the economy. Errors in expectation typically cause people to reassert conscious control, but that is far from automatic. Reasserting conscious control involves a comparison of the objective cost and subjective importance from having a less accurate expectation with the loss from not consciously attending to some other desired outcome. Even a minimum level of constant conscious monitoring for errors in expectations incurs substantial opportunity costs. People are known to rationally accept rather large errors in expectations rather than incur losses in some other areas (Kahneman & Lovallo, 1993). Moreover, since people tailor their expectations to a specific decision context, they judge the accuracy of the expectations from its impact on the final outcome. People cannot be expected to incur the cost of improving the accuracy of an economic expectation if it would not materially affect the outcome. This implies that people's responses must be evaluated in a broader and more unified context to make a robust assessment. Partial analysis will be necessarily incomplete and often misleading.

It is important to note that the ability to nonconsciously process and learn from economic information does not depend in any way on an understanding of how to interpret the information, make sophisticated calculations, or have the knowledge and ability to use a causal framework – the elements that largely define the so-called bounds on rationality. There is no presumption that the nonconscious is knowledgeable about economic theory in any respect. The singular strength of the nonconscious is its ability to distill information, form associations, and decipher patterns. The unconscious uses information on specific observations to form expectations by the bottom-up logic of inductive reasoning. Unlike the top-down approach of deductive reasoning, inductive logic does not require knowledge of a causal model or sophisticated calculations to form economic expectations. The challenge people face is to anticipate as accurately as possible how future economic events may affect their own economic situation. Lacking sophisticated knowledge of economic theory, the ability to interpret data, or make complex calculations, people simply rely on associations to tailored economic expectations to their own situation.

Perhaps the more important underlying reason for the dismissal of nonconscious processes is their reliance on inductive rather than deductive logic. The preference for deductive logic is widespread. Whether scientist or layman, everyone explains their expectations using a causal description of the underlying factors. In contrast, the nonconscious mind bases its learning on associations not causation. Every school child is taught that correlation does not mean causation. It is easy to understand why scholars and laymen believe that expectations based on associations are fraught with error. The superiority of the deductive method, however, depends on whether the causal model is accurate and can be reliably estimated. Unfortunately, while current economic models are the best they have ever been, they still have a relatively poor predictive performance. Not surprisingly, econometric estimates that avoid knowledge of causal structures and simply rely on associations have become widely accepted in the profession. While these factor models are unsatisfactory from a theoretical standpoint, they are nonetheless used to increase the accuracy of the estimates. Without causal structures, however, it is impossible to do simulations that test different economic scenarios or policies, a task that is of importance to both scholars and laymen alike.

There is no inherent opposition between inductive and deductive reasoning. They are different approaches to the same end. Evolution has equipped the human mind with both processes. This was not a mistake. Nor have evolutionary trends favored an increase in deductive reasoning capacity of the conscious mind at the expense of inductive capacity of the nonconscious mind. While the neocortex is a relatively recent addition, it neither replaced nor diminished the nonconscious mental capacities of the limbic system, brain stem, or cerebellum. It has been the seamless unification of the conscious, nonconscious, and emotional brain that constitutes the masterpiece of evolution. Each of these interdependent forms of reasoning serves an adaptive purpose. None can be discarded.

The importance of inductive as well as deductive reasoning for human decision making has been recently mirrored by a significant rebalancing of those two methodologies in scientific research. Like many research advances, it came as the unexpected consequence of the spread of new technologies. The digitization of nearly every facet of human life, covering every economic transaction, social and political behavior, and subjective assessment imaginable has created a virtual cornucopia of readily available data. Moreover, for the first time in human history, detailed real time data is being collected on social networks that can trace the source of information, the extent of influence patterns, contextual factors, and the affective and cognitive content of communications. This new era of "big data" means that these massive collections are so large and so complex that it is difficult, if not impossible, to achieve the full research potential using conventional approaches based on traditional scientific methodologies. The required shift in methodology is epochal. It requires moving from small representative samples, carefully measured variables, and the ability to make robust statistical inferences to a research paradigm dominated by massive convenience samples, an overabundance of error prone measures, and no pretense of being able to discover fundamental causes. It is not that quantity dominates quality. Big data offers the promise of being able to describe what might happen, not why it happens, as it moves the research goal from causation to correlation. This shift is by necessity, not by choice. The avoidance of deductive logic is due to the improbability of hypothesizing the massively complex theories that big data requires, and even if such theories were forthcoming, the use of convenience samples provides no statistical basis to make causal inferences. Inductive reasoning is the only alternative. Moreover, it is a far easier approach as computer programs can readily search the data for correlation and patterns that yield insights into human behavior that had previously escaped detection. While causal knowledge is always preferred, in most cases it is simply the occurrence of some event that is the primary prediction goal. While errors exist in all estimates, causal models in the social sciences have not provided a clear prediction advantage. Despite the odds against acquiring a true understanding, big data nonetheless provides robust estimates of events that no theory has ever contemplated.

The distinction between the methods used by big data and traditional analysis mirrors the same division between conscious and nonconscious information processing. Like big data, nonconscious information processes use correlations and pattern detection among relatively large accumulations of data. In contrast, traditional analysis and conscious processes are more likely to favor causal relationships among much smaller and less complex sets of data. One uses inductive logic and the other deductive reasoning, and one is nearly effortless and the other requires significant time and effort to accomplish. Although each is prone to prediction errors, there is an asymmetry in their evaluations. The lack of a causal structure is typically deemed the more serious scientific error, even when the predictions are less accurate, from the standpoint of traditional methods. The inductive method implicitly acknowledges the tradeoff between errors from incorrectly specified models with errors when predictions are based on association rather than causation. Perhaps science will accept decision theory's compromise that intuitive judgments are subject to conscious review depending on the losses associated with incorrect decisions. Traditional causal analysis combined with big data's fast and frugal approach can mimic the full mental capacities of the human brain. This marriage can be expected to lower the current aversion to nonconscious processes as a legitimate source of information for forming accurate economic expectations. Scientific progress emanates from unexpected bedfellows!

A NEW THEORY OF ECONOMIC EXPECTATIONS

Expectations are an inherent part of human life. Forming expectations is innate. Every human forms a countless number of expectations about a wide variety of events. People start forming expectations soon after birth and continue to form expectations throughout their lifetimes. Expectations are tailored to an individual's need to make a decision in a specific context. This allows people to take immediate and appropriate actions in response to most situations they encounter. All expectations are formed as the outcome of an information processing task that depends on conscious and nonconscious processes, incorporating cognitive as well as affective components. Revisions to expectations are driven by people's desire to maintain a reasonable degree of accuracy, otherwise expectations would be useless as a guide for their behavior. People use the same mental resources and procedures to process information to form all types of expectations pertaining to all aspects of their lives. There is nothing special about how people form economic expectations.

The revised theory includes ten essential factors that guide the formation of economic expectations. First, the primary function of expectations is to improve the efficiency of the human brain as an information processing engine. All of life's decisions depend on the acquisition and interpretation of information. Since the capacity for rational deliberation is limited, every decision cannot be consciously decided. The larger the share of information processing that can be made effortless and automatic, the greater the potential payoff from the more robust but limited ability for rational deliberation. Expectations enable people to make efficient use of their most constrained and valuable resource: the capacity to make conscious deliberative decisions.

Second, forming economic expectations is a natural and automatic process that utilizes all the mental resources of the human mind. It is generally impossible to parse the relative influence of conscious and nonconscious processes in the formation of economic expectations. The interplay of the various processes is especially true when forming expectations for complex economic events. Such expectations are rarely formed by an uninterrupted stream of conscious awareness, interpretation, and calculation. Nonconscious processes and affective states inevitably play a role. Conventional theories that solely focus on the conscious cognitive aspects of the formation process provide an incomplete and misleading assessment of the formation process.

Third, all mental resources, whether conscious or nonconscious, cognitive or affective, are capable of forming accurate expectations. This fact is essential to our evolutionary development. If nonconscious and affective processes were completely dysfunctional, human advancement would be impossible. To be sure, biased expectations can be produced by the nonconscious or the conscious mind as well as by cognitive or affective influences. Inaccurate expectations, no matter their pedigree, are automatically subject to revision because they represent an inefficient use of their mental capacity and are no longer useful guides to make decisions.

Fourth, the resources devoted to forming expectations aim to balance costs with benefits. Other than the costs of acquiring the necessary information, the main mental costs are defined by the decisions that were not consciously considered because of the limits on rational deliberation. Since these limits are severe compared with the relatively unlimited nonconscious resources, people have an abiding preference to process information nonconsciously. Even if the accuracy of nonconsciously formed economic expectations is lower than if they were formed consciously, the diminished decision benefits would need to exceed the opportunity costs of using more of their conscious attention. The many trivial economic expectations – trivial in the sense of their impact on people's economic decisions – have near zero decision benefits and as a consequence, people would expend nearly no resources and tolerate large errors.

Fifth, expectations are formed to make specific decisions in a given context. It is the decision context that determines how the acquired information is interpreted in the construction of an expectation for that specific use. The importance of the decision context means that the most critical information is the economic circumstances faced by the individual. Context dependent expectations are not a source of bias but simply represent expectations that are tailored to an individual's specific needs, including their assessments of costs and benefits of a more or less accurate expectation.

Sixth, the accuracy of expectations is paramount. Judgments about accuracy are derived from their impact on the decisions for which they were formed. Assessments of accuracy are decision specific; they are tailored to the same context and circumstances for which the expectation was formed. The accuracy of an expectation is not measured by its departure from national data but by its impact on the decision for which the expectation was formed. Greater decision benefits justify greater formation costs, and this cost–benefit approach is a critical part of the rationale for tailoring expectations to specific decisions.

Seventh, the formation of expectations critically depends on affective as well as cognitive factors. Emotions define people's goals and motivate them to constantly monitor certain economic events while ignoring others. These emotional forces prompt people to cognitively process information, consciously and nonconsciously, that is relevant and important to their economic situation. The most ardent rationalist, the *homo economicus* of economic theory, depends on strong and unwavering motivations – an ideal that is impossible if it were limited to conscious rational deliberation. Nonconscious acquisition of information and nonconscious learning are also required to accomplish this important task.

Eighth, persistent affective states influence whether information about macroeconomic prospects is processed consciously or nonconsciously. Persistence can be defined in terms of macroeconomic cycles of decline and recovery and corresponds to the mood of the consumer. When economic pessimism prevails, economic information is more likely to be processed consciously; when economic optimism prevails, new economic developments are more likely to be processed nonconsciously. People cannot intentionally choose their mood; it represents a compilation of economic events integrated by their evaluative outcomes, whether it is their mood toward the inflation or unemployment rate or the growth rate of the entire economy. Mood creates momentum and resilience. Momentum promotes the cumulative changes that define economic cycles and resilience enhances people's ability to ignore events counter to the prevailing trend.

Ninth, affect acts as the nonconscious mind's unit of account that allows people to judge comparative values, performing the same functions as monetary units for the conscious mind. Affect provides the common denominator that allows the formation of associations among diverse bits of economic information and facilitates learning based on inductive methods. While the conscious mind prefers the causal explanations supported by the logic of deductive theories, everyone satisfices at times with the insights based on inductive methods. As always, satisficing, rather than optimizing, is a decision based on comparative costs and benefits and is context dependent.

Tenth, economic expectations are inherently social. They represent economic outcomes determined in large part by the interactions of very many people. Observing the economic expectations of other people is therefore an important source of information about potential trends. Evolution has given the human brain the unique ability to understand the situation of another person by merely observing the emotions expressed by facial and other body movements. As a result, changes in expectations can be promulgated much faster across a population than if they depended on each person gaining an explicit personal knowledge of the detailed circumstances. Unfortunately, this response is asymmetric. It is much more likely to spark a sudden collapse in confidence than a surge in optimism.

Overall, this revised theory of the formation of economic expectations is more compatible with the orthodox theory of rational expectations rather than the biases and heuristics approach of bounded rationality. The primary strength of the revised theory lies in its specification of how the human mind utilizes all its faculties to form accurate economic expectations. It is the defining criteria of accuracy that the revised theory shares with rational expectations as well as marks its distinctiveness from the biases and heuristics approach. In the revised theory, expectations are tailored to specific decisions, and it is this context sensitivity that enables people to align formation costs with benefits. The clear advantage of the new theory is that it provides a comprehensive account of how, when, and why people form economic expectations that can be subjected to rigorous empirical testing.

Section I of this book began with empirical evidence that time-series data on consumers' inflation and unemployment expectations were reasonably accurate forecasts of subsequent realizations and recognized that this achievement did not solely depend on their conscious cognitive abilities for rational deliberation. The section ended with an explanation of how consumers have accomplished this feat by their automatic use of the total capacity of the mind to form expectations that were best suited to their individual needs. The next section examines how the economic expectations of consumers have an influential and independent impact on the performance of the macroeconomy.

PART II

THE CONSUMER AND
THE MACROECONOMY

There is no greater divide between economic theory and consumer perceptions than on the topic of recessions. Recurrent economic cycles have been the dominant characteristic of the macroeconomy throughout recorded history. Nonetheless, economists have found it difficult to advance a theory of macroeconomic cycles that fits within the traditional rational equilibrium framework. Instead, economics has mostly relied on exogenous forces, autonomous shifts, or animal spirits to explain the occurrence of macroeconomic cycles. No conventional economic model is capable of producing a recession without the influence of some misstep in policy or some external force. Although economists have repeatedly claimed victory over the forces of recessionary downturns, the next recession has always proved those claims premature. At best, economics has followed a version of Leo Tolstoy's observation that while happy economies are all alike, every unhappy economy is unhappy in its own way. Each recession is the result of some special circumstance. Rather than prompting a comprehensive and inclusive theory, the equilibrium theories of economics hold that there is no rational basis for recessions.

Consumers view recessions quite differently. Recessions are viewed as the primary existential threat to their economic wellbeing. Nothing is of greater concern to people than the potential loss of their job and livelihood. Economic downturns have a profound impact on people's economic situation even if their job remains secure. Recessions are associated with declines in work hours and incomes, more limited opportunities for job changes and promotions, and decreases in the value of assets such as homes and stocks. Even in the unlikely event that all of these losses are quickly reversed in the following expansion, no recovery can reverse the anguish and uncertainty that accompany every economic downturn, let alone erase the real economic hardships suffered. No consumer can forget the danger that recessions pose, even if the most devastating of past recessions exist only in family folklore. Given the frequency of recessions in the past, every rational consumer would expect at least a few recessions to occur sometime in their lifetime.

Forecasting the occurrence of the next recessions is no easy task for economists, let alone for consumers. Econometric models must await sufficiently large changes in the underlying causal factors before a robust recession prediction is even possible. In contrast, the recession warning systems of consumers do not exclusively depend on last month's data published by a federal statistical agency. The human mind is adept at using its full mental faculties to decipher clues of potential danger and to motivate behavior that reduces the resulting threats. Like our forefathers long ago in the African savanna, consumers believe such existential dangers require constant monitoring. Moreover, emotion is a critical source of information in ambiguous situations in which rational calculations are impossible. This is what Keynes identified as the "urge to action" that was sparked by "animal spirits," his term for other non-rational mental faculties. Unfortunately, economic theory labeled these actions irrational because a rational judgment was impossible, as though inaction was always preferable in these situations. Although conventional economic models break down in the presence of ambiguity (non-quantifiable risk), consumers can still process the necessary information to form expectations about potential turning points in the economy. This is the crucial advantage of human information processing over econometric models. This advantage has enabled measures of consumer sentiment to act as a leading economic indicator of macroeconomic cycles across a diverse array of economies and cultures around the world.

It is only natural to assume that a steep recessionary downturn or a vigorous expansion would be impossible without the participation of consumers. After all, the consumer accounts for the vast majority of spending in the US economy. Indeed, most observers would not hesitate in naming the consumer as the most powerful force in the US economy; some would even go as far as to suggest that the American consumer has been the most powerful force in the global economy (who may soon be replaced by the Chinese consumer in the twenty-first century). Whenever the US economy begins to wobble, attention is focused on how to buttress consumer demand. A core element of the government's counter-cyclical policies is aimed at stimulating consumer demand. These policy imperatives were as common during the Great Recession as during the Great Depression.

Most observers would be surprised to learn that conventional economic theory precludes the possibility of a consumer-led recession. Economic theory holds that consumption is endogenous, meaning that the decisions of consumers are based solely on changes in other economic variables like incomes, prices, and interest rates. While the proximate cause of a downturn may be related to the behavior of consumers, the ultimate causes are changes in the economic determinants of consumer behavior. The same rationale underpinned stimulus spending: the ultimate cause of the added spending was the government's program. Thus, neither recessions nor expansions can originate in the consumer sector since their actions are ultimately caused by other economic events. Consumers are assumed to be a passive actor in the macroeconomy since they simply translate changes in economic factors such as incomes, prices, and interest rates into changes in their spending and saving behavior. The business sector and government economic policies, in contrast, are recognized by conventional theory as independent forces that can shape macroeconomic trends.

The rationale for believing consumers play a passive role in the macroeconomy is longstanding. It was initially sparked by conditions in the agrarian economy, which dominated at the time when the first economic theorists planted the roots of the modern discipline. Economic growth and rising living standards had no place in the theories of Adam Smith and David Ricardo. Barely sufficient life-sustaining provisions meant that consumers automatically consumed all their scarce resources simply to survive. All of that changed following the Industrial Revolution. Advances in industrial production technologies meant rising incomes and living standards, allowing substantial numbers of consumers to move well beyond mere subsistence. Investments in new technology required capital, and prompted the shift of the dominating paradigm from an agrarian to a capitalist economy.

What did not change, however, was the notion that consumers were passive actors in the macroeconomy. While Keynes shifted the focus to demand management, it was the demand of the entrepreneur that needed special consideration, not consumer demand, despite the fact that consumers invested amounts equal to firms in their own versions of "plant and equipment" needed to produce their living standard. It is still true that the investments made by firms to enhance the productivity of labor are prized, while the investments made by consumers to enhance their own productivity are largely disregarded. Investments in vehicles and household durables, for example, allow consumers to become more productive in increasing their living standards and to increase the amount of time devoted to employment outside the home.

The narrow conventional view of the role of the consumer sector in shaping the macroeconomy is challenged in Chapter 7. Moreover, the passive view of the consumer sector has been increasingly challenged by a wide range of observers following the Great Recession. Despite the record levels of stimulus spending, the US consumer did not promptly translate higher incomes and lower interest rates into increased consumer spending and a resurgence in indebtedness. Even if the aggressive spending by independent consumers in the prior several decades was not convincing, the insufficient consumer demand that plagued the economy in the years following the Great Recession clearly demonstrated that the consumer sector was anything but passive.

Measures of consumer sentiment were designed with the recognition that consumers were an independent force shaping trends in the economy, and that consumers used all of their mental faculties to monitor changing economic conditions. The worldwide measures of consumer sentiment are examined in detail in Chapter 8. Consumer sentiment measures now cover the vast majority of all inhabitants in the world and an even larger share of worldwide GDP. While there are some variations in the type and wording of the component questions, the consistency across countries is substantial. Perhaps the single most important common element across all surveys is that each aims to capture more than just a rational evaluation of some economic condition. All questions are framed in a way that prompts evaluative responses rather than solely focusing on objective economic assessments. The questions are designed to directly tap the full conscious and nonconscious resources of the human mind. Respondents do not find the questions burdensome or difficult to answer. In contrast, professional economists, who happen to be included in the survey, find the questions challenging, and typically provide long and qualified answers. Moreover, in their professional judgment, no ordinary consumer could provide accurate answers, and most consumers are incapable of providing detailed responses in the probabilistic terms preferred by economists. Nonetheless, the survey data have repeatedly confirmed the accuracy of consumers' economic expectations. Moreover, the scales used in the worldwide surveys and how the responses are combined into an index based on a simple and transparent technique have been found to be robust when compared with other statistical techniques for index construction. These innovations in question design and index construction were due to George Katona, who established the field of behavioral economics in the 1940s.

The initial measures of consumer expectations engendered a debate in the 1950s about the appropriate methodology of science. James Tobin and George Katona, who enjoyed a lasting friendship, held opposite views on this topic. Tobin's view was that statistical proof of the merit of survey measures had to be confirmed at the micro as well as the macro level; a view that is still widely held in the profession. George Katona held that while expectations were measured at the micro level, the measurement intent was to form estimates of expectations that had predictive power only at the macro level. Katona was solely interested in those expectations that changed among masses of people at the same time and in the same direction and thus could influence the course of the macroeconomy. This eliminated a vast array of factors that determined micro spending decisions would ultimately disappear at the macro level: at any given time, consumers who would judge the factor positively would be offset by others who would judge it negatively. These divergent views reflect differences in how the micro foundations were conceptualized. For Tobin, the macro was simply an aggregation of micro units; for Katona, there was no straightforward relationship between micro and macro developments.

Compared with the economic situation of most households in the middle of the last century, today's consumers face a more diverse and demanding set of economic challenges. More households own a broader array of financial and non-financial assets as well as various forms of credit. They are faced with the constant task of developing new employable skills to match changing technology as well as being increasingly responsible for building and growing their own retirement investments. The globalization of markets, moreover, has made consumers more vulnerable to international economic events. Economics, for its part, has integrated various economic expectations into more complex economic models, demanding greater precision; the ideal expectation measure would specify the complete probability distribution for a precisely defined future economic event. Moreover, the ideal economic measure would eliminate the influence of emotion, focusing entirely on conscious rational calculations of model-consistent expectations.

There is no universally correct method to measure expectations. Expectations must be measured for a specific purpose. In the context of time-series models for the study of macroeconomic cycles, probability measures of consumer expectations did not perform any better, and in some cases much worse, than expectations measured using the conventional verbal likelihood scale. For example, whether responses were based on a three-point evaluative scale or a 100-point probability scale, the time-series changes in expectations were identical. This may simply reflect the well-known French proverb "plus ça change, plus c'est la même chose" commonly translated as "the more things change, the more they stay the same." Did consumers bend their probability estimates to their evaluation, or did they bend their evaluations to match their probability estimates? The most likely answer is that they adapted their responses to both questions based on the same information. The key issue then becomes which response scale more efficiently captures the available information with the least measurement error.

The questions now included in the University of Michigan's consumer surveys have expanded to include a wide array of additional questions and response scales. The additional questions were added to more fully cover the economic decisions faced by growing numbers of consumers. The type of response scale was chosen to match both how consumers naturally thought about the underlying issues as well as the growing demands of economic models for specific measures and scales.

There is substantial interest in whether the broader array of questions shows distinctive trends based on the demographic and economic characteristics of the individual or household. Conventional economic models suggest that there should be no differences assuming that each person rationally forms their expectations based on national data. The bounded rationality hypothesis anticipated differences across population subgroups based on cognitive, interpretive, and computational skills. In this case, differences could be reasonably expected to be related to education as well as economic experience. The tailored expectations hypothesis holds that insofar as differences exist in the economic conditions faced by individuals, their expectations would also differ. Finally, social factors have been emphasized by those who contend that consumers simply adopt the expectations of experts, with lesser, but nonetheless some, variations since expectations formed in this manner would require at least some attention to economic news.

Since macroeconomic analysis is concerned with change over time, the primary standard would be whether the time trends among two socioeconomic subgroups were identical or divergent. If the trends over time were identical, or nearly so, the trend information would be indistinguishable across subgroups. If, on the other hand, the trends in the expectations of the two subgroups were completely different, or nearly so, one or the other group's data may be a significant predictor of some macro event, but not the data from both subgroups. Many economists favor the divergent hypothesis; they believe some socioeconomic subgroups, say those with little education, would only add noise or random error to the measured expectation.

Whether the correlation is near unity or close to zero between two subgroups, the correlation has no bearing on differences in the mean level of the economic expectation. Some people may well be on average more optimistic or more pessimistic about some economic outcome, but nonetheless, how one group's optimism or pessimism changes over time could be fully synchronized with another group. As detailed in Chapter 9, the primary finding was that there was widespread agreement in the time trends in the various measures of economic expectations from 1978 to 2016 across education, age, income, marital status, and gender subgroups. At the same time, there were significant differences in the mean levels of these measures of economic expectations across all of the socioeconomic subgroups.

The data indicate that there was a broad agreement among socioeconomic subgroups about the expected direction and extent of change across a wide range of economic expectations. The distinctive experiences of the socio-economic subgroups were indicated by the significant differences in the group's mean level of various economic expectations. These differences reflect the formation of expectations that were tailored to the economic conditions each socioeconomic subgroup faced, while at the same time, time-series changes in expectations, regardless of their levels, were highly synchronized reflecting trends in the macroeconomy. The theory of tailored expectations, in contrast to orthodox theories, is able to explain differences across individuals as meaningful not irrational, and the consistency over time across socioeconomic groups is explained by the use of their full mental capacity not appeals to heuristics.

The final chapter in this section summarizes the need for a new and more comprehensive paradigm governing the formation of expectations and the independent role consumers play in determining the course of the macroeconomy. The inadequacies of orthodox theories are documented as well as the superiority of the new theories. The most basic elements of orthodox economic theories are largely preserved, although the new paradigm offers a more compelling rationale for accuracy as the defining goal of the formation process. The new paradigm provides a unique accounting of why, how, and when economic expectations are formed that sharply differs from the existing paradigm. In addition, the new paradigm holds that the consumer is a powerful actor in the macroeconomy rather than a passive re-actor, self-fulfilling expectations are a common occurrence, consumers are adept at making decisions in the presence of ambiguous information, and that consumer demand, rather than business investment, represents the more fundamental driving force behind economic growth.

7

Expectations of Macroeconomic Cycles

The defining feature of the macroeconomy is its cyclical nature. This has been true from the dawn of civilization. The pharaohs of ancient Egypt first acknowledged the recurrence of cycles of abundance and famine thousands of years ago (Sedlacek, 2011). Variations in weather drove cyclical changes in agricultural economies until the start of the Industrial Revolution about 200 years ago. Although the influence of weather on agriculture has not changed, the influence of agriculture on the macroeconomy receded as the pace of the Industrial Revolution accelerated. Despite the many fundamental changes in the structure of the modern economy, cyclical downturns in production, income, and employment remain the unconquered nemesis of economic advancement.

Eliminating recessions, or at least diminishing their impact, has long been an avowed goal of economic policy. Over the past 150 years, the US economy has sunk into thirty-three recessions, accounting for nearly one-third of the entire period. Some progress has been made as there were twenty-one recessions in the first half of the last 150 years and just twelve recession in the last seventy-five years. Moreover, in the last quarter century, the US economy has fallen victim to just three recessions. It is easy to understand that following exceptionally long periods without an economic downturn, economists declared at least partial victory. This has happened twice, following the two longest expansions in the past 150 years. The first record expansion occurred in the 1960s, which lasted nearly nine years, and the second occurred in the 1990s, which lasted ten years. In comparison, the length of all other expansions averaged just under three years. Each declaration of victory, however, was quickly retracted. Following the 1960s record expansion, the economy slipped into recession four times in the next dozen years. And following the 1990s expansion, the economy has so far fallen into two recessions. Despite these setbacks, Robert Lucas, in his 2003 presidential address to the American Economic Association, declared that the "central problem of depression-prevention has been solved, for all practical purposes, and has in fact been solved for many decades." A few short years later, the US economy plunged into the Great Recession, earning that moniker to indicate that its unusual severity was only comparable to the Great Depression of the 1930s.

The problem of cyclical instability has proved to be just as resistant to economic policies in the twentieth and twenty-first centuries as it has since the dawn of civilization. Indeed, there is still no consensus among economists that recessions are unavoidable nor undesirable. Everyone recognizes that recessions can have a devastating impact on the welfare of consumers; that is not at issue. Some believe, however, that recessions are necessary to purge the economy of imbalances and inefficiencies that would otherwise limit more robust economic growth in the future. More believe that recessions can be mitigated by appropriate economic policies without damage to future prospects for economic growth. These differences have deep roots in their underlying economic theories about rationality, with adherents being colorfully categorized as either freshwater or saltwater economists. Unfortunately, neither camp views consumers as having an independent role in shaping the course of the macroeconomy. Unlike the active role of businesses and governments in shaping the course of the macroeconomy, conventional economic theory assumes the consumer is a passive bystander.

Could it be true that the onset of each recession takes consumers by surprise, leaving them completely unprepared for the economic consequences? That would be the height of irrationality on the part of consumers. There is no reason to presume that rational consumers would not assume that a series of recessions would likely occur during their lifetime. Moreover, consumers would need to determine not only the likelihood of occurrence, but the probable duration and the extent of the impact on their own finances. To assume otherwise would mean that people held irrational economic beliefs.

Economic theory provides little guidance for consumers or economists in anticipating the start of a recession. Most econometric models rarely, if ever, produce a forecast that contains an economic downturn starting in say two or more years after the date of the forecast. Indeed, most long-term econometric forecasts have the economy growing at trend levels. Most economic downturns are identified in econometric models only after they have already begun (but well before the National Bureau of Economic Research [NBER] announces the official start data about a year after the recession actually began). Of course, in retrospect, empirical models have identified when recessions started and when recoveries began, but there has never been a consensus forecast that a recession would start sometime in the next year or so, and certainly no recessions are included in long-range forecasts.

While conventional economic theory has not directly dealt with expectations for economy-wide recessions, it has emphasized the import-ance of expectations about the various components of economic cycles. Clearly not all recessions are exactly similar, neither in their economic con-tent, nor in their duration or depth. Nonetheless, all of the major actors in the macroeconomy – consumers, business, and the government – look toward conditions in the overall economy for early warning signs of a potential downturn. Those early warning signs may be found in rising infla-tion, interest rates, or unemployment rates, or in falling values of homes or equities, or in weaknesses in economic sectors or even in non-economic events that may potentially influence the course of the national economy.

Hard-to-predict events as consequential as recessions require constant monitoring of the economic environment for any signs of an incipient cyc-lical downturn. Economic agents have been found to constantly update their expectations when hearing news of unusual economic events (Nimark, 2014). No economist finds it surprising that a sizable industry has emerged to closely monitor the economy for any signs of unusual episodes of poten-tial weakness. Wall Street and financial market traders have supported a vast network of firms and consultants who constantly update the forecast implications from the latest economic events. While many users of these forecasts do not fully understand the sophisticated models and complex statistical procedures behind the estimates, it is the credibility of the pro-vider and media outlets that commands attention to the resulting forecasts. These monitoring efforts are believed to be best left to experts. Ordinary consumers are assumed to be unwilling to exert the time and effort required to gain the necessary knowledge to predict when future economy-wide downturns would start or when the economic recovery would begin. After all, how could ordinary consumers do what formal econometric models were often unable to accomplish?

The main purpose of this chapter is to explore how the revised view of how people form their economic expectations provides a new foundation for understanding economic cycles. What traditional economic theory has failed to recognize is that reactions to these cyclical economic threats are as much rational as emotional. Indeed, it is the emotional reaction that has been shown to be critical in motivating consumers, firms, and governments to take actions to mitigate potential losses. Moreover, since recessions are as much a social as an economic phenomenon, people naturally monitor and are influenced by how other people evaluate these potential threats. This new foundation indicates that consumers actively monitor the economy based on information that is known to consumers but not yet reflected in the public releases of economic data by governmental agencies. This basic fact has prompted the measurement and use of consumer sentiment as a leading economic indicator in all inhabited continents in the world.

The chapter begins with a discussion of the reasons behind the emergence of the passive consumer in conventional economic theory. Early developments in the theory of the consumer by Adam Smith and David Ricardo focused on the fact that subsistence required nearly all consumers to spend their entire income to simply survive. Indeed, before the Industrial Revolution, sustained economic growth and rising consumer incomes were not even considered a theoretical possibility (Lucas, 2002). Subsistence was the pressing objective of consumers and the clear goal of a successful economic system. It was the increased productivity due to the Industrial Revolution that made it possible for people to achieve a better economic life than their parents and to expect their children to have an even higher standard of living.

It took a long time for income to rise from the amount that was adequate for subsistence to an amount that ordinary people could make discretionary purchases. By the time of Keynes, discretionary consumer investments in homes, vehicles, and household durables slightly exceeded the level of investments in plant and equipment by businesses. Since the share of the economy accounted for by consumer investments has not changed since the 1930s, it is somewhat surprising that Keynes did not include a more active role for the consumer sector in determining the course of the aggregate economy. This is especially troubling since investments by consumers and firms share many of the same characteristics: these investments represent large discretionary purchases that are typically financed by debt and represent a critical claim on future incomes for both consumers and firms. Even small differences in the pace of consumer investments can have a powerful impact on cyclical swings in the economy. Nonetheless, the type of demand management advocated by Keynes was distinctly different for consumers.

Keynes thought that entrepreneurs alone had the psychological capacity to act when reason and evidence were insufficient to justify investment decisions (Dow, 2013). This "urge to action" was what Keynes meant by animal spirits, which combined reason and emotion as complementary rather than antagonistic. When it came to understanding the actions of consumers, however, Keynes thought that current income was the main determinant of consumption – what he called the "fundamental psychological law."[1] Of course, the "fundamental psychological law" was quickly proved incorrect, but the notion has persisted that current income is the sole determinant of consumption and therefore consumers could not play an independent role in shaping the macroeconomy. Even the later theoretical revisions that placed permanent or lifetime income as the centerpiece of consumption theory came to be viewed as based on the past history of income trends. Consumer expectations of future income were simply viewed as the outputs of the economic system; they were not viewed as independent inputs that could shape future decisions and the course of the macroeconomy.

When animal spirits are referenced with regard to consumer behavior, it is not the blend of reason and emotion that is recognized as necessary to motivate action in uncertain times. Rather, it is meant to indicate irrational and suboptimal behavior. It is when risks are immeasurable that emotion is essential to motivate behavior. Too often economic theory is implemented by substituting measurable and probabilistic risks for ambiguity that cannot be quantified. There is no area in which this is truer than in how changes in confidence influence the macroeconomy. Some have estimated that nearly three-quarters of the variations in economic cycles are due to changes in confidence (Ilut & Schneider, 2014).

It is worth emphasizing that the overall objective is to challenge some basic elements of the orthodox economic theory as well as how that theory has been conceptualized in empirical research. The goal is to free the micro foundations of macroeconomic theory from the constraints imposed by these conventional implementations. The new theory of how expectations are formed infuses macroeconomic theory with a more robust and more realistic micro foundation. A critical departure is to assume that, along with business and the government, consumers take an active part in determining the course of the macroeconomy. Each of these actors is assumed to have an autonomous role in shaping economic outcomes (Frydman & Phelps, 2013). Assuming that the consumer sector plays no independent role in determining the course of the macroeconomy may have been appropriate

---

[1] Keynes (1936) said "The fundamental psychological law, upon which we are entitled to depend with great confidence both a priori from our knowledge of human nature and from the detailed facts of experience, is that men are disposed, as a rule and on the average, to increase their consumption as their income increases but not by as much as the increase in the income."

before the Industrial Revolution, but in the modern economy it is no longer possible to ignore the power of the consumer.

CONSUMERS SHIFT FROM SUBSISTENCE TO DISCRETION

For most of human history, people expected their economic lot in life to be the same as their parents. For more than 500 years prior to the Industrial Revolution, real wages in England varied within a narrow range, showing no long-term trend (Phelps, 2013). Thomas Malthus in 1798 postulated that the limited growth potential of the economy would act to contain population growth, keeping the income of the population close to subsistence levels. Around the same time, the economic theories proposed by Adam Smith and David Ricardo did not even admit to the theoretical possibility of sustained economic growth and rising living standards (Lucas, 2002). It was the Industrial Revolution that permanently changed life's prospects. The new industrial methods increased the productivity of labor, which enabled rising living standards. For the first time in human history, people aspired to a better economic life than their parents and hoped that their children would enjoy an even higher standard of living than they achieved. It took a long time for income to rise above the level that was necessary to merely sustain life to a level whereby ordinary people could make discretionary expenditures on investments in "plant and equipment" to increase their living standards.

By the start of the twentieth century, there were substantial numbers of people whose economic choices were much like today's consumers. Indeed, in the 1920s, consumers used debt to finance purchases of cars as well as homes, and had charge accounts at department stores and shops. While a broader array of financial products are now available to consumers, the ability of consumers to smooth consumption by the use of debt has been available for a century or more. More importantly, consumers have varied their pace of discretionary purchases and their use of debt as a means to adjust their budgets to expected changes in their incomes.

The Industrial Revolution was accompanied by pronounced cyclical swings in the economy. There were nineteen recession-recovery cycles from 1854 to 1928, with the downturns lasting nearly as long as the upturns (20.5 versus 25.5 months on average).[2] It should not be surprising that the theories

---

[2] The National Bureau of Economic Research determines cyclical dating. A recession is defined by a significant decline in economic activity spread across the economy, lasting more than a few months, normally visible in real GDP, real income, employment, industrial production, and wholesale-retail sales.

that emerged following the Industrial Revolution put primary emphasis on changes in the productive capacity of the economy. While overall productivity depends on labor, capital, and technology, only changes in technology and capital were thought to play the most decisive roles in generating economic growth. Moreover, classical theories thought that flexible prices and wages would automatically adjust and eventually correct any cyclical divergences in the economy. These initial theories established consumers as passive actors, who would automatically adjust their economic decisions to the wages and the prices they faced in the marketplace.

Reacting to the failure of classical theory to explain the Great Depression, Keynes shifted the main emphasis from the factors that shaped the productive capacity of an economy to the factors that shaped demand.[3] Keynes believed that the wants of consumers were greater than the ability of the economy to satisfy those needs, and were consistent with the passive view of consumers from subsistence theories of consumption. Keynes coined the phrase "supply creates its own demand" (now known as Say's Law), as a means to criticize Jean-Baptiste Say's overriding importance of the supply side in economic theories. While Keynes emphasized demand, he did not include a more active and independent role for the consumer. Indeed, his "fundamental psychological law" held that current income determined consumption (Keynes, 1936). Keynes advanced the notion that aggregate demand was dependent on the expectations of producers, but not on the expectations of consumers. Consumers, Keynes argued, were not forward looking; their demand depended on current incomes, prices, and interest rates which could be managed by government policies. New business investments, in contrast, were quite dependent on the expected future rate of return. This dependence on expected rates of return was a critical factor in Keynes' revised theory. The notion of animal spirits indicated how investment decisions are made in the face of Knightian uncertainty, or non-quantifiable risk (as opposed to making decisions among choices whose risks are quantifiable). Although Keynes primarily discussed his notion of "animal spirits" in relation to business investment decisions, economists are now much more likely to use the term to associate the decisions of consumers with irrationality. Keynesian theory still plays a crucial role

---

[3] Milton Friedman challenged the Keynesian view of the Great Depression, claiming that monetary policy could have prevented the Great Depression by providing more liquidity and preventing the sharp fall in the money supply. Ben Bernanke, Governor and then Chairman of the Federal Reserve, famously apologized to Milton Friedman on his ninetieth birthday in 2002: "You're right, we [the Federal Reserve] did it. We're very sorry. But thanks to you, we won't do it again."

in promoting expanded fiscal stimulus during a recession to bolster consumers' current incomes and hence their spending.

The "fundamental psychological law," however, fell into disrepute because it failed as a description of long-term economic trends (Curtin, 2004). The Keynesian prediction that the average propensity to consume (the ratio of consumption to income) would fall as income rose was based on the observation that the average propensity to consume was lower at higher income levels. It was this absolute income interpretation of Keynes that led to the prediction that shortfalls in consumer demand would precipitate another depression following World War II. In truth, the ratio of consumption to income has shown no such tendency to decline over time, and it was the constancy of this ratio that became the centerpiece of the permanent income hypothesis. More importantly, the dominating role of current income was displaced in favor of expected future incomes.

Friedman's permanent income hypothesis (Friedman, 1957) and Modigliani's life-cycle theory (Modigliani & Brumberg, 1954) emphasized the role of expectations in determining consumers' current spending and saving decisions. The driving force of both theories by these Nobel Prize-winning economists was the assumption that rational consumers would attempt to maximize utility by allocating their lifetime stream of income into an optimal pattern of lifetime consumption. Although numerous empirical studies of the life-cycle permanent income hypothesis, both at the macro and micro level, have rejected the general premise that consumption is equal to the annuity value of lifetime resources (or permanent income), this theory still remains a centerpiece of conventional theory.[4] The assumption that has not been subjected to much criticism was that consumers' expectations of lifetime income could be proxied by rational expectations. Moreover, such rational expectations of lifetime incomes were best estimated from the past history of incomes and other economic variables, as was done by Milton Friedman (1957). Thus, income expectations were assumed to be

---

[4] This finding prompted greater attention to potential sources of mis-specification, such as the failure to account for liquidity constraints (an inability to borrow against future income), the presence of myopic or rule-of-thumb consumers (who based their consumption decisions on current income rather than permanent income), non-stationary income processes, and other potential mis-specifications (Curtin, 2004). Some of these factors were found to be quantitatively large, for example Campbell and Mankiw (1989) estimate that about half of all disposable income accrues to rule-of-thumb consumers, with consumption mainly responding to innovations in current income. Based on PSID data, Zeldes (1989) finds the same split between liquidity-constrained and -unconstrained consumers, with the behavior of the latter approximating what would be expected based on the life-cycle permanent income hypothesis.

endogenous. This had the effect of keeping the consumer sector as a passive actor, unable to independently set the course of the macroeconomy.

Another hypothesis about the causes of cyclical economic swings, championed by the Nobel Prize-winning economists Edward Prescott and Finn Kydland, incorporated rational expectations into the debates about appropriate counter-cyclical policies. Their theories emphasized technological shocks to the economy as a fundamental cause of recessions. Real business cycle theory views recessions as an efficient response to exogenous changes in the economic environment. This theory shifts the primary emphasis back toward supply shocks and away from demand shocks, and shifts emphasis of government policy toward the promotion of growth and away from the prevention of recession. Indeed, this theory holds that recession prevention by fiscal or monetary policies would only delay the necessary adjustments. The real business cycle theory was easily generalized to include confidence shocks in addition to technology shocks (Barsky & Sims, 2012). Thus, when consumer spending behavior inexplicably changed, for example, it could be assumed that there was an autonomous shift in expectations, with the autonomous shift defined as the unexplained residuals of equations describing the rational formation process. For example, economists have described the 1990–1991 recession as due to an "autonomous" drop in consumer sentiment (Hall, 1993; Blanchard, 1993).

WHAT CAUSES RECESSIONS?

There is no consensus among economists on the actual causes of recessions (Christiano & Fitzgerald, 1999). None of the usual suspects – monetary, fiscal, credit, price, or technology shocks – account for the bulk of the cyclical fluctuations (Curtin, 2004). Consumption shocks, however, do account for a relatively large share of the fluctuations (Cochrane, 1994). Moreover, changes in confidence have been found to account for 70% of the variations in economic cycles (Ilut & Schneider, 2014). This is a troublesome finding given that conventional economic theories assume that consumption is endogenously determined by other economic factors. The clear implication of conventional economic theory since the Industrial Revolution is that there is no channel by which changes in consumer demand can cause economy-wide recessions. Even modern intertemporal theories of consumer behavior cannot produce consumer-led recessions. The consensus holds that consumption is endogenous. Unlike the active and independent decisions of government policies and business firms that can shape the course of the macroeconomy, consumers are assumed to have no independent effect on the economy.

This stands in sharp contrast to the widely held public belief that shifts in consumer spending have been a primary cause of recessions. Not every recession is the result of a downturn in consumer spending as other factors can precede and cause the falloff in consumption. Nonetheless, the credibility of conventional economic theory has been too often strained by appeals to factors that are outside the domain of economics. While the impact of events such as wars and natural disasters are commonly understood as being outside the realm of economic theory, it is not true for consumer expectations about a turning point in the economy. Shifts in confidence have been credited as causing a large share of cyclical downturn, and those shifts are increasingly viewed as being caused by ambiguity about future economic conditions (Ilut & Schneider, 2014). Ambiguity demands more than just our rational faculties to make economic decisions; such decisions demand the use of the full capabilities of the human mind.

Elephants and Fleas

Keynes' insight that demand rather than supply played a pivotal role is hardly surprising given conditions in the economy at that time. Keynes, however, did not have the advantage of the national income and product accounts to inform his theorizing. Simon Kuznets only established the national accounts in 1934, for which he won the Noble Prize in 1971. Given the data we now have, his insights about demand are hardly surprising. In the 1930s, consumption accounted for 78% of all GDP spending (the same was true for 1929, the earliest year Bureau of Economic Analysis data are available). As Table 7.1 shows, consumer spending has always dominated the economy. Even during the 1940s, when government war expenditures reached extraordinary levels, consumption still accounted for 62% of all spending. What is more surprising is that Keynes gave the nod to the economy's flea (business fixed investment) rather than the elephant (consumer spending) in determining the course of the aggregate economy. Even small differences in the rate of consumption can have a powerful impact on cyclical swings in the economy. Consumer spending accounted for two-thirds of total GDP on average, compared with business fixed investment, which accounts for just over one-tenth of GDP. Even consumer expenditures for residential investment, vehicles, and household durables exceeded business fixed investments on average dating back to 1929, although in the 1980s and 1990s the business investment share of GDP was slightly above consumer investments.

Table 7.1 *Percentage Shares of GDP by Decade*

Decade	Personal Consumption (%)		Business Investment (%)
	Total	Housing & Durables	
1930–1939	78.1	9.6	7.1
1940–1949	62.3	9.7	7.3
1950–1959	66.3	14.4	10.2
1960–1969	64.4	13.2	10.9
1970–1979	65.5	13.8	12.2
1980–1989	67.0	13.0	13.6
1990–1999	69.0	12.5	12.6
2000–2009	72.3	13.4	12.7

Source: Bureau of Economic Analysis.

It is the change rather than the level of consumption or business investment that demands most attention. The conventional theories suggest that the change in business investment, despite its rather small level, dominates cyclical changes in the overall economy. How much does the change in business investment contribute to the overall percentage change in GDP? Conventional theories suggest that investment decisions by businesses would dominate decisions by consumers to invest in new homes, vehicles, and household durables.

The US Bureau of Economic Analysis calculates the share of total GDP growth attributable to various spending flows. Figure 7.1 shows the share of total annual GDP growth attributable to business fixed investments and to investments by consumers in new homes, vehicles, and household durables from 1930 to 2013. While the variance in consumer investments was greater in the late 1940s and early 1950s, since the 1960s, both series showed more similar variations. Note, however, that consumer investments tend to lead business investments by about one year (since the data is annual, the estimated lead time is very approximate). A Granger causality test performed on the quarterly series from 1947:2 to 2017:4 found significant mutual causation, running from the consumer to business investments and from business to consumer investments. While this result was not unexpected, it is surprising that economic theory still provides no role whatsoever for the consumer in shaping aggregate economic trends.

It should be noted that inventory adjustments were excluded from the above discussion. Most goods-producing firms must maintain inventories of products available for sale. While seasonal patterns may well affect production, inventory data is seasonally adjusted. Firms adjust inventory levels

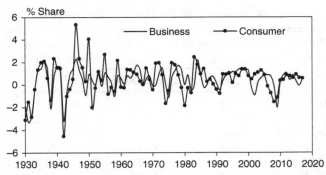

Figure 7.1 Contributions to Total Change in GDP from Changes in Personal Consumption and Business Investment

to expected sales volumes, and when sales are more or less than expected, inventories rise or fall. A rise in the value of inventories adds to GDP growth, and a fall subtracts from the rate of GDP growth. While some of the changes in inventories are intended, these adjustments often represent unintended changes due to unexpected variations in sales. Unintended changes in inventories mirror unexpected changes in consumption. While changes in inventories are a proximate cause of changes in investments, the ultimate cause was that firms did not predict sales trends accurately. Unintended inventory investments hardly represent a decision to invest but merely reflect the unexpected actions of their customers. Indeed, if the standard rational interpretation is extended to inventories, the residuals from the inventory equation would represent "autonomous" shifts in sales! In any event, in terms of the characteristics of investment decisions, consumer investments in homes, vehicles, and household durables are most comparable to business fixed investments excluding inventories.

Restricted Empirical Tests

The empirical tests that have guided the development of economic theory have been restricted in ways that act to reinforce the notion that the consumer sector does not have an independent impact on shaping the course of the macroeconomy (Curtin, 2004). Most of the empirical work relied on two simplifying assumptions that acted to exclude the crucial impact that measures of income uncertainty were designed to explain. The first was the so-called "certainty equivalence" assumption. This assumption meant that only the mean of the expected future income stream had an impact on current consumption decisions; the impact from uncertainty about future income was simply excluded from consideration. Although traditional theory left no room for considerations of uncertainty about future income, it has been shown that with more plausible assumptions about the utility function, consumers could be expected to accumulate precautionary savings as a hedge against uncertainty (Kimball, 1990; Yaari, 1965).[5] Once uncertainty about future incomes was incorporated, the variance of future income streams was also recognized as having an impact on current consumption decisions depending on the extent of accumulated assets and the level of current income relative to expected future income. The second simplifying assumption was that consumers' utility functions were assumed to be additive and time separable. Based on this assumption, expenditures on homes, vehicles, and household durables were simply eliminated from the empirical analysis of consumption. The rationale was that these expenditures did not represent consumption but were correctly viewed as investments.

Economic theory attributes an independent influence to firms' expectations about investment returns in shaping the macroeconomy, but does not concede a similar role for the expectations of consumers about their future incomes. When an inexplicable change in investment spending occurs, it is due to a sudden shift in profit expectations; when an inexplicable change in consumer spending occurs, it is called an autonomous shift due to factors outside the domain of economics. Consumers are even seen as bystanders during economic booms and subsequent busts, who passively participated in, but did not cause, the unusually large gains or losses. Economic theory has never considered waves of consumer optimism or pessimism capable of causing macroeconomic cycles, although those same waves in business sentiment have been mentioned as potential causes by Pigou, J. S. Mill, and Keynes. Just as the long economic expansions during the last half of the twentieth century occasioned the dismissal of these expectations from economic theory, reactions to the Great Depression and the Great Recession again focused attention on these potential sources.

As will be discussed in the next chapter, measures of consumer sentiment were initially conceptualized as representing a dimension that ran from one extreme of optimism and confidence to the other extreme of pessimism and uncertainty. Future income uncertainty and pessimism were hypothesized to have a substantial negative impact on the willingness of consumers to

---

[5] The exclusion of income uncertainty was based on the form of the utility function, which was hypothesized to be a quadratic. The more plausible utility function was assumed to be a conventional, time-separable concave utility function with a positive third derivative. The strength of the precautionary saving motive depends on the variance of consumption and interest rates.

make investments in homes, vehicles, and household durables. These expenditures occurred at the discretion of the consumer, whereas most expenditures on food, clothing, and so forth were necessary. In contrast, necessary expenditures are the most comparable with the standard definition of consumption used in economic theories. In a similar fashion to investment decisions by firms, the timing of "investment" decisions by consumers is heavily influenced by their uncertainty about future income flows. And similar to firms, consumers derive their independent influence on the macroeconomy by changes in these assessments and their spending behavior. Importantly, shifts in consumer sentiment, similar to business sentiment, occur too rapidly to be fully predicted in advance from prior changes in the economy. Indeed, to be qualified as a leading economic indicator, sentiment must turn negative when the economy is nearing its peak, and turn positive when the economy is at its worst.

Consumers mainly exert their influence on the macroeconomy through variations in the timing of investment expenditures. The timing of consumer investments is heavily influenced by consumers' economic expectations. Postponing the purchases of a new home, vehicle, or household durable typically has little immediate impact on their living standards, but has a large and immediate impact on savings. Indeed, varying the timing of investment expenditures is the dominant method used by consumers to adjust the amount of their precautionary savings in reaction to cyclical economic developments. If such changes in precautionary motives were random across consumers and over time, there would be no impact on the economy because the individual changes would cancel when aggregated. While many of the changes do cancel, it has been repeatedly observed that very many consumers change their views at the same time and in the same direction, either toward optimism or toward pessimism. It is this synchronization of change that can produce recessions or expansions. This recognition of the macro power of the consumer does not mean that every cyclical change is due to the consumer. It is only a recognition that changes in consumer expectations can, and sometimes do, propel the economy into downturns or upturns.

Self-Fulfilling Expectations

Conventional economic theory has always been wary of consumer expectations that were thought to be unrelated to economic fundamentals. The rational economic paradigm specifically excludes any role for self-fulfilling expectations. Expecting recessions or expansions, unmoored from economic trends, are treated as delusions, incapable of having an impact on subsequent trends. Conventional theory holds that an expectation cannot influence the economy simply because consumers think it should matter. Even if the "delusion" is commonplace, rational actors, at the margin, will dominate markets and end the fantasy.

These unjustified expectations have been referred to as "sunspots" in economic theory. The name comes from William Stanley Jevons, who tried to correlate variations in agricultural output with actual counts of sunspots (Jevons, 1878). While no relationship between sunspots and economic cycles was found, the term came to signify the influence on the economy by expectations that were unrelated to economic reality. Research based on the possibility of sunspots has shown that the potential for multiple rational expectations equilibria does exist (Cass & Shell, 1983). As a result, the potential impact of self-fulfilling expectations has become an important area of research in the past few decades (Shiller, 2000; Howitt & McAfee, 1992). Most of this research, however, has not focused on consumers but instead on the employment and investment decisions of firms or the actions of investors in financial markets. Importantly, when any positive results were confirmed, they have always been considered temporary anomalies or autonomous shifts in preferences, not a refutation of standard theory. Even the housing boom and bust associated with the Great Recession were viewed by many economists as mainly caused by the practices of financial firms; consumers were simply considered eager lemmings who rushed over the housing cliff.

Self-fulfilling expectations represent an interesting and challenging line of research. At the level of the individual consumer, self-fulfilling expectations affect spending and saving behavior in exactly the same way as expectations that were fully based on economic causes. The shifts in consumers' economic outlook as well as the changes in their spending and saving are identical; indeed, the two situations are indistinguishable to the individuals involved. It is of course true that sometimes their expectations are incorrect, and they inappropriately cut back or advance their spending. Most people would find it more difficult if they advanced their spending inappropriately, since many spending decisions are difficult to reverse. In contrast, exercising greater spending caution than was necessary is easy to correct in the future. This asymmetry in consumers' optimal responses to potential changes in the macroeconomy is responsible for the preoccupation of economics with negative self-fulfilling expectations. Indeed, confidence is seen as a prerequisite for a well-functioning economy. Positive self-fulfilling expectations are required as part of the natural course of economic growth, but they are typically referred to simply as optimistic expectations. Only when people become too confident, or "over confident," is it a problem. Overconfidence leads to inappropriate decisions on the part of consumers as well as by firms and the government. The booms and busts that may result will be the focus of a later chapter.

Even at the macro level of analysis, it would be difficult to robustly determine whether changes in consumer behavior were actually due to self-fulfilling expectations. For example, it would be impossible to determine when spending cutbacks by consumers in anticipation of a recession and a recession occurs, whether the initial expectation was based on true or imagined economic fundamentals. Moreover, shifts in expectations arise from changes in economic fundamentals as well as from other factors due to heightened ambiguity around turning points in the macroeconomy. What share of the determination of expectations needs to be attributed to economic fundamentals to call it a "true" economic expectation? Since the expectations of economic agents at turning points most likely represent a combination of reason and emotion, how can they be defined as completely true or completely self-fulfilling? What if consumers based their expectations on what they believed to be the views of the majority – the Keynesian beauty contest: would these consumers hold self-fulfilling expectations because they cut their spending and increased their precautionary savings since they perceived others would cut back on their spending and potentially cause a downturn? Why is it that economic theory is more likely to accept the rationality of a business cutback in anticipation of slower sales than when consumers cut back on their discretionary spending due to the same anticipated slowdown? The surprising answer is that economic theory is simply more likely to presume rationality on the part of businesses than on the part of consumers.

Even if expectations were based on economic fundamentals, the motivation to act on those expectations is due to emotions and other non-rational processes. Since economists favor behavior as a true measure of expectations, it is impossible to parse reason from passion. It is insufficient to merely hold that a false expectation is one that could not be produced by current economic data. If that were the case, as few turning points in the macroeconomy would be actually observed as have been projected by economic models. All expectations would simply point toward the reestablishment of the underlying rate of trend growth.

The underlying tension about self-fulfilling expectations is misplaced. The expectations of consumers are often identified as self-fulfilling merely because they were not formed according to conventional economic theories. As was documented in the preceding chapters, it is likely that economic theory underestimates the ability of consumers to form accurate expectations based on private information. Economists typically assume that consumers base their economic expectations on the public information released by governmental agencies; that is, on the same sources of information used by economists. Despite this standard assumption, the most important source of economic information for consumers is not the official statistics. Personal experience, direct knowledge of changes in local employment conditions, changes in prices and the availability of goods in local markets, and the numerous other direct connections that consumers have with changing economic conditions are most influential. It would not be rational for consumers to base their expectations on anything other than their own economic prospects and circumstances. Not only is this information more germane, but it is also more timely. This is not to deny that official statistics have no impact, nor the possibility that expectations may sometimes lack an economic basis. It only postulates that such private information is available well in advance of national economic statistics, and it is this private information on which consumers are more likely to base their expectations. Moreover, if economic fluctuations are primarily driven by private, unobserved information, this would explain the persistent puzzle about the determinants of business cycles (Cochrane, 1994).

EXPECTATIONS OF MACROECONOMIC CYCLES

A central tenet of modern economic theory is that people use information about their lifetime (permanent) income to make optimal intertemporal consumption decisions. The theory presumes that people's expectations of their lifetime income are formed rationally and are accurate given the information available when the expectations were formed. People are thought to engage in an ongoing evaluation process to determine if any adjustments to their current estimates are required. The crucial task for consumers when evaluating incremental information is whether a recent income change signifies a permanent change in lifetime income or a temporary aberration. Permanent changes in income, unlike transitory changes, should have a lasting impact on consumption.

Many of the economic risks that people face are likely to occur randomly across the population and over time. While some of these events will result in changes in people's estimates of their lifetime income, most signal only transitory income changes. As often happens in economic matters, someone's gain is another's loss so many random shifts in people's incomes are typically offset at the macro level. For some of the more important risks, people commonly purchase insurance to blunt the potential for substantial losses in lifetime incomes. Life and health insurance as well as home and vehicle policies are the usual examples. Other important risks are uninsurable, at least currently. People cannot purchase private insurance to protect themselves from job loss, for example; government unemployment insurance programs do provide limited and minimum aid. Indeed, most of the economic risks people face associated with business cycles are uninsurable. These risks, of course, go well beyond job loss. Nearly every aspect of people's economic lives are affected by economic cycles, from job and wage prospects, returns on financial assets, pensions, and real estate, to the adequacy of the social safety net, entitlements, tax obligations, and so forth.

How do people guard against the risks associated with economic cycles? There is no reason to presume that rational consumers would not anticipate that a series of recessions would occur during their lifetimes. Few people believe that they are invincible, totally unaffected by recessions and expansions. It could be argued, however, that recessions are primarily associated with a transitory change in income, with any temporary losses offset by gains during the ensuing expansion. This implies that permanent income remains unchanged, and so consumption decisions would be unaffected, at least in theory. Others argue that recessionary losses may never be fully recouped, or that cyclical losses and gains are generally associated with different people, and as a result, business cycles often lead to permanent change in an individual's estimate of lifetime income. While a very mild downturn may only have a transitory impact, a severe downturn is more likely to be associated with permanent changes. This means that people need to determine not only the likelihood of occurrences of recessions, but also the probable duration and the extent of the recession's impact on their own finances. People form these expectations by the same processes detailed in the first section of this book.

The data collected by the University of Michigan as well as scores of other countries have documented that people are intensely interested in the current state and expected direction of the macroeconomy. Forecasting a recession is no easy task. Few, if any, econometric models have forecasted a recession a year or more in advance of its official start date, a date that is determined approximately a year following its actual start by NBER. Moreover, virtually no government agency or private organization has ever predicted that a recession would start in two, three, five, or ten years. Indeed, the longer the forecast horizon, the more likely econometric models converge to a positive long-term growth trend. The occurrence of a recession may be more like the risk of illness: there is no reason to anticipate that a serious disease will strike at any given time, but the potential costs are high, even if the probability of a serious illness is low in any given year. Thus, most forecasters as well as ordinary individuals may think that it is highly likely that a recession will occur sometime in the future without knowing exactly when it may occur. Moreover, until more information is available about a specific downturn, the defining characteristics of a recession, its length and depth, would also be unknown.

Just as early detection of illness increases the likelihood of recovery, people have learned to carefully monitor the ongoing flow of economic information for warning signs of a potential downturn. Needless to say, people also pay careful attention to signs of recovery and economic expansion. But, as documented in prior chapters, humans are uniquely attuned and react faster to potential threats. The reactions of consumers are not limited to how much of their current income they consume and save. What future challenges and opportunities they expect from the macroeconomy affect many other behaviors, including motivations to work and invest in human capital, choices between different types of investments, preferences for government spending programs and tax policies, and so forth.

Given the long persistence of economic cycles in market economies, one might think that conventional economic theory would include the actions that rational consumers should take to prepare for an economy-wide downturn, and include how their actions should differ by the recession's expected length and depth. No such theorizing has ever taken place on the appropriate actions of consumers. This should not be surprising since the standard euphemism for macroeconomic cycles is *business cycles*, a term that focuses attention away from consumers. The term "business cycles" was first used at the start of the Industrial Revolution when most consumers were thought to be at subsistence levels, with the macroeconomy incapable of providing for all their needs. Rather than focusing on the expectations of consumers, economic theory focused on the profit expectations of business firms. Moreover, while firms were expected to be capable of making rational economic judgments, the consumer sector was hypothesized to lack the necessary information and ability to form realistic expectations.

It should be noted that the exclusion of consumers does not emanate as much from the basic theory, but rather from how the theory has been implemented in empirical research. When analysts conclude that firms decide not to invest because their expected return would not match their costs, it is treated as a rational decision. In the aftermath of the Great

Recession, the cutback in employment reflected the expectation of firms that there would be "insufficient demand." Needless to say, the reduction in employment was in turn used to justify the spending cutbacks undertaken by consumers. Just like firms, consumers are most likely to cut back on "investment" goods that are typically financed by debt. These forward-looking expenditures are trimmed by consumers due to concerns about future incomes, the same concerns that prompt firms to trim their future investments. Nonetheless, self-fulfilling prophecies are a more common description when consumers rather than firms cut back on their spending due to fears of a downturn. This prognosis is often justified by the notion that the expectations of consumers are based on irrational fears, unlike the rational calculations assumed to take place in firms.

Consumers' Expectations as a Leading Economic Indicator

How much do consumers know about the expected direction of change in the macroeconomy? While a rational consumer would certainly devote attention to information about potential changes in the economy, how much could we reasonably expect the average consumer to know? The University of Michigan has collected data on the expectations of consumers about the macroeconomy for decades. Rather simple comparisons of quarterly data from 1960 to 2017 showing year-to-year changes in the Index of Consumer Sentiment and changes in Gross Domestic Product (GDP) are shown in Figure 7.2. To be sure, the two series do not move in lock-step, but the correspondence is substantial. The survey data is noisy in that it often varies by generally small amounts due to measurement and sampling errors. It is generally assumed that these variations are much larger than those contained in the GDP data. Nonetheless the overall patterns of change indicate that consumers expected economy-wide downturns in advance of the decline in GDP.

Note that the annual change in both series is shown, largely to smooth both series in order to more clearly display the underlying relationship. A more rigorous test was performed between the quarterly changes in GDP at seasonally adjusted annual rates and the level of the Consumer Sentiment Index. This focuses solely on the new information in each series. Also note that the latest revised figure for GDP was used, not the value from the initial release.[6] This is more consistent with the basic idea that consumers use

---

6   Versions of economic data that were available on specific dates in history are available
    from FRED, a database maintained by the St. Louis Federal Reserve Bank.

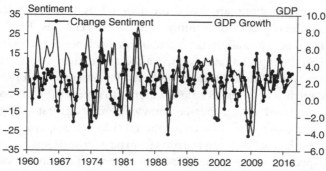

Figure 7.2 Annual Change in Consumer Sentiment and Annual Growth in Gross Domestic Product

"informal" information about the potential direction of the economy and how it affects their own economic situation as shown in prior chapters. It is somewhat puzzling that analysts believe expectations are formed based on national data and that people typically use the data as initially released instead of assuming that each of the several subsequent revisions of the data also affect the formation of expectations.

The data demonstrate a strong correspondence between the Index of Consumer Sentiment and quarterly changes in GDP at seasonally adjusted annual rates. A Granger causality test based on five lags, estimated from 1960 to 2017, indicates that the quarterly Index of Consumer Sentiment significantly predicts subsequent changes in quarterly GDP, while changes in GDP do not predict subsequent changes in the Sentiment Index.[7]

The implication that consumer sentiment acts as a leading economic indicator has been utilized in the United States as well as other countries. The University of Michigan survey has been part of the US Index of Leading Indicators for decades. Series were selected for inclusion based on their economic significance, consistent timing and conformity to economic cycles, statistical reliability, and timely availability. The other series selected for inclusion are average weekly hours in manufacturing, initial claims for unemployment insurance, new orders for consumer goods and non-defense capital goods, building permits, stock prices, a credit index, and interest rate spread (Levanon et al., 2011).

---

[7] The Granger test rejected the hypothesis that the Sentiment Index does not predict GDP ($p < 0.000$), while the data could not reject the hypothesis that GDP does not predict the Sentiment Index ($p = 0.23$).

Whether expectations are based on national or local considerations, people have the objective of forming accurate expectations. Each process is rational in that expectations are based on all available and relevant information when the expectation is formed, although neither process can guarantee accuracy even under ideal conditions. Presumably, the information burden is much less for expectations tailored to an agent's own economic situation compared with a greater knowledge and understanding of the national economy required by conventional theories. Imperfect information affects both processes, and learning from past errors is just as important whether expectations are formed based on national or locally relevant data.

There is one critical difference between expectations formed based on national data and those based on local information. The formation of expectations that is dependent on national statistical information means that every agent uses the same criterion for accuracy, whereas the tailored formation of expectations incorporates multiple accuracy criteria depending on the specific circumstances for which the expectation was formed. For example, the accuracy criteria for expectations about unemployment and inflation are uniform across all agents under the national criteria, but would vary depending on the unique characteristics and the economic situation of each individual. Some individuals may naturally expect a higher or lower rate of inflation or unemployment depending on their specific situation and the characteristics of local markets. Importantly, despite the diversity of circumstances, the sum of these individual expectations would approximate the national average when properly aggregated.

Conventional economics considers the key strength of its theories to be the potential to use powerful deductive logic to generalize how expectations are formed by all agents in the economy. Moreover, conventional theory can consider consumer expectations endogenous since the formation process only depends on national economic information. No separate measurement of income, employment, or inflation expectations is needed since these expectations are assumed to be generated based on the same global information that is already contained in economic models. This significant implication created the rational expectations revolution in conventional economic theory, whereby every aspect of economic theory was infused with the powerful force of expectations. Paul De Grauwe (2010) has termed this a top-down approach to macroeconomic theory. A bottom-up approach is more consistent with the new theory of tailored expectations.

De Grauwe explored agent-based macroeconomic models as a means to incorporate local formation of expectations and compared the results with the national models based on rational expectations. The agent-based model used simple heuristics and learning rules that were generated based on the accuracy of past expectations. The agent-based model generated waves of optimism and pessimism based on these learning rules that were found to be essentially similar to the survey data of expectations collected by the University of Michigan (De Grauwe, 2010). One of his key findings was that agent-based models led to systematic correlations in beliefs that created peaks and troughs that corresponded with conventional rational expectations dynamic stochastic general equilibrium (DSGE) models of inflation and national output.

Subgroup Variations in the Index of Consumer Sentiment

Does the relationship between Consumer Sentiment and GDP indicate that all consumers hold reasonably accurate economic forecasts, or does the overall relationship primarily depend on the views of more informed population subgroups? It could be hypothesized that trends in economic expectations among many, if not most, consumers simply represent random "guesses" in response to survey questions, with optimistic replies acting to offset pessimistic replies in the aggregate. Against such a trendless background, a much smaller group of informed consumers could determine the actual trends in the survey measures. This hypothesis implies that, for example, those with limited cognitive abilities or understanding of the economy, would essentially provide trendless responses, while those with higher cognitive abilities or more information about prospective trends in the economy are primarily responsible for the observed trends in the data.

A more comprehensive view would be that trends in expectations may differ in two distinct ways: differences in the average level of expectations across socioeconomic subgroups, as well as differences in how expectations change over time across subgroups. For example, two subgroups may indicate very different average levels of the expected performance of the economy based on personal experiences, say those with high and low job skills. Whether the two subgroups change their overall expectations in a similar manner over time is a separate issue. Similar time trends would not be anticipated if it was thought that the subgroups differed in their ability to access the relevant economic information and draw the necessary implications for the future course of the economy. In contrast, the conjecture that similar time-series changes in expectations across subgroups, even if the level of their expectations remained quite different, would require that all people attend to information and form expectations about cyclical economic developments based on their own perspectives. Perhaps the more common hypothesis would be that socioeconomic subgroups differed in both the absolute level of their expectations as well as how they changed over time.

It should be noted that the analysis that follows does not preclude the fact that a particular individual could be totally unaware of some economic development. Based on hundreds of thousands of interviews conducted as part of the University of Michigan surveys, such uninformed individuals are always present; some even proudly proclaim their ignorance as well as their disdain for the material world. There are others, of course, who believe that they possess accurate knowledge, and even tout their expertise, since their jobs or investments depend on up-to-date knowledge about the economy. What is at issue is whether the majority of consumers, not every single consumer, forms expectations about the potential direction of the economy. In particular, do the bounds on rationality limit some groups more than others from forming an accurate economic expectation? The literature has long emphasized differences in cognitive skills, computational abilities, and knowledge of ongoing events as well as economic theory for the formation of accurate expectations. Do differences in educational attainment, as a proxy for cognitive skills, or differences in age as a proxy for experience, or differences in income as a proxy for economic exposure have a significant impact on how people process information about potential economic cycles? More importantly, do these differences result in different absolute levels of economic optimism or pessimism about potential economic cycles, or differential trends in expectations, or both?

How does the Index of Consumer Sentiment vary across socioeconomic subgroups? Although the Sentiment Index is a reasonable predictor of subsequent changes in GDP, is that true for all education, age, and income subgroups? Focusing on the thirty-nine-year period from 1978 to 2016, the data indicate that the average levels of the Sentiment Index did differ significantly across education, age, and income subgroups (right side of Table 7.2), but the time-series correlations among these groups were uniformly quite high, ranging from 0.91 to 0.98 (left side of Table 7.2). For each time-series correlation, two groups were formed from the raw data: one group was defined as all respondents in a particular education, age, or income subgroup, and the second group was defined as all other respondents. For example, the time-series correlation of 0.912 for those without a high school degree was calculated from two series: the Index values among those without a high school degree and the Index scores of all those with more than a high school degree. The same procedure was followed for each education, age, and income subgroup. This procedure meant that these

Table 7.2 *Index of Consumer Sentiment: Means and Correlations among Socioeconomic Subgroups (Quarterly Data, 1978–2016)*

Education of Householder

	Times Series Correlation between Subgroup and All Other Subgroups					Mean Levels within Subgroups (Standard Errors)				
	Less than High School	High School	Some College	College Degree	Graduate Studies	Less than High School	High School	Some College	College Degree	Graduate Studies
	0.912	0.958	0.950	0.970	0.959	73.3 (0.81)	82.2 (1.00)	87.1 (1.05)	92.3 (1.07)	91.4 (1.12)

Age of Householder

	18–34	35–44	45–54	55–64	65 +	18–34	35–44	45–54	55–64	65 +
	0.961	0.958	0.974	0.961	0.958	95.2 (1.01)	88.4 (1.08)	83.8 (1.07)	80.6 (0.98)	75.8 (0.82)

Income of Household[a]

	Bottom Fifth	2nd Fifth	Middle Fifth	4th Fifth	Top Fifth	Bottom Fifth	2nd Fifth	Middle Fifth	4th Fifth	Top Fifth
	0.931	0.968	0.980	0.979	0.960	74.9 (0.84)	82.4 (1.00)	87.6 (1.10)	90.9 (1.12)	95.9 (1.17)

[a] The data for household income is for 1979:4 to 2016:4; all other data is for 1978:1 to 2016:4.

correlations were not biased by including the same households in both variables: households in each education subgroup were excluded from figures for "all other households."

The results for education indicated that the Sentiment Index for each educational subgroup was highly correlated with all other groups: the correlations ranged from 0.91 to 0.97. Note that trends in the Sentiment Index had the lowest correlation among those without a high school degree, but that correlation was still substantial, high enough to indicate virtually identical trends. The same is true for differences in ages, with the correlations barely different, ranging from 0.96 to 0.97. Across income subgroups, the same applies, with the correlations ranging between 0.93 and 0.98. The data provide rather strong confirmation that changes over time in the Sentiment Index are virtually identical across the population. As previously noted, particular individuals are likely to differ significantly from the group averages, and the questions comprising the Sentiment Index only ask the respondent to make judgments about basic differences in the direction of the economy. Nonetheless, the data provide support for the notion that most people are aware of the same underlying trends in the economy, and just as importantly, that awareness is predictive of subsequent changes in the actual performance of the economy.

Importantly, there were significant differences in the absolute level of economic expectations across population subgroups. As educational attainment increased, optimism about the economy was more prevalent. The difference in mean levels between those without a high school diploma and those with a college degree was 18.1 Index points. Note that the mean level of the Sentiment Index is slightly lower among those with graduate degrees, although the difference was not significant. As might be anticipated, the differences in mean levels in the Sentiment Index were largest across income subgroups. The range from the bottom to top income quintile was 21.0 points in the thirty-nine years from 1978 to 2016. This difference was nearly evenly split between the overall mean and were all about 20 Index points.[8] This difference is quite large in terms of lowest income quintile (-10.6 points) and the highest quintile (+10.4 points). The mean differences in the Sentiment Index across age groups indicate that the youngest age groups were more optimistic than older age groups. This pattern reflects the fact that younger households generally receive larger

---

[8] Note that since the sample sizes were identical, the standard errors also provide an estimate of the standard deviation of the Index within subgroups. To convert to standard deviations, simply multiply the standard errors by 12.5 for education and age subgroups and by 12.2 for the income subgroups.

income increments, no matter the stage of the economic cycle. The mean differences between those under age thirty-five and those sixty-five years or older was 19.4 Index points from 1978 to 2016. Note that the largest mean differences across education, age, and income subgroups in the overall Sentiment Index were approximately equal to the inter-quartile range.

NEW MICRO FOUNDATIONS FOR MACROECONOMICS

The purpose of this chapter was to assert that consumer spending is a primary driving force behind economic cycles and that forming expectations about future economic cycles is an essential task undertaken by all consumers. These two facts are often ignored by conventional economic theory.

Consumers directly account for two-thirds of all spending in the economy, with the amount of their investment spending as large as investments made by the business sector. Moreover, cyclical trends in investment spending, whether by consumers or firms, have been nearly identical over the past century. The enduring distinction in economic theory between the two sectors in generating expansions or contractions has been largely due to the economic conditions that prevailed at the birth of economic theory. Prior to the Industrial Revolution, when Adam Smith and David Ricardo first elaborated economic theory, the clear goal of a successful economic system was to provide a subsistence living standard to all consumers. That situation changed radically due to the Industrial Revolution. Sustained cumulative increases in productivity made it possible for succeeding generations to achieve ever higher living standards. Rising incomes meant that consumption no longer changed in lockstep with incomes. The constraints of the "fundamental psychological law" were gradually counteracted by increases in discretionary incomes and the growing availability of credit. The growing power of the consumer to shape trends in the macroeconomy was masked by two developments in economic theory. First, subsistence became a relative rather than an absolute concept, defined to include rising material desires rather than being limited to what was needed for survival. This was meant to resurrect the fundamental implications of Keynes' discredited law. The rational expectation revolution found the notion that consumer investment spending did not depend on expectations unacceptable. The second means to neutralize the power of the consumer was to assert that consumers' expectations were themselves a product of the overall economic system. Once their expectations were determined endogenously, consumers simply became passive transmitters of inputs to outputs, losing any independent power to shape the future course of the economy. The expectations of consumers were rendered useless as predictive tools, they simply became window-dressing, having no independent power to explain economic cycles. The only option left to explain economic cycles associated with consumer spending was to assert some autonomous shift had occurred in the economic environment. Indeed, autonomous shifts were specifically designed to explain discontinuous breaks from past trends, the very definition of a cyclical turning point in the macroeconomy.

Economic downturns affect people in many ways; no one is immune. Some are affected by changes in their jobs and incomes, others by changes in inflation or credit conditions, or by changes in equities and home values, and still others by changes in taxes and entitlement programs. While governments claim that economic policies can avoid or counter the impact of economy-wide downturns, an assertion harking back to Keynes' fundamental law, the historical record, however, argues otherwise. It is true that economic policy experts offer no comprehensive theory on the origins of recessions. These experts routinely predict a smooth sailing economy at trend levels over the longer term, a forecast that has repeatedly missed the mark. Indeed, claims that policy experts can ensure economic growth and avoid financial disasters have followed their own cycle, peaking near the end of very long expansions and reaching a low in the midst of deep recessions. This is not to say that progress has not been made to minimize the toll of recession paid by consumers; in fact, the progress that began during the Great Depression and continues to this day has been substantial. Nonetheless, the hardship suffered by families due to economic downturns is still quite significant. The only rational response by consumers is to carefully monitor changes in the economic environment for any potential signs of an emerging downturn. Most consumers have already taken defensive actions by the time public officials admit to the occurrence of a recessionary downturn.

The data collected by the University of Michigan clearly indicates that consumers have displayed a remarkable awareness of cyclical economic trends. Importantly, the trends in consumer assessments were nearly identical across all education, income, and age subgroups. No evidence was found that some consumers suffered from an inability to comprehend economic trends or from a lack of relevant information. Moreover, the expectations of consumers were found to accurately predict future trends in the economy. There were differences in the level of optimism or pessimism, indicating that some socioeconomic subgroups expected better economic times on average, and some consistently expected less favorable conditions. Whatever the level, the change in expectations across all groups was uniform. Whether rich or poor, old or young, with less than a high school education or a graduate degree, consumers consistently monitored the economic landscape for signs of cyclical change. Extreme differences in socioeconomic characteristics were not investigated, say among those in the bottom few percent of the income distribution, or among householders over age ninety, or among those who were illiterate. Such extreme differences may indeed be related to their willingness or their ability to form expectations. Economy-wide recessions do not depend on changes at the fringes, but rather on changes across the mass of consumers.

If one assumed that consumers' expectations were based on national economic data collected and published by federal statistical agencies, this feat would be impossible to believe. As already shown in Chapter 3, few consumers pay close attention to the official national economic data. This accomplishment is reasonable only if one assumes that people based their expectations on information they personally encounter and that affects their own economic situation. This information is more relevant and more accessible, and allows people to tailor their expectations to their own needs. While some economic decisions are primarily sensitive to interest rates, other decisions on potential inflation rates, or income growth, and still others on investment gains, there is no other economic event as all-encompassing as an economy-wide recession. History has taught consumers that recessions can be ignored only at their peril.

The social nature of expectations is especially important for understanding how people anticipate cyclical developments in the economy. Recessions and recoveries are as much social as they are economic events. Every recession and recovery requires that very many people decide at approximately the same time to either cut back or increase their spending. This coordination of behavior acts to define economic cycles. Conventional economic theory makes the assumption that every agent simultaneously and independently reacts in the same way to the same underlying changes in the economy. The observed coordination among economic agents is only a mirage; it is due to the simultaneous reaction of all agents to the same publicly available national economic information. This would simply be a convenient ruse if all it entailed was knowledge of other people's assessments, and that knowledge had no influence on their own expectations and behavior. That is not the case, however. Surveillance for potential threats is more effectively and efficiently accomplished by groups of people rather than by individuals. People have an economic incentive to take precautionary actions. There is no symmetry: people want to react faster to secure their own economic welfare in anticipation of a downturn, but those same cautionary motives reduce their incentive to be the first to act in anticipation of an upturn.

Discounting the importance of private information has sometimes been justified by the longstanding desire to isolate reason from emotion. Rationality assumes emotionless agents, which is an impossible state of affairs. No decision is possible without the influence of emotion (Damasio, 1994). Economics has long recognized this basic fact, but nonetheless counsels that every effort should be made to extract emotion from economic expectations. Economic decisions, however, always reflect emotions as well as rational analysis. Most of the time rational analysis completely dominates, but not always. Rational assessments may be especially inappropriate for expectations regarding the possibility, the extent, and the timing of macroeconomic cycles. This point was convincingly made by Keynes at the time of the Great Depression and by many others at the time of the Great Recession. These economic catastrophes would seem to make the dual role of reason and passion impossible to avoid. Nonetheless, apart from these two extraordinary economic events, economics tried its best to eliminate emotion as a potential cause of economic cycles. The self-imposed restrictions that barred the full range of mental faculties to form expectations is a critical theoretical omission.

Recessions represent a significant and recurrent threat to economic well-being. Most people would find it preferable to hold cyclical expectations that under-predict the strength of a recovery and over-predict the severity of a recession. This view is consistent with the potential economic disruption caused by unanticipated gains compared with unanticipated losses. The willingness of people to take precautionary actions in the face of potential threats may result in an economic slowdown or even a downturn when it would otherwise be unjustified strictly based on past economic trends. Of course, this zealousness about hedging potential negative risks is not limited to consumers, as business firms may also act out of a sense of precaution which was later recognized as unrelated to their true economic situation. Moreover, governments may also act in a similar manner, especially by instigating changes in regulations or stimulus spending that were unjustified by current economic circumstances. To simply label all these occurrences as self-fulfilling expectations and outside the domain of economics is self-defeating. This applies not only to the spectacular booms and busts that have occasionally occurred in the US economy, but to the far more common marginal adjustments in the length and extent of economic cycles. Subsequent chapters will discuss these factors in more detail.

The notion that consumer expectations are endogenous, merely reflecting changes in other known economic variables, means that consumers will always be surprised at turning points in the economy. More importantly, this means that consumers will always suffer the largest unmoderated losses since no precautionary behavior is envisioned before the start of a recession. This view is a hangover from economic theories developed for subsistence economies where consumers had little if any spending discretion. In contrast, there exists substantial discretion in modern economies with the widespread availability of various forms of credit as well as savings and investment options. These characteristics of the modern economy break the lockstep link between income and consumption, and are essential components of life-cycle and permanent income theories. It also means that consumer expectations can have a substantial and independent impact on shaping trends in the macroeconomy.

Several reactions of consumers to the macroeconomy are contrary to conventional economic theory. Perhaps the most well-known is what has been termed "inflationary psychology," which implies that in the face of product price increases, consumers increase their demand, acting to exaggerate both cyclical peaks, and as a consequence, make the ultimate downturn deeper. In addition, why during periods of record growth in personal incomes do households raise instead of lower their labor force participation rates? Just as interesting, why during periods of record slow growth in incomes, do households lower their labor force participation? Why are self-fulfilling expectations mainly discussed as a potential cause of recessions but not of recoveries? Why do booms occur when everyone realizes that they cannot continue forever?

These and other anomalies are due to incorrectly specified micro foundations of the macroeconomy. The rational paradigm of economics can be faulted for excluding the influence of passion on human decisions, for its dismissal of the social nature of economic decisions, and for many other imperfections. It is not the omission of any one of these factors that represents the critical fault. The crucial error is the denial that consumers can have an independent effect on the course of the macroeconomy. It is long past due that economic theory include the possibility that consumer spending, which accounts for the vast majority of the economy, has a significant and independent impact on cyclical economic developments. Theory must recognize that economic recessions as well as recoveries can result from self-fulfilling expectations, whether those expectations guide business investments, consumer investments, or government economic policies.

8

The Measurement of Expectations

What is consumer confidence? The term is now part of popular culture. Consumer confidence is cited by government officials, business executives, and the media, as well as by ordinary consumers to describe national economic conditions. It has become a global phenomenon as consumer confidence is measured in scores of countries representing every inhabited continent in the world. Consumer confidence is now so much a part of the economic dialog that many people believe that measures of consumer confidence have a specific and widely agreed upon definition. Nonetheless, it should be no surprise that the definition of consumer confidence has remained elusive since the "confidence" of consumers can never be directly observed. It is only the behavior of consumers that can be observed. How could the single definition of consumer confidence adequately capture the wide array of economic behaviors across developed, developing, and underdeveloped economies? Even the economic behavior of consumers within any one country has significantly changed since consumer confidence was first measured in the middle of the last century. It would seem obvious that economic decisions, made by populations that differ in their economic attainment, sophistication, and access to information would require different measures of consumer sentiment.

How have measures of consumer confidence adapted to significant variations in economic conditions both over time and across countries? This is the core issue that will be investigated in this chapter. Some elements of consumer confidence can be expected to remain unchanged, no matter the circumstances. Personal economic progress and financial security are core elements that are important to everyone. Income and job prospects as well as trends in prices and interest rates reflect these universal concerns. These factors were reflected in the basic conceptualization of consumer confidence when it was initially proposed by George Katona in the middle

234

of the twentieth century. When people are confident and optimistic about their economic situation, their willingness to spend increases, and when people are pessimistic and uncertain, their willingness to spend declines. Even small changes in the willingness of consumers to spend, when it occurs among many consumers at the same time, have the ability to drive the entire economy toward expansion or contraction. This is what makes the consumer sector a powerful force in shaping the macroeconomy. It also explains why it commands the attention of everyone interested in fostering a growing and prosperous economy.

Psychologists and economists have framed how changes in consumer expectations affect the macroeconomy using different terminology. Psychologists have focused on discretionary purchases as opposed to necessary expenditures, whereas economists have focused on investment spending as opposed to consumption expenditures. Not every discretionary purchase is considered an investment by economists, and not every investment expenditure is considered discretionary by psychologists, but there is substantial agreement. Most would agree that homes, vehicles, and major household durables represent discretionary purchases as well as investment expenditures. Necessary purchases reflect life's essentials, such as spending for food, clothing, and shelter; they are the archetypical examples of consumption.[1] While this distinction may be clear in theory, nearly all categories of necessities have discretionary elements and likewise, investment spending sometimes represents necessary expenditures. Some people spend more on food, clothing, and shelter than is necessary, for example, by eating at an expensive restaurant, buying designer clothing, or owning a luxurious home. Other people may find it necessary to immediately purchase homes, vehicles, or household durables due to a host of reasons, ranging from storm losses to mechanical failure.

The critical property of discretionary expenditures is their dependence on expected future economic developments. Since these purchases typically involve the use of accumulated savings or the incurrence of debt, the timing of these purchases is sensitive to how consumers view their future economic prospects. This allows even small shifts in economic expectations to have an impact on the macroeconomy when the shift occurs simultaneously across

---

[1] Economists consider the purchase of a house as an investment expenditure and it is not included in consumption. The flow of housing services from the house is estimated and counted as consumption in official accounts. In contrast, purchases of vehicles and large household durables are counted as consumption, not investments, in the national accounts.

many individual consumers. The sensitivity of these investment expenditures to changes in optimism or pessimism forms the basis of the predictive ability of the confidence index. This is what gives the consumer sector an independent and powerful influence on shaping trends in the macroeconomy.

Some have argued that in addition to being viewed as an input to economic decisions, maintaining confidence and optimism at high levels could be regarded as a valuable output of the economy. It is now widely believed that the national income accounts should not be the sole arbiter of economic welfare. An appropriate societal goal is to encourage economic conditions that promote a confident and optimistic citizenry. Consumer confidence in this perspective could be considered a social indicator that has important implications for society apart from any impact it has on economic behavior. These added benefits from positive expectations, however, go well beyond the scope of this book. This book is focused solely on expectations as an input to consumer decisions. Nonetheless, it is perhaps this dual role as both an economic and a social indicator that underlies the worldwide adoption of these measurements.

Valid measures of economic expectations are impossible without the guidance of theory (Koopmans, 1947). Although measurement without theory is a strong and growing impulse as our economic lives become increasingly digitized and the resulting "big data" becomes more widely available, theory is still required to give meaning to the measures. Economic theory defines what expectations should be measured, how to assess the validity of the observed measures, and how to interpret the results. This chapter begins with a review of the theoretical foundations and economic circumstances that promote the use of expectations in economic decisions.

From the earliest of times, people have commonly stated their expectations using verbal qualifications to indicate their degree of certainty in their beliefs about the future. It was not until the development of probability theory in the seventeenth century that expectations were quantitatively defined as probabilistic judgments about uncertain events or outcomes. Although it is still much more common for people to express uncertainty using non-quantitative verbal descriptions, the use of probability statements in everyday conversations has increased over time, and is now common in at least a few areas, such as in forecasts of weather and sports. People also commonly express their expectations as contingent on the information available to them, consistent with the generally accepted view that expectations are conditional probability statements.

While theorists and consumers have always shared the same conceptualization of expectations, how consumer expectations should be measured has long been the subject of scientific debate. At first, theorists thought that it would be foolish to ask consumers about their economic expectations as they would not have the knowledge or skill to form coherent economic expectations. In this view, the measured expectation would essentially be random guesses, and when aggregated across individuals, positive expectations would likely offset negative expectations. With the arrival of the rational expectations hypothesis, conventional economic theory did an about-face by assuming people held rational expectations that were accurate given the current available information. Rather than advocating measurement, the conclusion drawn from the rational expectations hypothesis was that there was no need to actually measure consumer expectations since they could be estimated from the readily available economic data, based on the same information that consumers would use (or should use) to form their expectations.

More recently, as expectations have become more central components in economic theories, economists have renewed their interest in the measurement of expectations. The theoretical specifications of the desired expectation measures, however, have become much more exacting. The ideal measure would specify the characteristics of the complete probability distribution for a precisely defined future event or outcome. Given an estimate of the entire probability distribution, the theoretically desired measure could be constructed, including measures of central tendency as well as the dispersion of the distribution to capture the associated uncertainty of the expectations. Although the measurement debate has now completed a full circle, there has never been any doubt that expectations influence the spending and saving behavior of consumers. This critical fact underscores the importance of expectations for explaining economic behavior, regardless of data measurement specifications.

An important limitation to probability-based measures of expectations is called Knightian uncertainty. Forming rational expectations requires that potential risks be measurable, with known probabilities of occurrence. When risks are impossible to calculate, no rational expectation can be formed due to the ambiguity. Conventional theories of expectations recognize the difference, but view situations in which risks are incalculable as rare and these situations are treated as special cases. As Keynes noted, other non-rational processes must be used to make economic decisions when risks are not calculable and ambiguity prevails. Keynes used the term "animal spirits" to invoke these other non-rational processes, a colorful metaphor to indicate the importance of other mental processes not dependent on conscious rational probability calculations. Keynes thought that ambiguity is a dominant characteristic surrounding turning points in the economy, and unfortunately, we know that those instances are not all that rare in the history of the macroeconomy nor in many other decisions faced by consumers. It was the growing recognition that all mental faculties are used to form expectations that inspired the creation of behavioral economics by George Katona shortly after the end of the Great Depression of the 1930s. It also formed the rationale for the comprehensive description of how the full range of mental assets are employed to form economic expectations, which was the subject of the first section of this book. The development of behavioral economics is the first topic of this chapter.

The basic types of expectations that are measured and form the consumer confidence indices are similar across a broad range of countries. The indices represent an additive combination of the responses, with the time-series results interpreted in terms of period-to-period change. The conformity across nations represents the influence of the measurement programs at both the University of Michigan and the European Union. The countries that measure consumer confidence and the questions used in their confidence indices represent the next topic of this chapter. Some countries have expanded the range of expectations measured, due to changing economic circumstances, an increase in the economic sophistication of the population, or an increase in the availability and quality of relevant economic information. The survey program at the University of Michigan, which includes the broadest range of economic expectations of any country, will be highlighted as an example. Following this, the results from several experimental questions and response scales are reviewed.

The two biggest challenges in measuring consumer expectations are how the survey questions describe the relevant economic concept and what type of response scale is used to measure the expectation. How consumers construct expectations has been discussed in theoretical terms in previous chapters; now it will be discussed in more practical terms. First, the economic concept under investigation – income, job, or inflation prospects, for example – must be presented in population language, avoiding the jargon of economics. It would be foolish to design a question that asks consumers about the expected quarterly percentage change at annual rates in personal disposable income in constant 2016 dollars. The question must be phrased in terms of how the economic concept is understood by consumers. Some scholars object to the loss of "face validity" of the question, meaning that the question did not exactly match the economist's definition. For example, the question on unemployment expectations, which was analyzed in Chapter 2, includes no instruction for framing the answer as a proportion of all people who were actively seeking and available for work during the prior four weeks. Since survey respondents would have no way of knowing who was actively seeking employment, that criteria of the official unemployment rate was simply ignored. Ultimately, the validity of measures of expectations is judged by its predictive ability, by its correspondence with aggregate trends in the objective measurement. The success of these predictive measures depend on the choice of response scales as well as question wording.

The simple verbal likelihood response scales widely used to measure consumer expectations could be easily improved. Rather than asking "increase, same, or decrease," for example, the survey could ask "increase a lot, increase a little, same, decrease a little, or decrease a lot." Or the survey could ask "What percentage change do you expect?" Or "What is the probability of an increase?" Or even, several questions could be asked to uncover the complete probability distribution. As was discussed in previous chapters, the simplest formulations take advantage of nonconscious processes and automatic evaluations, while the more demanding response scales require more concentrated conscious deliberation and computational skills. Economists typically prefer response scales that require conscious deliberation on the assumption that only conscious thought can yield rational responses. A clear implication of this position is that the accuracy of expectations measured by a three-point verbal likelihood scale would be significantly less than based on a 100-point probability scale. An empirical experiment that compared different response scales found essentially identical time-series results for two questions on income expectations measured in surveys for over fifteen years. There was a wider dispersion of responses based on the probability response scales within any single survey, but the time-series means trace virtually identical paths. Even if the entire difference is contained in the cross-section variance, it is how the mean of the expectation series evolves over time that is most relevant for macroeconomic analysis.

A third experiment on questions about unemployment expectations found the two response scales to move independently over time, with the verbal likelihood measure offering a closer correspondence to changes in the national unemployment rate. In this case, the two questions differed in that the verbal likelihood questions asked about overall trends in unemployment, whereas the probability question asked about the chances that the respondent would become unemployed. The aggregation of each respondent's unemployment expectations should track overall prospects for unemployment. The primary divergence occurred during the Great Recession when the probability assessments did not increase as much as might have been expected.

What could explain the nearly identical time-series movements in income expectations regardless of the response scale? Could each scale tap the same nonconscious or conscious response processes? The economic sophistication of the population has been advanced by increases in human capital and by innovations in technology. The technology of the information age has meant that an increasing array of economic information is instantly available. Everyone has access to more detailed economic information than was available even to experts and government statisticians in the past. Just as importantly, people have become more knowledgeable users of this information. Today's population is less limited by the classic bounds on rationality (acquiring, calculating, and interpreting data) than the populations a hundred or even fifty years ago. As shown in prior chapters, the increases in cognitive capacity enhance both conscious and nonconscious information processing. Moreover, the digital information age has vastly increased the ability of people to find others in comparable situations that are facing the same economic issues and decisions. The vast increase in the availability of such private information is likely to be more important to consumers than the greater availability of data from federal statistical agencies.

This chapter concludes with a discussion of future opportunities and challenges to the measurement of consumer expectations. The primary advantage of basing measures on representative sample surveys is that the derived estimates can employ standard statistical methods to generalize the results to the national or supra-national levels. Unfortunately, the cost of population sample surveys is now high and growing, and the proportion of selected respondents that agree to be interviewed is low and falling. Surveys conducted on the internet would seem to be an obvious solution, but the methods to select representative samples of internet users are based on older sampling techniques that have increasingly suffered from high costs and low response rates.

There is every reason to anticipate new measurement methods will be developed in the future. It is likely that non-probability samples will increase in importance, especially as big data collections become more readily available in digitized forms on the internet. While some progress has been made on deriving robust statistical tests for non-probability samples, these efforts are still in their infancy. Despite these drawbacks, economists place most emphasis on the predictive ability of the alternative measures in econometric models. Moreover, the derived measures would necessarily be proxies for the expectation, as no direct measure is possible. Proxies could include verbal reports, such as internet search behavior, or behaviors, such as items purchased. It is likely that successful measurement strategies will be built on new and radically different forms of data collection and analysis. Indeed, there have already been attempts to replicate the Index of Consumer Sentiment based on a variety of "big data" sources with mixed success.

It is only natural to begin the discussion of measurement issues by focusing on the key developments in economic theory.

BEHAVIORAL ECONOMICS

George Katona founded the discipline of behavioral economics in the 1940s.[2] His theoretical focus was on the role that the consumer plays in determining the course of the macroeconomy. Many feared that the post-World War II economy would again give rise to the same deflationary spiral and mass unemployment that characterized the Great Depression of the 1930s. Indeed, press headlines in mid-1945 proclaimed, "Government economists predict 8 million unemployed by 1946." After all, millions of soldiers and sailors would soon be returning home and looking for work in what was already a full-employment economy that had satisfied domestic needs as well as equipped and supported US forces overseas. What actually occurred was quite different. In the first half of 1946, the unemployed numbered 3, not 8, million, and instead of deflation, the economy faced strong inflationary pressures. Rather than harboring the same fears of economists, consumers exhibited a renewed sense of confidence. Acting on that optimism, consumers spent an increasing fraction of their incomes, as the savings rate plunged to a low that would not again be recorded for fifty years (Curtin, 2010). In explaining the forecast error, the Nobel Laureate Lawrence Klein (1946) noted that it was due to an incorrect prediction of consumer expenditures, which led to disastrous economic policy recommendations (Curtin, 2004).

Rather than being confined by the Keynesian emphasis on current income, Katona focused on two developments in the US economy that gave consumers the power to shape the course of the macroeconomy. First, growth in incomes, liquid assets holdings, and increased access to credit provided households with financial latitude. Incremental gains or losses in consumers' incomes could no longer be expected to result in

[2] Katona documented the development of his theories in a series of books: *Psychological Analysis of Economic Behavior* (1951), *The Powerful Consumers* (1960), *The Mass Consumption Society* (1964), and *Psychological Economics* (1975). For an overview of Katona's theoretical contributions, as well as a complete list of his publications and biographical information see Curtin (1983; 2016).

immediate changes in consumption. This financial latitude enabled consumers to become active and independent decision makers, able to time their spending decisions to best meet their needs. Katona developed these important theories of household financial management long before the appearance of life-cycle and permanent income theories were put forth in the 1950s. The second change involved the growing importance of consumer investment goods – purchases of homes, vehicles, and other large household durables. These large and infrequent purchases were more likely to be planned decisions and the timing of the purchase could easily be advanced or postponed without much harm to living standards. Moreover, these purchases frequently involved risks associated with the use of credit or accumulated savings. Indeed, consumers favored postponement of these large purchases as the most effective means to vary their net savings and financial obligations.

As a result, the timing of these large purchases became dependent on consumers' current incomes and asset holdings as well as on their expectations about future trends in their income and employment. Rational consumers would also base the timing of their purchases on expected trends in prices, interest rates, and other relevant factors. Although each individual may only make a marginal change in their own spending, when aggregated across all consumers, the impact from changing economic expectations could shape expansionary or contractionary cycles in the macroeconomy.

George Katona devised measures of consumer expectations in the early 1940s so that they could be directly incorporated into macro empirical models of spending and saving behavior (Katona, 1951; 1960; 1964; 1975). Katona summarized his views by saying that consumer spending depends on consumers' "ability and willingness to buy." By spending, he meant discretionary purchases; by ability, he meant the current income and assets of consumers; and by willingness, he meant consumers' assessments of their future economic prospects. Katona hypothesized that spending would increase when people viewed future economic conditions with optimism, and precautionary savings would rise when they became pessimistic. Moreover, Katona held that it was not simply the expected level of a consumer's future income, but also the certainty or uncertainty that was attached to those expectations. Katona enshrined this dual criterion by defining the dimension of consumer sentiment as ranging from optimism and confidence to pessimism and uncertainty.

Importantly, Katona believed that consumers' expectations were not completely predictable by current or past economic conditions nor were they the product of "animal spirits." Katona never believed that consumers had the needed information, computational skills, or the motivation to consciously form rational economic expectations. Nonetheless, Katona did believe that the informational content of consumer expectations was enough to make their expectations influential factors in shaping their spending and saving decisions and, as such, should be measured and incorporated into forecast models. Moreover, Katona ascribed to the consumer sector the same independent power shared by the government and business sectors to determine the course of the macroeconomy. Indeed, Katona entitled one of his books *The Powerful Consumer* (1960). Despite the common and widespread public belief in the power of the consumer, conventional economic theory to this day is still not compatible with consumer-led recessions.

INDEX OF CONSUMER SENTIMENT

George Katona and Eva Muller (1956) formed the first Consumer Confidence Index in 1952 based on data from household surveys that began in 1946. Shortly thereafter, the Index was renamed the Index of Consumer Sentiment. The renaming reflected Katona's belief that the underlying dimension had affective as well as cognitive components and he thought the word sentiment rather than confidence was the more appropriate term to convey that duality. While Katona would have preferred to report the detailed findings from the survey, he recognized that a summary index was needed for both ease of dissemination as well as empirical testing. He believed that no single question could adequately measure consumer sentiment. Although consumers' financial prospects were at the center of the proposed concept, changes in the overall economy and employment conditions were also important in determining future prospects, and price and credit conditions were important in influencing buying plans. Based on empirical research, five questions were ultimately selected, two on personal finances, two on prospects for the economy and jobs, and one question on buying conditions for durables. From a methodological point of view, multiple measures provided a more reliable estimate of the underlying concept. The Michigan surveys have always included many more questions touching on every aspect of people's economic lives, covering a wide array of economic expectations, including expectations about inflation and interest rates, home price appreciation, financial and non-financial assets, and impacts of government economic policies, among many other topics.

The research methodology has been adopted by many other countries. There are three general areas that are critical for the interpretation of the survey findings: the sample design and survey methodology, question wording, and transformations of the raw data into indices of consumer sentiment.

Survey Methodology

The seventy-two countries that have measured consumer sentiment are listed in Table 8.1. The countries represent all six inhabited continents, with most of the recent additions in Eastern Europe, Asia, and in South and Central America; a few of these countries, especially those in South and Central America, have yet to mount programs that have consistently measured expectations over time. The ideal design for internationally comparative surveys would be if all countries used a nationally representative sample, asked comparable questions, used a common method for index construction and seasonal adjustment, and provided information on response rates and procedures used to construct non-response weights. While the actual surveys include many variations of these standards, the data are broadly comparable. The European countries use the most consistent survey methodology across all members due to the guidance of the European Commission. Surveys conducted in other parts of the world are generally not harmonized, although the Organization for Economic Cooperation and Development (OECD) has made progress in recent years in convincing countries to conform to the accepted standards. Nonetheless, there are considerable differences in the economic and population characteristics of the countries which should be reflected in variations in the research design that recognize differences in the stage of development in the economy and in the population.

Sample Design and Interview Methodology

Most countries have designed their sample so that every adult member of the population or every private household has an equal chance of being selected. Nationally representative samples are standard in all developed countries; in emerging economies, the samples are often limited to urban centers, such as in Brazil, Malaysia, Mexico, and Peru. Such limitations of the national samples are not critical omissions if the areas excluded from the sample do not fully participate in their market economies. Most nations conduct the interviews by telephone, although some conduct in-person interviews, especially in lesser developed countries.

Sample weights are widely used to correct for differential non-response, and in some cases, to align samples with actual population distributions.

Table 8.1 *Countries Conducting Consumer Sentiment Surveys*

Albania	Ecuador	Japan	Portugal
Argentina	El Salvador	Kazakhstan	Romania
Armenia	Estonia	Latvia	Russia
Australia	Finland	Lithuania	Slovak Republic
Austria	France	Luxembourg	Slovenia
Belgium	Georgia	Malaysia	South Africa
Bolivia	Germany	Malta	South Korea
Brazil	Greece	Mexico	Spain
Bulgaria	Guatemala	Mongolia	Sweden
Canada	Hong Kong	Morocco	Switzerland
Chile	Hungary	Netherlands	Taiwan
China	Iceland	New Zealand	Thailand
Colombia	India	Norway	Trinidad & Tobago
Costa Rica	Indonesia	Pakistan	Turkey
Croatia	Ireland	Panama	Ukraine
Cyprus	Israel	Peru	United Kingdom
Czech Republic	Italy	Philippines	United States
Denmark	Jamaica	Poland	Uruguay

Some experiments have been done using the survey data collected in the United States, which indicates that measures of consumer sentiment are not very sensitive to coverage or non-response bias. In fact, no significant time-series differences in the consumer sentiment index were uncovered when the overall response rate was reduced by two-thirds (Curtin et al., 2000). This is, of course, no guarantee that the damaging impact of non-response and coverage biases will not be present in any other country or even in the United States in future surveys.

Questions Used to Measure Consumer Sentiment[3]

There were several variations in the types of questions that are now being used to measure consumer confidence. In nearly all of the countries, the questions focus on personal finances, general conditions in the economy including jobs and inflation, and intentions to spend or save. Of course, there are slightly different versions of these basic themes across the countries; nonetheless, all of the questions in all countries addressed similar

[3] The text describing the questions used to measure consumer sentiment and the methods used for index calculations was adapted from Curtin (2007) and used with the permission of OECD, Public Affairs and Communications Directorate.

topics. Indeed, the major differences involved variations in the frame of reference: some countries included questions about past as well as expected future changes, and some countries asked about time horizons of six months instead of the more typical twelve-month reference period. It should be noted that the questions used to calculate the sentiment indexes are typically drawn from surveys that include a broader range of questions that could be used to supplement or reformulate the current sentiment index.

For the purposes of this discussion, the countries were separated into three main groups largely based on differences in reference periods. The first group, accounting for more than half of all the countries, uses the harmonized European Union questionnaire; the second group uses questions on both past and expected future changes as well as a longer time horizon; and the final group uses similar questions, but with a six-month time horizon. The questions in all groups were modeled after the University of Michigan's survey to a varying extent. These basic groups also differ in the number of questions used in the overall confidence index, with the number ranging from three to six.

The basic rationale for the selection of questions to include in an index was that consumers first and foremost base their spending decisions on how they assess their financial situation. This is a much broader concept than wages or money income; it was meant to be all-inclusive. The term "financial situation" was meant to include not only wage and non-wage incomes but also how changes in assets, debts, and prices affect respondents' living standards as well as the impact from presence or absence of spouses, children, and other adults. When asking respondents to explain their responses, the University of Michigan surveys regularly recorded these reasons and other similar rationales. Questions about prospects for the overall economy are important since these general conditions define expected changes in the economic environment. Even consumers who believe that their jobs and incomes are secure expect to benefit more from a prosperous economy than a contracting economy. The first signs of economic difficulties do not directly affect everyone, but everyone pays attention to these cautionary indicators. Finally, the indices typically include a question on spending or savings preferences.

Question Variant 1: EU Harmonized. The European Commission governs the methodological standards for more than half of all countries that now conduct consumer tendency surveys. A recent review of the properties of the consumer sentiment index led to recommending a change from five questions comparable to the University of Michigan survey, to the following four questions (Goldrian et al., 2001):

- expected change in financial situation over the next twelve months;
- expected change in general economic situation over the next twelve months;
- expected change in unemployment over next twelve months;
- expected saving over next twelve months.

The sentiment index is defined as the arithmetic average of the four series. This new formulation was derived based on an analysis that used real private consumption as the criterion variable. The EU uses a weighting procedure to aggregate the indices from the individual countries, with the weights depending on the relative size of total personal consumption expenditures.

Question Variant 2: University of Michigan. The second major grouping of countries generally follows the University of Michigan version of the questions. These countries are: Argentina, Australia, Brazil, Canada (Decima), Hong Kong, Indonesia, Mexico, New Zealand, South Africa, Russia, and the United States. Hong Kong and South Africa only use the three forward-looking expectation questions in their confidence indicator. These countries all generally use a form of the following questions:

- personal financial situation over the past twelve months;
- expected change in personal finances in the next twelve months;
- expected change in general economic conditions in the next twelve months;
- expected change in general economic conditions in the next five years;
- buying conditions for consumer durables.

Question Variant 3: Six-Month Reference Periods. The countries in this group include Canada (Conference Board), China, Japan, Korea, Malaysia, Taiwan, and the United States (Conference Board). The questions in these countries include the following:

- expected change in family living standards in six months;
- expected change in income in six months;
- expected change in price level in six months;
- current and expected change in business conditions in six months;
- current and expected change in employment in six months;
- buying plans for durables in six months.

No country in this group includes questions on all of these topics; typically five questions are used. The single common element was the six-month horizon.

Index Construction

Nearly all of the countries allow for five potential responses to their questions, ranging from very positive (PP), positive (P), neutral, negative (N) to very negative (NN). Typically, two steps are involved in the computation of the overall consumer confidence index for each country. First, for each question a balance score is computed based on the percentage distribution as:

$$B = (PP + \tfrac{1}{2} P) - (\tfrac{1}{2} N + NN)$$

The overall confidence index is then simply the average of the balance scores:

$$CCI = \sum_{i=1}^{n} B_i / n$$

For countries that coded three instead of five response categories – positive (PP), neutral, and negative (NN) – the same index formula applies except the half-weight terms are simply dropped. More generally, the index formula can be written as:

$$CCI = \sum_{i} w_i B_i^s$$

where w is the weight and is the standardized balance score. The standardization is sometimes necessary to equalize the variance contributed by each component to the overall index. For example, an equal variance index would mean that each component question would be normalized by subtracting the mean and dividing by the variance. The standardized balance score could also include the application of a smoothing factor, such as a moving average that represents the number of months to cyclical dominance (which is the number of months for the percentage change in the cyclical component to exceed the irregular component without regard to sign). For the EU sentiment index, the length of time to cyclical dominance has been estimated at two to three months (Nilsson, 2000).

Alternate Methods of Index Construction

Instead of equally weighting each component question in the overall sentiment index, some have favored differential weights based on some statistical criteria. Psychologists have a long history in developing statistical methods for index construction, and economists have long favored each question's predictive ability to decide relative weights. Psychologists have preferred to posit that the ideal weights would be determined by how each question conforms to the unobserved subjective construct of consumer sentiment, while economists have thought it necessary to first convert the qualitative responses into quantitative scales for use in econometric analysis. Each of the proposed variants has been extensively investigated, and has been shown to be so highly correlated with indices based on equal weights that the revised weighting schemes provided no advantage in time-series analyses.

Dimensional Analysis. The Index of Consumer Sentiment was designed to represent a single dimension, ranging from optimism to pessimism. Psychologists have long favored the use of multiple questions to reliably estimate a single dimension index, with the weight accorded to each question calculated based on the common dimensional structure of the observed data. Common factor analysis is typically used to estimate the number of unique underlying dimensions represented by a set of questions. A finding of multiple dimensions among the five questions used to measure consumer sentiment would reduce the predictive power of the Sentiment Index.

The critical difference in the common factor approach was whether the structure of the data was best analyzed in its cross-section or time-series format. Most psychologists preferred the cross-section data format, while most economists preferred the time-series format. In the cross-section format, the correlations are based on the individual deviations from the survey means; in the time-series format, the correlations are based on the deviations in sample means across surveys over time. The former focuses on individual differences, the latter on sample differences. These two sets of correlations are quite distinctive, as shown in Tables 8.2 and 8.3.

The time-series correlations are between two and three times larger than the cross-section correlations. Although some of the cross-section correlations are quite low, they are all highly significant given that the estimates were based on quite large sample sizes (over 250,000). Importantly, if estimates were based on just a few surveys, the correlation may be quite

Table 8.2 *Cross-Section Correlations among Index Components*
(Pooled Data, 1978:1 to 2016:4)

	Current Personal Finances	Expected Personal Finances	Economic Outlook in Year	Economic Outlook in Five Years
Expected Personal Finances	0.231			
Economic Outlook in Year	0.244	0.270		
Economic Outlook in Five Years	0.196	0.225	0.459	
Durable Buying Conditions	0.161	0.116	0.205	0.163

Table 8.3 *Time-Series Correlations among Index Components*
(Quarterly Data, 1978:1 to 2016:4)

	Current Personal Finances	Expected Personal Finances	Economic Outlook in Year	Economic Outlook in Five Years
Expected Personal Finances	0.801			
Economic Outlook in Year	0.862	0.837		
Economic Outlook in Five Years	0.774	0.868	0.888	
Durable Buying Conditions	0.894	0.732	0.826	0.749

different due to contemporaneous economic circumstances or the larger sampling errors inherent in smaller samples. In contrast, while the time-series correlations have been more stable over the past several decades, they too show variability depending on the time period selected. By a simple inspection of the correlations, one may have guessed that there was a high likelihood of a single underlying common factor for the time-series, but that the cross-section correlation may not represent a single common factor. The most common suggestion over the years is that the question on durable buying conditions represents a separate dimension. Yet when the data was analyzed to determine whether a common factor was present, a single underlying dimension was found for both the time-series and cross-section correlations. Moreover, the optimal weights given to each question to form an index were roughly consistent across the two approaches in relative terms (see Table 8.4). It should be no surprise that the correlations between indices that were formed using the optimal question weights and the conventional equal weighting of the questions were high. Indeed, the indices were correlated at 0.99 over the 1978 to 2016 time period.

Table 8.4 *Optimal Question Weighting Based on Common Factor Approach*

	Cross-Section	Time-Series
Current Personal Finances	0.19	0.27
Expected Personal Finances	0.19	0.15
Economic Outlook in Year Ahead	0.36	0.26
Economic Outlook in Five Years	0.30	0.23
Durable Buying Conditions	0.14	0.15
Addendum	0.997	0.999

Time-series correlation of Index calculated with
common factor weights and equal weighted
balance scores

Quantification of Qualitative Scale. Some think that it is imperative to translate qualitative survey data into quantitative estimates of the underlying distribution. The argument is that balance scores rely on unrealistic assumptions about the underlying distribution of responses. This argument dates back to Theil (1952), and grew more influential after Carlson and Parkin (1975) proposed a convenient technique that could be used to quantify the survey data based on an underlying probability distribution. This quantification was seen as essential before using the survey data in an econometric analysis. Several other variations have been proposed including a time varying parameter model and the regression technique of Pesaran (1984). Each of these extensions was aimed at correcting deficits in the Carlson and Parkin technique (see Nardo, 2003 for a review). All of the alternatives, however, provide similar results. Table 8.5 shows the correlations between the usual balance score method and the Carlson and Parkin probability method for each question in the Sentiment Index as well as for the overall Sentiment Index calculated using each method. If the two measures exhibited low correlations then the two measures have some opportunity to show distinctive relationships with other economic variables, but if they were perfectly correlated they would provide identical results. The correlation for the overall Sentiment Index was quite high at 0.96, indicating little difference between the two methods of index construction. The advantages of using balance scores and equal weighting of the component questions is not only transparency but having indices that are not subject to revision. All of the alternative index scoring and index construction methods would necessarily differ depending on which cross-section surveys were used in the estimation or which time periods in the time-series methods.

Table 8.5 *Correlations of Component Scores Formed by Carlson-Parkin Technique and Standard Balance Scores (1978:1 to 2016:4)*

Current Personal Finances	0.992
Expected Personal Finances	0.998
Economic Outlook in Year Ahead	0.961
Economic Outlook in Next Five Years	0.928
Durable Buying Conditions	0.670
Index of Consumer Sentiment	0.936

Cross-Section Time-Series Equality. An advantage of the balance scoring method is that the questions and the Sentiment Index can be calculated in a similar fashion. This can be easily illustrated using the University of Michigan surveys. The basic formula for the most well-known Index of Consumer Sentiment is:

$$ICS_t = \sum_{j=1}^{5} \left(P_{jt}^f - P_{jt}^u \right)$$

where

P_{jt}^f = the sample proportion giving favorable replies to the *j*th question at time *t*, and

P_{jt}^u = the sample proportion giving unfavorable replies to the *j*th question at time *t*.

Equivalently, the formula can be expressed in terms of the individual responses and analysis can be carried out at the level of the individual respondent:

$$ICS_t = \sum_{J=1}^{5} \sum_{i=1}^{n} \frac{x_{ijt}}{n}$$

where

X^{ijt} = 1 if favorable response to *j*th question by *i*th respondent at time *t*,

X^{ijt} = −1 if unfavorable response to *j*th question by *i*th respondent at time *t*,

X^{ijt} = 0 for all other responses to *j*th question by *i*th respondent at time *t*.

Some observers have incorrectly assumed that the "same" responses get a zero score and are therefore eliminated from the analysis. Note that any linear transformation of the scores would yield an index that gave exactly the same results: instead of −1, 0, +1, it could have been scored +1, +2, +3 and so forth. In addition, an important strength of this method of scoring is that it allows comparable measures of variances and standard errors to be computed for both cross-section analysis as well as time-series analysis.

Case Elimination Methods. Finally, it is useful to note the procedure used by the Conference Board in constructing the Consumer Confidence Index. The scoring procedure for the component questions is equal to the proportion that gave "favorable" replies out of the total number of respondents who either gave favorable or unfavorable replies. This essentially eliminated the responses of any respondent who replied "same." This is inherently a time-series method, since no index can be calculated for any respondent who chooses the "same" response. The conventional balance scores discussed above can be calculated for every respondent, with the mean of the cases equal to the overall index.

EXPECTATIONS AND MEASUREMENT METHODS

The University of Michigan research program on the measurement of economic expectations continuously adapts to the introduction of new theories and new measurement methodologies. The sheer range of questions asked in the surveys has expanded significantly over the years, as have the types of response scales utilized. Careful experimentation has accompanied the expanded repertoire of economic expectations as well as the new response scales. The expansion partly reflects the different economic circumstances faced by consumers, and partly the growing sophistication of consumers. Questions on inflation expectations, for example, started out a half century ago by just asking consumers whether they expected prices to increase or decrease. Some years later, consumers were asked if prices would go up/ down "a little or a lot," and then consumers were given bracketed amounts of change (1–2%, 3–4%, 5%, and so forth). Finally, in the mid-1970s, consumers were simply asked for the expected percentage change.

Table 8.6 includes the list of questions and response scales currently used in the survey. These are the survivors; many more potential measures were eliminated due to their inability to produce valid and reliable data. A major experiment that is currently underway involves the use of probability response scales; half of those questions have already been eliminated and it is possible that more deletions will occur in the future.

The survey has always had additional questions that are included from time to time about recurrent economic topics, such as prospective changes in taxes or other fiscal or monetary policies, allowing comparisons among

Table 8.6 *University of Michigan Survey Measures*

Question		Response Scales
	Summary Indices	
1	Index of Consumer Sentiment	Index
2	Index of Current Economic Conditions	Index
3	Index of Consumer Expectations	Index
	Personal Finances	
4	Current Financial Situation Compared with a Year Ago	Verbal Likelihood
5	Reasons for Current Financial Situation	Free Response
6	Expected Change in Financial Situation in a Year	Verbal Likelihood
7	Current Financial Situation Compared with Five Years Ago	Verbal Likelihood
8	Expected Change in Financial Situation in Five Years	Verbal Likelihood
9	Expected Change in Household Income in Next Year	Verbal Likelihood and Percent
10	Expected Change in Real Income in the Next Year	Verbal Likelihood
11	Probability That Income Will Increase in Next Year	Probability
12	Probability of Real Income Gains during the Next Five Years	Probability
13	Probability of Losing a Job during the Next Five Years	Probability
14	Total Household Income	Dollar Amount
	Savings and Retirement	
15	Probability that Social Security/Pensions Provide Adequate Retirement Income	Probability
16	Change in Likelihood of a Comfortable Retirement Compared with Five Years Ago	Verbal Likelihood
17	Probability of Increase in the Stock Market Prices in the Next Year	Probability
18	Current Value of Stock Market Investments	Dollar Amount
19	Current Market Value of Primary Residence	Dollar Amount
	Economic Conditions	
20	News Heard of Recent Changes in Business Conditions	Verbal Likelihood
21	Items of News Heard of Recent Changes in Conditions	Free Response
22	Current Business Conditions Compared with a Year Ago	Verbal Likelihood
23	Expected Change in Business Conditions in a Year	Verbal Likelihood
24	Business Conditions Expected during the Next Year	Verbal Likelihood
25	Business Conditions Expected during the Next Five Years	Verbal Likelihood

Table 8.6　(*cont.*)

Question	Response Scales
Unemployment, Interest Rates, Prices, Government Policy	
26　Expected Change in Unemployment in the Next Year	Verbal Likelihood
27　Expected Change in Interest Rates during the Next Year	Verbal Likelihood
28　Expected Change in Prices during the Next Year	Verbal Likelihood and Percent
29　Expected Change in Prices during the Next Five Years	Verbal Likelihood and Percent
30　Opinions about the Government's Economic Policy	Verbal Likelihood
Household Durables Buying Conditions	
31　Buying Conditions for Large Household Durables	Verbal Likelihood
32　Reasons for Durable Buying Conditions	Free Response
Vehicle Buying Conditions	
33　Buying Conditions for Vehicles	Verbal Likelihood
34　Reasons for Vehicle Buying Conditions	Free Response
35　Expected Change in Gasoline Prices in the Next Year	Percentage
36　Expected Change in Gasoline Prices in the Next Five Years	Percentage
Home Buying and Selling Conditions	
37　Buying Conditions for Houses	Verbal Likelihood
38　Reasons for Home Buying Conditions	Free Response
39　Selling Conditions for Houses	Verbal Likelihood
40　Reasons for Home Selling Conditions	Free Response
41　Change in Home Values during the Past Year	Verbal Likelihood
42　Expected Change in Home Values in the Next Year	Verbal Likelihood and Percent
43　Expected Change in Home Values in the Next Five Years	Verbal Likelihood and Percent

the impacts on expectations from the Kennedy tax cuts and those advanced by Carter, Reagan, Bush, Obama, and Trump. Finally, the questionnaire has always included questions on large and small economic events that were quite unusual and had the potential to influence economic expectations, with the most important events related to war, terrorism, oil, financial crises, and other social and political events.

The measurement of the economic expectations held by consumers began in the United States in 1946, immediately following World War II and the Great Depression. At that time, most consumers judged economic conditions by how they affected their current job and income prospects. The University of Michigan surveys have always included a broader range of questions, but most questions asked in those early years dealt in some fashion with the economic factors behind consumers' job and income expectations. Over time, consumers have come to view their future economic prospects as dependent on a much broader range of expectations, including expected returns on financial assets and real estate holdings, the future value of private and public pensions and health care entitlements, future taxes, government subsidies, and job and income prospects. Moreover, consumers have increasingly made distinctions between near and long-term prospects when making their economic decisions. While all of these factors normally move in the same direction, either becoming more positive or negative, they often exhibit different rates of change, and sometimes move in opposite directions.

The expanded range of expectations has been due to the increasing prevalence of asset ownership and accrued entitlements, accelerated by an aging population. In addition, consumers have an increased recognition of potential risks originating in private markets as well as government policies. Presumably, the importance of the full array of expectations asked in the Michigan surveys would not be as relevant among lesser developed countries or those with younger populations. Nonetheless, along with a growing global interdependence of trade and finance, no consumer can be fully immune from international economic developments.

It is an empirical question as to whether any expectation on the expanded list would play a role in shaping the course of a county's macroeconomy. Many of the newer measures do not have a long enough time series to robustly test the merit of all the expectations now collected by the University of Michigan (see Table 8.6). Some, such as measures of household wealth have been shown to boost spending by US consumers (Curtin, 2013). Moreover, concerns about federal economic policies have been reported as frequently as complaints about the lack of job prospects for the first time in the US surveys conducted in 2013. While there is evidence of the rising importance of these additional economic expectations, there is no evidence that job and income prospects have been displaced.

An aging population will cause several shifts in the relative importance of different expectations. As people near retirement age, the importance of labor income declines while the importance of assets and pension entitlements rise. As a consequence, people will increasingly shift their attention from income uncertainties originating in the labor markets to uncertainties about future rates of return on financial assets. Moreover, compared with variations in labor market conditions, variations in the value of financial assets are more likely to exhibit abrupt and larger changes in response to both local and global financial markets. Little is known, however, about how consumers form expectations about future rates of return on various assets, let alone variations of returns adjusted for inflation.

Uncertainty about future rates of return on assets will prompt consumers to engage in precautionary declines in spending during retirement in much the same way that it prompted precautionary increases in savings prior to retirement. Understanding how people assess uncertainty must incorporate information on how people form expectations about future needs and how those expectations change as they age. Expectations about longevity and disability, and *in vivo* transfers and bequests, as well as changes in expectations about the provisions of private and public pensions and health care programs will all play a more important role.

Response Scales

There are four basic response scales that are now used in the University of Michigan surveys: verbal likelihood, percentages, probability, dollar amounts. The verbal likelihood response scale is evaluative, asking consumers whether they expect some economic condition to be better or worse, favorable or unfavorable. This type of response scale combines the affective and cognitive components of expectations in a way that requires the least conscious cognitive effort, as discussed in prior chapters. Evaluative scales are inherently dynamic, automatically adjusting to past experience and prior expectations. Conventional economic theory has no provision for this flexibility, but holds to an absolute standard that is independent of past experience or prior expectations. Such context independence means that any positive outcome, however small or unexpected, must be judged favorably, and any negative comparison must be judged unfavorably. No economist believes this to be an accurate portrayal other than in the state of equilibrium. Modern psychological theory holds that the reference used in comparative judgments varies over time and across people according to their past experience and expectations (Koszegi & Rabin, 2006; 2007; 2009).

Another commonly used response scale is percentages, asking, for example, the percent by which consumers expect income or prices to change. This response scale requires a greater cognitive effort on the part of consumers, although for changes in incomes and prices, most consumers normally refer to this information in terms of percentage changes. Moreover, as discussed in prior chapters, people have a natural affinity to use percentages (logs) when thinking about larger quantities. Although probability and percent response scales are quite close in meaning, people don't have the same innate abilities to think in terms of probabilities; people naturally think in terms of frequencies rather than probabilities. It does not mean that people cannot or are unwilling to calculate probabilities; it simply takes effortful conscious deliberation whereas frequencies can be handled effortlessly by nonconscious cognitive processes.

A non-numerical response scale used in the University of Michigan surveys simply asks consumers to explain their views in their own words. These responses are then grouped into codes that reflect comparable responses. The benefit of the free-response scales is that these questions measure the relative importance of recent economic developments as well as indicate the growing importance of new factors affecting expectations. Just as importantly, unanticipated events, such as the impact of a stock market plunge or a natural disaster, are automatically identified in the data.

The measurement of inflation expectations represents a good example of the evolution of response scales over time. When this question was first asked in 1946, the question simply asked whether prices were expected to increase or decrease. Then consumers were asked whether they judged the change favorably or unfavorably. Given that prices fell during the Great Depression, some consumers could have interpreted price declines as unfavorable and price increases as favorable. The negative reaction to price declines soon disappeared, but a half century later, renewed concerns about deflation may make that question relevant again. In the late 1940s, the follow-up question was changed to determine whether consumers expected prices to change a lot or a little. In the early 1960s, a new follow-up question asked consumers who expected price increases to estimate the expected percentage gain from pre-selected categories ranging from 1%–2% to 10% or more. Price declines were expected by so few consumers, that the extent of the expected decline was never initially asked. Finally, in the mid-1970s, the follow-up question simply asked consumers to provide answers in percentage terms as to how much they expected prices to increase or decrease, without indicating any pre-selected amounts. The pace of change toward more detailed scales was determined by the validity of the responses. As shown in Chapter 2, the current measures of inflation expectations have proven to be remarkably accurate predictors of actual inflation trends.

PROBABILITY MEASURES OF EXPECTATIONS

While economic theorists and consumers share the same general conceptualization of expectations, theorists have always desired greater measurement precision than was thought attainable from ordinary consumers

(Curtin, 2004; 2007). The ideal measure would specify the characteristics of the complete probability distribution for a precisely defined future event or outcome. Some surveys of economists now measure the complete probability distributions of future changes in GDP, personal income, and so forth, allowing estimates of the central tendency as well as the dispersion of expectations among professional economic forecasters. It should be no surprise that comparable measures of the probability distributions of expectations held by consumers have not been as successful. Some progress toward this end has been made. Nonetheless, the measurement of the complete probability distribution places much greater demand on survey respondents, in terms of the cognitive burden as well as a greater number of required questions. Importantly, these increased burdens entail high opportunity costs, both in terms of the ability of people to sustain high levels of cognitive deliberation as well as the number of different expectations that can be expressed in any given survey.

Cognitive Burden

Reliable and valid probability measures of expectations are subject to all of the problems usually associated with sample surveys. Aside from the more general issues of survey methodology, the crucial measurement issue has involved judgments about the capacity of individuals to provide meaningful responses using probability response scales. The goal of achieving the greatest possible precision must be balanced against the prevalence of measurement errors. Increased measurement precision relies on the motivation of respondents to engage in effortful conscious cognitive activity. The respondent burden is likely to be large insofar as people do not naturally conceptualize most economic expectations as probability distributions. While properly constructed questions, however demanding, may be free of systematic measurement errors among those respondents that provide answers, the fraction of respondents that do not provide any response typically increases along with the difficulty of the response scale presented to the respondent. If item non-response is relatively small, it is clearly preferable to record missing data rather than forcing uninformed guesses on the part of respondents. Although the same reasoning may hold when the fraction of item non-response is extraordinarily high, say by half of all respondents, the analytic potential of the measure is considerably diminished, and the potential non-response bias is considerably increased.

The presumed trade-off between the greater precision of numerical probability scales and the reduction in measurement error by using verbal scales has repeatedly been challenged as misguided.[4] The concerns have centered on the imprecision of verbal descriptions compared with numeric scales, and the resulting loss of interpersonal comparability as well as intrapersonal comparability across events or over time. Much of the research on the imprecision of verbal response codes has taken the form of asking respondents to match numerical probabilities to points on verbal likelihood scales. The results typically indicate that a broad and overlapping range of probabilities are associated with each point on the verbal scale (Fischhoff, 1994; Wallsten et al., 1986; Beyth-Marom, 1982). For example, the probabilities associated with the term "almost certain" differed significantly across respondents and extended over a relatively broad range, and overlapped with the range of probabilities assigned to the term "probable." Moreover, the range and overlap of probabilities varied depending on the specific verbal descriptions used in the scale.

Although numerical scales are assumed to allow the comparability of responses among people, across situations, and over time, it is not clear that they do. Just as two respondents may associate different numerical probabilities with a given verbal scale category, respondents may well differ in their understanding of the meaning of a given numeric probability. More convincing evidence would be that the meanings that people attach to different points on numeric probability scales show less variation than different points on verbal scales. For example, is there more or less variation in how people interpret a probability of 5% than how they interpret "very unlikely?" Moreover, methodological research has rarely focused on whether verbal likelihood scales or numeric probability scales show a greater correspondence to behavioral decisions. Another variant of this same issue is the presumption that the algebra of modern probability theory can be used to interpret the results (Dominitz & Manski, 1997). As Kahneman and Tversky (1982:48) have noted, "In making predictions and judgments under uncertainty, people do not appear to follow the calculus of chance or the statistical theory of prediction." Indeed, rational decision making is impossible in the presence of Knightian uncertainty. Since decisions around turning points in the macroeconomy often need to be made in the midst of ambiguity, measurement scales must be flexible enough to capture these judgments.

Overall, numeric probability scales are said to have clear theoretical advantages for a broad range of research topics, and have long been

---

[4] The balance of this subsection as well as the two following subsections on "Measurement of Uncertainty" and "Framing and Context Effects" are drawn from Curtin (2004:143–146). Reprinted with the permission of the University of Michigan Press.

advocated by Fischhoff (1994), Manski (1990), Savage (1971), and Juster (1966). Although simply shifting from a verbal response scale to a numeric probability scale may have merit, insofar as the question asks respondents for a single-point estimate of the likelihood of an event or outcome, the numeric response may still be vulnerable to misinterpretation. Strict interpersonal comparability would require the assumption that all respondents' replies were based on the same measure of the probability distribution's central tendency (the mean, mode, or median) or that all respondents viewed the underlying probabilities as being normally distributed, so that the mean, mode, and median were identical. The proposed remedy to the potential misinterpretation is to estimate the entire shape of the probability distribution, giving researchers the ability to consistently compute the measure of central tendency that is appropriate for their research design.

Measurement of Uncertainty

The resolution to these measurement issues, however, was not the primary motivation to move toward the measurement of the complete probability distribution. The impetus has mainly come from developments in economic theory that have increasingly stressed the importance of the degree of uncertainty associated with consumers' expectations. The measurement of uncertainty at the level of the individual consumer requires the specification of the complete probability distribution for each person. Given the entire distribution, measures of central tendency can then be supplemented by measures of dispersion to capture the impact of the uncertainty with which expectations are held. This distinction dates back to at least Pigou and Keynes. Keynes drew the distinction between the implications of evidence based on the probabilities and the weight of evidence based on people's confidence in the assessment, and questioned whether both aspects could be captured by a single probability number (Camerer & Weber, 1992).

Researchers have typically focused on two techniques to elicit numeric probabilities to estimate the entire cumulative distribution function (Lichtenstein et al., 1982). The first asks respondents to attach "values" to various points on the percentile distribution, say at 1%, 25%, 50%, 75%, and 99%. The other method asks respondents to attach probabilities to selected values (say, an income of $10,000, $25,000, $50,000, and so forth). Research on these two approaches indicates that the former method yields more narrow interquartile ranges, while the latter is subject to anchoring effects. In a comparison of several variants of each method, Seaver, Winterfeldt, and Edwards (1978) found that for continuous variables, the superior approach was to ask respondents to attach probabilities to selected values. This is the measurement approach that has been used by Dominitz and Manski (1997) and Guiso, Japelli, and Terlizzese (1992).

Estimates of the full probability distribution are typically based on questions that ask respondents to identify a limited number of points along the distribution. Guiso, Japelli, and Terlizzese (1992) asked respondents to allocate probabilities across a fixed set of values, forcing the sum to equal 100. In contrast, Dominitz and Manski (1997) took advantage of computer-assisted interviewing protocols to dynamically adjust the values on which respondents were asked to provide probability estimates. Based on information provided by respondents about the relevant range of potential outcomes, a midpoint anchor was selected and respondents were asked to specify probabilities over a fixed set of intervals surrounding the midpoint. The choice of the number of measured points on the underlying distribution reflects the usual tradeoffs between precision, judgments about the ability of respondents to reliably distinguish ever finer differences in probabilities, and how much interview time should be devoted to these measures compared with other competing measures.

While the overall results of these initial attempts are quite promising, the results are not without some drawbacks. A presumably correctable problem is that the detailed questions prompted unusually large amounts of item non-response, and among those that provided answers, an unusually large number of respondents reported a 100% probability for a single value rather than probabilities spread over a range of possible outcomes.[5] In reviewing the results of the survey conducted by Guiso et al., Carroll (1994:135) interpreted the results as an indication that consumers did not understand the survey question rather than

---

[5] The frequency of item non-response in the Italian Survey of Household Income and Wealth was high by any standard: 55% of eligible respondents did not answer the questions, and among those that did provide answers, 63% gave a point estimate for expected change in income, inflation, or both (Guiso et al., 1992). Dominitz and Manski (1997) measured current and expected income *levels*, taking the difference as a measure of expected *change* in income. The resulting item non-response rate was 47% for the measure of expected income change. Calculating the expected change as the difference in levels is likely to yield estimates that are coarse and imprecise compared with direct measures of the expected change in income. This is an especially important problem for time-series analysis since defining income expectations as the difference between two relatively noisy level estimates may lead to high and spurious variability in income expectations (Curtin, 2004).

an indication of the absence of uncertainty. Careful methodological experimentation is likely to provide question sequences that minimize the item non-response as well as provide measures that reliably capture variations in uncertainty. Dominitz and Manski achieved higher response rates by use of a computer-assisted approach that tailored questions to each individual's economic situation, and their approach holds the most promise for future development. This methodological task is not trivial since overconfidence in probability assessments has been widely documented. Overconfidence is typically measured by the width of the interquartile range, the same metric used by Dominitz and Manski as a proxy for uncertainty. There has been a good deal of research on what is termed the "debiasing" or "calibration" of probability scales, which indicates that even extended instructions to respondents has only a modest impact on reducing overconfidence or certainty of expectations (Lichtenstein et al., 1982).

Framing and Context Effects

Another rather straightforward methodological concern involves the issue of question framing. There has been little research on the impact of different frames of reference that could be used in the measurement of expectations. It is unlikely that shifting the frame of reference from gains to losses would yield the same probability distributions. For example, asking about the probability of losing a job versus asking about the probability of keeping a job, the probability of income gains versus losses, or the probability of living to age eighty-five compared with asking about the probability of dying before age eighty-five, and so forth. Nor has there been much research on whether expectations based on one or the other frame of reference would show greater correspondence with subsequent behavior. Indeed, it is likely that responses to questions about gains and losses are not symmetrical, so that measures based on one or the other frame might show stronger or weaker behavioral associations.

A more difficult challenge involves the measurement of expected changes in real rather than just nominal economic variables. Economic theory typically focuses on expected changes in inflation-adjusted measures, such as real income. If changes in income and inflation were independent, separate measures of expected changes in nominal income and inflation would suffice. Such economic variables are rarely independent, however, and combining the separate measures requires assumptions about the covariance of the growth rate of nominal income and inflation expected by each

respondent.[6] Clearly, for some respondents, the covariance could be positive and quite high, at least for that part of their income that was indexed
to inflation, while for others, the covariance could be negative. This measurement problem is avoided if all consumers were assumed to expect the
same inflation rate (with certainty); with this assumption, differences in real
income uncertainty would be equivalent to differences in nominal income
uncertainty. While it is commonplace to calculate past real income growth
by applying the same inflation adjustment factor to all consumers, it would
defeat the very purpose of measures of real income uncertainty to assume no
variation in expected inflation rates. Although this measurement problem
could also be avoided by simply asking respondents to state their expected
probability distributions in *real* terms, the difficulty of such questions may
result in even greater item non-response. Moreover, it is clearly of some
interest to distinguish between these two sources of uncertainty. When real
income uncertainty is primarily driven by uncertainty about inflation, consumers may adopt characteristically different behaviors than when it is primarily due to uncertainty about their future wages. How to best estimate
the joint probability distributions that are needed to determine real income
uncertainty deserves a high priority on future research agendas.

Another measurement challenge lies in the recognition that household
income is derived from many different sources and that uncertainty may
differ significantly for each income source. Focusing only on the labor
income of the respondent may represent a comprehensive measure among
young single adult households, but just a fraction among older two-earner
households. While it may be more realistic to assume independence between
different sources of household income than between each income source
and inflation, it still represents a significant task to estimate the uncertainty
associated with total household income. Of course, the ideal measure would
be of uncertainty about the future lifetime path of human and non-human
wealth, rather than simply focusing on uncertainty about next year's income.

EXPERIMENTAL TESTS OF PROBABILITY MEASURES

To assess the potential of probability measures, the University of Michigan
has experimented with several probability questions to determine an
optimal format of the questions, to assess their cognitive burden, and to

---

[6] This is what was done by Guiso et al. (1992) to estimate uncertainty about expected real
incomes. While the lack of variance in income and inflation expectations may have been
an unfortunate methodological artifact, it meant that for the majority of cases the covariance term could be unambiguously defined since the variance of income, inflation, or both
were zero (Curtin, 2004).

determine how best to minimize any systematic biases in the responses.[7] The costs to achieve greater detail in measures of expectations is two-fold. The first cost is in terms of the sustained amount of time during which people can be expected to provide the required conscious cognitive effort to answer probability questions. As already documented, the conscious cognitive effort required to answer probability questions implies unusually strict limitations on the number of questions people will devote to this effortful task. These cognitive burdens typically result in increases in item non-response and measurement errors. More precise questions are typically more difficult questions. More demanding questions require a high degree of motivation on the part of respondents to provide accurate answers, often require respondents to access a greater amount of information from memory, and demand that respondents have greater conceptual and computational skills. These higher demands may cause respondents to refuse to answer the questions, resulting in more missing data.

The second cost is the lost opportunity to measure another concept. Most surveys have many more potential questions than they have room to accommodate, and most surveys favor designs that cover all important topics in some detail rather than measure fewer concepts in greater detail. While estimates of the complete probability distribution of the typical economic expectation can be based on as few as five to seven questions, this would mean that a substantial number of other questions could not be asked. Adding new questions to a continuing monthly survey is very expensive, especially since a large number of observations are needed before any time-series tests can be performed.

As a result of these considerations, the initial experiments were designed to ask consumers to attach a probability to a defined future event, such as an increase in income, loss of a job, or the probability of stock market gains. No attempt has yet been made to measure the complete probability distribution for any economic expectation given the substantial costs involved. The experiments did provide one crucial test that has rarely been investigated: do the central tendencies of probability or verbal likelihood measures show greater time-series correspondence with behavioral decisions?

The tests have shown mixed results. On the positive side, probability questions were easily adapted to population surveys and respondents did not find them too onerous to provide an answer. On the negative side, there were several questions where a comparison of the probability and verbal likelihood response scales found virtually identical times-series results.

---

[7] Small portions of this section were drawn from Curtin (2007) and used with permission of OECD, Public Affairs and Communications Directorate.

Probability Measures

Eleven probability questions have been asked during the past decade covering three core areas: employment, income, and financial investments. Each question asked respondents to assess the probability that the:

Y1: Household income will increase by more than overall prices during the next five years

Y2: Personal income will increase during the next twelve months

Y3: Personal income will increase by more than 10% during the year ahead

Y4: Personal income will increase by more than overall prices during the year ahead

Y5: Income from social security and job pensions will be adequate for retirement

J1: Respondent or spouse will lose a job within the next five years that they wanted to keep

J2: Respondent will lose a job within the next twelve months that they wanted to keep

J3: Respondent will get a new job at least as good in terms of wages and benefits

M1: Mutual fund of $1,000 will increase in value during the next twelve months

M2: Mutual fund of $1,000 will increase by at least 10% during the next twelve months

M3: Mutual fund of $1,000 will increase by more than overall prices during the next twelve months

Note that all the questions asked about "one-sided" probabilities: the probability of a job loss, the probability of an increase in income, or the probability of a gain in the value of mutual funds. The questions did not attempt to determine the probability distribution across all potential outcomes. Rather the questions focused on the probability of a single outcome (for example, a 10% increase in income). The first set of experiments thus fell short of specifying the entire probability distribution. This decision was based on the trade-off between the much larger number of questions that would be needed to measure the entire probability distribution of a single topic and the number of topic areas that could be covered in the experiment. The time period in which each question was asked is shown in Table 8.7, along with the mean and median of the replies, the extent of missing data and the number of cases.

Table 8.7 *Summary Statistics for Probability Measures of Expectations*

	Probability That ...	Time	Mean	Median	%Miss	Cases
Y1	Household income will increase by more than overall prices during the next five years	1998:01–2013:09	37.0	30.0	2.4%	94,951
Y2	Personal income will increase during the next twelve months	2002:06–2013:09	45.1	49.7	2.0%	68,410
Y3	Personal income will increase by more than 10% during the year ahead	2002:06–2003:05	30.2	19.0	3.9%	6,015
Y4	Personal income will increase by more than prices during the year ahead	2003:06–2004:09	36.2	30.1	2.8%	8,043
Y5	Income from social security/pensions will be adequate for retirement	1998:01–2013:09	35.5	29.3	2.9%	94,951
J1	Respondent/spouse will lose job within the next five years that they wanted to keep	1998:01–2013:09	18.6	9.6	1.0%	94,951
J2	Respondent will lose a job within the next twelve months that they wanted to keep	2002:06–2004:09	15.0	4.9	1.1%	9,052
J3	Get a new job at least as good as job lost in terms of wages and benefits	2002:06–2004:09	47.0	49.8	2.3%	9,052
M1	Mutual fund of $1,000 will increase in value during the next twelve months	2002:06–2013:09	46.2	49.9	5.1%	68,410
M2	Mutual fund of $1,000 will increase by at least 10% during the next twelve months	2002:06–2003:05	31.1	25.0	7.6%	6,015
M3	Mutual fund of $1,000 will increase by more than overall prices during the next twelve months	2003:06–2004:09	40.3	49.5	6.0%	8,043

It should also be noted that it is unlikely that the same probability distributions would be measured if the frame of reference were shifted from gains to losses (Kahneman & Tversky, 1979). For example, it is likely that asking about the probability of losing a job is not the inverse of asking about the probability of keeping a job, nor asking the probability of income or investment gain equivalent to asking about losses. It is likely that responses to questions about gains and losses are not symmetrical. For these initial experiments, the questions used what is the most common frame of reference for the respondents, namely losses about jobs and gains about income and investments.

Incomplete Use of Probability Scales

The extent of "don't know" responses is typically taken as an indication of the difficulty of the question, and in this case, the relatively low missing data rates suggest that most respondents did not find these questions too difficult (see Table 8.8). For the probability questions about job prospects, missing data rates ranged from 1.0% to 2.3%, while missing data rates on income prospects were higher, ranging from 2.0% to 3.9%, and missing data rates for the questions on returns to investments in mutual funds were the highest, ranging from 5.1% to 7.6%. This pattern was not surprising and indicates the greater difficulty in estimating stock market returns than income or job prospects. Nonetheless, the relatively low levels of missing data indicate that these questions were not perceived as being too difficult to answer by most respondents.

A closer inspection of the data does raise more concerns. More troublesome was that the full range of the probability scale was not utilized by respondents (see Table 8.8). Across the eleven questions, just 2% to 6% of all respondents gave answers that did not indicate near certainty (probabilities of 0% to 5% or 95% to 100%) or were not rounded responses (multiples of 10 or 25 and 75). Indeed, about half of all respondents gave certain or near certain responses or responded 25%, 50%, or 75%, a virtual five-point scale. Most of the rest of the responses were multiples of 10.

Why did the vast majority of respondents choose so few points out of the range from 0 to 100? The most common answer is that the responses represent "rounded" estimates. Several hypotheses have been suggested to account for this pattern. Given the potentially high cognitive burden of these questions, some have suggested that respondents simply report the first satisfactory answer that comes to mind and these estimates are often rounded (Krosnick, 1999). Others have suggested that digit preference is a

Table 8.8 *Limited Range of Responses for Probability Measures of Expectations*

Probability That	Certain (0% or 100%)	Near Certain (1–5% or 95–99%)	Quarter Rounding (25%, 50%, 75%)	Ten Rounding (10,20,30, 40,50,60, 70,80,90)	All Other Codes	Total (%)
Y1 Real household income in five years	19	5	25	48	3	100
Y2 Real personal income in year	34	7	19	38	2	100
Y3 Income increases by more than 10%	36	7	17	37	3	100
Y4 Income increase more than prices	26	7	23	40	4	100
Y5 Social Security and job pensions adequate	23	6	23	45	3	100
J1 Lose job in five years	47	4	14	32	3	100
J2 Lose a job in next year	45	12	10	31	2	100
J3 Get a new job as good as job lost	21	5	25	45	4	100
M1 Mutual fund gains in year	11	6	30	47	6	100
M2 Mutual fund rises by 10% in year	15	8	25	47	5	100
M3 Mutual fund rises more than prices in year	11	7	31	46	5	100

widespread phenomenon, exhibited by nearly all responses to open-ended numeric questions of all types (Edouard & Senthilselvan, 1997; Baker, 1992). The digits that are favored are precisely those that constituted the vast majority of the responses to the probability questions, namely multiples of 10 plus 5, 25, and 75. Others have suggested that people retrieve the most accessible data from memory, and that is the mode rather than the mean or median of the underlying probability distribution (Lillard & Willis, 2001). This "modal choice" hypothesis suggests that the data that is easiest to retrieve is where the probability distribution reaches its peak.

Economists have interpreted such results as exhibiting a "near rationality," whereby the rounding represents the level of precision that is associated with differences that matter to the respondent. A more traditional economic interpretation involves balancing costs and benefits: people want to minimize computational costs so they compute detailed probabilities only to the extent that the finer detail would affect their decisions. These explanations also favor rounded numbers.

There is another explanation emerging from neuroscience that asserts that people do not possess such fine detail but rather hold coarser probabilities in memory. In this explanation, rounding does not reflect the additional cost of cognitive processing but rather reflects the true state of their knowledge as most people only maintain "rounded" numbers in memory (Dehaene, 1997). This hypothesis has other implications, including that probabilities would not generally adjust to small changes unless some threshold was reached, and that sudden and unusually large changes in probabilities could result when the new information exceeded the threshold. Another possibility is that since people don't typically use expectations defined as probabilities, but rely on expectations defined by frequencies, probabilistic expectations are not routinely updated nor subject to the same automatic nonconscious error correction processes according to expectations that people actually use for decision making.

Errors in Probability Assessments

The experimental questions allowed another test of how well the respondents understood the underlying task. Respondents were asked about the probability that their income would increase during the year ahead and then were asked about the probability that their income would increase by more than 10% during the year ahead (questions Y2 and Y3). A conjunctive error appears if a respondent judged the probability of getting any increase in income to be lower than the probability of getting

Table 8.9 *Consistent and Inconsistent Probability Responses to Questions on Expected Income Gains and Expected Gains in the Value of Mutual Funds*

	Personal Income		Mutual Fund	
	10% Gain	Real Gain	10% Gain	Real Gain
Consistent with probability of any increase in income/mutual fund – Total	73	69	60	56
Both 0%	14	12	5	2
Both 100%	6	5	1	2
Other consistent replies	53	52	54	52
Inconsistent with probability of any increase in income/mutual fund – Total	27	31	40	44
Equal probabilities	19	20	24	27
Other inconsistent replies	8	11	16	17
Total	100%	100%	100%	100%
Cases	5,724	7,731	5,438	7,359

a 10% increase in income. There are two possible exceptions to this test of the conjunction fallacy. The first is if a respondent expected an income decline with certainty, then the probability of any increases as well as the probability of an increase of 10% could be zero; the second is if the respondent expected an increase of more than 10% with certainty, then both probabilities could be 100%.

When the two responses were compared on more than 5,000 cases, 53% of all replies were consistent in that respondents assigned a lower probability to getting a 10% increase than to getting any income increase at all. Another 14% reported zero probabilities to both questions, and 6% reported that both probabilities were 100%. If these are also assumed to be consistent, a total of 73% provided consistent probabilities (first data columns in each panel of Table 8.9).

Inconsistent replies to the two probability questions on income gains were given by a total of 27%, but the majority of these errors were recorded when a respondent assigned the same probability to both expecting any increase as well as expecting a 10% increase. Just 8% of the sample gave different probabilities that were inconsistent. Some of these equal probabilities may have resulted from the tendency of respondents to round their answers and may not reflect a true inconsistency. Nonetheless, providing equal probabilities to two questions that span a relatively large difference in income expectations seems to indicate that these respondents did not understand the underlying notion of probabilities or were unwilling to undertake the required cognitive burden to provide accurate answers.

The same overall pattern was found in the questions on the probability of any positive increase in a mutual fund and the probability of a 10% gain (questions M1 and M2, third column in Table 8.9). Although nearly equal proportions gave consistent non-zero or 100% replies (54% for mutual fund gains and 53% for income gains), there were many fewer respondents who responded with a 0% probability for mutual fund gains than income gains (5% versus 14%) and 100% replies (1% versus 5%). As a result, the total number with consistent replies was much lower (60% versus 73%), and a correspondingly higher percentage gave inconsistent replies (40% versus 27%). Again, most of the inconsistent replies involved identical probabilities. Inconsistent replies that were not equal were recorded twice as frequently for mutual fund investments compared with income expectations (16% versus 8%). While rounding and digit preference may be expected to be even more likely to influence responses to questions about future returns on investments, it is still rather discouraging that even a 10% gain was judged equal to any gain at all by one-quarter of all respondents. Again, it may be just as likely that respondents were unwilling to exert the necessary conscious cognitive effort to properly answer the two questions, but simply provided the same answer.

The questions on the probability of income and mutual fund increases were also followed by an alternative set of questions about real gains, that is, the probabilities of gains after an adjustment was made for changes in the overall level of inflation (questions Y2 and Y4 and questions M1 and M3). The consistency test is much less rigorous in this case since the level of inflation was relatively low; at the time these data were collected, the inflation rate averaged about 2.5% (CPI-u). Surprisingly, the number of consistent replies, excluding 0% and 100%, were quite close to what was observed in the 10% experiment for both the income question (52% versus 53%) and the mutual fund question (54% versus 52%). Inconsistent replies were very close, although there was a slight increase for real income gains (31% versus 27%) and real mutual fund gains (44% versus 40%). Again the data suggest that either the probabilities given by respondents were rounded and cover a broad range or that a significant number of respondents didn't understand the concept of probabilities.

The data on whether the respondent gave consistent or inconsistent replies can also be examined within demographic subgroups. The standard hypothesis is that the higher the education, the higher the cognitive capacity, and the less likely the respondent would provide inconsistent answers.

Table 8.10 *Consistent and Inconsistent Replies to Probabilities by Education (Probability of Any Size Gain versus a 10%+ Gain)*

	Probability of Income Gain			Probability of Mutual Fund Gain		
	High School	Some College	College Grad	High School	Some College	College Grad
Consistent Replies						
Both 0%	18	13	12	6	5	5
Both 100%	4	6	7	2	1	1
Other Consistent	46	52	58	41	55	62
Subtotal	68	71	77	49	61	68
Inconsistent Replies						
Equal Probabilities	21	20	17	30	23	19
Other Inconsistent	11	9	6	21	16	13
Subtotal	32	29	23	51	39	32
Total	100%	100%	100%	100%	100%	100%
Cases	1,928	1,301	2,472	1,759	1,239	2,415

The proportion giving consistent replies on the income and mutual fund questions does suggest that cognitive skills play an important role. Consistent replies were the most common among college graduates, and inconsistent replies most common among those with a high school degree or less (see Table 8.10). For the questions on the probability of an income increase, the total with consistent replies was 77% among college grads and 68% among those with no more than a high school education; for mutual fund gains, the difference was even larger, with 68% of college grads versus 49% among those with high school education.

While greater cognitive skills appear to be significantly related to higher quality answers to the probability questions, it is still true that among college graduates, nearly one in four gave inconsistent replies to the questions on income and nearly one in three provided inconsistent replies to the questions on mutual funds. These results suggest that probability measures of economic expectations are error prone, presumably to a greater degree than the verbal likelihood response scales. This presumption is based on the idea that probability response scales require a good deal of conscious cognitive effort, whereas verbal likelihood scales are more likely to be partly based on automatic nonconscious evaluations. It may well be true that some of the inconsistencies of probability scales may be due to rounding, although a rounding rule would need to be capable of providing inconsistent results.

More widely accepted hypotheses are that people do not fully understand probabilities, or that they do not want to expend the cognitive effort needed to answer the questions accurately. If either of these hypotheses is true, it would imply that, even for college graduates, the probability measure asked for a level of detail that they were incapable or unwilling to deliver.

Comparisons of Probability versus Verbal Likelihood Scales

While no rigorous comparisons between the results based on probability scales and verbal likelihood scales are possible with the collected data, comparisons of broadly similar questions are possible. The best evidence would have come from using the same question wording but with two different response scales: the probability response scale and the verbal likelihood scale. Instead, the probability and verbal likelihood questions asked about slightly different versions of the same question. Income expectations were assessed for the "household" using the verbal likelihood scale and for "personal" income for the probability scale. Inflation-adjusted income expectations and unemployment expectations were asked for the year ahead using the verbal likelihood scale and for the next five years using the probability scale. How important are these differences in wording? Certainly, personal income is equivalent to household income for one person households, but could be quite different for households with multiple earners. Nonetheless, the questions only ask about the direction of change or the probability of an increase in income. The difference between a one-year and a five-year horizon is more substantial, with questions about the longer horizon being more difficult. Importantly, the five-year probability question on potential job loss asks about the respondent's own prospects whereas the verbal likelihood question asks about national trends in unemployment.

Given that the data are intended to act as a leading indicator of changes in a macroeconomic analysis framework, time-series comparisons are the most appropriate tests. Time-series tests are essentially about changes in the monthly sample means, not the variance of results across people within a month. While the potential range of responses to the probability scale greatly exceeded the three-point verbal likelihood scales, it may well be true that the probability scales may perform better in the analysis of individual responses within a survey. For the time-series analysis, the mean probabilities were computed and compared to the likelihood scores calculated as balance statistics (% increase − % decline +100).

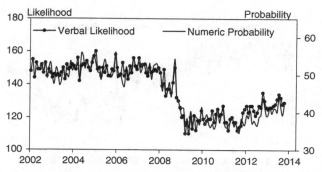

Figure 8.1 Nominal Income Expectations – Numeric Probability versus Verbal Likelihood Measures

Figure 8.1 shows the correspondence between the probability of personal income increases (Y2) and the three-point verbal likelihood question on expected change in household incomes. Although both questions use a twelve-month horizon, one asks about the probability of an increase in personal income while the other asks whether household income will increase or decrease. It is surprising how close the correspondence was over the eleven-year period between these two monthly series. The time-series correlation is 0.95, indicating that the two series give virtually identical information. Even for a single person household, many would have expected a larger difference between the probability of an income increase and the expected direction of change in income during the year ahead. The much greater detail contained in the probability scales added nothing to the time-series information. The 100 different gradations in probability were totally captured by the time-series changes in the three-point verbal likelihood scale. It may be true that the more detailed probability responses are helpful in the micro analysis of an individual's behavior, but any such advantage disappeared at the macro level. It is hard to believe that this could occur by chance in nearly 200 monthly surveys.

Figure 8.2 shows the time-series data for the probability and likelihood scales for the two questions on inflation-adjusted incomes. Again the correspondence is quite high, with a time-series correlation of 0.96. The greater detail of the probability responses added no time-series information to the verbal likelihood scoring. The close correspondence is all the more surprising given the significant difference between the two questions: the probability question asks about changes in real income within the next five years and the verbal likelihood questions about the year ahead; the probability

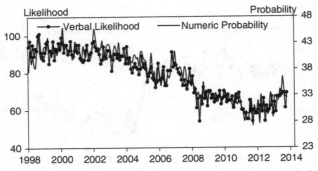

Figure 8.2 Real Income Expectations – Numeric Probability versus Verbal Likelihood Measures

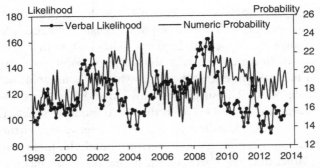

Figure 8.3 Unemployment Expectations – Numeric Probability versus Verbal Likelihood Measures

scale only asks about expected gains, not expected gains and declines in real income; and the probability scale allows 100 different gradations of responses compared with just a three-point verbal likelihood scale.

Perhaps the biggest difference in question wording involved job expectations. The probability question specifically asked about how likely it would be that the respondent (or spouse) would lose a job in the next five years (J1), whereas the verbal likelihood question asked whether unemployment in general was expected to increase, remain unchanged, or decrease (this was the question that proved to be a significant predictor of the unemployment rate in Chapter 2). Here the difference between the probability and verbal likelihood measures was significant. As shown in Figure 8.3, the two series were basically independent, with a time-series correlation of 0.04. In comparison with the nearly identical data on income expectations in response to the probability and verbal likelihood scales,

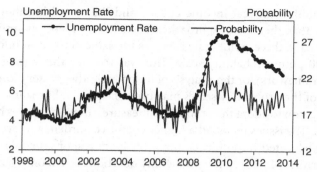

Figure 8.4 Probability of Unemployment versus National Unemployment Rate

job expectations questions appear to be heavily influenced by whether the question referred to people's own job or jobs in general. It is likely that the longer time horizon of the probability question (five years versus the next year) also had a significant impact. Some may think the disjointed results are hardly surprising. Nonetheless, why the differences showed up in unemployment expectations and not in income expectations that had comparable differences in question wording is still a puzzle.

It could also be anticipated that since people possess more information about their own job than for the nation as a whole, the probability measure may be a better predictor of the national unemployment rate than the verbal likelihood measure discussed in Chapter 2. Figure 8.4 shows the correspondence between the probability of job loss and the national unemployment rate. It is apparent that there is no close correspondence between the two over the past dozen years. The series could have been scaled so that either people judged the probability of job loss too low in the early period or too low in the later part of the period; the scaling simply reflects which period had a closer fit for the longest period. The peak of the probability series occurred in 2003 (at 24.6 when the unemployment rate was 5.7%); during the Great Recession, it came close but never topped that earlier peak (24.2 when the unemployment rate was 8.7%). It could be argued that unemployment was so widespread and labor force dropouts rose so much following 2009 that the probability of losing a job decreased since the job had been already lost or abandoned. Whatever the cause of the difference, it is clear that the verbal likelihood question on unemployment expectations is significantly related to subsequent changes in the unemployment rate. The same cannot be said for the probability measure.

Although these experiments are not complete, the preliminary results are as challenging as they are promising. The time-series comparisons of the probabilities of real income change and the verbal likelihood scales indicated that these two approaches yield nearly identical results. This suggests that a three-point scale captures the same amount of information as the 100-point probability scale. This was true for the macroeconomic analysis framework; for the analysis of individuals, the greater cross-section variance of the probability scales may prove helpful. While some may take this as a reason to adopt the probability measures, those measures had other problems. The issues included a higher cognitive burden, and even among the most educated respondents, the probability responses contained substantial errors. Moreover, the probability questions tested only asked about one side of the distribution, meaning that a full implementation would require at least several more questions. Unfortunately, this amounts to a one-sided comparison since the more traditional likelihood measures were not subjected to such scrutiny. Nonetheless, Occam's razor would favor the more parsimonious verbal likelihood scale for time-series analysis.

CHALLENGES IN THE TWENTY-FIRST CENTURY

The measurement of consumer expectations will become even more challenging in the twenty-first century. What constitutes consumer confidence will continue to expand into a broader and more complex assessment of economic prospects. The identification of which expectations will increase in importance as predictors of consumers' economic behavior during the years ahead is a difficult task. No one sentiment index is likely to be optimal for all uses, for all population subgroups, nor for all nations. Moreover, decisions about how samples of consumers are selected and the methodology used to measure expectation will be more difficult in the years ahead. Traditional methods that rely on probability samples, direct questioning, and the voluntary participation of respondents are already faced with declining population coverage, low response rates, and high costs. Even if coverage and response rates can be improved in the future, costs to obtain representative samples are likely to still be an issue.

These issues have led some researchers to favor non-probability samples as an acceptable alternative even if traditional statistical significance tests no longer apply. Indeed, it will be hard to avoid the use of "big data" from readily available digital information to extract some proxies for economic expectations. Already there have been many attempts to replicate consumer confidence measures from Google, Twitter, and other readily available digital data sources. Such a shift toward the use of "big data" would mean that the new measures of "expectations" would not be accepted based on theoretical considerations but on their association with some subsequent outcome behavior. As described in detail in prior chapters, this represents a radical shift from deductive to inductive logic. Moreover, it would mean the loss of important auxiliary data on which socioeconomic subgroups hold positive or negative expectations, a critical element for the interpretation of the data.

Finally, the challenges to traditional methods of analysis and statistical inference will be substantial, as methods have yet to be developed that allow robust statistical inference in the absence of probability samples. For some, this is not a liability since the use of big data is not predicated on deductive theory but on the improved accuracy of economic forecasts based on observed associations. Indeed, no Kuhnian scientific revolution is required to recognize the long known fact that probability sampling is not necessary for scientific advancement.

New Sentiment Measures

The basic measures of consumer confidence have survived largely unchanged since the middle of the last century. Confidence measures have withstood substantial changes in the economic and regulatory environments as well as more knowledgeable consumers with much greater access to economic information. They have thus far survived due to their universal importance in determining economic behavior. The basic premise is that expectations about future job and income prospects determine consumers' discretionary spending decisions, and as a result, act to shape aggregate trends in the macroeconomy. Income and employment prospects are still the main driving force, although the potential sources of income have expanded beyond wages and the locus of job prospects has increasingly shifted from local to global markets. No longer do consumers believe that their nation's borders will automatically protect them from changing international economic conditions. Consumers can be expected to increasingly incorporate into their expectations information that originates in international markets. This tendency is already apparent among nations with formal links such as the European Union or strong connections involving trade or financial markets.

While a confidence index quite similar to what is now in worldwide use may still be appropriate in the decade ahead, it is unlikely that the current measures would still be appropriate fifty years from now. Future empirical models of consumer behavior are likely to be better specified by utilizing a broader range of expectations. The challenge is that candidates have to be measured over an extended period of time before their predictive ability can be ascertained in time-series models. The University of Michigan surveys have always included a wide range of questions and published the detailed results so that interested scholars could test and compare new measures. Rather than attempting to enshrine any current definition of consumer confidence, a range of new measures should be developed that cover a broad range of expectations that may be relevant in the coming decades. One technique that is used by the Michigan surveys enables automatic detection by simply asking consumers to describe in their own words the factors underlying their economic decisions. The higher costs of these free-response questions turn out to be less expensive than asking a larger number of questions about various expectations that ultimately demonstrate no link to macroeconomic trends.

New Analytic Strategies

Macro models that use "consumer sentiment" for all purposes miss one simple fact: no single index of consumer sentiment can be devised to accurately predict all types of consumer expenditures at all times. Most macro models do not sufficiently disaggregate the components of consumer demand, and most macro models do not disaggregate households into demographic and economic subgroups to make those forecasts. Consumer expectations for interest rates, inflation, income, jobs, stock prices, home values, economic policies, to name just a few, are all important components of people's expectations about their future living standards or real income prospects. But many of these economic variables have a very different impact on spending on homes, vehicles, household durables, travel, and so forth. More accurate forecasts require disaggregating consumer expenditures into its components and then utilizing the most appropriate information on consumer expectations to forecast each component. Moreover, the data should be disaggregated by demographic and economic subgroups. The individual forecasts of the component series can then be combined to produce estimates at higher levels of aggregation.

This same goal could be approached from an entirely different angle. Consumer survey data are typically published so that the results are representative of all households in a particular country. No recognition is given to the differential economic impact of these households as the highest income household is given the same weight in the index as the lowest income household. Case weights could be devised to account for the differential economic status of individual households. The EU now does something similar when combining the data from different countries to form a sentiment index for the entire community; only in that case, each country's data is weighted by the proportion of total spending. The same type of procedure could be applied within countries as well as across countries. Thus, for example, the income and age groups that spent the highest amounts on discretionary purchases would be given correspondingly higher weight in computing the index within each country.

New Data Collection Methods

Along with the challenges of developing new questionnaire content and analysis strategies, the confidence surveys face increasing pressure to change the sample design and how the surveys are administered. Just as few argued a quarter century ago that telephone surveys were superior to face-to-face in-home surveys in terms of data quality, few would now argue that internet surveys are superior to telephone surveys in terms of data quality and statistical inference. Change in research designs is sometimes motivated by the push from deteriorating conditions, and sometimes by the pull of potential improvements. The move from in-home surveys to telephone surveys was due to push from rising costs; there was little if any pull from the greater research potential of telephone surveys. The shift away from telephone surveys that is now in full swing is due to push from higher costs, declining population coverage, and falling response rates as well as from the pull of the enhanced research potential of internet surveys.

Internet surveys have the ability to handle more complex research designs. Researchers could utilize design questions and response codes using graphical as well as verbal methods, provide background information, provide definitions and question instructions, and automatically generate additional probes to clarify and resolve any inconsistencies. Respondents could view online information about the research project, check the project's credentials, consult privacy and confidentiality pledges and other information about the protection of human subjects, and complete the interview at a time that best meets their own schedule. The promise of internet surveys is as great as the methodological innovations that will be required to produce statistically reliable inferences for the entire population. The selection bias in non-probability samples creates a substantial risk that the estimated results will differ from the true population values. The use of non-probability samples means that inferences must be model-based, and the estimated variables are only as valid as the model's assumptions.

The appeal of internet surveys may be offset by future changes in technology. The ongoing shift toward hand-held devices may pose severe limits on the type and number of questions that can be asked. Perhaps future technology will permit delivering the survey questions in the form of a video and collecting spoken responses to questions that can be automatically sorted into different response codes. Moreover, the willingness of people to devote the time and effort to complete surveys delivered over the internet is still a limiting factor. There is no reason to believe that people will become more cooperative in the future.

Economists are more comfortable with the type of model-based inferences required for non-probability samples. While this will accelerate the use of internet samples to estimate economic expectations, it will have an even greater impact on the use of readily available digitized big data. Throughout the history of the University of Michigan's surveys, the critical issue for economists was not the theoretical role of expectations in decisions, but the practical issue of whether the data could accurately predict consumer spending and trends in the macroeconomy. Given a methodological preference for accurate prediction, long championed by Milton Friedman, economists may find using readily available digitized data a satisfactory means to identify optimal proxies for expectations.

The strength of this research program is that it is based on the premise that the description and prediction of consumer behavior represent the best means to foster advances in theory. While there is nothing more useful than good theory, there is nothing more productive in generating theoretical advances than good data. The unique contributions of the research program at Michigan will continue to be built on the collection of data that enables rigorous tests of established theory as well as allows the unexpected to emerge and energize new theoretical advances. Rather than being confined to the armchair of the theorist, the research program continues to seek advances from the armchairs of respondents as they explain the factors underlying their economic decisions.

9

Tailored Economic Expectations

The basic thesis of the last few chapters was that people view macroeconomic downturns as serious threats to their economic welfare, and as a result, they actively search for information and act on that information to lessen their financial risks. The data indicated that the expectations of consumers successfully anticipated cyclical turning points in the economy. Although the data did not provide a flawless signal, it was sufficient to be included, along with other measures, as a leading indicator of macroeconomic trends. As a consequence, consumer sentiment surveys have been adopted in every inhabited continent, accounting for the vast majority of worldwide GDP.

The ability to foreshadow economic cycles implies that consumers pay careful attention to national economic conditions, presumably the data released by federal statistical agencies on trends in the national economy. The traditional view has been that it would be impossible to predict trends in GDP, for example, if people did not pay close attention to the official statistics. The first section of this book, however, came to exactly the opposite conclusion. Namely, that expectations were tailored to an individual's own situation rather than economy-wide outcomes. People preferred to base their expectations on the economic conditions they personally faced, and it was unusual for people to pay close attention to the data released of federal statistical agencies. Indeed, the new theory of tailored expectations emphasized the overwhelming importance of personalized economic information for optimal decisions.

The main purpose of this chapter is to reconcile the macro-level accuracy with the micro-level personalization of expectations. How can people form expectations that are both optimal for their own economic decisions, and when aggregate across the population, form optimal predictions for the economy as a whole?

This duality goes against conventional theory which holds that the economic expectations of all agents are based on identical sources of public information. The new theory holds that the diversity in the economic conditions that people face translates into an array of expectations for the same economic outcome. While diverse expectations are taken by conventional theories to reflect people's lack of knowledge about economic conditions, the new theory holds that the diversity in expectations allows people to make more optimal decisions. Diverse expectations do not represent bias as much as the ability of agents to customize expectations for specific decision purposes.

The analysis contained in this chapter encompasses a wide variety of expectations from the University of Michigan surveys, detailing results across an array of socioeconomic characteristics. The analysis is intended to allow many of the implied hypotheses of rational expectations, bounded rationality, and tailored expectations to be examined. Importantly, the University of Michigan surveys can produce two independent views of the differences in economic expectations across socioeconomic subgroups: a cross-section and a time-series perspective. The common element is the mean of the individual responses. In cross-sectional analysis, variances are computed as differences of individual responses from the sample mean. A typical cross-sectional analysis focuses on how individual differences in expectations influence a person's behavior; alternatively, traditional theories hold that those individual differences indicate biased expectations. In contrast, time-series analysis focuses on how the mean expectation of each survey differs from the mean across all surveys. Time-series analysis typically focuses on how changes in the sample mean of the expectation measure relate to changes in aggregate behavior; alternatively, it can indicate how accurately the expectation mirrors actual subsequent developments. Thus, cross-section and time-series analyses represent two different perspectives of the same data.

The theory of tailored expectations holds that the mean of the expectation measure represents the economic conditions that people face. For example, those with substantial work skills may anticipate a stronger labor market and hence expect a lower unemployment rate than someone with marginal work skills. The pattern of how unemployment expectations change over time, however, is similar for both high- and low-skilled workers; similar in proportional, not absolute change. If that hypothesis is true, then the time-series correlation between high- and low-skilled workers would be very high despite the difference in mean levels. These hypotheses are unique to the theory of tailored expectations.

Given that the focus of this book is on macroeconomic trends over time, the time-series approach conforms to how the data would be used in econometric models. In addition, only the time-series approach allows the computation of correlations between, for example, the mean expectation of one educational subgroup with another educational subgroup over time. Since conventional economic theories place an emphasis on how different levels of education influence the accuracy of expectations, the time-series approach provides a more appropriate test of that conjecture. Moreover, the tailored expectations hypothesis holds both that differences in expectations are related to differences in economic conditions that different groups face as well as that changes in expectations over time are primarily influenced by trends in the overall economy. This hypothesis can be tested by the observation of persistent differences in mean levels of expectations that still demonstrate highly correlated changes over time. The tailored expectations hypothesis also implies that these two characteristics would apply to a broader array of socioeconomic characteristics, including education, income, age, and geographic location.

Time-series differences in economic expectations across socioeconomic subgroups may be classified in three distinct ways: differences in mean levels, differences in variance, and differences in correlations between subcategories of each socioeconomic characteristic. Each of these measures was computed based on quarterly observations over a thirty-nine-year period. Differences in the average level of expectations may well occur in any single survey due to a variety of substantive reasons as well as due to sampling and measurement errors. Differences in mean levels across decades, however, are more likely to result from persistent differences across socioeconomic subgroups. Such persistent differences across education subgroups, for example, could reflect cognitive constraints or represent differences in work skills and in employment opportunities. More generally, the central issue is whether differences in the mean levels of expectations reflect biases due to bounds on cognitive abilities or simply reflect differences in the economic conditions people actually face. The data suggest a limited influence of conscious cognitive bounds on the formation of economic expectations.

The second potential difference is the extent to which different socioeconomic subgroups exhibit similar trends over time in their economic expectations. If the correlation over time is high, it would indicate that those socioeconomic subgroups changed their expectations in the same way at the same time, presumably in response to the same information, whether from official statistics or from personal experience. Highly correlated changes across subgroups can occur despite persistent differences in mean levels.

For example, as the economy enters an expansion or contraction, all education subgroups could increase or decrease their employment prospects by a comparable amount, even if one group consistently expects a much higher level over time. In this case, whether a subgroup's expectations improved or worsened would be independent from the mean differences between the subgroups. Some subgroups would still have higher unemployment expectations, and others lower unemployment expectations. Indeed, a critical property of time-series correlations is their independence of the mean of each series.

The third difference is in the degree of variation over time in a subgroup's mean expectations. Conventional theories of expectations imply that where bounds on rationality are greatest, expectations should sow greater instability over time insofar as they represent mostly uninformed and random guesses on the part of survey respondents. This would imply that the variance of expectations would be greater for lower than for higher educational subgroups. As will be shown, this was exactly the opposite of what was typically observed. Indeed, higher variance was much more common among the subgroups that held the most favorable expectations. This implies that those subgroups experienced greater variations in their economic situations across economic cycles; in contrast, those with the least favorable economic expectations on average, were less likely to benefit from variations in the macroeconomy.

How differences in these three characteristics are interpreted critically depend on the underlying theories of how expectations are formed. The rational expectations hypothesis is the most restrictive in that it implies that the means and variances should be identical and all expectations should be perfectly correlated across socioeconomic groups. This reflects the fact that conventional economic theories assume that expectations conform to the data published by official statistical agencies, say for GDP, inflation, or unemployment. These theories hold that the expectations of every socioeconomic subgroup should converge to these national figures. Persistent differences in expectations across socioeconomic groups have been taken as an indication of biased expectations. Others have argued that such biases reflect limits on people's rationality, which restrict their ability to acquire all the needed information, perform the necessary calculations, and understand the relevant theory essential for interpreting the data. Thus, while theories of full rationality anticipate no differences across subgroups, theories of bounded rationality anticipate persistent biases in both levels and trends.

The theory advanced in this book takes a different approach, based on a broader conceptualization of people's mental faculties. Expectations are based more on private than on public announcements of official statistics. Information about people's own economic situation is constantly accumulated by nonconscious processes and, along with conscious deliberations, is used to form expectations. This hypothesis anticipates that significant differences in the mean levels of economic expectations will correspond to differences in people's economic situation, but that correlations over time will nonetheless be substantial. Importantly, these relationship will hold across a broad array of expectations, not just a few. As we will find, observations of how people change their economic expectations provide even stronger evidence that all people, regardless of their socioeconomic characteristics, adjust their economic expectations over time in a uniform manner. It is important to note that all tailored expectations are contingent on available information, and are thus just as fallible as rational expectations. The key difference is that judging errors in expectations cannot be done by a simple comparison to national data sources. Moreover, the intended degree of accuracy depends on the sensitivity of the specific decision for which the expectation is used.

MACROECONOMIC EMPHASIS

While the average levels of expectations and their variances are critical to the analysis of individual households, macroeconomic models place most emphasis on correspondence of the period-to-period change in the model's variables. It is the correlations among the variables that are primarily responsible for the coefficient estimates in macro models. Any differences in the mean levels are subsumed into the estimates of the equation's constants. A perfect time-series correlation between the expectations of two socioeconomic subgroups would mean that the two groups provide exactly the same information on how their expectations change over time, even if the expectations of one group were persistently higher or lower than the other group. Moreover, if the expectations of two subgroups were perfectly correlated, entering the data on both subgroups in a macro model would not only be redundant but could be harmful to statistical estimates based on regression methodology.[1]

---

[1] The addition of perfectly correlated explanatory variables to a regression model represents the classic definition of perfect multicollinearity. Under this condition, regression models would fail. Even if the explanatory variables are not perfectly correlated, but the correlation is very high, the multicollinearity among the explanatory variables would cause the model to produce inefficient coefficient estimates. The standard assumption of regression models is that the explanatory variables are independent, meaning that

In contrast, a zero or near zero correlation over time would mean that the expectations of each socioeconomic subgroup provided independent information. Data on the expectations from both groups could be entered into macro models to indicate which group had the greater forecasting power. It is not uncommon for analysts to assume that one socioeconomic subgroup, say those with higher incomes or more education, leads other subgroups in becoming more optimistic or more pessimistic about future economic trends. If this were so, the expectations of higher income and more educated groups would be a leading indicator for changes in the other groups. Another example would be if spending on some specific product was more likely among a certain subgroup, say younger or older consumers, and the expectations of those subgroups moved independently, forecast models should only focus on the data from that subgroup.

Conventional economic theories as well as the revised theory of tailored expectations do have some implications about what could be expected. The rational expectations hypothesis suggests that correlations across subgroups should be insignificantly different from 1.0 and differences in mean levels should be 0.0. Theories of bounded rationality suggest that differences in cognitive abilities should affect the level of expectations, randomly biasing some upward and others downward. There would also be differences in correlations as those with the least cognitive abilities would essentially respond with random guesses about future expected changes, which would be unrelated to the more rational estimates of those with higher cognitive abilities. The bounded rationality postulate implies neither zero mean differences nor uniform responses to official economic statistics; the analysis is limited to documenting the degree of bias present for any given socioeconomic characteristic. The theory on tailored expectations, however, suggests that the main difference in expectations would be in their observed levels, which would correspond to the different economic circumstances faced by each subgroup. Nonetheless, all groups can be expected to change their expectations in the same direction at the same time. This high degree of correlation across subgroups is due in large part to the social dynamics that underpin changes in economic expectations.

----

their correlation is zero. While most explanatory variables in econometric models are correlated to some degree, the correlations are typically substantially less than a perfect 1.0. The estimation problems become critical whenever the inter-correlation among the explanatory variables is higher than the correlation of the explanatory variables with the dependent variable.

EXPECTATIONS AMONG SOCIOECONOMIC SUBGROUPS

The socioeconomic characteristics selected for this analysis include income, education, age, geographic location, gender, and marital status. The quarterly samples were divided into five subgroups based on household income, education, and age of the respondent. The division into five groups reflected the constraint due to the cross-section sample size of about 1,500 households per quarter. Gender and the combination of gender and marital status were also used to define subgroups. Finally, the four Census regions were used to test geographic variations in expectations. While other socio-economic characteristics could have been selected, the selection was made based on the characteristics' relevance to the formation of expectations and macroeconomic analysis.

It is of course true that larger differences in expectations may be observed if the socioeconomic characteristics of the population were divided into more groups. Unfortunately, the sample and research design of the surveys were not suitable to capture the extremes of the population defined in terms of most any socioeconomic characteristics. The extremely wealthy or extremely poor individuals are not well represented, nor are the illiterate or the very oldest. It is not that the sample design excludes any of these groups, but the very small number of interviews meant that there would be too few for a robust analysis. The samples for the University of Michigan surveys were designed to be representative of all private households in the nation. It should be emphasized that the analysis does not follow the same individuals over long time spans; no panel or cohort analysis was undertaken, not even the creation of synthetic cohorts. This was not done since economic expectations primarily reflect time-period effects rather than aging or cohort experiences.

Based on the pooled cross-section samples, each subgroup's expectation was calculated to form a quarterly time-series that was used in the analysis. The data are typically used in this format in macroeconomic models. The time period covered was from 1978 to 2016. Importantly, the selected period includes both the 1980s recessionary downturn as well as the financial crisis of 2007–2009. Breaking the thirty-nine-year period into sub-periods provided no significant differences in the analysis. The analysis was meant to conform to how the data are usually used in macroeconomic models. Balance scores were defined for most of the economic expectations measures, with higher scores indicating more favorable economic expectations. The only exception was for the expected inflation rate.

Data on every inter-correlation across each socioeconomic subgroup for all expectations would be voluminous and difficult to interpret. The goal of the correlation analysis was to determine whether the change over time in an expectation for one socioeconomic subgroup was consistent with the change recorded among all other subgroups. For example, the analysis is focused on whether the expectations of households with the lowest educations changed in the same manner as all other households. Such an analysis would indicate whether changes in the expectations of any one of the subgroups contained independent or different information.

In addition, for each socioeconomic subgroup, the mean level of the expectation is reported. Note that the standard errors are reported below each mean to enable a determination of statistically significant differences. Also note that since the total number of time points or time-series observations is the same for each variable, differences in the standard errors mirror differences in the variance of the time-series. For most of the socio-economic subgroups, the total time points was 156, so the standard deviation of the subgroup can be estimated by multiplying the standard errors by 12.5, the square root of the case count. For income, the total time points were 148, yielding a slightly different multiplicative factor of 12.2. The coefficient of variation, a measure of the relative variability, is perhaps the best measure for comparisons across subgroups, and can be calculated by dividing the subgroup's standard deviations by its mean.

Sixteen different expectations were selected for this examination of differences across socioeconomic subgroups. The first group of expectations is related to the personal financial situation of households (questions 1 to 4). The second group of questions is about how people evaluate overall conditions in the economy (questions 5 to 9), the third group involves expectations for unemployment, inflation, and interest rates (questions 10 to 13), and the fourth group covers assessments of buying conditions (questions 14 to 16). These variables were selected due to their availability throughout the 1978 to 2016 time period. Note that nearly all of the variables ask respondents for a qualitative judgment, typically better or worse, or good or bad. There are a few exceptions that ask respondents to answer in percentage terms; this was done for income expectations and for inflation expectations.

The problem is that the bias can only be calculated based on knowledge of the "true" expectation. By conventional economic assumptions, the "true" value would be ascertained from data published by the official statistical agency. For the tailored expectations hypothesis, it is generally not possible to ascertain the "true" expectation, since it is based on the actual circumstances faced by individuals in the context of a specific economic decision. In any event, the purpose of this analysis is not to estimate bias; it is to determine how closely the expectations of various socioeconomic subgroups mirror the rest of the population. As already mentioned, the most important element for macroeconomic analysis is the inter-correlations of any socioeconomic subgroup with the rest of the population. As long as the correlation is close to 1.0, differences in the mean levels or the relative variance of the time-series will not influence the estimates of the model's basic parameters. If the inter-correlation was close to 0.0, it would indicate independent time-series information, and it could potentially add to the forecast's accuracy.

Differences by Education

The data on differences in the means, variances, and correlations across educational subgroups indicate significant differences in means and variances, but generally very highly correlated changes over time (see Table 9.1). Across the sixteen questions, higher education subgroups typically held more optimistic expectations than the least educated. Since education corresponds with differences in work skills, more optimistic expectations among those with higher educations would be anticipated based on the tailored expectations hypothesis. Insofar as education can be viewed as a proxy for bounded rationality, the data provide, at best, limited support. One might anticipate that those with less than a high school degree and those with advanced degrees beyond college would be the most and least affected by bounds on their cognitive abilities. While these two groups demonstrated somewhat lower correlations with the rest of the population, the differences were quite marginal, with the sole exception of expected percentage change in nominal incomes. The data clearly suggest a much more limited role of cognitive limitations on the formation of economic expectations. Importantly, the impact of cognitive limitations may have been reduced since most of the questions were likely to be answered based on nonconscious processes without much conscious deliberation involved.

Level of Expectations. Expectations regarding the general economy and buying conditions generally rose with the education of the respondent, although the highest expectation levels were recorded for college graduates rather than graduate degree holders. Importantly, there was no significant difference in responses to the question on economic news, indicating that all education subgroups comparably evaluated the news they heard

Table 9.1 *Economic Expectations: Means and Correlations by Education of Householder*
(Quarterly Data, 1978:1 to 2016:4)

	Times Series Correlation: Subgroup and All Other Subgroups					Mean Levels within Subgroups (Standard Errors)				
	Less H. Sch.	High Sch.	Some Col.	Col. Degr.	Grad. Sch.	Less H. Sch.	High Sch.	Some Col.	Col. Degr.	Grad. Sch.
1. Current Personal Finances[a*]	0.817	0.906	0.896	0.921	0.907	84.3 (1.07)	99.9 (1.35)	106.9 (1.41)	120.7 (1.45)	119.2 (1.50)
2. Expected Personal Finances[a*]	0.670	0.888	0.845	0.883	0.824	106.0 (0.85)	116.9 (0.86)	126.2 (0.89)	130.2 (0.91)	127.4 (0.91)
3. Nominal Income Expectations[b]	−0.008	0.890	0.907	0.904	0.890	0.0% (0.09)	1.9% (0.12)	3.1% (0.14)	4.0% (0.16)	3.9% (0.18)
4. Real Income Expectations[a]	0.623	0.857	0.800	0.877	0.879	67.2 (0.61)	67.7 (0.81)	78.4 (1.04)	94.0 (1.06)	97.6 (1.24)
5. Economic News[a]	0.815	0.931	0.957	0.957	0.915	76.0 (1.35)	72.5 (1.85)	70.3 (2.37)	71.8 (2.94)	72.4 (3.51)
6. Current Economic Conditions[a]	0.903	0.953	0.977	0.970	0.938	83.0 (2.24)	90.6 (2.83)	95.3 (3.05)	100.8 (3.25)	100.8 (3.49)
7. Expected Change in Economy[a]	0.719	0.882	0.908	0.906	0.855	101.2 (0.94)	105.3 (0.95)	109.0 (1.14)	111.5 (1.22)	111.1 (1.39)
8. Economic Outlook in Year Ahead[a*]	0.847	0.961	0.967	0.972	0.958	90.0 (1.68)	97.0 (2.25)	101.6 (2.49)	106.8 (2.60)	105.3 (2.71)

9. Economic Outlook in Next Five Years[a][*]	0.740	0.917	0.915	0.919	0.907	70.8 (1.23)	82.8 (1.42)	92.3 (1.46)	101.8 (1.51)	101.8 (1.67)
10. Unemployment Expectations[a]	0.768	0.902	0.928	0.940	0.898	79.1 (1.09)	79.6 (1.17)	82.1 (1.30)	85.5 (1.52)	85.5 (1.79)
11. Interest Rate Expectations[a]	0.881	0.971	0.980	0.970	0.950	60.9 (1.39)	63.5 (1.75)	64.9 (2.01)	67.1 (2.24)	67.4 (2.34)
12. Inflation Rate Expected Next Year[b]	0.871	0.965	0.978	0.977	0.959	3.9% (0.12)	3.7% (0.13)	3.7% (0.14)	3.6% (0.15)	3.7% (0.16)
13. Economic Policy Evaluations[a]	0.820	0.963	0.961	0.946	0.890	89.1 (1.34)	86.3 (1.59)	88.3 (1.78)	95.5 (1.97)	97.5 (2.08)
14. Durable Buying Conditions[a][*]	0.887	0.952	0.951	0.944	0.892	130.4 (1.75)	144.8 (1.57)	147.3 (1.51)	150.1 (1.46)	149.6 (1.56)
15. Vehicle Buying Conditions[a]	0.822	0.920	0.911	0.914	0.885	109.7 (1.50)	125.9 (1.44)	132.2 (1.42)	140.2 (1.35)	142.3 (1.49)
16. Home Buying Conditions[a]	0.884	0.955	0.976	0.960	0.961	108.8 (2.20)	132.9 (2.37)	144.6 (2.34)	152.5 (2.42)	154.4 (2.56)

[a] Balance scores: % Favorable – % Unfavorable + 100.
[b] Annual percentage increase.
[*] Sentiment Index variable.

of recent changes in economic conditions. Nonetheless, the higher education subgroups held more favorable economic expectations. Important exceptions were for inflation, unemployment, and interest rate expectations, all of which were more favorable among the top education subgroup, but those differences did not reach the level of statistical significance across the thirty-nine-year period. Moreover, rather than recording larger and more significant differences by educational subgroups instead of across age and income groups, as will be shown shortly, the data found just the opposite was true. This is a troubling finding for the theory of bounded rationality.

Time-Series Correlations. Nearly all time-series correlations were quite high across education subgroups, with only one exception among eighty correlations reported: among respondents with less than a high school degree, their nominal income expectations were nearly perfectly uncorrelated (-0.008) with the income expectations of all other educational groups. For all questions aside from those about personal finances, the average correlation of the expectations among those with less than a high school degree and the balance of the population was 0.83. While lower than the average of 0.94 recorded by other education subgroups, it was still quite substantial. Thus, there was some marginal evidence of the impact of cognitive limitations among those without a high school degree, but that evidence largely disappears among those with just a high school degree.

Differences by Household Income

Households in the top income quintile gave more favorable replies on all sixteen questions than those in the lowest income quintile during the 1979 to 2016 period (see Table 9.2). Despite consistently expressing more favorable expectations, the correlations for each income quintile with all other households were uniformly high. The sole exception was for the questions about expected percentage increase in household income. As might be anticipated, those in the highest income quintile expected the largest annual gains, an average increase of 4.1%, while those in the lowest quintile expected the smallest annual gain, just 0.4% over the 1978 to 2016 time period. In addition, the time-series correlations for income expectations among those in the lowest income quintile changed independently from the other income quintiles; the correlation between those in the lowest income quintile and all other households was -0.195 from 1978 to 2016. The other questions about personal finances had very high correlations over time across income quintiles, with each quintile demonstrating more

Table 9.2 *Economic Expectations: Means and Correlations by Household Income (Quarterly Data, 1979:4 to 2016:4)*

	Times Series Correlation between Subgroup and All Other Subgroups					Mean Levels within Subgroups (Standard Errors)				
	Bottom Fifth	2nd Fifth	Middle Fifth	4th Fifth	Top Fifth	Bottom Fifth	2nd Fifth	Middle Fifth	4th Fifth	Top Fifth
1. Current Personal Finances[a]*	0.852	0.920	0.945	0.946	0.904	81.6 (1.07)	96.5 (1.35)	109.7 (1.48)	118.9 (1.59)	129.3 (1.62)
2. Expected Personal Finances[a]*	0.767	0.894	0.905	0.901	0.838	112.7 (0.75)	120.2 (0.88)	125.0 (0.91)	126.4 (0.87)	130.5 (0.88)
3. Nominal Income Expectation[b]	−0.195	0.711	0.919	0.941	0.900	0.4% (0.08)	1.7% (0.10)	2.7% (0.11)	3.1% (0.12)	4.1% (0.13)
4. Real Income Expectations[a]	0.748	0.825	0.887	0.883	0.836	65.5 (0.74)	69.2 (0.84)	76.2 (0.95)	84.3 (0.99)	105.3 (1.06)
5. Economic News[a]	0.897	0.941	0.963	0.963	0.947	73.6 (1.59)	71.8 (2.10)	71.2 (2.42)	72.2 (2.71)	75.6 (3.34)
6. Current Economic Conditions[a]	0.945	0.973	0.987	0.986	0.948	84.1 (2.50)	91.5 (2.92)	96.7 (3.17)	99.1 (3.29)	103.7 (3.58)
7. Expected Change in Economy[a]	0.728	0.870	0.930	0.917	0.873	103.4 (0.85)	106.8 (0.94)	108.9 (1.06)	110.6 (1.12)	115.1 (1.26)
8. Economic Outlook in Year Ahead[a]*	0.928	0.966	0.976	0.978	0.963	90.0 (1.78)	97.7 (2.24)	102.5 (2.47)	106.3 (2.60)	112.3 (2.84)

(continued)

Table 9.2 (cont.)

	Times Series Correlation between Subgroup and All Other Subgroups					Mean Levels within Subgroups (Standard Errors)				
	Bottom Fifth	2nd Fifth	Middle Fifth	4th Fifth	Top Fifth	Bottom Fifth	2nd Fifth	Middle Fifth	4th Fifth	Top Fifth
9. Economic Outlook in Next Five Years[a*]	0.842	0.908	0.941	0.933	0.922	74.9 (1.18)	84.6 (1.36)	92.3 (1.58)	98.1 (1.58)	108.2 (1.71)
10. Unemployment Expectations[a]	0.862	0.925	0.952	0.955	0.918	78.2 (1.09)	80.8 (1.23)	82.8 (1.31)	84.6 (1.44)	88.2 (1.77)
11. Interest Rate Expectations[a]	0.915	0.963	0.976	0.979	0.955	62.3 (1.44)	63.8 (1.81)	64.9 (1.99)	66.5 (2.24)	68.3 (2.51)
12. Inflation Rate Expected Next Year[b]	0.883	0.950	0.984	0.980	0.960	3.9% (0.10)	3.6% (0.11)	3.5% (0.12)	3.3% (0.12)	3.2% (0.13)
13. Economic Policy Evaluations[a]	0.855	0.958	0.973	0.963	0.951	85.6 (1.36)	87.2 (1.60)	89.9 (1.73)	94.0 (1.88)	101.1 (2.16)
14. Durable Buying Conditions[a*]	0.906	0.946	0.952	0.962	0.925	133.1 (1.70)	144.0 (1.70)	148.4 (1.65)	150.5 (1.61)	154.1 (1.55)
15. Vehicle Buying Conditions[a]	0.900	0.932	0.944	0.934	0.906	115.5 (1.48)	126.7 (1.53)	133.9 (1.47)	138.4 (1.50)	147.6 (1.38)
16. Home Buying Conditions[a]	0.920	0.974	0.977	0.979	0.944	116.3 (2.31)	135.5 (2.52)	145.7 (2.61)	152.3 (2.75)	158.9 (2.63)

[a] Balance scores: % Favorable – % Unfavorable + 100.
[b] Annual percentage increase.
* Sentiment Index variable.

positive evaluations as incomes rose. These results are consistent with the view that people tailor their own financial expectations to their situation.

Level of Expectations. Higher income households held more favorable expectations on all sixteen questions, whether about their own personal finances or about expected trends in the general economy. Only a few differences were not statistically significant. The most interesting non-significant difference was on the question about what recent economic news consumers had heard. This suggests that all income subgroups reported hearing the same degree of positive or negative news on the economy.

How they used that information was similar in that all groups changed their expectations in the same direction at the same time as indicated by the high time-series correlations, but dissimilar in that income groups still maintained differences in the level of their expectations. This would be surprising if everyone based their expectations on official statistics about national economic conditions, but not so surprising if people tailored their economic expectations to their own situation. The data suggests that consumers do tailor their economic expectations to their own situation, with higher income households more likely to report more favorable economic conditions on a consistent basis.

Time-Series Correlations. The correlations across income subgroups on people's assessments about the overall economy and buying conditions were uniformly high. The average correlation across the twelve questions for the five income groups was 0.94. The average correlation among the bottom income quintile was the lowest of any subgroup, but it nonetheless averaged 0.88 across the twelve questions. Indeed, only eight out of the sixty correlations were below 0.90, with six of those correlations recorded by the lowest income quintile (only two were below 0.9 when the correlation was rounded to one decimal). The data thus indicate widespread agreement about how various facets of the economy are expected to change across all income subgroups.

Differences by Age

Life-cycle theories suggest that younger age groups should hold more favorable expectations about changes in their own financial situation. The mean levels for personal financial expectations confirm this presumption (see Table 9.3). Younger households were universally more likely to

Table 9.3 *Economic Expectations: Means and Correlations by Age of Householder (Quarterly Data, 1978:1 to 2016:4)*

	Times Series Correlation Between Subgroup and All Other Subgroups					Mean Levels within Subgroups (Standard Errors)				
	18–34	35–44	45–54	55–64	65+	18–34	35–44	45–54	55–64	65+
1. Current Personal Finances[a]*	0.915	0.853	0.928	0.906	0.848	129.6 (1.33)	113.2 (1.50)	102.1 (1.45)	93.1 (1.24)	83.8 (0.91)
2. Expected Personal Finances[a]*	0.856	0.835	0.868	0.778	0.760	143.1 (0.70)	131.6 (0.93)	121.7 (1.03)	108.8 (0.99)	93.0 (0.62)
3. Nominal Income Expectations[b]	0.558	0.868	0.832	−0.021	−0.290	5.3% (0.14)	3.8% (0.11)	2.8% (0.10)	0.6% (0.08)	0.0% (0.04)
4. Real Income Expectations[a]	0.790	0.703	0.855	0.845	0.753	99.8 (0.84)	87.5 (0.89)	76.1 (0.85)	63.9 (0.76)	59.5 (0.65)
5. Economic News[a]	0.948	0.963	0.968	0.937	0.933	79.7 (2.19)	73.3 (2.68)	67.9 (2.52)	67.1 (2.28)	69.5 (1.83)
6. Current Economic Conditions[a]	0.976	0.983	0.985	0.979	0.973	104.9 (3.06)	97.7 (3.07)	92.0 (2.96)	88.4 (2.87)	85.9 (2.64)
7. Expected Change in Economy[a]	0.890	0.934	0.927	0.910	0.878	111.2 (1.01)	108.2 (1.09)	106.5 (1.08)	106.3 (1.13)	105.9 (1.00)
8. Economic Outlook in Year Ahead[a]*	0.932	0.963	0.967	0.951	0.934	110.2 (2.44)	101.8 (2.44)	96.9 (2.37)	96.1 (2.25)	94.5 (1.95)
9. Economic Outlook in Next Five Years[a]*	0.891	0.923	0.924	0.890	0.876	95.8 (1.66)	91.5 (1.52)	87.3 (1.48)	88.1 (1.42)	87.6 (1.24)

10. Unemployment Expectations[a]	0.914	0.960	0.956	0.924	0.925	86.4 (1.27)	81.6 (1.45)	79.7 (1.36)	79.8 (1.32)	82.7 (1.18)
11. Interest Rate Expectations[a]	0.952	0.978	0.978	0.964	0.943	60.9 (1.75)	63.5 (1.92)	65.0 (1.97)	65.5 (2.11)	69.1 (2.02)
12. Inflation Rate Expected Next Year[b]	0.962	0.981	0.982	0.947	0.864	3.7% (0.15)	3.7% (0.15)	3.6% (0.14)	3.4% (0.12)	3.3% (0.11)
13. Economic Policy Evaluations[a]	0.952	0.951	0.975	0.970	0.937	92.5 (1.47)	91.7 (1.70)	89.5 (1.75)	89.5 (1.76)	90.4 (1.66)
14. Durable Buying Conditions[a][*]	0.907	0.950	0.943	0.937	0.892	150.5 (1.40)	145.2 (1.64)	143.9 (1.67)	144.3 (1.63)	139.2 (1.75)
15. Vehicle Buying Conditions[a]	0.870	0.936	0.931	0.916	0.900	134.2 (1.40)	131.9 (1.52)	129.6 (1.53)	128.5 (1.58)	124.9 (1.61)
16. Home Buying Conditions[a]	0.940	0.976	0.980	0.959	0.945	142.8 (2.24)	144.2 (2.48)	140.7 (2.68)	138.5 (2.70)	129.9 (2.62)

[a] Balance scores: % Favorable – % Unfavorable + 100.
[b] Annual percentage increase.
[*] Sentiment Index variable.

report that their current financial situation had improved and they were more likely to expect greater financial gains in the future than older age groups. For example, householders under age thirty-five anticipated an annual income increase of 5.3% on average from 1978 to 2016, with the annual expected income gains declining in each older age group until it fell to zero among those aged sixty-five or older. The time-series correlations for the question on nominal income expectations were much lower than for any of the other questions on personal finance, ranging from 0.56 among the youngest age group to –0.29 among the oldest age group. For the other three questions on personal finances, the correlations were still quite high, ranging from 0.70 to 0.93. These other personal financial questions only asked about the direction of change, not the magnitude of expected change, as did the question on the percentage change in nominal incomes.

Levels of Expectations. In contrast to the common trends in consumers' assessments of economic conditions, the data confirmed that younger consumers generally held more favorable expectations. The pattern of greater optimism among younger consumers extended well beyond personal finance to include nearly all of the expectations examined.

There were a few notable exceptions. Younger consumers expected a higher rate of inflation than older consumers, and younger consumers were more pessimistic about interest rate trends than older consumers. While these expectations of higher interest and inflation rates are consistent with economic theory, these expectations are usually associated with less optimistic expectations about economic prospects. Importantly, since younger consumers expect higher percentage gains in wages, the impact on their overall financial situation would not be as negative as among older workers.

Time-Series Correlations. For the questions about the economy and buying conditions, the time-series correlations were uniformly higher, with nearly all correlations in the mid to high 0.90s – of the sixty correlations, only eight were below 0.90, with the lowest being 0.86. The correlations were somewhat higher for the youngest age subgroup than the oldest, although the differences were quite small. Overall, the youngest as well as the oldest consumers judged trends in whether economic conditions were improving or worsening quite similarly, including expectations for interest rates, unemployment and inflation rates.

Differences by Gender and Marital Status

There is no economic theory that holds that men and women would perceive the same economic event differently. The data in Table 9.4, however, clearly suggest a consistent difference in the economic expectations of men and women. Most of these differences can be explained by differences in the economic status of the household. While no robust analysis was conducted of these differences, the sample design for the University of Michigan surveys enables an easy method to abstract from some of the potentially confounding effects. The sample design gives each US household an equal probability of being selected, and within each household, it gives each adult an equal probability of being chosen as the respondent. This means that in married households, there was an equal chance that the male or female spouse would be selected. Although the survey questions were about the household's financial situation, why would the responses differ depending on whether the married male or married female provided the answer? Moreover, gender influenced people's expectations for the national economy as well. Although differences in risk aversion between men and women have been hypothesized (Loewenstein et al., 2001), there is no clear reason to believe that it would have a differential impact on the economic expectations held by people. Nor is it apparent whether men tailor their expectations too optimistically or women too pessimistically.

Level of Expectations. On every question, women held less favorable views than men, although the gap was not always statistically significant. More than half of the sixteen questions recorded a significant difference between all men and women, and more than a third of the differences were significant for married men and women. When asked about expected changes in household income, for example, married men on average reported that they anticipated a gain of 3.1%, while married women expected an average gain of 2.4%. The differential of 0.7 percentage points was just over half the differential of 1.2 percentage points between all men and women. Nonetheless, the 0.7 percentage point difference was surprisingly high. Interestingly, the data recorded the same difference between men and women, whether married or not, for inflation expectations: men on average from 1978 to 2016 expected an inflation rate of 3.5% while women a rate of 3.8%.

Time-Series Correlations. The correlations between trends in men's and women's economic expectations were uniformly high, recording an average

Table 9.4 *Economic Expectations: Means and Correlations by Gender and Marital Status of Householder (Quarterly Data, 1978:1 to 2016:4)*

	Times Series Correlation Between Subgroup and All Others				Mean Levels within Subgroups (Standard Errors)			
	Male	Female	Married Male	Married Female	Male	Female	Married Male	Married Female
1. Current Personal Finances[a]		0.961		0.943	112.4 (1.32)	101.4 (1.27)	112.6 (1.39)	108.6 (1.40)
2. Expected Personal Finances[a]		0.926		0.912	125.1 (0.87)	118.3 (0.80)	122.8 (0.93)	119.8 (0.81)
3. Income Expectations[b]		0.856		0.893	3.2% (0.13)	2.0% (0.10)	3.1% (0.13)	2.4% (0.11)
4. Real Income Expectations[a]		0.918		0.900	86.7 (0.93)	72.7 (0.77)	86.5 (0.97)	76.9 (0.86)
5. Economic News[a]		0.923		0.915	76.9 (2.43)	68.5 (2.16)	76.4 (2.48)	67.4 (2.35)
6. Current Economic Conditions[a]		0.972		0.967	101.0 (2.98)	89.4 (2.86)	100.5 (3.00)	91.0 (2.97)
7. Expected Change in Economy[a]		0.894		0.878	112.0 (1.13)	104.2 (0.94)	117.7 (1.20)	104.1 (1.02)
8. Economic Outlook in Year Ahead[a]		0.968		0.964	108.7 (2.36)	93.8 (2.22)	108.9 (2.40)	95.9 (2.38)

9. Economic Outlook in Next Five Years[a]	0.896	0.886	101.5 (1.44)	81.2 (1.41)	102.4 (1.48)	83.5 (1.57)
10. Unemployment Expectations[a]	0.909	0.883	85.8 (1.41)	79.5 (1.19)	86.1 (1.46)	80.0 (1.26)
11. Interest Rate Expectations[a]	0.939	0.925	66.9 (2.15)	62.6 (1.72)	66.6 (2.29)	62.1 (1.84)
12. Inflation Rate Expected Next Year[b]	0.979	0.966	3.5% (0.14)	3.8% (0.13)	3.4% (0.14)	3.8% (0.14)
13. Economic Policy Evaluations[a]	0.948	0.958	91.5 (1.84)	90.1 (1.49)	92.1 (1.95)	91.4 (1.60)
14. Durable Buying Attitudes[a]	0.962	0.942	151.1 (1.35)	140.4 (1.66)	151.9 (1.38)	141.9 (1.69)
15. Vehicle Buying Attitudes[a]	0.942	0.922	136.4 (1.35)	126.1 (1.49)	137.4 (1.42)	127.5 (1.54)
16. Home Buying Attitudes[a]	0.981	0.982	146.3 (2.38)	134.8 (2.47)	148.9 (2.48)	139.9 (2.61)

[a] Balance scores: % Favorable – % Unfavorable + 100.
[b] Annual percentage increase.

correlation of 0.94 across all sixteen questions among all respondents and 0.93 among married respondents. How men and women changed their expectations over time was highly synchronized regardless of their economic situation or differences in their perspectives. While the differences are not a concern for macroeconomic analysis, they do represent a significant challenge for microeconomics

Differences across Geographic Regions

Differences across geographic regions in economic conditions are often noted, but those differences are usually based on much smaller geographic areas than the Census definition of US regions. Each of the four US regions are large, multi-state areas that encompass significant economic diversity. While there have been numerous instances of isolated favorable or unfavorable economic conditions in various regions, they have been, for the most part, temporary. Most of the geographic variations are based on city or metro differences, especially within areas that are now or have been dominated by a particular industry.

Level of Expectations. There were no differences across regions in the levels of nearly all of the economic expectations (see Table 9.5). Perhaps the biggest difference was in the expected percentage change in incomes. Western residents recorded the highest average level at 2.9%, while those residing in the North Central regions reported the lowest income expectations at 2.3%. The Northeast was close to the West, at 2.8%, and the South intermediate at 2.6%. Note that inflation expectations did not differ across the regions, similar to most of the other economic expectations.

Time-series Correlations. The average correlation between any region and the rest of the country was 0.94 on the sixteen questions measured in the thirty-nine years from 1978 to 2016. The correlations were quite similar for each region with the rest of the country, in the narrow range of 0.93 to 0.95. For the personal financial expectations, the average correlation was 0.90, with the lowest correlation at 0.86. For the expectations about the general economy and buying conditions, the average correlation was 0.96, with the lowest being 0.90. Overall, changes in economic expectations were nearly identical across all regions.

A RISING TIDE …

The impact of socioeconomic characteristics on economic expectations can be easily summarized: the quarterly changes in a broad range of

Table 9.5 *Economic Expectations: Means and Correlations by Region of Residence (Quarterly Data, 1978:1 to 2016:4)*

	Times Series Correlation Between Subgroup and All Other Subgroups				Mean Levels within Subgroups (Standard Errors)			
	West	North Central	North East	South	West	North Central	North East	South
1. Current Personal Finances[a]	0.925	0.926	0.920	0.934	107.6 (1.28)	105.9 (1.29)	103.3 (1.48)	107.9 (1.33)
2. Expected Personal Finances[a]	0.876	0.911	0.886	0.915	124.6 (0.79)	118.6 (0.85)	118.8 (0.86)	123.2 (0.92)
3. Income Expectations[b]	0.921	0.878	0.874	0.923	2.9% (0.14)	2.3% (0.11)	2.8% (0.12)	2.6% (0.11)
4. Real Income Expectations[a]	0.893	0.895	0.862	0.907	82.0 (0.85)	75.4 (0.87)	81.0 (0.95)	79.2 (0.86)
5. Economic News[a]	0.961	0.962	0.956	0.963	72.2 (2.47)	72.2 (2.27)	70.7 (2.45)	73.4 (2.09)
6. Current Economic Conditions[a]	0.976	0.981	0.968	0.978	96.3 (3.01)	94.3 (3.00)	92.5 (3.07)	95.2 (2.75)
7. Expected Change in Economy[a]	0.937	0.933	0.900	0.925	108.3 (1.11)	106.3 (1.02)	108.6 (1.05)	108 (1.00)
8. Economic Outlook in Year Ahead[a]	0.972	0.969	0.950	0.974	101.5 (2.37)	99.5 (2.32)	98.3 (2.41)	101.9 (2.20)

(continued)

Table 9.5 (cont.)

	Times Series Correlation Between Subgroup and All Other Subgroups				Mean Levels within Subgroups (Standard Errors)			
	West	North Central	North East	South	West	North Central	North East	South
9. Economic Outlook in Next Five Years[a]	0.941	0.947	0.902	0.946	91.0 (1.42)	89.8 (1.50)	91.0 (1.53)	89.8 (1.39)
10. Unemployment Expectations[a]	0.941	0.949	0.938	0.947	83.0 (1.34)	82.2 (1.35)	81.2 (1.37)	82.9 (1.22)
11. Interest Rate Expectations[a]	0.975	0.980	0.971	0.982	64.2 (2.00)	65.3 (1.94)	66.7 (1.93)	62.7 (1.81)
12. Inflation Rate Expected Next Year[b]	0.985	0.979	0.975	0.988	3.7% (0.15)	3.6% (0.13)	3.6% (0.14)	3.6% (0.14)
13. Economic Policy Evaluations[a]	0.966	0.971	0.939	0.944	89.3 (1.70)	89.9 (1.65)	91.4 (1.75)	91.9 (1.61)
14. Durable Buying Attitudes[a]	0.941	0.948	0.947	0.965	144.7 (1.49)	146.2 (1.58)	145.2 (1.62)	144.7 (1.54)
15. Vehicle Buying Attitudes[a]	0.920	0.943	0.934	0.956	130.4 (1.37)	131.5 (1.48)	131.9 (1.57)	129.6 (1.44)
16. Home Buying Attitudes[a]	0.955	0.975	0.952	0.963	140.2 (2.25)	143.1 (2.60)	135.5 (2.53)	140.0 (2.49)

[a] Balance scores: % Favorable − % Unfavorable + 100.
[b] Annual percentage increase.

economic expectations followed a nearly identical time-series path across all socioeconomic subgroups. Despite this synchronization of trends, socioeconomic subgroups exhibited persistent differences in the extent of their economic optimism. Perhaps the most surprising finding was that the higher variances were due to higher peaks among the subgroups that held more favorable expectations rather than due to lower troughs among those with less favorable expectations. While the results of any one survey may differ, these results were based on the analysis of thirty-nine years of surveys.

The data provide no reason to believe that when used in macroeconomic analysis, the time-series trends of any one subgroup significantly differs from the balance of the population. For microeconomic analysis, the data provide just as convincing evidence that different socioeconomic subgroups hold distinctive economic expectations. Given these survey measures were designed to aid in the explanation of macroeconomic trends, the synchronization of changes across all socioeconomic subgroups streamlines the data requirements for macro analysis to population totals. This simplifies analysis strategies as well as survey designs since smaller sample sizes are needed to provide the same precision than if subgroup estimates were required.

What implications do these results have for the competing theories on the formation of expectations? Considering only the economy-wide expectations, the overall results are mixed. The rational expectations hypothesis would imply that all socioeconomic subgroups should change their expectations in a similar fashion, which was confirmed by the data. The persistent differences in the means, however, were not consistent with the rational expectations hypothesis. The implications are just the opposite for the bounded rationality hypothesis: mean differences across socioeconomic subgroups would confirm that "biased" expectations were common, but the synchronization of changes in expectations does not suggest that some subgroups unduly suffer from cognitive limitations, an inability to calculate and forecast, or a lack of understanding of economic matters. To be sure, among those with the least education, their expectations had somewhat lower time-series correlations with the rest of the population, but the falloff was quite small.

The alternative theory of tailored expectations is consistent with the observed data across socioeconomic subgroups. The data hardly represent robust proof, however. By their very nature, tailored expectations are anticipated to be responsive to the individual's own economic situation. So it is not surprising that groups most favored by their income position or work skills would generally hold more optimistic economic expectations, nor is it surprising that the young see the economy more optimistically than the aged. Moreover, the higher peak but comparable troughs indicate that those who would benefit most from expansions voiced the most favorable expectations, while recessions were equally recognized by all subgroups. The synchronization of changes in expectations over time indicates a high degree of uniformity in how new economic information is processed by every subgroup. Indeed, the synchronization suggests a broad agreement across subgroups about processing new economic information regardless of the decision context. This may suggest that it is the level of expectations rather than the change in expectations that is more subject to contextual effects.

A rising economic tide does indeed lift all expectations. Nonetheless, some boats still take on water and are in danger of capsizing, while other boats ride high on the waves, positioned to reach ever higher crests. Regardless of their situation, no one is ignorant of economic conditions, and no one wants to be caught by an unexpected storm. While the economic circumstances in which people find themselves differ widely across the population, people are nonetheless well aware of whether the economic tide is rising or receding.

10

Economic Expectations

Paradigms and Theories

The objective of this book was to propose a new comprehensive paradigm about the formation of economic expectations and how those expectations influence the macroeconomy. Scientific paradigms encompass much more than just theories as they also specify the appropriate concepts, methodologies, and testing procedures to advance a discipline. Paradigms represent the intellectual culture of a discipline. Like all cultures, paradigms provide continuity to scientific disciplines even as they evolve over time. Most theoretical advances occur within the confines of an established paradigm, with each new advance building on past accomplishments. Isaac Newton, as many others both before and since, credited his ability to advance science to "standing on the shoulders of the giants" who had preceded him. The recognized work of scientists is to advance their discipline by the accumulation of empirically confirmed facts and theories.

The notion that scientific knowledge advances in an incremental fashion within discipline boundaries was challenged by Thomas Kuhn (1962). Kuhn argued that, for mature sciences, the usual path to scientific advancement was through "paradigm shifts." A paradigm shift can alter how theories are conceptualized or interpreted, define new relationships, provide new theoretical implications, or offer new methods for testing and verification. New paradigms open disciplines to fresh approaches for interpreting the anomalies accumulated under existing paradigms. These fresh interpretations are often enabled by new concepts or additional factors that the old paradigm had dismissed as irrelevant. Importantly, a new paradigm can often provide inferences across a greater range of phenomena than were possible under the existing paradigm. Kuhn noted that the hallmark of a successful paradigm shift was one that provided explanations that were more accurate, concise, consistent, and generalizable. The introduction of rational expectations established a paradigm shift that significantly altered the discipline's perspective on expectations and also had a more general and pervasive impact on economic theory.

FORMATION OF EXPECTATIONS

The paradigm shift that has been detailed in this book does not challenge the preeminent role of rationality in economic theory. Unlike traditional critiques of rationality, the new paradigm offers a new, and more compelling, rationale for the accuracy of expectations. The main challenge to the existing paradigm involves how economic expectations have been conceptualized and the methodologies used in empirical tests. The existing paradigm prompted incorrect inferences about the formation process and incorrect assessments of the accuracy of expectations. The revised theory of tailored expectations avoids these defects while remaining fully consistent with the basic tenets of orthodox economic theory. Expectations were theorized to focus on the economic conditions people actually face, to be dynamically formed for specific decisions, and to balance the formation costs against the decision benefits. While these criteria are familiar elements of economic theory, the new paradigm did not limit the use of people's mental faculties to conscious deliberation. Indeed, it was found that variations in conscious cognitive skills could not fully account for the observed differences in people's expectations nor the widespread synchronization of changes in people's economic expectations over time. To be sure, the absolute levels of economic expectations differed across population subgroups; these differences were based on variations in the economic situations that people actually faced. Examining how economic expectations changed over time among people who differed markedly in their conscious cognitive abilities produced results with extraordinarily high time-series correlations. The conclusion from these observations is that, despite differences in levels, the expectations changed in unison across all population groups. What could cause this surprising result? Measurement and other assorted survey errors, while no doubt present, were judged relatively unobtrusive given the correspondence of the expectation data with the economic data published by state statistical agencies. Nor was it satisfactory to simply claim that the bounds on rationality were not as limited as generally claimed. Rather, the fault was found in the existing paradigm that excluded from consideration how most information was actually processed, by the cognitive nonconscious.

The new paradigm holds that most economic expectations are formed by nonconscious cognitive activity. Conscious deliberation, however, is

likely to dominate when people initially learn to form a specific expectation, or when there is a sudden change in the underlying economic
circumstances, and in other unusual situations. Of course, when people
have reason to use a specific expectation, a conscious cognitive review is
also likely to occur. For the most part, however, expectations are automatically and effortlessly formed by nonconscious cognitive processes.
The evolutionary purpose of expectations is to free conscious deliberation from the repetitive tasks of monitoring changing conditions in a
wide variety of areas, with economics being just one of the many areas for
which expectations are formed and maintained. Nonconscious cognitive
processes have demonstrated ability to acquire and organize information, learn patterns and relationships, and form and revise expectations.
This allows people to maximize the potential of conscious deliberation,
their most limited and their most prized mental faculty. The inclusion of
nonconscious cognitive processes is consistent with rational expectations,
since the theory is silent on how expectations are formed, and, more
importantly, both theories hold that the accuracy of expectations is the
sole objective. The impact from the exclusion of nonconscious cognitive
processes is most notable in theories and empirical investigations about
how people learn to form rational expectations.

Since the goal is to form expectations about the economic conditions
people actually face, the most relevant data does not come from state
statistical agencies but from their own interactions with the economy.
This represents another significant departure from the existing paradigm. Moreover, rather than being sparked by the timing of data
releases from statistical agencies, expectations are constantly updated
as people are confronted with new economic information in their daily
lives. Receiving economic information as it occurs rather than from the
delayed reporting from statistical agencies provides economic agents an
advance warning and a forecasting advantage, especially if the news is
negative. Despite the heterogeneity in the expected levels, when properly aggregated across the population, expectations are likely to closely
approximate national averages published by the statistical agencies. The
correspondence with macroeconomics depends solely on the evolution
of expectations over time. In this regard, all population subgroups exhibit
nearly identical changes in their expectation. The data thus strongly indicate that despite the differences in economic situations or the presumed
differences in their capacities to form accurate expectations, all population subgroups demonstrated the same ability to discern prospective
changes across a broad range of economic conditions.

IMPACT ON MACROECONOMY

The other major challenges to the existing paradigm involve the assumption that consumers play a passive role in the macroeconomy, and that economic agents are unable to form rational expectations when economic risks are immeasurable, especially at cyclical turning points in the macroeconomy. The new paradigm asserts that the course of the macroeconomy is shaped by the consumer sector along with the business, government, and international sectors. The data suggests that consumer spending on investments in homes, vehicles, and durables was generally larger than business investment spending and has generally preceded business investments over the past century. The independent power of the consumers to help determine economic cycles is inconsistent with orthodox theory. The new paradigm holds that in developed economies it is more likely that expected increases in consumer demand prompt firms to make productive investment so they can maximize their profits from higher sales. This is in contrast to the existing paradigm which holds that business investments act to expand employment and income and hence result in higher consumption. The new paradigm recognizes that a mutual interdependence exists between the consumer and business sectors.

Indeed, cyclical downturns in the macroeconomy are inconsistent with orthodox economic theory. The traditional view was that external shocks were necessary to produce recessions, rather than being produced by endogenous factors. The new paradigm does not discount external shocks, but holds that economic cycles can also be caused by changes in expectations that have endogenous roots. The most important elements involve how economic risks are assessed and the role of self-fulfilling expectations. The existing paradigm misjudges people's ability to handle situations where risks are immeasurable, what has been called Knightian uncertainty. Under the old paradigm, ambiguity neutralized people's ability to make rational assessments, but this is not true under the revised paradigm. Evolutionary developments have conferred an innate ability to rationally respond to ambiguous information, especially when it could result in harm. Moreover, situations that present ambiguous information are much more common than envisioned in orthodox economic theory. Economic agents do not simply suspend behavior in the presence of ambiguity, but have learned how to use their full mental faculties to make rational expectations despite the prevailing uncertainty. Evolutionary forces have favored caution in the face of potential loss as the most rational response. As more cautious expectations are expressed in behavior, they create outcomes that increase the likelihood of even more cautious expectations among other people, creating cascades across the population. A significant characteristic of the new paradigm is that it does not rule out self-fulfilling expectations as a powerful determinant of trends in the macroeconomy. Moreover, under certain situations, self-fulfilling expectations can become so extreme that they prompt economic booms and subsequent busts.

All of the above has been discussed in detail in the preceding chapters. No mention in this closing chapter has yet been made of the important role of social and emotional factors nor the impact of contextual factors in shaping expectations. This discussion must await a brief review of the benefits and drawbacks of the equilibrium nature of orthodox economic theory.

EQUILIBRIUM AS CONTEXT

All of orthodox economic theory exists within the context of equilibrium. Equilibrium is defined as a steady state, characterized by a stable balance of opposing economic forces. The most typical example of equilibrium is the balance of supply and demand such that prices will remain unchanged in the absence of some exogenous force. All implications drawn from orthodox economic theory are valid only in the context of equilibrium. The most important advantage of the equilibrium context is that it enables economic theory to specify relationships and outcomes as if the economic system was completely unaffected by any and all non-economic variables or processes. The concept of equilibrium is unique in the social sciences and provides economics with an unparalleled theoretical advantage. Indeed, it is a *tour de force* that enables economics to focus on how economic factors must be arrayed to rationally maximize the welfare of individuals across the entire economy. Economic agents are assumed to possess all relevant information, evaluate information without regard to any other context, understand its potential importance, know how to use the information to make optimal economic decisions, and act independently from other agents. Economics readily admits that this is a normative view based on how people and markets ought to behave, and recognizes that many agents and markets fall short of this ideal.

Other disciplines use similar concepts that mediate relationships, generally referred to as "contexts." A general definition is that different contexts or frames of reference influence the interpretation of information and the resulting decisions. The archetypical example is differences in decisions depending on whether a positive or negative frame was used to describe the alternatives; another example is whether an economic or political context was used to evaluate a proposed policy. The key disciplinary difference is that economics defines equilibrium by the absence of all non-economic contexts, while other social sciences define it by the presence of some specific context or frame of reference. The state of equilibrium is understood by economists to represent a global context that holds tastes, preferences, and all other non-economic variables, fixed or constant. Regardless of whether "contexts" are defined by inclusion or exclusion, they both act to mediate relationships among variables.

Other social science disciplines could employ techniques similar to economics and describe theoretical deductions as if all other elements were fixed. Psychology, for example, could substitute homeostasis for equilibrium and derive theoretical relationships among psychological variables assuming all non-psychological variables were unchanged. This is a theoretical not an empirical choice since all would agree that equilibrium exists only in theory and not in observable behavior. Indeed, most people live their entire lives in a state of disequilibrium, a permanent state of transition between some presumed past and projected future equilibriums. That fact alone, however, is insufficient to disregard the theoretical merits of equilibrium. There is a more important factor that limits the appeal of equilibrium for the study of economic expectations: equilibrium trivializes the importance of expectations in decision making. Since equilibriums define steady states, expectations lose their distinctive meaning since the future value of a variable would be the same as its current value, whether defined in terms of levels or rates of change.

The unquestioned usefulness of economic expectations is to aid decision making when disequilibrium exists. Economic theory can presuppose expectations in the state of equilibrium, but those expectations would simply replicate current realizations and provide no unique information. While redundant in equilibrium, orthodox theory provides no definitive guidance about expectations, or any other economic variable, when disequilibrium exists. Since the presumption is that a new equilibrium will ultimately be established, it is only reasonable to anticipate that agents will act in ways that would reestablish equilibrium, although no aspect of orthodox theory uniquely guarantees such a result. More importantly, this would imply that the processes that govern the formation of expectations in disequilibrium are not bound by orthodox equilibrium theory. This does not diminish the importance of the accuracy of expectations, but if the equilibrium context can no longer be assumed to exist, there is no theoretical basis for prohibiting non-economic influences on the formation of expectations.

Indeed, since economic theory is silent on the optimal path back toward equilibrium, it can hardly prohibit the use of any means to form accurate expectations. This view is consistent with the rational expectations hypothesis which only specifies the characteristics of the resulting expectations, leaving the process used to form those expectations unspecified. More importantly, this represents the basic rationale for maintaining the hypothesis status of rational expectations since it presumes equilibrium like outcomes in the midst of disequilibrium.

ORTHODOX DEFENSE OF RATIONAL EXPECTATIONS

Rationality has long been a basic tenet of economic theory. Classical economics held that consumers and firms made decisions that rationally maximized their benefits. Initially, those same assumptions of rationality did not extend to expectations, and classical economics generally held the accuracy and usefulness of observed expectations in low regard for 200 years. It was only in the last half of the twentieth century that John Muth extended the assumption of rationality to expectations. The introduction of rational expectations constituted a paradigm shift that revolutionized economics. Rational expectations helped transform static economic models into dynamic models, and fostered the incorporation of the complete array of economic behaviors into an integrated theory. The new paradigm demonstrated all the characteristics that Kuhn had outlined: the paradigm shift provided explanations that were more accurate, concise, consistent, and generalizable. While it took several hundred years to extend the concept of rationality to expectations, it only took a few decades for the new rational expectations paradigm to expand the scope and usefulness of economic theory.

The assumption of rationality has always been contentious among other social scientists. Many have wondered why countless rejections in empirical studies have not convinced the discipline to abandon the rationality assumption as a description of economic behavior. The most general answer is that accurate behavioral predictions do not constitute the sole criterion for acceptance. Theoretical assumptions play two critical roles in the advancement of a discipline. The first criterion is its ability to predict behavior, and the second is its ability to expand the scope and usefulness of the preexisting theory. Of the two, other social scientists most often cited the inability of the rationality assumption to accurately describe behavioral outcomes. On this count, critics have repeatedly called for the liberation of economic theory from its extreme assumptions about human rationality;

of course, these complaints about the assumptions of rational maximization by consumers and firms date back hundreds of years. The debate about rational expectation, however, was fueled by the notion that expectations could be observed and compared to realizations, whereas no generally valid observations of utility were possible. On the second criterion, economists consider the rationality assumption a significant advance in economic theory. Indeed, rational decision making ensures the optimal outcome, which is the normative goal of utility or profit maximization. Moreover, the rationality assumption allows the dynamic extension of economic theory so as to incorporate many other aspects of economic and market behaviors.

Economics as a discipline took several approaches to maintain its core belief in rationality. Perhaps the easiest reconciliation was that expectations only converged to rationality in the steady state of equilibrium. The basic argument was that when in disequilibrium, there was no presumption that all agents would hold rational expectations. As a result, the common finding that expectations were dominated by biases rather than by rational calculations, was not interpreted as definitive evidence since it could be viewed as a consequence of disequilibrium. This view prompted the emergence of learning theories to demonstrate how economic agents could ultimately achieve rational expectations. Unfortunately, learning theories, like economics, could not identify the existence of any path that would guarantee the reestablishment of equilibrium. Moreover, learning theories focused exclusively on conscious cognitive deliberation, dismissing the more expansive, and dominant influence of nonconscious cognitive processes.

Economists have proposed several practical solutions to avoid the pitfalls of survey measures. One solution was to replace the expectations of economic agents with expectations calculated by economic models. "Model-consistent" expectations, generated by econometric models, could fully meet the demanding criteria of rational expectations without the inefficiencies and inaccuracies of expectations obtained directly from economic agents. Indeed, since the theory of rational expectations only places constraints on the outcomes, not the formation processes, it was quite natural that estimates that meet the outcome criteria would be preferred. This alternative completely avoids any issues surrounding the formation of expectations in favor of defining the outcomes in terms of the past histories of the variables included in the model. The drawback of this approach was that expectations contained no insights that were independent of past economic developments of the included variables. This limitation meant that model-consistent expectations typically could not forecast cyclical turning points in advance. Model-consistent expectations mirrored the orthodox view that recessions were created by exogenous forces.

Another alternative was to determine the expectations of economic experts: they presumably have extensive knowledge of the data, know how to interpret the data, and could easily do the necessary calculations. This procedure would allow judgments to be incorporated about future trends that went beyond the current data available to econometric models. Moreover, the survey response scales could be designed to exactly match what would be considered optimal measures. It is true that there is no shortage of data on expert opinions, but they have largely failed to demonstrate their superiority against the expectations of random samples of adults. This finding had a negative impact on the assumption that knowledge of the economy, the interpretation of the data, and the calculation of expectations were exclusively associated with conscious cognitive deliberation.

Conventional economic theory provides no guidance for empirical research on the formation of expectations. In fact, the appeal of model-consistent expectations as well as the use of experts and reliance on national data reinforced misconceptions about the formation process. Since the accuracy of expectations were solely judged by national data, it encouraged the inappropriate use of the "representative agent" assumption, and discouraged the use of alternate means to explain how people acquire, interpret, and use information when in disequilibrium. The new paradigm contained in this book provides a more generalized framework that can guide empirical investigations and test competing propositions.

RESISTANCE TO AND ACCEPTANCE OF THE NEW PARADIGM

Some readers may find the anomalies, faulty conceptualizations, and the flawed testing procedures of the theory of rational expectations to be superficial, and easily accounted for by small modifications of conventional theory. This defense of orthodoxy would start by noting that forming accurate expectations is the ultimate goal of both the new and revised theories. Some might argue that this commonality is enough to discount all of the other misspecifications since the orthodox theory never specified how expectations were formed. In addition, defenders of the orthodox paradigm may consider it a trivial difference if expectations were formed about the economic conditions people actually faced rather than for the overall economy. To personalize expectations, people could simply calculate them as deviations from the national benchmarks. The defenders of orthodoxy would hold that the use of national data and "representative agents" were simply convenient devices for exposition purposes, and not intended to be used as guides for empirical testing. Moreover, conventional theory views cost–benefit comparisons as a central component of any economic decision. The dismissal of the costs associated with forming expectations reflected the absence of any reliable data on the costs of mental calculations, including opportunity costs. While the benefits may be better specified in the context of the specific decisions in which they are used, multiple uses of the same expectation meant that it was more efficient and cost effective for agents to form expectations that were as accurate as possible even if that degree of accuracy was unnecessary for some of the decisions. Overall, defenders would hold that these criticisms do not challenge the core theory of rational expectations, but mainly involve secondary concerns about how the theory was conceptualized in empirical tests. Improper testing can never invalidate theory.

In direct contrast, this book held that it has been poor conceptualizations, inappropriate methodologies and empirical testing procedures that have acted to block theoretical advances. The purpose of a discipline's scientific paradigm is to promote the advancement of the disciple. While theories represent the main component of a paradigm, scientific advancement critically depends on the other components, including acceptable conceptualizations, suitable methodologies, and appropriate testing procedures. Indeed, as a discipline matures, theoretical advancement becomes more dependent on fresh conceptualizations, innovative methodologies, and new testing procedures. To resist change simply increases the number of findings that must be treated as unexplained anomalies. The acceptance of significant anomalies are symptoms of a more serious disease that weakens the discipline's ability to produce future scientific advancement. To restore prospects for robust advancements in the future, a paradigm shift is often required to reinvigorate the discipline by establishing new conceptualizations, methodologies, and testing procedure.

Many of the findings from past research on expectations have been misinterpreted due to incorrect guidelines contained in the existing paradigm. More importantly, if that research was based on the revised paradigm contained in this book, the empirical data would more often lead the new paradigm to the opposite conclusions than obtained from the existing paradigm. The two most common findings under the existing paradigm are that the quantitative levels of people's expectations are typically inaccurate, and even if the overall levels are accurate, the large variations across the population are inconsistent with rational expectations. In sharp contrast, the new paradigm draws the crucial distinction between observed levels of expectations – which mirrors the actual economic conditions faced by an individual – and how those expectations change over time – which reflects the rationality of expectations. In this new paradigm, heterogeneity of expectations is not a sign of inaccuracy but is anticipated based on differences in the economic conditions faced by different people. Moreover, the correlations over time between people's expectations and national economic statistics is a more accurate measure of the rationality of expectations.

How do people obtain the necessary information about the economic conditions they face? The old paradigm holds that the amount of information required to personalize expectations amounts to a herculean task that few, if any, people could accomplish. Indeed, only state statistical agencies could cost-effectively produce timely and accurate results. The best method to personalize expectations advocated by the conventional paradigm would be as deviations from the benchmarks defined by either the national data or from the more detailed data collected by the state agencies. This amounts to an indirect means to keep the primary focus of the research paradigm on national data. While this would salvage one aspect of the old paradigm, it would impose even greater costs for forming expectations. Moreover, no empirical evidence has supported this view.

Economic theory provides no incentive for people to be knowledgeable about national statistics that do not influence their own economic situation. People do have an incentive to directly monitor economic conditions that affect their own situation, and this incentive existed long before the innovation in the mid-twentieth century of national economic accounts and state statistical agencies. It is not that people are completely uninterested or find national economic statistics useless, it is that these data do not represent their only source of information about their economic situation. Importantly, the use of private information does not imply that these perceptions are unrelated to the economic statistics produced by state agencies. Indeed, the new paradigm does not make macro analysis intractable. An accurate assessment of the economic conditions faced by each individual implies that the appropriate weighted sum across the population would equal the national average. It was the old paradigm that produced the faulty implication that rationality required all individuals to hold the same expectation. While the use of national data and representative agents are convenient devices for exposition purposes, unfortunately these shortcuts also spawned flawed guidelines for empirical tests.

Even orthodox economic theory recognizes that people have had to form economic expectations long before the advent of state statistical agencies. While the content of people's expectations have changed over time, individuals have always been motivated to anticipate changes in their economic environment in order to make optimal decisions by the least costly method, including the opportunity cost of what could have been accomplished by one's mental faculties.

Conscious deliberations represent people's most prized and most limited mental resource, whereas the nonconscious commands a much greater capacity for information processing and learning. The new paradigm holds that people's ability to form and continuously revise expectations is an innate and automatic process aimed at maximizing the usefulness of their mental faculties. Economic expectations, along with a multitude of other expectations, are routinely formed by the same cognitive processes, with the choice between conscious and nonconscious largely independent from the potential benefits or costs of a decision. Although most economic expectations are formed by a combination of conscious and nonconscious cognitive processes, people cannot consciously recall the details of the formation process due to nonconscious processing, only the outcome can be consciously recalled. In most cases, people are likely to describe their expectations as intuitions since they have no conscious awareness of the information they actually used in the formation process. Nonetheless, since most people favor causal explanations, they are apt to provide some reasons that supports the expectation.

There are also timing differences in the formation of expectations between the old and new paradigms. The existing paradigm holds that expectations are typically formed prior to any decision, and the new paradigm holds that the formation usually awaits the identification of a decision. Under the old paradigm, people are assumed to incur the costs of keeping a full array of expectations updated and ready for any potential use. Expectations are assumed to be revised upon the release of new estimates or revisions from statistical agencies. The new paradigm holds that decisions must first be identified so that people can determine the degree of accuracy required and hence any added costs they are willing to incur. Although people continuously update information about the economy, largely by nonconscious processes, the sensitivity of the decision to economic expectations still matters. Decisions that critically depend on some economic expectation, however, are more likely to require explicit conscious deliberation. A moderate dependence may require a small degree of conscious deliberation to supplement nonconscious processes; most everyday economic decisions, however, are typically based on nonconscious acquisition of information and nonconscious learning. If all expectations, economic and otherwise, were formed solely by conscious deliberation, that drain would exhaust people's limited mental capacity for conscious cognitive processing. No person would use their mental resources so inefficiently.

The existing paradigm recognizes the limitations on conscious deliberation, but ignores the much more extensive nonconscious capacity of the human mind. Indeed, perhaps the most significant criticism of rational expectations over the past half century involved limitations on people's ability to obtain the appropriate information, interpret that information, and to calculate expectations based on their conscious cognitive resources. These limitations represent the critical preconditions in support of theories of bounded rationality. Bounded rationality is conceptualized as representing limitations on conscious cognitive deliberations, and more importantly, all nonconscious processes are assumed to result in biased expectations resulting from the use of inappropriate heuristics. No attempt is made to explain why people would form and maintain heuristics that were dysfunctional, nor why rationality would require conscious deliberation.

The new paradigm comes to the opposite conclusions. While affirming the role of conscious deliberation, the new paradigm holds that expectations largely result from the nonconscious accumulation and interpretation of economic data. Nonconscious cognitive processes have the ability to synthesize information and learn how to form and revise economic expectations. Moreover, the choice between conscious and nonconscious processing is not primarily dependent on the importance of the decision or the size of the economic stake, the favored hypotheses of the traditional paradigm. Rather, the choice is related to past experience with the same or similar decisions. Nonconscious processes quickly take over repetitive tasks even when the stakes are the highest, as the driving examples demonstrated. First-time or unique events are more likely to prompt conscious information seeking and deliberation. To be sure, all expectations can be defined as representing conscious processes if the very verbal description of an economic expectation implies that conscious deliberation had the opportunity to intervene.

Another related difference concerns how people can be taught to form rational expectations. Learning theories are intended to demonstrate that people can learn how to overcome bounded rationality to form accurate economic expectations. The outcome of the learning process is thought to be improved conscious deliberation. While it is not surprising that guided conscious learning can produce greater accuracy, it would be surprising if once learned, people would consistently repeat the process solely by conscious deliberation rather than by utilizing nonconscious processes. People would not be maximizing the potential of their mental faculties if they relied exclusively on their relatively scarce resource of conscious deliberation.

The existing paradigm holds that emotions are the root cause of irrationality; the new paradigm holds that emotions are critical elements that motivate the formation process. Reason needs passion to form expectations. Emotion motivates and defines the desired goals, a necessary precursor for the calculus of expectation. Even conscious rational deliberation requires a mental discipline that is guided by an emotional attachment to rationality. As goals change over time, emotions ensure those shifts are represented in the information obtained and expectations formed. Without these emotional guideposts, choice is impossible. Moreover, emotions occupy a preferential position in the interpretation of new information. People's mental faculties give precedence to nonconscious evaluations of new information even before people become consciously aware of that same information. This allows physiological reactions to the information to begin without conscious contemplation; it readies the body for actions that enable people to quickly and automatically respond to economic opportunity or distress. More importantly, these evaluations automatically sort information between those bits that require conscious attention and those that can be processed nonconsciously. The more past experience a person has in forming a specific expectation, the more likely it is that nonconscious processes will be preferred. Without these essential functions of emotions, people's conscious processing would be overwhelmed.

As readers of this book already know, contextual factors have a significant impact on the how, when, and why expectations are formed. How information is acquired, processed, and acted upon is not independent of contextual factors; indeed, context and framing are not the bane of rationality, but its benefactor. In sharp contrast, conventional economics generally views context effects on information processing as an indication of irrationality. Yet, nearly every economist uses the context associated with economic information to interpret its meaning: how a sudden spurt in inflation is interpreted depending on whether it was in core or headline inflation, how a sudden surge or slump in employment is interpreted differently depending on its cause, or why some income changes are interpreted differently than others, and so forth.

The existing paradigm holds that social influences are irrelevant for the formation of expectations, whereas the revised paradigm holds that the defining element of expectations is their social nature. Social interactions enable greater accuracy and prompt faster responses, both critical components for economic decisions. The costs of monitoring the economic environment by groups, as opposed to separate monitoring by individuals, are lower and result in more accurate expectations. The orthodox paradigm does not deny these advantages, but holds that they are superfluous since all individuals face the same (national) economic conditions, all agents have the same (nearly costless) mental capacity, and all arrive at the same rational outcomes. While this is a perfectly reasonable assumption in the context of equilibrium, it is not so in the typical state of disequilibrium, where, by definition, there is no general consensus about economic conditions. In disequilibrium, how an individual's expectation differs from what other people expect is crucial information. When divergences exist, it would only be rational for people to take into account the risk that their expectations may prove incorrect. Indeed, precautionary reactions are required whenever an individual's expectation runs counter to the majority. The excesses of booms and busts indicate that contrarian expectations are sometimes rational; timing, however, is crucial since contrarian expectations provide poor guidance except just before cyclical peaks and troughs.

Importantly, the social nature of expectations facilitates self-fulfilling expectations in the new paradigm. A self-fulfilling expectation prompts a response that acts to confirm that very expectation. Conventional economics accepts the notion that a prevailing inflationary expectation can itself cause higher inflation, and the expectation of deflation can itself cause lower inflation. This acceptance was simply the recognition of an important anomaly, as orthodox economic theory cannot endogenously produce self-fulfilling expectations. In the revised paradigm, the role of self-fulfilling expectations is more broadly defined to include the expectations of consumers and producers, and more importantly, to include self-fulfilling expectations that promote stronger as well as weaker economic growth. The conventional paradigm holds that since economic growth represents an unassailable goal, it therefore cannot be a false expectation that became self-fulling during expansions. The same does not hold true for economic contractions as they are implicitly considered to be false expectations that only in very rare circumstances can be self-fulfilling. The revised paradigm holds that self-fulfilling expectations driven by social factors play an important role in secular growth as well as secular stagnation.

Finally, the orthodox and revised paradigms differ in people's reactions to economic situations where decision risks are incalculable. The conventional paradigm indicates that the appropriate reaction is inaction given the ambiguous nature of the economic signals. Since no rational action is possible in the presence of ambiguity, any action taken must be due to "animal spirits." Since these situations are assumed to be extraordinarily rare, the non-rational patch of animal spirits is tolerated, although often disputed. The new paradigm holds the opposite view: ambiguity is assumed to be much more common, and could even be described as commonplace. Moreover, ambiguity is more properly defined in terms of probability ranges, not just where probability is undefined. Once the probability range reaches a significant width, although calculations may still technically be made, its meaning for behavioral decisions is indistinct from situations where the probability is undefined. The recognition that ambiguity is more commonplace needs to be accompanied by the recognition that people have the mental faculties to form accurate expectations in the face of what the old paradigm considered incalculable risks.

BEHAVIORAL ECONOMICS

This book exemplified the importance of the human factor in economic theory, an example of the merits of behavioral economics. The field of behavioral economics was initiated in the 1940s by George Katona (Curtin, 2016). His designation had the simple purpose of distinguishing the behavior of economic agents from economic markets. Economic theory has long recognized that outcomes depend on both the behavior of agents as well as the actions of markets. Katona believed the mission of behavioral economics was to explore how agents acquire, process, and act on economic information. This mission was undertaken with the explicit aim to enhance economic theory based on empirical observations. Although behavioral economics had become an essential component of the discipline by the start of the twenty-first century, behavioral economics has not fully achieved Katona's original goal of challenging and replacing some elements of orthodox economic theory. Instead, behavioral economics has become a sub-discipline that mainly catalogues divergences from rational behavior. Unfortunately, it was this shift in focus from the old objective of theory development to the new objective of documenting divergences from rational behavior that has been identified as the reason for the resurgent popularity of behavioral economics. Rather than spark new innovative theories, behavioral economics has become a field guide to design policies that optimally take advantage of these presumed biases to achieve the desired goals of government policies, the marketing goals of private firms, and even how people can achieve the desired behaviors among other family members, friends, and acquaintances.

Past research on economic expectations has documented a long list of heuristics and biases that constitute divergences from rationality according to the existing paradigm. Few scholars have delved into the mechanisms that produce these divergences, with the implicit notion that no robust theory could reliably explain errors in expectations. That judgment is not based on the pure theory of rational expectations, but on a scientific paradigm that excluded the importance of nonconscious cognitive processes, that dismissed the impact of relative costs and benefits of expectations formed for specific decisions, and insisted that empirical tests be based on national data rather than the conditions actually faced by economic agents. The new paradigm advanced in this book does not rule out irrational behavior, but it does make that judgment more dependent on a complete assessment of the relevant facts. Answers to why, how, and when expectations are formed have been anchored to a more solid scientific foundation, as well as answers to why, how, and when expectations can have an independent influence on the course of the macroeconomy. The new scientific paradigm is in its infancy awaiting further development by economists as well as other social scientists.

Paradigm shifts occur endogenously. It is usually a slow process of acceptance by the scholars within a discipline. Some features of the new paradigm will be readily accepted, others may take longer to be accepted, and presumably some will be rejected for good cause. It is hard to imagine, however, a rejection of all of the elements of the new paradigm presented in this book. The hope is that the more robust description of how, when, and why expectations are formed as well as the independent role expectations play in shaping trends in the macroeconomy will find ready acceptance. Moreover, it is hoped that the new paradigm will have a positive impact on future theory development and foster revised research methodologies and testing protocols.

References

Akerlof, G., Dickens, W., & Perry, G. (2001). Options for stabilization policy. The Brookings Institution Policy Brief, *69*.

Akerlof, G., & Shiller, R. J. (2010). *Animal spirits: How human psychology drives the economy, and why it matters for global capitalism (new edition).* Princeton, NJ: Princeton University Press.

Allen, R., & Reber, A. (1980). Very long term memory for tacit knowledge. *Cognition, 8*(2), 175–185.

Aslin, R. N., Saffran, J. R., & Newport, E. L. (1998). Computation of conditional probability statistics by 8-month-old infants. *Psychological Science, 9*(4), 321–324.

Bacchetta, P., & van Wincoop, E. (2005). Rational inattention: A solution to the forward discount puzzle. NBER Working Paper Series, 11633.

Baghestani, H. (1992). Survey evidence on the Muthian rationality of the inflation forecasts of US consumers. *Oxford Bulletin of Economics and Statistics, 54*(2), 173–186.

Baker, M. (1992). *Digit preference in CPS unemployment data.* Toronto, Ontario: University of Toronto Press.

Bargh, J. A., & Chartrand, T. L. (1999). The unbearable automaticity of being. *American Psychologist, 54*(7), 462–479.

Bargh, J. A., & Ferguson, M. J. (2000). Beyond behaviorism: On the automaticity of higher mental processes. *Psychological Bulletin, 126*(6), 925–945.

Bargh, J. A., & Morsella, E. (2008). The unconscious mind. *Perspectives on Psychological Science, 3*(1), 73–79.

Bargh, J. A., & Williams, E. L. (2006). The automaticity of social life. *Current Directions in Psychological Science, 15*(1), 1–4.

Barsky, R. B., & Sims, E. R. (2012). Information, animal spirits, and the meaning of innovations in consumer confidence. *American Economic Review, 102*(4), 1343–1377.

Batchelor, R., & Dua, P. (1989). Household versus economists' forecasts of inflation: A reassessment. *Journal of Money, Credit and Banking, 21*(2), 252–257.

Baumeister, R. F., & Vohs, K. D. (2004). *Handbook of self-regulation: Research, theory, and applications.* New York, NY: Guilford.

Baumeister, R. F., Bratslavsky, E., Muraven, M., & Tice, D. M. (1998). Ego depletion: Is the active self a limited resource? *Journal of Personality and Social Psychology, 74*(5), 1252–1265.

Bechara, A., Damasio, H., Tranel, D., & Damasio, A. R. (1997). Deciding advantageously before knowing the advantageous strategy. *Science*, *275*(5304), 1293–1295.

Bernanke, B. S. (1983). Irreversibility, uncertainty, and cyclical investment. *Quarterly Journal of Economics*, *97*(1), 85–106.

Bernheim, B., & Rangel, A. (2004). Addiction and cue-triggered decision processes. *The American Economic Review*, *94*(5), 1558–1590.

Berridge, K. C., & Robinson, T. E. (1998). What is the role of dopamine in reward: Hedonic impact, reward learning, or incentive salience? *Brain Research Reviews*, *28*(3), 309–369.

Berry, D. C., & Broadbent, D. (1984). On the relationship between task performance and associated verbalizable knowledge. *The Quarterly Journal of Experimental Psychology Section A*, *36*(2), 209–231.

   (1988). Interactive tasks and the implicit–explicit distinction. *British Journal of Psychology*, *79*(2), 251–272.

Berry, D. C., & Dienes, Z. P. (1993). *Implicit learning: Theoretical and empirical issues.* East Sussex, UK: Lawrence Erlbaum Associates.

Betsch, T., Plessner, H., Schwieren, C., & Gutig, R. (2001). I like it but I don't know why: A value-account approach to implicit attitude formation. *Personality Social Psychology Bulletin*, *27*(2), 242–253.

Beyth-Marom, R. (1982). How probable is probable? Numerical translations of verbal probability expressions. *Journal of Forecasting*, *1*, 257–269.

Bikhchandani, S., Hirshleifer, D., & Welch, I. (1992). A theory of fads, fashion, custom, and cultural change as informational cascades. *The Journal of Political Economy*, *100*(5), 992–1026.

Blanchard, O. (1993). Consumption and the recession of 1990–1991. *American Economic Review*, *83*(2), 270–274.

Blendon, R. J., Benson, J. M., Brodie, M., Morin, R., Altman, D. E., Gitterman, D., et al. (1997). Bridging the gap between the public's and economists' views of the economy. *Journal of Economic Perspectives*, *11*(3), 105–118.

Bless, H., Schwarz, N., Clore, G. L., Golisano, V., Rabe, C., & Wölk, M. (1996). Mood and the use of scripts: Does a happy mood really lead to mindlessness? *Journal of Personality and Social Psychology*, *71*(4), 665–679.

Blinder, A. S., & Krueger, A. B. (2004). What does the public know about economic policy, and how does it know it? *Brookings Papers on Economic Activity*, *2004*(1), 327–397.

Branch, W. A. (2007). Sticky information and model uncertainty in survey data on inflation expectations. *Journal of Economic Dynamics and Control*, *31*(1), 245–276.

Brase, G. L., Cosmides, L., & Tooby, J. (1998). Individuation, counting, and statistical inference: The role of frequency and whole-object representations in judgment under uncertainty. *Journal of Experimental Psychology: General*, *127*(1), 3–21.

Bryan, M. F., & Gavin, W. T. (1986). Models of inflation expectations formation: A comparison of household and economist forecasts. *Journal of Money, Credit and Banking*, *18*(4), 539–544.

Bryan, M. F., & Venkatu, G. (2001). The demographics of inflation opinion surveys. Federal Reserve Bank of Cleveland, Economic Commentary.

Cacioppo, J. T., & Petty, R. E. (1982). The need for cognition. *Journal of Personality and Social Psychology*, *42*(1), 116–131.

Cagan, P. (1956). The monetary dynamics of hyperinflation. In M. Friedman (Ed.), *Studies in the quantity theory of money* (pp. 25–117). Chicago, IL: University of Chicago Press.

Camerer, C. F., & Hogarth, R. M. (1999). The effects of financial incentives in experiments: A review and capital-labor-production framework. *Journal of Risk and Uncertainty, 19*(1), 7–42.

Camerer, C. F., Loewenstein, G., & Prelec, D. (2005). Neuroeconomics: How neuroscience can inform economics. *Journal of Economic Literature, 43*, 9–64.

Camerer, C., & Weber, M. (1992). Recent developments in modeling preferences: Uncertainty and ambiguity. *Journal of Risk and Uncertainty, 5*(4), 325–370.

Campbell, J. Y., & Mankiw, N. G. (1989). Consumption, income, and interest rates: Reinterpreting the time series evidence. In S. Fischer, & O. Blanchard (Eds.), *NBER macroeconomics annual 1989* (volume 4, pp. 185–246). Cambridge, MA: MIT Press.

Caplin, A., & Dean, M. (2008). Dopamine, reward prediction error, and economics. *The Quarterly Journal of Economics, 123*(2), 663–701.

Carey, S. (2001). Bridging the gap between cognition and developmental neuroscience: The example of number representation. In C. A. Nelson, & M. Luciana (Eds.), *The handbook of developmental cognitive neuroscience* (pp. 413–432). Cambridge, MA: MIT Press.

Carlson, J. A., & Parkin, M. (1975). Inflationary expectations. *Economica, 42*, 123–138.

Carroll, C. D. (1994). How does future income affect current consumption. *Quarterly Journal of Economics, 109*(1), 111–147.

(2001). The epidemiology of macroeconomic expectations. NBER Working Paper Series, 8695.

(2003). Macroeconomic expectations of households and professional forecasters. *The Quarterly Journal of Economics, 118*(1), 269–298.

Carter, R., & Frith, C. D. (1998). *Mapping the mind.* Berkeley and Los Angeles, CA: University of California Press.

Cass, D., & Shell, K. (1983). Do sunspots matter? *Journal of Political Economy, 91*(2), 193–227.

Ceci, S. J. (1991). How much does schooling influence general intelligence and its cognitive components? A reassessment of the evidence. *Developmental Psychology, 27*(5), 703–722.

Chaiken, S., & Trope, Y. (1999). *Dual-process theories in social psychology.* New York, NY: Guilford Press.

Christiano, L. J., & Fitzgerald, T. J. (1999). The business cycle: It's still a puzzle. *Economic Perspectives, Federal Reserve Bank of Chicago, 22*(4), 56–83.

Cleeremans, A., Destrebecqz, A., & Boyer, M. (1998). Implicit learning: News from the front. *Trends in Cognitive Science, 2*(10), 406–416.

Cochrane, J. H. (1994). Shocks. *Carnegie-Rochester Conference Series on Public Policy, 41*, 295–364.

Conlisk, J. (1996). Why bounded rationality? *Journal of Economic Literature, 34*, 669–700.

Cosmides, L., & Tooby, J. (1996). Are humans good intuitive statisticians after all? Rethinking some conclusions from the literature on judgment under uncertainty. *Cognition, 58*, 1–73.

Croushore, D. (1998). Evaluating inflation expectations. Federal Reserve Bank of Philadelphia, Working Paper 98-14.

Cukierman, A., & Meltzer, A. (1986). A theory of ambiguity, credibility, and inflation under discretion and asymmetric information. *Econmetrica, 54*(5), 1099–1128.

Curtin, R. T. (1983). Curtin on Katona. In H. W. Spiegel & W. J. Samuels (Eds.), *Contemporary economists in perspective* (pp. 495–522). New York, NY: Jai Press.

(1999). The outlook for consumption in 2000. In S. Hymans (Ed.), *The economic outlook for 2000*. Ann Arbor, MI: University of Michigan.

(2003). Unemployment expectations: The impact of private information on income uncertainty. *Review of Income and Wealth, 49*(4), 539–554.

(2004). Psychology and macroeconomics. In R. Kahn, F. T. Juster, J. House, & E. Singer (Eds.), *A telescope on society: Survey research and social science at the University of Michigan* (pp. 131–155). Ann Arbor, MI: University of Michigan Press.

(2007). Consumer sentiment surveys: Worldwide review and assessment. *Journal of Business Cycle Measurement and Analysis, 3*(1) 7–42.

(2008). What US consumers know about economic conditions. In E. Giovannini (Ed.), *Statistics, knowledge and policy 2007: Measuring and fostering the progress of societies*. Paris: OECD.

(2010). Inflation expectations and empirical tests: Theoretical models and empirical tests. In P. Sinclair (Ed.), *Inflation expectations*, Routledge International Studies in Money and Banking 56 (pp. 34–61). London: Routledge.

(2013). Consumer behavior adapts to fundamental changes in expectations. In G. Fulton (Ed.), *The economic outlook for 2014*. Ann Arbor, MI: University of Michigan.

(2016). George Katona: A founder of behavioral economics. In Roger Frantz, et al. (Eds.), *Routledge handbook of behavioral economics* (pp. 18–35). London, UK: Routledge.

Curtin, R. T., Presser, S., & Singer, E. (2000). The effects of response rate changes on the index of consumer sentiment. *Public Opinion Quarterly, 64*, 413–428.

Damasio, A. R. (1994). *Descartes' error*. New York, NY: Putnam.

Darwin, C. (1872). *The expression of the emotions in man and animal*. London, UK: John Murray.

De Cruz, H. (2006). Why are some numerical concepts more successful than others? An evolutionary perspective on the history of number concepts. *Evolution and Human Behavior, 27*(4), 306–323.

De Grauwe, P. (2010). Top-down versus bottom-up macroeconomics. *CESifo Economic Studies, 56*(4), 465–497.

Dehaene, S. (1997). *The number sense: How the mind creates mathematics*. New York, NY: Oxford University Press.

(2003). The neural basis of the Weber–Fechner law: A logarithmic mental number line. *Trends in Cognitive Sciences, 7*(4), 145–147.

Dehaene, S., & Akhavein, R. (1995). Attention, automaticity, and levels of representation in number processing. *Journal of Experimental Psychology: Learning, Memory and Cognition, 21*(2), 314–326.

Dehaene, S., Dehaene-Lambertz, G., & Cohen, L. (1998). Abstract representations of numbers in the animal and human brain. *Trends in Neuroscience, 21*(8), 355–361.

Dehaene, S., Molko, N., Cohen, L., & Wilson, A. J. (2004). Arithmetic and the brain. *Current Opinion in Neurobiology, 14*, 218–224.

Dehaene, S., Changeux, J., Naccache, L., & Sackur, J. (2006). Conscious, preconscious, and subliminal processing: A testable taxonomy. *Trends in Cognitive Science, 10*(5), 204–211.

Delli Carpini, M., & Keeter, S. (1996). *What Americans know about politics and why it matters.* New Haven, CT: Yale University Press.

Di Chiara, G. (1997). Alcohol and dopamine. *Alcohol Health and Research World, 21*(2), 108–114.

Dijksterhuis, A. (2004). Think different: The merits of unconscious thought in preference development and decision making. *Journal of Personality and Social Psychology, 87*(5), 586–598.

Dominitz, J., & Manski, C. F. (1997). Perceptions of economic insecurity. *Public Opinion Quarterly, 61*, 261–287.

Dow, G. (2013). Marx, Keynes and heterodoxy. *The Journal of Australian Political Theory* (75), 69–98.

Easley, D., & Kleinberg, J. (2010). *Networks, crowds, and markets: Reasoning about a highly connected world.* New York, NY: Cambridge University Press.

Edouard, L., & Senthilselvan, A. (1997). Observer error and birthweight: Digit preference in recording. *Public Health, 111*(2), 77–79.

Ekman, P. (1972). Universals and cultural differences in facial expressions of emotion. *Nebraska symposium on motivation* (pp. 207–286). Lincoln, NE: University of Nebraska Press.

(1992). *Cognition and emotions.* San Francisco, CA: Lawrence Erlbaum Associates.

Elster, J. (1998). Emotions and economic theory. *Journal of Economic Literature, 36*(1), 47–74.

Enticott, P. G., Johnston, P. J., Herring, S. E., Hoy, K. E., & Fitzgerald, P. B. (2008). Mirror neuron activation is associated with facial emotion processing. *Neuropsychologia, 46*(11), 2851–2854.

Epstein, S. (1994). Integration of the cognitive and psychodynamic unconscious. *American Psychologist, 49*(8), 709–724.

Feigenson, L., Dehaene, S., & Spelke, E. (2004). Core systems of number. *Trends in Cognitive Sciences, 8*(7), 307–314.

Fischer, S., Drosopoulos, S., Tsen, J., & Born, J. (2006). Implicit learning – explicit knowledge: A role for sleep in memory system interaction. *Journal of Cognitive Neuroscience, 18*(3), 311–319.

Fischhoff, B. (1994). What forecasts (seem to) mean. *International Journal of Forecasting, 10*(3), 387–403.

Fisher, I. (1930). *The theory of interest as determined by impatience to spend income and opportunity to invest it.* New York, NY: Macmillan.

French, E., Kelley, T., & Qi, A. (2013). Expected income growth and the great recession. *Economic Perspectives, 37*(1), 14–29.

Freud, S. (1900). *The interpretation of dreams.* Leipzig & Vienna: Franz Deuticke.

Friedman, M. (1953). *Essays in positive economics.* Chicago, IL: University of Chicago Press.

(1957). *A theory of the consumption function.* Princeton, NJ: Princeton University Press.

Frijda, N. H. (1986). *The emotions: Studies in emotion and social interaction*. London & Paris: Cambridge University Press & Editions de la Maison des Sciences de l'Homme.

Frydman, R., & Phelps, E. S. (2013). *Rethinking expectations: The way forward for macroeconomics*. Princeton, NJ: Princeton University Press.

Gallagher, D., & Clore, G. (1985). Effects of fear and anger on judgments of risk and evaluations of blame. Annual Meeting of the Midwestern Psychological Association, Chicago, IL.

Gallese, V., Keysers, C., & Rizzolatti, G. (2004). A unifying view of the basis of social cognition. *Trends in Cognitive Sciences, 8*(9), 396–403.

Gallistel, C. R., & Gelman, R. (1992). Preverbal and verbal counting and computation. *Cognition, 44*, 43–74.

Geweke, J., Meese, R., & Dent, W. (1983). Comparing alternative tests of causality in temporal systems. *Journal of Econometrics, 21*(2), 161–194.

Gigerenzer, G. (1996). On narrow norms and vague heuristics: A reply to Kahneman and Tversky. *Psychological Review, 103*(3), 592–596.

(1998). Ecological intelligence: An adaptation for frequencies. In D. D. Cummins, & C. Allen (Eds.), *The evolution of mind* (pp. 9–29). New York, NY: Oxford University Press.

Gigerenzer, G., & Hoffrage, U. (1995). How to improve Bayesian reasoning without instruction: Frequency formats. *Psychological Review, 102*(4), 684–704.

(1999). Overcoming difficulties in Bayesian reasoning: A reply to Lewis and Keren (1999) and Mellers and McGraw (1999). *Psychological Review, 106*(2), 425–430.

Gigerenzer, G., Swijtink, Z., Porter, T., Daston, L., Beatty, J. & Krüger, L. (1989). *The empire of chance: How probability changed science and everyday life*. Cambridge: Cambridge University Press.

Gilbert, D. T. (1999). What the mind's not. In S. Chaiken, & Y. Trope (Eds.), *Dual-process theories in social psychology* (pp. 3–11). New York, NY: Guilford.

Goldrian, G., Lindbauer, J. D., & Nerb, G. (2001). *Evaluation and development of confidence indicators based on harmonised business and consumer surveys*. Munich: IFO Institute for Economic Research.

Gordon, P. (2004). Numerical cognition without words: Evidence from Amazonia. *Science, 306*(5695), 496–499.

Gramlich, E. (1983). Models of inflation expectations formation. *Journal of Money, Credit and Banking, 15*(2), 155–173.

Grant, A. P., & Thomas, L. B. (1999). Inflation expectations and rationality revisited. *Economics Letters, 62*, 331–338.

Guiso, L., Japelli, T., & Terlizzese, D. (1992). Earnings uncertainty and precautionary saving. *Journal of Monetary Economics, 30*, 307–337.

Hagemann, R. P. (1982). The variability of inflation rates across household types. *Journal of Money, Credit and Banking, 14*(4), 494–510.

Hamilton, J. T. (2003). *All the news that's fit to sell: How the market transforms information into news*. Princeton, NJ: Princeton University Press.

Hall, R. E. (1993). Macro theory and the recession of 1990–1991. *The American Economic Review, 83*(2), 275–279.

Hasher, L., & Zacks, R. T. (1984). Automatic processing of fundamental information: The case of frequency of occurrence. *American Psychologist, 39*(12), 1372–1388.

Hendry, D. F., & Krolzig, H. M. (2005). The properties of automatic GETS modelling. *The Economic Journal, 115*(502), C32–C61.

Hinsz, V. B., Tindale, R. S., & Vollrath, D. A. (1997). The emerging conceptualization of groups as information processors. *Psychological Bulletin, 121*(1), 43–64.

Hirshleifer, D., & Slumway, T. (2003). Good day sunshine: Stock returns and the weather. *Journal of Finance, 58*(3), 1009–1032.

Hobijn, B., & Lagakos, D. (2005). Inflation inequality in the united states. *Review of Income and Wealth, 51*(4), 581–606.

Hodgkinson, G. P., Langan-Fox, J., & Sadler-Smith, E. (2008). Intuition: A fundamental bridging construct in the behavioural sciences. *British Journal of Psychology, 99*(1), 1–27.

Hoffmann, J., & Sebald, A. (2005). When obvious covariations are not even learned implicitly. *European Journal of Cognitive Psychology, 17*(4), 449–480.

Hogarth, R. M. (2001). *Educating intuition.* Chicago, IL: University of Chicago Press.

Howitt, P., & McAfee, P. (1992). Animal spirits. *American Economic Review, 82*(3), 493–507.

Iacoboni, M., Molnar-Szakacs, I., Gallese, V., Buccino, G., Mazziotta, J. C., & Rizzolatti, G. (2005). Grasping the intentions of others with one's own mirror neuron system. *PLoS Biology, 3*(3), 529–535.

Ilut, C. L., & Schneider, M. (2014). Ambiguous business cycles. *American Economic Review, 104*(8), 2368–2399.

Izard, V., & Dehaene, S. (2008). Calibrating the mental number line. *Cognition, 106*(3), 1221–1247.

Jevons, W. S. (1878). Commercial crisis and sun-spots. *Nature, 19,* 33–37.

Juster, F. T. (1966). Consumer buying intentions and purchase probability: An experiment in survey design. *Journal of the American Statistical Association, 61*(315), 658–696.

Kahneman, D. (2011). *Thinking, fast and slow.* New York, NY: Farrar, Straus and Giroux.
    (2013). Behavioral economics and investor protection: Keynote address. *Loyola University Chicago Law Journal, 44,* 1333–1509.

Kahneman, D., & Lovallo, D. (1993). Timid choices and bold forecasts: A cognitive perspective on risk taking. *Management Science, 39*(1), 17–31.

Kahneman, D., & Miller, D. T. (1986). Norm theory: Comparing reality to its alternatives. *Psychological Review, 93*(2), 136–153.

Kahneman, D., Slovic, P., & Tversky, A. (1985). *Judgment under uncertainty: Heuristics and biases.* Cambridge: Cambridge University Press.

Kahneman, D., & Tversky, A. (1979). Prospect theory: An analysis of decision under risk. *Econometrica, 47*(2), 263–292.
    (1982). On the psychology of prediction. In D. Kahneman, P. Slovic, & A. Tversky (Eds.), *Judgment under uncertainty: Heuristics and biases* (pp. 48–68). Cambridge: Cambridge University Press.

Kareev, Y., Lieberman, I., & Lev, M. (1997). Through a narrow window: Sample size and the perception of correlation. *Journal of Experimental Psychology, 126*(3), 278–287.

Karlsson, N., Loewenstein, G., & Seppi, D. (2009). The ostrich effect: Selective attention to information about investments. *Journal of Risk and Uncertainty, 38*(2), 95–115.

Katona, G. (1940). *Organizing and memorizing: Studies in the psychology of learning and teaching.* New York, NY: Columbia University Press.

(1951). *Psychological analysis of economic behavior*. New York, NY: McGraw-Hill.

(1960). *The powerful consumer: Psychological studies of the American economy.* New York, NY: McGraw-Hill.

(1964). *The mass consumption society*. New York, NY: McGraw-Hill.

(1975). *Psychological economics*. New York, NY: Elsevier.

Katona, G., & Mueller, E. (1956). *Consumer expectations, 1953–56.* Ann Arbor, MI: Survey Research Center, University of Michigan.

Keane, M. P., & Runkle, D. E. (1990). Testing the rationality of price forecasts: New evidence from panel data. *American Economic Review, 80*(4), 714–735.

Keynes, J. M. (1936). *The general theory of employment, interest, and money*. New York, NY: Harcourt, Brace.

Khan, H., & Zhu, Z. (2002). Estimates of the sticky-information Phillips curve for the United States, Canada, and the United Kingdom. Bank of Canada, Working Paper 2002-19.

Kihlstrom, J. F. (1987). The cognitive unconscious. *Science, 237*(4821), 1445–1452.

Kimball, M. S. (1990). Precautionary saving in the small and in the large. *Econometrica, 58*(1), 53–73.

Kirkham, N. Z., Slemmer, J. A., & Johnson, S. P. (2002). Visual statistical learning in infancy: Evidence for a domain general learning mechanism. *Cognition, 83*, B35–B42.

Klein, L. R. (1946). A post-mortem on transition predictions of national product. *The Journal of Political Economy, 54*(4), 289–308.

Koch, C., & Tsuchiya, N. (2006). Attention and consciousness: Two distinct brain processes. *Trends in Cognitive Sciences, 11*(1), 16–22.

Koopmans, T. C. (1947). Measurement without theory. *The Review of Economics and Statistics, 29*(3), 161–172.

Koppl, R. (1991). Retrospectives: Animal spirits. *Journal of Economic Perspectives, 5*(3), 203–210.

Koszegi, B., & Rabin, M. (2006). A model of reference-dependent preferences. *The Quarterly Journal of Economics, 121*(4), 1133–1165.

(2007). Mistakes in choice based welfare analysis. *The American Economic Review, 97*(2), 477–481.

(2009). Reference-dependent consumption plans. *The American Economic Review, 99*(3), 909–936.

Koyck, L. M. (1954). *Distributed lags and investment analysis.* Amsterdam: North-Holland.

Krosnick, J. A. (1999). Survey research. *Annual Review of Psychology, 50*, 537–567.

Kuhl, P. K. (2004). Early language acquisition: Cracking the speech code. *Nature Reviews Neuroscience, 5*, 831–843.

Kuhn, T. S. (1962). *International encyclopedia of unified science*. Chicago, IL: University of Chicago Press.

Lahiri, K., & Zhao, Y. (2016) Determinants of consumer sentiment over business cycles: Evidence from the US surveys of consumers. *Journal of Business Cycle Research, 12*, 187–215.

LeDoux, J. (1996). *The emotional brain: The mysterious underpinnings of emotional life.* New York, NY: Simon and Schuster.

Lepage, J., & Théoret, H. (2007). The mirror neuron system: Grasping others' actions from birth? *Developmental Science, 10*(5), 513–523.

Lerner, J. S., Small, D. A., & Loewenstein, G. (2004). Heart strings and purse strings: Carryover effects of emotions on economic decisions. *Psychological Science, 15*(5), 337.

Levanon, G., Ozyildirim, A., Schaitkin, B., & Zabinska, J. (2011). *Comprehensive benchmarks revisions for the Conference Board Learning Economic Index for the United States.* New York, NY: The Conference Board.

Lewicki, P. (1986). Processing information about covariations that cannot be articulated. *Journal of Experimental Psychology, 12*(1), 135–146.

Lewicki, P., & Hill, T. (1989). On the status of nonconscious processes in human cognition: Comment on Reber. *Journal of Experimental Psychology,* 118(3), 239–241.

Lewicki, P., Hill, T., & Czyzewska, M. (1992). Nonconscious acquisition of information. *American Psychologist, 47*(6), 796–801.

(1994). Nonconscious indirect inferences in encoding. *Journal of Experimental Psychology: General, 123*(3), 257–263.

(1997). Hidden covariation detection: A fundamental and ubiquitous phenomenon. *Journal of Experimental Psychology: Learning, Memory and Cognition, 21*(1), 221–228.

Lewin, S. B. (1996). Economics and psychology: Lessons for our own day from the early twentieth century. *Journal of Economic Literature, 34*(3), 1293–1323.

Lichtenstein, S., Fischhoff, B., & Phillips, L. D. (1982). Calibration of probabilities: The state of the art to 1980. In D. Kahneman, & A. Tversky (Eds.), *Judgment under uncertainty: Heuristics and biases* (pp. 306–334). Cambridge: Cambridge University Press.

Lieberman, M. D. (2000). Intuition: A social cognitive neuroscience approach. *Psychological Bulletin, 126*(1), 109–137.

Lillard, L. A., & Willis, R. J. (2001). *Cognition and wealth: The importance of probabilistic thinking.* Ann Arbor, MI: Michigan Retirement Research Center & Health and Retirement Study.

Loewenstein, G. F., & O'Donoghue, T. (2004). Animal spirits: Affective and deliberative processes in economic behavior. SSRN 539843.

Loewenstein, G. F., Hsee, C. K., Weber, E. U., & Welch, N. (2001). Risk as feelings. *Psychological Bulletin, 127*(2), 267–286.

Lott, W., & Miller, S. (1982). Are workers more accurate forecasters of inflation than capitalists? *Applied Economics, 14*(5), 437–446.

Lucas, A. (1987). Public knowledge of biology. *Journal of Biological Education, 21*(1), 41–45.

Lucas, A. M. (1988). Public knowledge of elementary physics. *Physics Education, 23*(1), 10–16.

Lucas, R. J. (2002). *Lectures on economic growth.* Cambridge, MA: Harvard University Press.

Mankiw, N. G., & Reis, R. (2002). Sticky information versus sticky prices: A proposal to replace the new Keynesian-Phillips curve. *The Quarterly Journal of Economics, 117*(4), 1295–1328.

(2003). What measure of inflation should a central bank target? *Journal of the European Economic Association, 1*(5), 1058–1086.

Mankiw, N. G., Reis, R., & Wolfers, J. (2004). Disagreement about inflation expectations. *NBER Macroeconomic Annual 2003, 18*, 209–270.

Manski, C. F. (1990). The use of intentions data to predict behavior: A best-case analysis. *Journal of the American Statistical Association, 85*(412), 934–990.

Massey, D. S. (2002). A brief history of human society: The origin and role of emotion in social life. *American Sociological Review, 67*(1), 1–29.

Mathews, R. C., Roussel, L. G., Cochran, B. P., Cook, A. E., & Dunaway, D. L. (2000). The role of implicit learning in the acquisition of generative knowledge. *Journal of Cognitive Systems Research, 1*(3), 161–174.

Mehra, Y. P. (2002). Survey measures of expected inflation: Revisiting the issues of predictive content and rationality. *Economic Quarterly-Federal Reserve Bank of Richmond, 88*(3), 17–36.

Menzies, G. D., & Zizzo, D. J. (2009). Inferential expectations. *The BE Journal of Macroeconomics, 9*(1), 1–25.

Michael, R. T. (1979). Variation across households in the rate of inflation. *Journal of Money, Credit and Banking, 11*, 32–46.

Midford, R., & Kirsner, K. (2005). Implicit and explicit learning in aged and young adults. *Aging, Neuropsychology, and Cognition, 12*(4), 359–387.

Mirenowicz, K., & Schultz, W. (1994). Importance of unpredictability for reward and response in primate dopamine neurons. *Journal of Neurophysiology, 72*, 1024–1027.

Modigliani, F., & Brumberg, R. (1954). Utility analysis and the consumption function: An interpretation of cross-section data. In K. Kurihara (Ed.), *Post-Keynesian economics* (pp. 388–436). New Brunswick, NJ: Rutgers University Press.

Montague, P. R., & Berns, G. S. (2002). Neural economics and the biological substrates of valuation. *Neuron, 36*(2), 265–284.

Muth, J. F. (1961). Rational expectations and the theory of price movements. *Econometrica, 29*(3), 315–335.

Nakahara, H., Itoh, H., Kawagoe, R., Takikawa, Y., & Hikosaka, O. (2004). Dopamine neurons can represent context-dependent prediction error. *Neuron, 41*(2), 269–280.

Nardo, M. (2003). The quantification of qualitative survey data: A critical assessment. *Journal of Economic Surveys, 17*(5), 645–668.

Neisser, U. (1967). *Cognitive psychology (4th edition).* Urbana, IL: University of Illinois Press.

Nerlove, M. (1958). Adaptive expectations and cobweb phenomena. *Quarterly Journal of Economics, 72*(2), 227–240.

Nilsson, R. (2000). Confidence indicators and composite indicators. Paper presented at the CIRET Conference, Paris.

Nimark, K. P. (2014). Man-bites-dog business cycles. *American Economic Review, 104*(8), 2320–2367.

Nisbett, R. E., & Wilson, T. D. (1977). The halo effect: Evidence for unconscious alteration of judgments. *Journal of Personality and Social Psychology, 35*(4), 250–256.

Nisbett, R. E., Krantz, D. H., Jepson, C., & Kunda, Z. (1983). The use of statistical heuristics in everyday inductive reasoning. *Psychological Review, 90*, 339.

Noble, N. R., & Fields, T. W. (1982). Testing the rationality of inflation expectations derived from survey data: A structure-based approach. *Southern Economic Journal, 49*(2), 361–373.

Onishi, K. H., & Baillargeon, R. (2005). Do 15-month-old infants understand false beliefs? *Science, 308*(5719), 255.

Organization for Economic Cooperation and Development. (2006). *PISA: Assessing scientific, reading, and mathematical literacy.* OECD.

Pesaran, M. H. (1984). *Formation of inflation expectations in British manufacturing industries.* Cambridge: Faculty of Economics, University of Cambridge.

Petty, R. E., Briñol, P., Loersch, C., & McCaslin, M. J. (2009). The need for cognition. In M. R. Leary, & R. H. Hoyle (Eds.), *Handbook of individual differences in social behavior* (pp. 318–329). New York, NY: Guilford.

PEW Research Center. (2009). *Evening news viewership.* Washington, DC.

Phelps, E. S. (2013). *Mass flourishing: How grassroots innovation created jobs, challenge, and change.* Princeton, NJ: Princeton University Press.

Pica, P., Lemer, C., Izard, V., & Dehaene, S. (2004). Exact and approximate arithmetic in an Amazonian Indigene group. *Science, 306*(5695), 499–503.

Popper, K. R. (1935). *The logic of scientific discovery.* New York, NY: Harper & Roy.

Presenti, M., Thioux, M., Seron, X., and De Volder, A. (2000). Neuroanatomical substrates of Arabic number processing, numerical comparison, and simple addition: A PET study. *Journal of Cognitive Neuroscience, 12,* 461–479.

Reber, A. S. (1967). Implicit learning of artificial grammars. *Journal of Verbal Learning and Verbal Behavior, 6*(6), 855–863.

(1992). The cognitive unconscious: An evolutionary perspective. *Consciousness and Cognition, 1*(2), 93–133.

Reber, A., Kassin, S. M., Lewis, S., & Cantor, G. (1980). On the relationship between implicit and explicit modes in the learning of a complex rule structure. *Journal of Experimental Psychology: Learning, Memory and Cognition, 6*(5), 492–502.

Redgrave, P., & Gurney, K. (2006). The short-latency dopamine signal: A role in discovering novel actions? *Nature Reviews Neuroscience, 7*(12), 967–975.

Rescorla, R., & Wagner, A. (1972). *A theory of Pavlovian conditioning: Variations in the effectiveness of reinforcement and nonreinforcement.* New York, NY: Appleton-Century-Crofts.

Rizzolatti, G., & Craighero, L. (2004). The mirror-neuron system. *Annual Review of Neuroscience, 27*(1), 169–192.

Rizzolatti, G., Fogassi, L., & Gallese, V. (2001). Neurophysiological mechanisms underlying the understanding and imitation of action. *Nature Reviews Neuroscience, 2*(9), 661–670.

Roberts, J. M. (1997). Is inflation sticky? *Journal of Monetary Economics, 39*(2), 173–196.

Ross, D., & Dumouchel, P. (2004). Emotions as strategic signals. *Rationality and Society, 16*(3), 251–286.

Roßnagel, C. S. (2001). Revealing hidden covariation detection: Evidence for implicit abstraction at study. *Journal of Experimental Psychology: Learning, Memory and Cognition, 27*(5), 1276–1288.

Sargent, T. J., & Sims, C. A. (1977). Business cycle modeling without pretending to have too much a priori economic theory. *New Methods in Business Cycle Research, 1,* 145–168.

Savage, L. J. (1971). Elicitation of personal probabilities and expectations. *Journal of the American Statistical Association, 66*(336), 783–801.

Schwarz, N. (2007). Attitude construction: Evaluation in context. *Social Cognition*, *25*(5), 638–656.

Schwarz, N., & Clore, G. L. (1996). Feelings and phenomenal experiences. *Social Psychology: Handbook of Basic Principles*, *2*, 385–400.

(2003). Mood as information: 20 years later. *Psychological Inquiry*, *14*(3/4), 296–303.

Seaver, D. A., Winterfeldt, W., & Edwards, W. (1978). Eliciting subjective probability distributions on continuous variables. *Organizational Behavior and Human Performance*, *21*(3), 379–391.

Sedlacek, T. (2011). *Economics of good and evil: The quest for economic meaning from Gilgamesh to Wall Street*. New York, NY: Oxford University Press.

Shefrin, H. M., & Thaler, R. H. (1988). The behavioral life-cycle hypothesis. *Economic Inquiry*, *26*(4), 609–643.

Shiller, R. J. (2000). *Irrational exuberance*. Princeton, NJ: Princeton University Press.

Simon, H. A. (1955). A behavioral model of rational choice. *The Quarterly Journal of Economics*, *69*(1), 99–118.

(1987). Satisficing. *The New Palgrave: A Dictionary of Economics*, *4*, 243–245.

(1997). Models of bounded rationality. In H. A. Simon (Ed.), *Models of bounded rationality*. Cambridge, MA: MIT Press.

Simon, T. J., Hespos, S. J., & Rochat, P. (1995). Do infants understand simple arithmetic? A replication of Wynn (1992). *Cognitive Development*, *10*, 253–269.

Sims, C. A. (1980). Macroeconomics and reality. *Econometrica*, *48*(1), 1–48.

(2003). Implications of rational inattention. *Journal of Monetary Economics*, *50*(3), 665–690.

Smith, N. K., Cacioppo, J. T., Larsen, J. T., & Chartrand, T. L. (2003). May I have your attention, please: Electrocortical responses to positive and negative stimuli. *Neuropsychologia*, *41*(2), 171–183.

Souleles, N. S. (2001). Consumer sentiment: Its rationality and usefulness in forecasting expenditure-evidence from the Michigan micro data. NBER Working Paper Series, 8410.

Spelke, E. S., Breinlinger, K., Macomber, J., & Jacobson, K. (1992). Origins of knowledge. *Psychological Review*, *99*, 605.

Stanovich, K. E., & West, R. F. (2000). Individual differences in reasoning: Implications for the rationality debate? *Behavioral and Brain Sciences*, *23*(5), 645–665.

Stark, T., & Croushore, D. (2002). Forecasting with a real-time data set for macroeconomists. *Journal of Macroeconomics*, *24*(4), 507–531.

Starkey, P., Spelke, E. S., & Gelman, R. (1990). Numerical abstraction by human infants. *Cognition*, *36*(2), 97–127.

Sterman, J. D. (1989). Misperceptions of feedback in dynamic decision making. *Organizational Behavior and Human Decision Processes*, *43*(3), 301–335.

Stickgold, R. (2005). Sleep-dependent memory consolidation. *Nature*, *437*(7063), 1272–1278.

Stock, J. H., & Watson, M. W. (1998). Diffusion indexes. NBER Working Paper Series, 6702.

(2002). Forecasting using principal components from a large number of predictors. *Journal of the American Statistical Association*, *97*(460), 1167–1179.

(2007). Forecasting in dynamic factor models subject to structural instability. In N. Shephard, & J. Castle (Eds.), *The methodology and practice of econometrics: Festschrift in honor of D. F. Hendry* (pp. 173–205). Oxford: Oxford University Press.

Surowiecki, J. (2004). *The wisdom of crowds: Why the many are smarter than the few and how collective wisdom shapes business.* New York, NY: Random House.

Symeonidis, L., Daskalakis, G., & Markellos, R. N. (2010). Does the weather affect the stock market volatility? *Finance Research Letters, 7*(4), 214–223.

Tarde, G. (1902). *Psychologie économique.* Félix Alcan, ed., Ancienne Libr. Germer Baillière et Cie.

Teglas, E., Girotto, V., Gonzalez, M., & Bonatti, L. L. (2007). Intuitions of probabilities shape expectations about the future at 12 months and beyond. *Proceedings of the National Academy of Sciences of the United States of America, 104*(48), 19156–19159.

Theil, H. (1952). On the time shape of economic microvariables and the Munich business test. *Review of the International Statistical Institute, 20*, 105–120.

Thomas, Jr., L. B. (1999). Survey measures of expected US inflation. *Journal of Economic Perspectives, 13*(4), 125–144.

Thorndike, E. L. (1911). *Animal intelligence: Experimental studies.* New York, NY: Macmillan.

Tooby, J., & Cosmides, L. (1992). The psychological foundations of culture. In J. Barkow, L. Cosmides, & J. Tooby (Eds.). *The adapted mind: Evolutionary psychology and the generation of culture* (pp. 19–136) New York, NY: Oxford University Press.

Turk-Browne, N. B., Junge, J. A., & Scholl, B. J. (2005). The automaticity of visual statistical learning. *Journal of Experimental Psychology: General, 134*(4), 552–564.

Turner, J. H. (2000). *On the origins of human emotions: A sociological inquiry into the evolution of human affect.* Stanford, CA: Stanford University Press.

Vanoli, A. (2005). *A history of national accounting.* Amsterdam: IOS Press.

Varley, R. A., Klessinger, N. J. C., Romanowski, C. A. J., & Siegal, M. (2005). Agrammatic but numerate. *Proceedings of the National Academy of Sciences of the United States of America, 102*(9), 3519–3524.

Velmans, M. (1991). Is human information processing conscious? *Behavioral and Brain Sciences, 14*, 651–726.

Wagner, U., Gais, S., Haider, H., Verleger, R., & Born, J. (2004). Sleep inspires insight. *Nature, 427*(6972), 352–355.

Walker, M. P., & Stickgold, R. (2004). Sleep-dependent learning and memory consolidation. *Neuron, 44*(1), 121–133.

Wallsten, T. S., Budescu, D. V., Rapoport, A., Zwick, R., & Forsyth, B. (1986). Measuring the vague meanings of probability terms. *Journal of Experimental Psychology: General, 115*(4), 348–365.

Wilson, T. (2002). *Strangers to ourselves: Discovering the adaptive unconscious.* Cambridge, MA: The Belknap Press of Harvard University Press.

Wynn, K. (1992). Addition and subtraction by human infants. *Nature, 358*(5389), 749–750.

Xu, F., & Garcia, V. (2008). Intuitive statistics by 8-month-old infants. *Proceedings of the National Academy of Sciences of the United States of America, 105*(13), 5012–5015.

References

Xu, F., & Spelke, E. (2000). Large number discrimination in 6-month-old infants. *Cognition*, *74*(1).

Yaari, M. E. (1965). Uncertain lifetime, life insurance, and the theory of the consumer. *Review of Economics and Statistics*, *32*(2), 137–150.

Zajonc, R. B. (1965). Social facilitation. *Science*, *149*(3681), 269–274.

(1980). Feeling and thinking: Preferences need no inferences. *American Psychologist*, *35*(2), 151.

(1984). On the primacy of affect. *American Psychologist*, *39*(2), 117–123.

Zarnowitz, V. (1985). Rational expectations and macroeconomic forecasts. *Journal of Business & Economic Statistics*, *3*(4), 293–311.

Zeldes, S. P. (1989). Consumption and liquidity constraints: An empirical investigation. *Journal of Political Economy*, *97*(2), 305–346.

Index

Printed in the United States
by Baker & Taylor Publisher Services